Sexualities in Context

Sexualities
IN CONTEXT

A Social Perspective

Rebecca F. Plante

Ithaca College, Ithaca NY

A Member of the Perseus Books Group

Published by Westview Press,
A Member of the Perseus Books Group

Westview Press books are available at special discounts for bulk purchases in the United States by
corporations, institutions, and other organizations. For more information, please contact the Special
Markets Department at the Perseus Books Group, 11 Cambridge Center, Cambridge MA 02142, or
call (617) 252-5298 or (800) 255-1514, or e-mail special.markets@perseusbooks.com.

Designed by Deborah Gayle

Library of Congress Cataloging-in-Publication Data
Plante, Rebecca F.
   Sexualities in context : a social perspective / Rebecca F. Plante.
      p. cm.
   ISBN 10: 0-8133-4293-7
   ISBN-13: 978-0-8133-4293-1 (pbk.)
   1. Sex. 2. Sex—Social aspects. 3. Sexual orientation. I. Title.
   HQ21.P554 2006
   306.76—dc22

                                                                                    2005033651

06 07 08 / 10 9 8 7 6 5 4 3 2 1

For M, T, B and B,

with love

Contents

Introduction: Setting the Scene   *ix*

Section I
The Basics of Sexuality

   1. **Why Sex Matters:** A Brief History of Sex/uality   *3*
   2. **Studying the Sexual:** Classifying and Theorizing   *31*
   3. **Boys, Girls, Men and Women:** Variables of Experience   *67*

Section II
Becoming Sexual

   4. **Birds Do It, Bees Do It:** Learning about "It"   *99*
   5. **Finding a *Playboy* under a Rock in the Woods:** Sex in the Mind   *133*
   6. **Hooking It Up:** Sex in the Bedroom   *163*

Section III
Outside Ourselves: Sex in Social Context

   7. **LGBTQQPA(H), BDSM:** The Alphabet Soup of Sexualities   *195*
   8. **Bunnies, Bytes, and Beaches:** Representations of Sex   *241*
   9. **Screwing with Sex:** Some Politics of Sexualities   *267*

Acknowledgments   *289*
Notes   *291*
Index   *319*

Introduction

SETTING THE SCENE

In chapter 1, I write, "Culturally, our discussions of all things sexual are marked by ambivalence, confusion, and contradictions." This book counts too—it is part of that discussion, that conversation about sex. Clearly, I cannot escape my own point of view in terms of content, rhythm, topics, and even choices of words, images, and ideas. This conflicts with the *usual* purpose of a textbook, even a brief, specialized one like this, which is to (objectively) state the facts, fully describe a series of issues, and marshall more library sources than the average reader has ever seen. As a part of United States society, and as a woman socialized into femininity, my own point of view is larger than just my own experiences. My culture has given me much ambivalence, confusion, and contradictory information about sex. My story reads a bit like this . . .

The advent of new technologies, like the contraceptive pill and the Internet, has combined with politics and social forces to create a new sexual citizen in the United States (and in other industrialized nations). The Pill gives heterosexually active women some measure of freedom, autonomy, and control of the body. Liberalization in attitudes and policies enables all of us to see ourselves differently, as "liberated," sexually knowledgeable, and sexually aware. We are bombarded with sexy television images: Samantha, from *Sex and the City.* On *Desperate Housewives,* there's an affair with a gardener, eroticizing both "housewives" and working-class men. On *Will & Grace,* the main character is a gay man; *Ellen* is a popular talk show starring one of the only "out" lesbians in Hollywood. Sex is democratized, it seems—can't each of us just have it all?

But then the pendulum swings back to something darker, as real as all the rest of this. It's not too late—10 p.m.—but I am watching former *Playboy* Playmate Jenny McCarthy get a lap dance while interviewing a *Survivor: Palau* cast member. The dancers have the bored, banal "sexy" looks on their faces, the grim half smiles, half smirks of employees simply being paid to do a job. Jenny and her guest don't look at the dancers. They crane their necks to make eye contact with each other while the dancers grind and writhe. Jenny asks her guest "about 'Aunt Flo' . . . did you get to bring. . . you know. . . feminine hygiene products?. . . " I cannot tell whether Jenny is trying to be coy and ironic, knowing that it seems insane to be getting a lap dance while stumbling over the words "tampon" and "menstruate." Jenny asks whether there were any Pocket Rockets on the island, small vibrators that some women enjoy. I am confused.

Then Jenny shows us what I guess is the new "bachelorette party"—where the bride's friends buy her an exotic dancer, a young blonde dressed like a Hollywood film executive's fantasy of a schoolgirl. The blonde rubs herself all over the bride, who clutches dollar bills in her teeth; the dancer leans in to grab the bills. Am I watching a lesbian moment? My confusion grows when the bride is literally chained to a stripper pole while the dancer writhes on her. The camera closes in on the bride, who looks into the camera and says, "You asked to see me with another girl, honey—well here ya go." It wasn't really what I thought it was—it was just a same-sex role play, in effect. It was performance for "his"—the groom's—benefit, and that of other male viewers.

Addicted to television now, I flip the channels and the seasons, in my mind. One fall there was that reality show, *Boy Meets Boy*. A cute young guy, with the help of his female friend, selected men to date from a pool of eligibles chosen by the network. The catch was that some of the men were gay and some were straight and acting; the endearingly sweet main character had no idea of this at first. Once he got over feeling betrayed, he began devising tests of his gaydar—take his date to sit in the hot tub, go to the gym together—hoping that these settings would reveal if his date was a straight man and therefore uncomfortable. But there was no French kissing, no green, grainy, night-vision cameras revealing men groping each other under the sheets. One network heterosexual reality show, about a construction worker tricking women into thinking he was wealthy, showed him walking into the woods with his date. The sounds of groans and moans, a zipper being unzipped, and the unmistakable slurping noises of fellatio followed.

We would never see this on a network dating show for gay men or lesbians, though watching heterosexually identified women getting lap dances and being chained to stripper poles is probably the stuff of high ratings. Though there are several gay male characters on mainstream television now, *none* of them are sexual or romantic in front of the camera. In the comedy *Will & Grace*, gay characters Will and Jack "locked lips" in one episode, but it was far from what anyone would call a sexual or romantic "make-out" session. (In fact, the kiss was a protest over the fact that the characters' favorite NBC show failed to show a much-hyped kiss between two men, and instead cut away to another scene.) Except for *Queer as Folk,* which is only available on premium cable or DVD, we rarely see same-sex couples share the kind of extended romantic kiss that is so common between other-sex couples on other television shows.

All of these portrayals of sex on television remind me of the oft-repeated cliché that knowledge is power, knowledge will set us free. Have we really illuminated the mysteries of sex by being able to see "sex" on television or in movies? Have we opened up dark closets of repression and fear by being able to find "sex" in a host of nonpornographic magazines or in any number of songs? If I can hear rapper Lil' Kim saying, "If I was a dude, I'd tell y'all to suck my dick," or Foxy Brown being "bent over the sink with my panties in your mouth," it's a good thing, right? Men have been rapping about sex for years, so turnabout is fair play, right? But I am a little confused. If Lil' Kim was a guy, she would insult people by telling them to suck her dick—meaning, to be in the vulnerable or weak position of being like a woman—because only women or gay men "suck dick." I'm not really sure this makes me feel empowered.

I go to the bookstore to sit in the café and read some magazines. The articles describe some new operations—genital surgeries for men and women. The women featured in the articles are paying $5,000 or more for "vaginal rejuvenation," hymen reconstruction, and labiaplasty. They want to tighten their vaginas after childbirth because they want to be firmer "for their husbands," or they don't like the way their vaginal lips look in thongs and tight jeans. The men in the articles are getting penile enlargements by having their suspensatory ligaments severed, freeing up an extra inch or so. Some get treated cadaver skin wrapped around their penises to achieve more girth. The equation seems very simple: sexuality is all about the body, the genitalia. If the genitalia look good and feel right then sex will be good and will feel right. Maybe this is at the heart of what psychologists and sex therapists call "sexual dysfunctions." Our bodies are to blame, not our cultural values or our context. This is really a conundrum. Shouldn't we feel good about Americans being able to do whatever makes them happy, including willingly allowing sharp surgical instruments near their genitals? That is true freedom, true individuality. But what about women who have kids and don't get vaginal rejuvenations? Will they be judged and looked down on and accused of not wanting to "please their husbands"?

At the bookstore I also find some sex self-help books. Most of them seem like they are written for women. Those books keep describing how "low desire" is practically an epidemic, that there are millions of women who have little to no interest in sex with their male partners. Then there are the millions of women who may be interested in sex, but they cannot reliably have orgasms. Given that the same books contain chapters of advice on having better, more, and more exotic orgasms (G-spot, ejaculatory, X-spot, multiples), it is obvious that it would be problematic to have no orgasms. So the authors recommend all kinds of things for women, including Viagra and testosterone creams and patches. The message seems twofold. There is a new set of expectations for women—want sex, need sex, insist on orgasms, and if it doesn't work, call a doctor, who can medicate the problem. I am a little confused. If sex is supposed to be a private, intimate thing, why invite doctors into my bedroom? And what about the pressure to perform? Men already have to deal with that and being subjected to that sort of pressure doesn't seem to work out well ("the mind is willing but the flesh is not"). Why put this pressure on women, too?

All of this seems as if it is in service of the belief that there was a "sexual revolution" from the 1960s to the 1970s. We liberated sexuality from repression, fear, and ignorance, didn't we? We got the opportunity for heterosexual women to "have sex like men," to have sex on their terms (which may not be that different from men's). We can learn about vibrators and "depressed vaginas" and anal sex and oral sex—all from just one television show, HBO's *Sex and the City.* We stole sex from shame, guilt, and double standards, especially for women, right? We got the right to "hook up"—to have ambiguously defined, exciting sex without the hassles of relationships. And the Internet—that topic is an entire lengthy book all its own—but I decided to delve into it anyway, to read some blogs.

I find the blog of someone I will call "Wantingtobegood."[1] She had just gotten out of a four-year relationship with someone who never really treated her as she wished. He ended their relationship, via an email, for another woman. Wantingtobegood describes her first real hook-up one wintry night around the Christmas holidays. Her unhappy mood, the need to escape from her parents' house, and a few strong cocktails combined to get her into bed with a guy she met at a bar. When she drove home at six in the morning, she felt smugly satisfied, impressed by her ability to hook up; she had always been in long-term relationships and never imagined she was capable of hook-ups or friends-with-benefits (FWB) scenarios. But as I read her blog, it became clear that Wantingtobegood was struggling, rationalizing her newly uncommitted sex life. She was experimenting with different kinds of hook-ups and finding herself troubled by "catching feelings" for Guy One, not having enough feelings of any kind for Guy Two, and feeling used by Guy Three.

I will paraphrase her talking about Guy Three, to protect her anonymity; this particular blog is representative of the 15 or so (focused on young women's sexual exploits) that I read. He "booty called" with only a half-hour to spare for it, and Wantingtobegood thought that "fifteen minute fucking" would make her "feel rather cheap." About Guy One, she wondered why it couldn't be something more than it was, something more than a very noncommittal relationship where he called the shots and decided when and if they would get together. Guy One had already announced that he had no intention of dating exclusively, that the whole point of FWB was to have multiple sexual relationships. Wantingtobegood tried to consider his request that she simply sleep with him and his female friend if she wanted more from him. She wrote about the realities of hook-ups—that she would be unable to do so with someone she did not generally respect.

Between her attempts to rationalize her feelings, Wantingtobegood wrote about her friends, who all seemed to have settled down, gotten engaged or married, begun their adult lives. She watched *Sex and the City,* noticing how different her life was from what was depicted on television. As I read, I thought that things would almost certainly change for her as she got older—people *are* marrying later than ever (average age for men is about 28.5, for women it is 26.5 or so), but weddings still happen. Then I read the entry in which she wrote that she is in her early 30s. She seemed so torn between wanting to be able to hook up on men's terms, wanting to be capable of sex without feelings and emotions, wanting to be capable of the kind of reserve she noticed in her partners. She seemed unhappy.

Back to the television. As I write this, ABC is airing *Hooking Up,* "the online dating adventures of 11 single women" in New York City. Ubiquitous shots of women typing at their computers are interspersed with reality TV–style commentaries about chemistry, attraction, and discussions of when to go *offline* and when to delete online personal ads. "I'm just having too much fun not to sleep with him tonight. He's expecting it and he's really nice. We're attracted to each other and it's not like we're 18; it's not like we haven't done this before," says Amy. After they sleep together, Amy waits for his call. At a meal with her sister, she says, "He slept over Friday, so when should he have called me?" Sister: "It was Friday? By Monday then." Amy: "It's Tuesday and he just called, and it was weird." Amy explained that he "just wants to shag. I don't want to be added to his list." Having already slept with him, but apparently overlooking that, Amy tells her sister that "if he doesn't want to be in commitment-mode, then he doesn't get to be in naked-mode." She seemed resolute but also confused about how best to get what she wanted—a commitment, a relationship leading to marriage and children. She is 27 years old.

Hooking Up has every heterosexual character you can imagine—a woman who pulls away from a consensual kiss because "it was getting a little hot and heavy, a little giddy," apparently playing the gatekeeper. One man tells his date that he went to a nudist resort with three of the women he was dating. He says he is just not used to being monogamous. I think most straight women fear men like this, words like this. His date later tells her friend, "I don't like sexual talk like that when I barely know someone." Her friend confidently announces, "That's a twenty-nine-year-old speaking. They don't mature until they're like forty-two. Forty-two is the new twenty-two."

So what am I confused about, and more importantly, troubled by? First, I am wondering if knowledge really is power. Does it help me to know that the stakes are very high for the average American's sex life? Have I gained any real power because I now have knowledge of five different orgasms, female strippers for brides-to-be, and I can laugh at Jack's gay stereotyping on *Will & Grace*? Have I really learned anything about sexuality? What I really want—and need—to know is what American sexuality is *really* like, right now, in 2005. I have questions like: How might the narratives of sexual liberation and revolution be helpful *and* dangerous to us? What role does the body play, when all the pills, gadgets, and potions do not seem to really be able to cure "sexual dysfunctions"? Why have we made sex so important to us that wars have been fought over it, people have been killed because of it, partners have been betrayed in the name of lust, and billions of global dollars have been spent on Viagra?

Format and Approach of This Book

What is *sexuality*? Isn't sex something to be kept private? Won't studying sex demystify it? What does it mean to talk about *sexualities* in the plural? What is *sex*—is it different from sexuality? What does it mean to argue that, regardless of terms, it is *socially constructed*? And seriously, *why* all these questions about something that's just a simple reflection of who we are and what our natural inclinations are? Isn't sex just about doing what comes naturally—responding to drives, hormones, horniness, and lust?

Evolutionary psychologists assert that *sex* is universal and can be understood by calculating the reproductive strategies of heterosexuals. Anthropologists argue that sexual practices develop meaning within cultural and local contexts. Psychologists discuss sexuality as a feature of individuals' experiences. But in everyday life, women and men negotiate complex terrain. We confront our sexualities in bedrooms, doctors' offices, and Victoria's Secret lingerie shops. "Sex"—whether in the plural or singular, whether medicalized or slangy—is not simple, and it is far from just a matter of doing what comes naturally. Sociologists John Gagnon and William Simon observed, ". . . in

United States society and perhaps in most western societies to learn about sex is to learn about guilt" (1973: 262).[2]

Increasingly around the country, college courses are exploring sex through the perspectives of social and interdisciplinary sciences—anthropology, history, women's studies, cultural studies, and sociology, among others. The organizing principles of courses in these disciplines differ from those in the natural sciences—including health studies—and nursing or medical programs. Whereas science-based courses focus on reproductive anatomy and the sexual body, courses in the social sciences focus on sexual identities and activities. But underlying these courses is the thesis that it is also necessary to examine the social construction of sexuality. Human sexuality is more than the apparently simple product of natural urges or drives; it is also shaped and constructed in social contexts. Hence there is a considerable range of sexual variations in our own society, and *even more* variation if we look across time and place at sexual attitudes and behaviors.

The intersections of the global, the individual, the universal and the culture-specific are central to *Sexualities in Context*. The sexual is intimately personal and infinitely social. It is also political, as the women's, gay, lesbian, transgender, and intersex movements have demonstrated. Some of the most widely discussed social issues in recent years involve the public nature of discussions about sexuality—think Monica Lewinsky and her blue, semen-stained "trophy" dress, featured in President Clinton's impeachment proceedings. (It seems amazing to look back at that event now—the idea that a president would be impeached for consensual oral sex is astonishing to me.) Sex also sometimes involves force—the proverbial "he said, she said"—and power differences.

F.A.Q.

Q. Why are you not discussing anatomy and physiology in the standard sexuality textbook fashion, one chapter on men and one on women (or "males and females")?
A. Most anatomy chapters unconsciously limit discussion of "sexual anatomy" to the genitalia—there are many other aspects of the body that are "sexual," including the skin, the fingertips, the tongue, the buttocks, the brain, and in effect, the whole body.

Q. Why is this book so brief? Why didn't you include my favorite topic or author?
A. This text was conceived of specifically as a brief text. It is intended to challenge the approach normally taken by standard 17- to 20-chapter sexuality textbooks. As a brief text, it is designed to be used in conjunction with other readings/sources appropriate

to the specific course and discipline. This feature should make up for the fact that your favorite topic or author may have been omitted.

Q. It seems as if there is a distinct argument in the book. Why don't you just summarize all the existing research instead of making inferences, thinking critically, and analyzing?
A. Yes, there is an argument and analytical themes featured throughout the book. The study of sexuality must include critical analysis of the things we often take for granted and an acknowledgment of how power, oppression, and inequalities are part of U.S. culture. The idea is that readers will learn how to develop their own arguments about the sexual issues that matter to them and focus on the range of issues raised in their classes. "Summarizing all the research" and "brief text" are oxymorons—one cannot co-occur with the other.

Some Words about the Words I Choose

You will notice that I use specific language in this book, some of which will inspire a reconsideration of certain assumptions about sex. As much as possible, I will clarify the usually unspoken adjectives of sexual orientation, race/ethnicity, nationality, and class where applicable. Too often when people write about sexuality, they mistakenly presume the universality of heterosexuality, whiteness, middle-class status, and U.S. citizenship. So ideas, statements, claims, and research findings assume and take for granted that "men" applies to all male persons, or that "men and women" refers to everyone. It is more accurate to address the reality that not every finding, statement, claim, or generalization applies equally to everyone. So you will see that I am as specific as I can be without being overly cumbersome. For example, I might say, "Researchers have studied desire in heterosexual men and women" to clarify that we cannot assume that the findings will apply to people with other sexual orientations.

Terms

Sex (Male, Female).   Here "sex" refers to biological concepts. We tend to think of "sex" as having two and only two forms, male and female, though it is not always the case.

Sex (as an Act).   We are familiar with this usage, as in "Did you have sex with him?" In this case, *sex* is shorthand for many things. It successfully replaces cumbersome communication about what we might really mean, to wit: "Did you engage in a series of progressively more intimate and arousing activities, in a relatively standard progression from kissing to hopefully some sort of climax or orgasm?" We tend to use *sex* to refer to penile-vaginal intercourse in this context. But we also use this as shorthand for *sexuality*, as in, "Sometimes sex can be awfully confusing." So depending on the context of the sentence, and the rhythm of the words, I may use *sex* to mean "sexual things people do together (or alone)" or as shorthand for *sexuality*. In the text I also distinguish usage by saying *biological sex* when I mean "male" or "female."

Sexuality. The best way to describe how I will use this term is by quoting the definition offered by the Sexuality Information and Education Council of the United States (SIECUS): "Human sexuality encompasses the sexual knowledge, beliefs, attitudes, values, and behaviors of individuals. Its various dimensions involve the anatomy, physiology, and biochemistry of the sexual response system; identity, orientation, roles, and personality; and thoughts, feelings, and relationships. Sexuality is influenced by ethical, spiritual, cultural, and moral concerns" (www.siecus.org).[3] *Sexuality* is a broader and more complete term, and in context, you should be able to grasp which of these dimensions, if any, I am specifically referring to.

Sexualities. Whereas *sexuality* is taken to be a singular term, *sexualities* is clearly plural. *Sexuality* may imply a monolithic, solitary form, that there is one (true) form of human sexual expression. *Sexualities* implies diversity, breadth, and complexity—the *plurality* of things encompassed by the SIECUS definition of "human sexuality."

Sexual. This is used as an adjective: sexual intercourse, sexual conduct, sexual activities, and so on.

Gender (Man/boy, Woman/girl). Gender is a "social" term, referring to socially constructed roles and portrayals of self. So a person may be born female but *woman* or even *girl* is something she is socialized into.

Other Sex vs. Opposite Sex. I reluctantly use *opposite sex* for clarity in most instances, but I do think it perpetuates the "men are from Mars, women are from Venus" ideologies (that we're opposites).

Sexual Orientation terms are fraught with difficulty due to the intersections of identity, behavior, self-concept, and role, or the public presentation of self.

- *Heterosexual.* The relevant terms you will see are *heterosexually oriented, heterosexually interested, heterosexually active,* and *heterosexual.* I will occasionally but infrequently use the term *straight.*
- *Sexual Minority.* This relates to a statistical observation and should not be viewed as having any value judgment.
- *Homosexual.* The relevant terms you will see are *lesbian, gay, same-sex oriented, same-sex behavior, men who have sex with men, women who have sex with women,* and infrequently, *homosexual.*

    Why the infrequent use of *homosexual?* The term *homosexual* has pejorative and negative connotations. It has been used as a label, a diagnosis, and a taunt. So I choose to be careful about using it for those reasons, though I do use it as an adjective, especially in chapter 7.

    Other terms, such as *bisexual, intersexual,* and *trans,* will be clarified when relevant. You will also note this term—*"casual sex"*—with quotations, because I am not really convinced anyone knows what it means (nor am I convinced it is always casual).

Race/Ethnicity Terms. I will tend to use *African American* and *black* somewhat interchangeably. The choice tends to be based on the flow of the sentence, along with an acknowledgement that not everyone agrees on which term to use or apply to themselves. I also use *Caucasian American* and *white* interchangeably. Since we tend to ignore the fact that "white" is a race (a large, overarching, unspecific race, but a race nevertheless), the language conventions here are less clearly defined. It is unlikely that a white person would be offended by either term. For the peoples of the Hispanic and Asian diasporas, I tend to stick to *Asian American* and *Latin American.* Note: Both terms are misleading, ignoring those new to the United States who may not apply the label to themselves. Each term is major shorthand for the many people contained within these umbrella designations.

This book addresses the issues central to social scientific approaches to sexuality: theory, methods, and issues of identity, behavior, culture, politics, power, oppression and context (while not totally ignoring the physiological). My primary purpose is to describe some aspects of human sexualities within a social constructionist argument, using gender as the key variable, along with sexual orientation, race, class, and ethnicity. Explicit critical thinking tools and the application of those tools are part of my approach as well (see chapters 1 and 2). Because it is a brief text, the content is necessarily more narrow than broad. By focusing on several issues with some depth, readers can sharpen their analytical skills. My hope is that you will develop critical thinking skills to apply to the sexual issues you find intriguing. By the time you finish this book, you will understand, among other things, how the basics of the sexual body are made complex in/by social and historical contexts, why it is more appropriate to use the plural "sexualities," and why sex is such a fascinating and vexing aspect of everyday life.

SECTION I

The Basics of Sexuality

1

Why Sex Matters

A BRIEF HISTORY OF SEX/UALITY

It was 1895 in Victorian London, England. The city was captivated by a trial happening in its midst—the libel trial of the Marquess of Queensberry, John Sholto Douglas. Novelist and playwright Oscar Wilde, a married father of two, had befriended Douglas's son, Lord Alfred, a young aspiring poet. The marquess was eccentric and easily infuriated and had begun harassing Wilde, assuming that his relationship with Lord Alfred was "indecent." He had told his son that "to pose as a thing is as bad as to be it," revealing a concern with how the relationship between Wilde and Alfred *appeared* to others. With Lord Alfred's encouragement, Wilde sued the marquess, who had been publicly and loudly claiming that Wilde was a *sodomite*, someone who engaged in sex with a member of the same sex. The marquess was accused of libel, written or oral statements that convey unjustly unfavorable impressions; Wilde was confident that he would win.

The problem was that Wilde had apparently been sexually intimate with men. When the defense brought out some men who could attest to their relationships with him, testimony cemented with exhibits of love letters and gifts, Wilde was ultimately accused of "gross indecency." In other trials, Wilde was the defendant, and a number of men testified that Wilde had paid them for sex. Following two trials, he was ultimately found guilty and sentenced to two years of hard labor in prison. After his release, Wilde's health suffered and he died in Paris, in his mid-forties, penniless, his work discredited.

This chapter on why sex matters starts with an event that had ripple effects far into the twentieth century. The events surrounding the trial highlight the role of culture, society, politics, and history in the formation of sexualities. The trial and the verdict ushered in a fear of homosexuality that replaced previous indifference and/or pity. People began conflating art and poetry with effeminacy and homosexuality. Suspicion of those with close, same-sex relationships spread. The trials also marked the beginning of a convention that persists today—the linking of sexual acts and desires with *identity* and the use of the term *homosexual* to describe a person. The significance of this shift in perceptions of identity will become clearer as you read this book, when we explore things like language, culture, history, and society.

The main purpose of this book is to invite you to think more critically and thoughtfully about what sexuality is. It is relatively easy—and it even seems to make sense—to assume that sex is fairly simple. It's about biology, anatomy, genes; uncontrollable drives, lust, and horniness. Sex is absolutely about all these things, but it's also about much, much more. Since I am confident that you can find plenty of information elsewhere about biology, anatomy, and sex drive, I will not spend a lot of time on these issues. But I am less confident and am somewhat skeptical that you can find a lot of information about the social, historical, and cultural contexts in which individuals develop their sexualities. In asking you to carefully examine sexuality more generally, I will be focusing specifically on the bigger picture.

SO WHAT *IS* THE BIGGER PICTURE?

Language. This is relatively simple to define. Merriam-Webster OnLine (http://www.m-w.com) reports that language is "words, their pronunciation, and the methods of combining them used and understood by a community." But language is more than the series of intelligible sounds one can verbalize. It is also a systematic process or method of communicating ideas (i.e., making common); language utilizes sound but also signs, gestures, and nonverbals. There is no way to really understand the broader context without spending a little time critically reflecting on the ways in which we discuss and describe all things sexual. Everything from English slang to Latin-derived medical terms is inflected with meaning, symbolism, and significance. What are we communicating—making common—and what assumptions pervade our interpretations?

Culture. From the Latin *cultura*, to cultivate. In the social sciences, culture and social structures are foundational concepts, hinting at things larger than any single individual in a specific time or era. Merriam-Webster OnLine defines culture as the "integrat-ed pattern of human knowledge, belief, and behavior that depends upon man's capac-ity for learning and transmitting knowledge to succeeding generations." In the social sciences, we tend to add some nuances to this definition, to clarify that we are describ-ing the "shared attitudes, values, goals, and practices" of particular groups or people. What role does culture play in controlling sexualities? How do we learn these atti-tudes, goals, and values?

Socialization. This is a process, dependent on social interactions, by which individuals learn (and internalize) the culture of particular societies, nations, and other social groups (such as subcultures). Socialization helps us become part of "the group"—whether that group is small and local, or larger and less defined. It is important to note that socialization, though most salient in childhood, is in fact a lifelong process. How do we teach new members of societies and groups, whether infants or immigrants? And importantly, *what* do we teach? What are our shared attitudes, goals, and values? How do we use socialization to attempt to control individual and social expressions of sexualities? What contradictions and conflicts can we identify? What kinds of *subcul-tures*, groups with characteristic patterns, norms, values, and behaviors somewhat dis-tinct from the overarching culture or society, exist in terms of sexualities?

Demographics and Variables. When we think about subcultures, we have to consider some of the elements of human experience that we have made meaningful through-out history: race, ethnicity, nationality, gender, biological sex, social class, age, physi-cal and/or mental ability, religion, geography, and sexual orientation. We classify our-selves and others on the basis of these characteristics; make judgments, laws, and policies; and develop subcultures, norms, sanctions, penalties, rewards, and rules with these things in mind.

So the perspective I will take in this book can be described in this way:

1. Everything that constitutes "sex" cannot and should not be boiled down or overly simplified. It is a mistake to assume that if we want to understand sex all we need to do is find a road map to our bodies and rely on our "sex drives" to guide us further. Acts of sex exist in all cultures and have existed throughout history, and these acts even involve the same basic set of body parts and hydraulic motion, in effect. But there is no universal, absolute, unchanging set of laws, attitudes, or perspectives about sex. We do not *just* "have sex," "do it," or "hook up." There is so much more to it than just drives, hormones, or reproductive imperatives.

2. Instead, we must explore, evaluate, and examine the bigger picture of social, historical, political, and cultural context. Discourses (or the conversations, narratives, and stories) of broader cultures construct systems of sexuality and identity, wherein particular acts, feelings, and interactions are given particular meaning and significance. Each of us, especially in contemporary society, is subject to societal expectations, politics, and morality, among other things. In this light, we each *interpret* our behaviors, feelings, and attitudes. *Power*—the ability to influence, to make one's will dominant, to assert one's interests and perspectives—is an absolutely key concept. We cannot understand any of these things without frequently reminding ourselves about how power operates. We will focus on the American context, though ideas and information from other cultures will be touched on occasionally.

3. Demographics and variables interact with this bigger context (and biology) to form the foundation on which all things sexual are built. We will consider gender at every juncture and it will be the basic variable in every chapter. Race, ethnicity, age, and sexual orientation are other variables that we will also address.

4. Finally, a systematic approach to critical thinking is necessary to look deeply into sexualities. To really see what is in our culture and subcultures, and see how "sexuality" has developed inside each of us, we must develop the regular habit of mind (or mental discipline) of systematically questioning what we read, hear, think, feel, and are taught about sexualities, gender, and biological sex.

ANOTHER MOMENT IN HISTORY

One of the most often cited claims about sexual history is that ancient Greeks were gay. While it is possible to see artwork and vases depicting sexual acts between men, and we can find texts describing sex and love between men, it is not entirely accurate to say that these men were gay, in the same way that we would use the word. Classics expert David Halperin writes that the sexual acts men engaged in served very specific sociocultural purposes, chief among them to signify social status (1990).[1] Ancient Athens had a sexual conduct code that "position[ed] social actors in the places assigned to them (by virtue of their political standing) in the hierarchical structure of the Athenian polity" (p. 50). Sexuality was not conceptualized in the way that it is in the contemporary United States. Sexuality was dichotomized not in terms of acts performed between males and females, or between males, but in terms of *active and passive* (Karras, 2000).[2] "The relevant features of a sexual object were not so much determined by a physical typology of genders as by the social articulation of power" (Halperin, 1990: 50). Sex was not merely about pleasure and the private exchange of feeling between two individuals; it was a way to cement public or social standing. As such, the most privileged form of sexual relations between men involved men of superior status solely engaging in penetrative activities (*active*). Interest in being penetrated (the misleading term *passive*) was akin to effeminacy or taking the female role, an inferior form of behavior. Relationships between men were seen as the highest form of love; women, and wives especially, were regarded as child bearers (Keuls, 1993).[3]

The Greek example shines a useful light on the argument that many aspects of sexualities are *socially constructed*. The best way to understand this concept is to start with a premise: some things are real (and true) independently of individual whims, decisions, or patterns. Gravity on Earth is one example. It is probably easy for you to accept that gravity on Earth is real. You may wish to challenge this proposition, but you would need to support your challenge with evidence or proof. The problem is that you would be unable to provide any single examples, let alone systematic patterns or trends, to challenge the existence of gravity. Accepting that some things are real, we can however move to the fundamental premise of *social construction(ism)*: there are things (ideas, propositions, and so forth) that appear to be "natural" and "obvious," that are, more accurately, specific inventions or artifacts of particular cultures or societies. These things require some collective, human practices to sustain their existence and have meaning, significance, and effects that are agreed upon by the majority of society. It is most likely harder for you to just accept this definition of social construction(ism) than it is to just accept that some things are real.

What kinds of things are we referring to? What significance or meaning? How do we know people agree on these things? I, for one, have never been formally surveyed or asked to contribute to an opinion poll on the meaning of things. Have you? Picture such a poll:

> Interviewer: "Ma'am, we're calling to find out what you think about sex. Today's item to be socially constructed, by virtue of cultural consensus, is oral sex. Are you willing to agree that 'oral sex' shall be an act that is not quite as important as penile-vaginal intercourse, which has otherwise already become known as 'hitting a home run' or 'going all the way'? If we gain consensus on this point, then oral sex will be placed in a continuum of behaviors and called 'foreplay,' clearly denoting its insignificance compared to penile-vaginal intercourse. Your participation is very important to us."

Since this is clearly *not* how we come to consensus, how can we really understand what it means to say that many aspects of sexualities are socially constructed? We can use the ancient Greek example to see that although men engaged in same-sex behavior and had romantic relationships with other men, the relationships were not viewed in the same light as contemporary, similar relationships. Individuals were not identified as "gay" or "heterosexual"—sexual behaviors simply did *not* define people; that was unfathomable in ancient Greek culture. Through the intersections and influences of culture, socialization, and history, sexualities have been socially constructed. Therefore, in Greek culture, it was agreed—via convention, expectation, and social interpretation—that same-sex behavior was a way to communicate superior status. Sexualities are created by the various practices and consensus of societies (Karras, 2000). So the meanings and interpretations of most of the things we call sexual are subject to changing consensus and belief systems.

Examples of change are abundant in modern culture. When Nathaniel Hawthorne wrote *The Scarlet Letter* in 1850, he told the tale of Hester Prynne's relationship with Reverend Arthur Dimmesdale. The problem was that Hester was married to Roger Chillingworth, making her guilty of the crime of *adultery*, sexual acts between persons not married to each other (but married to others). For her crime, Hester was jailed and forced to wear a red "A" on her clothing upon her release, forever communicating to others her sin. Fast forward to 2005 and imagine every married person who has been sexually intimate with a nonspouse wearing a red "A." We could expect to see tens of thousands of letters, if not millions. Though American attitudes about adultery seem uniform, with 93 percent of Americans in a Gallup poll saying that "married men and women having an affair" is morally unacceptable (Carroll, 2005),[4] the reality is that affairs are not generally punished in the same way they were in Hawthorne's time and earlier. In fact, it was newsworthy that in 2004, in a small Virginia town, the former town lawyer was prosecuted for adultery (Turley, 2004).[5] After 18 years of marriage, John Bushey had a relationship with Nellie Mae Hensley; when he ended it, she went to the police. Virginia is one of 23 states that retains laws regulating the sexual conduct of married citizens. After having initially pled guilty and then trying to fight the charge, Bushey ultimately decided to do 20 hours of community service for the misdemeanor offense.

We have seen changes in the social construction of other issues as well. A majority (more than 51 percent) of Americans now say that divorce, sex between unmarried men and women, and having a baby outside legal, heterosexual marriage is "morally acceptable" (Carroll, 2005). For example, in a 1969 Gallup poll of Americans, "only 21.4% of respondents said that premarital sex was 'not wrong'" (Pennington, 2003:

107).[6] By 1973, 43 percent said that it was not wrong. The rapid shift in perceptions of the morality of premarital, heterosexual conduct is an excellent example of social constructionism at work, to the extent that 58 percent of Americans in a recent Gallup poll believe that premarital sex is *not* wrong (Carroll, 2005). Has the actual behavior changed? No—we're essentially talking about unmarried heterosexuals engaging in various sexual acts, and that's what the Gallup poll referred to in 1969, 1973, and 2005. The acts are the same; it is the sociocultural perceptions, interpretations, and meanings that have changed. (The fact that 54 percent of Americans in the 2005 Gallup poll think pregnancy outside marriage is "morally acceptable" represents a huge change in attitudes.) We will return to the concept of sexual attitudes throughout the book.

CONTRADICTIONS AND CONFUSION

When we begin turning over rocks, looking underneath them to critically examine sex and society, we begin noticing some troubling things. Americans believe that gays and lesbians should not be discriminated against, but the majority still believes that homosexuality is "morally wrong" (Loftus, 2001).[7] A major element of the discourse on the American Dream is a belief in civil rights and equality for all, in spite of evidence to the contrary. This may explain Americans' attitude against discrimination, while a variety of complex factors may explain the majority's belief that homosexuality is "immoral." But if we simply focus on the findings themselves, it is rather confusing. With our adultery example, it is unequivocal that Americans' *attitudes* remain uniformly negative, despite societal changes in other respects. So it is confusing, troubling, and contradictory to note that nonetheless, Americans do step outside their partnerships regularly. It is almost impossible to tell how often this occurs, however, because the dominant, negative sociocultural attitude may prevent people from admitting infidelities. Barash and Lipton, in discussing the difficulty of maintaining monogamy, claim that studies average out to a 50 percent rate for heterosexual, married men, and perhaps a 30 percent rate for heterosexual, married women (2001).[8] The National Health and Social Life Survey (NHSLS) of the 1990s reported lifetime infidelity incidence rates of about 25 percent for heterosexual men overall and 15 percent for heterosexual women overall (Laumann, Gagnon, Michael, and Michaels, 1994).[9]

There are many other examples of the gaps between what we think and how we reason and what we actually do. What might explain the obvious disjuncture between the attitudes and behaviors of millions of people? Maybe there are differences between people based on generation, age, or peer groups. Maybe the people who get surveyed or polled about attitudes are different from those whose behaviors are reported in other studies. We will further consider the methods underlying studies like these in chapter 2, but for now, let's consider another possible explanation. I warn you—it is unsatisfying, but I think part of the gap between attitudes and behavior is explained by the fact that culturally, our discussions of sex are marked by ambivalence, confusion, and contradictions. We could become embroiled in a chicken-and-egg scenario. Which came first? Our confused discussions about sex or our confused sexual activities? As you read, you will certainly learn more to help clarify this, but I think it is unlikely that we can definitively solve the mystery by the end of the book.

What's So Confusing, Anyway?

Some of the social and cultural aspects of sexualities do not necessarily clear up any mysteries and in fact, may only lead to more confusion and more contradictions. Let's explore. . . .

The Verbal and Nonverbal World. Conversations, language, and the terminology of sexuality are central to our ability to communicate, as suggested above. In chapter 4, you will read about adolescent confusion, inspired by discussions with uncomfortable parents and peers with their points of view. What do we *really* learn about sex when one of the first things we may learn is that we are not allowed to openly discuss the questions we have? What about when we learn that penises are referred to as "wee-wees," "pee-pees" and "ding-dongs," and female genitalia are referred to as "down there" or as "vaginas" (thereby ignoring the vulva, clitoris, and mons)? When we ask about "where babies come from" and we are told that "when Mommies and Daddies are in love. . . ," what happens when we find ourselves sexually attracted to people for whom we have no such feelings? The ways in which we communicate about everything sexual can be carefully analyzed to reveal our cultural values.

Our language about gender, starting with the fact that we have two different terms (i.e., man and woman), is evidence that we value difference. When we name one class of people "men" and another class of people "women," we are communicating the belief that the individuals in these groups are not the same—that they need to be classified with separate terminologies. Then we further describe men and women largely on the basis of divergent characteristics and attributes. Why is this confusing? Probably because most of us know people (maybe even ourselves) who do not wholly embody the dominant cultural version of either masculinity or femininity. We know people who possess traits that we have assigned to the other gender. Although our language—terms like *man, woman, opposite sex*—does translate what society has "made common," language does not and cannot capture *all* our experiences.

This is especially clear when we consider the language of and for sexuality. We tend to use euphemisms such as "privates" when referring to women's genitalia, which require the listener to assume what is not said. The words we use may be morally and emotionally loaded. Men utilize a far more varied set of terms for genitalia and sexual acts (Cornog, 1986).[10] The slang for penis alone runs the gamut from aggressive terms to food terms to war and weaponry terms: for example, *prick, worm, snake, bone, wiener, pole, flute, meat* (Richter, 1987).[11] Philosophers Ronald De Sousa and Kathryn Pauly Morgan (1988) expand on the specifics of slang: "For a second example, consider the terms used most often by men to refer to women. Such terms may represent women as various kinds or parts of animal (e.g. 'chick,' 'bird,' 'fox,' 'pussy,' 'tail,' 'piece of ass,' 'cow'); as playthings (e.g. 'babe,' 'doll'); as fetishised body parts (e.g. 'cunt,' 'puss,' 'piece'); as frivolous edible products ('sugar,' 'honey,' 'cupcake,' 'cookie,' 'crumpet,' 'dish,' 'peach,' 'cherry,' 'tart')."[12] We have complicated etiquette for sexual terms. Some are solely medical or clinical and probably do not have much use outside a doctor's office—coitus, penile-vaginal intercourse (which would probably not be used outside this book), fellatio, premature ejaculation. Some could be offensive and insulting and are probably used mostly as insults—cunt, prick, dickhead. Some are relatively neutral but awkward, especially in an intimate setting—vagina, penis, testicles, labia. What terms do you and your friends use? Are the terms different depending on your audience and the setting? One confusing thing is that popular sex manuals and sex experts tell us to improve our sex lives via sexual communication. But they rarely address the discrepancies we have built into language—gender, race, and class differences in how we communicate about sex.

Add to this the confusion of slang like "suck my dick" as an insult, the practice of calling men "pussies," and the use of "fuck" or "fucked (over)" as a synonym for "take(n) advantage of." Consider the insult *suck my dick*. What does that really mean? Who normally "sucks dick"? Women, or men having sex with men . . . or men in the role of women. Telling someone to suck dick is, in effect, to suggest that they behave like a woman. The act, in this context, communicates, or makes common, the concept of inferiority for the person who "behaves like a woman." What about using *pussy* as an insult for men? When a man (or woman) calls another man a pussy, he is, in effect, saying that the man is acting "like a woman." He is apparently behaving in some way that indicates weakness, vulnerability, and/or emotionality.

Language is further confusing if we just consider *intercourse*, an apparently neutral term to be used in "polite" or medical company. De Sousa and Morgan write:

> . . . it is not surprising that our most common euphemism for erotic sexual activity is also "gender-corrupted." "Intercourse" is a fine word on the road to swift degradation. Not because of its use in a sexual context, but because of its systematic and now all but unavoidable misuse in that context. Properly used, any erotic mode of relating—whether heterosexual, gay or lesbian, and including not only the genital but also the ocular, the oscular, and even the merely jocular—ought to count as "sexual intercourse." The literal meaning of the phrase fits it to be used as one of the widest and vaguest terms available to describe erotic interaction. But in current usage, "sexual intercourse" (or worse, unqualified "intercourse") is very precisely Penile Intromission into the Vagina with Male Orgasm (or PIVMO, as a logically correct sexual discourse might have it). We need to struggle to become aware of the moral and political implications of our sexual vocabulary.[13]

One of these implications is the use of *fuck* to imply "taken advantage of." It suggests something about how we see the roles and statuses of men and women, argues philosopher Robert Baker ([1975] 2000).[14] Many of the common words for (heterosexual) intercourse—*fuck, screw, bang*, among others—imply the actors' socially expected roles—the initiator fucks, the recipient "is fucked." In this case, men are constructed as active and women are constructed as passive. This conception sheds new light on why it is significant for a man to say, "I got fucked [over]." Baker's examples include: Dick had Jane, Dick banged Jane, Dick screwed Jane; Jane was fucked by Dick, Jane was laid by Dick, Jane was humped by Dick. . . . "Male subjects play an active role in the language of screwing, fucking, having, doing it, and perhaps, laying [e.g., get laid], while female subjects play a passive role" (2000: 278). We know next to nothing about how language works for those with same-sex partners and orientations, by the way.

Baker argues that the gendered differences do not *just* reflect anatomical differences. "Thus one can easily imagine a society in which the female normally played the active role in intercourse, where . . . the standard metaphors were terms like 'engulfing'—that is, instead of saying 'he screwed her,' one would say 'she engulfed him'" (2000: 279). What does this suggest about heterosexually active women, who are normally referred to as having "gotten (or been) fucked"? Baker suggests that gender is inherent in the way that *fuck* is used when men say, "Yeah, I fucked her," and they mean a very different thing therefore when they say, "I got fucked." "The passive construction of verbs indicating coitus . . . can also be used to indicate that a person is being harmed. . . . Thus the female sexual role must have something in common with being conned or being sold shoddy merchandise. The only common property is that of being harmed, deceived, or taken advantage of" (2000: 279).

What are the implications of conceptualizing (hetero) sex in this way? One is that it can enable us to see sexual exchanges between men with this same lens—the man who fucks (orally or anally) is "more of a man," while the man who is fucked is "more of a woman." Sociologist Celia Kitzinger (2005) studied the ways in which language and conversation produces heterosexuality.[15] Routinely taking for granted that couples are heterosexual is evident in the use of sex-specific terms like *wife* and *husband.* Kitzinger's research, along with Baker's, reminds us that language is not merely a simple system of symbols and sounds. Uncritically and unreflectively using language—the ideas we have made common—that reflects power imbalances and gender differences dooms us to continue conceptualizing heterosexual sexual activities as something men "do to" women.

Approaches to Sex. Certainly, American cultural attitudes about sex have relaxed and become more liberal over time. We do not have much research about sexual conduct and attitudes in the United States before the 1950s, when Alfred Kinsey, a zoologist at Indiana University, released his research team's studies of the sexual behavior of thousands of adult Americans (1948, 1953).[16] But we can briefly piece together some evidence, starting with the way in which the United States was colonized and resettled by Europeans. The settlers privileged reproductive, marital sexual expression with penile-vaginal intercourse seen as a duty each spouse owed the other (D'Emilio and Freedman, 1988).[17] Significant social and religious sanctions combined with community morals (like those described in *The Scarlet Letter*) to provide consistent, unitary messages about the impropriety of extramarital sex and childbirth without marriage. Thus the incidence of these events was low. Interest in maintaining strict social controls on individual sexual expression was furthered by the colonists' realization that Native peoples' sexual cultures differed. Native peoples did not tend to conceptualize sex in terms of sin or morality, shame or guilt. Practices of polygamy, nonmarital intercourse, same-sex sexuality, and broader conceptualizations of gender could be found, though certainly not in every Native group. Generally Native peoples seemed to have more individual freedoms, personal choice, and less negativity regarding sex (D'Emilio and Freedman, 1988).

Gender began to have a certain kind of salience in the colonies in the 1600s to 1800s. Women literally bore the evidence of nonmarital sexuality. The proportion of births occurring within the first nine months of marriages rose steadily throughout the later 1600s and early 1700s (Godbeer, 2004).[18] Though prosecutions of couples did occur, it was parental concern for their daughters that dominated. What if the father of the child did not actually marry the mother before she gave birth? What if he refused to take responsibility? The practice of *bundling* may have begun in response to these worries. Bundling enabled parents to invite gentlemen to visit with their daughters, secure in the knowledge that though the couple would share a bed (if he had traveled a distance to call on her), physical intimacy would be inhibited because the couple would be fully clothed. Sometimes bundling included a board placed between him and her. The idea that women needed to be protected from men, along with the belief that men's sexuality was more animal-like and uncontrolled, was influential (Bloch, 2003).[19] Women began to be seen as the gatekeepers of men's sexuality, which had far-reaching consequences that we will explore more fully in subsequent chapters.

The clear and consistent social and legal norms of the early colonies gradually gave way to greater inconsistency, reflecting shifts in popular perceptions and approaches to sex. In the last 50 years alone, we have seen abortion legalized, although popular opinion reflects the contentious nature of the issue. Anywhere from 40 percent to 55 percent of Americans disapprove of abortion; the figures vary depending on how pollsters pose questions (Misra and Hohman, 2000).[20] American attitudes about sex outside of legal, heterosexual marriage are also inconsistent. Although age cohorts grew more and more liberal between the 1920s and the 1970s, most of that "liberalization" occurred between 1969 and 1973 (Harding and Jencks, 2003).[21] It appears as if liberal attitudes are an effect of chronological age, with more conservative attitudes starting to settle in around age 30 and older. So we are *not*, with each generation, growing more liberal about heterosexual sex before marriage (Harding and Jencks, 2003).

Attitudes about equality for gays and lesbians are just as confusing. In the General Social Survey, a study of about 2,000 adult Americans done yearly since 1972, we can see a shift in the percentages of respondents saying that "sexual relations between two adults of the same sex . . . [are] not wrong at all." In the 1998 GSS, 28 percent agreed with this, while in the 1988 GSS only 13 percent agreed.[22] Superficially, this seems like movement in a more socially accepting direction, but looking beneath the surface reveals further distinctions. In a national study of 1,335 heterosexuals' attitudes and impressions of gays and lesbians, Gregory Herek discovered significant differences between women and men (2002).[23] Heterosexual women supported gay and lesbian employment protection and adoption rights more than did heterosexual men and were less likely to hold stereotypical beliefs about gays and lesbians. Heterosexual men were more negative about recognition of same-sex relationships and adoption rights for gay men, more likely to believe that gay men are mentally ill and molest children, and were most negative in their feelings about gay men (Herek, 2002).

Another confusing aspect of the American approach to sexualities is the cluster of dominant attitudes, delineated in the NHSLS cited earlier. Researchers noticed certain attitudes and feelings that co-vary; people with a *procreational* approach, for example, believe that the primary purpose of sexual conduct is to reproduce and tend to disapprove of same-sex behavior (unsurprisingly, since same-sex conduct is not connected to reproduction). But those with a procreational approach have diverging opinions about pornography, abortion, and other matters. Those with *relational* approaches see sexual conduct as part of loving, committed relationships and generally approve of various behaviors in *that* context. Finally, those with *recreational* approaches tend to see any consenting sex act as acceptable, but do not necessarily have such broad acceptance of same-sex sexualities.

Sociocultural and Historical Variables

The apparently contradictory attitudes described above are indicative of broader social and historical changes that are at least somewhat confusing, if not wholly confusing! These conundrums would read like surreal newspaper headlines:

'Hot' Sex Saturates Media; Gov't Gives $1 Billion for Abstinence-Only Education

U.S. Tells World We're a 'Bastion of Freedom and Defender of Democracy'; Women's Reproductive Choice under Siege

Women and Men Striding toward Equality; About 90 percent of Sexual Assaults Committed by Lovers, Friends, or Relatives

U.S. Parents Overwhelmingly Support School Sex Ed; Say 'We Don't Want to Have to Talk about It!'

Youth Say It's 'No Big Deal' to Be Gay; Support for Same-Sex Marriage Falters

Reverend Fred Phelps Protests Murdered Teen's Funeral, Says Matthew Shepard Will 'Rot in Hell with Other Fags'; Spanish Legislature Approves Same-Sex Marriage Bill

Women, Inspired by 'Sex and the City,' Have Sex and Hook-Ups on 'Own Terms'; Pharmacists Deny Women 'Morning-After' Pills, RU–486, and Condoms

'Hot' Sex Saturates Media; Gov't Gives $1 Billion for Abstinence-Only Education and U.S. Parents Overwhelmingly Support School Sex Ed; Say 'We Don't Want to Have to Talk about It!'

Everything announced by these mock headlines is real, reported in studies or the popular press. As I write this, the television show *Desperate Housewives* is the hit of the entertainment media and late-night talk shows, captivating viewers with its depictions of housewives' affairs and sexual escapades. Yet the U.S. government spends about $1,000,000,000 a year on abstinence-only school "sex" education. Teachers are mandated to speak only about contraceptive failures, not the profound and regular success of most forms of contraception (Huberman, 2005).[24] Teachers must tell students of the damage that will surely befall them if they do not abstain from all sexual activity until legally, heterosexually married. Of the public school districts that actually have a policy about the teaching of sex ed, 86 percent require that abstinence be promoted (Landry, Kaeser, and Richards, 1999).[25] Fully 35 percent require that abstinence be taught as the *only option;* the other 51 percent teach that abstinence is the *preferred option* but allow discussion of contraception. Landry, Kaeser, and Richards clarify that more than 50 percent of the districts in the Southern United States "with a policy to teach sexuality education have an abstinence-only policy, compared with 20% of such districts in the Northeast."

This is all in spite of the persistent and well-documented fact that parents *want* sex education in the public schools, period. The Sexuality Information and Education Council of the United States (SIECUS) found that low-income parents support comprehensive sex education programs, along with middle-class parents and teens of all ethnicities and classes (2002).[26] The vast majority—81 percent—support education that goes beyond abstinence, though there were some racial differences, with African American parents (about 85 percent) supporting comprehensive education more so than Caucasian American and Latin American parents (about 80 percent each). Ready for the kicker? Less than half of all parents had actually discussed sex with their nine- and ten-year-old children. Maybe this is not so confusing after all—parents want schools to provide sex ed so that they don't have to!

U.S. Tells World We're a 'Bastion of Freedom and Defender of Democracy'; Women's Reproductive Choice under Siege

While the United States moves through the world attempting to gather allies for "the war on terrorism," we are told that this country is more free than any other in the world. As I write this, two Supreme Court justices are resigning, paving the way for appointments that may shift the balance of previous judicial interpretations of the Constitutional right to privacy. In 1973, the landmark federal case of *Roe v. Wade* extended that right, first argued in the 1965 Supreme Court case *Griswold v. Connecticut.* Estelle Griswold had opened a Planned Parenthood clinic precisely to test the state law prohibiting the dispensing of condoms to married heterosexuals. In ruling in favor of Griswold, the Court enabled people such as unmarried college students to have access to condoms, the Pill, lubricants, and spermicidal foam. *Roe v. Wade* established federal protections for the right to privacy—clarifying that state laws restricting a woman's right to have an abortion violated her right to (sexual) privacy. Although many states have subsequently eroded some of that right, in the form of things like parental consent laws and second-trimester restrictions, the federal right still stands. The current threat is real and imminent, however. What is confusing is how Americans feel about abortion.

We are split, virtually down the middle, regardless of how the attitude or "approval" questions are worded (Saad, 2004).[27] About 48 percent are "pro-choice," while 45 percent are "pro-life" and another 7 percent have no opinion or a mixed opinion. When asked about whether laws should be made more strict, about 40 percent think laws should remain as they are. "The plurality—40%—wants the laws to remain as they are, while a smaller percentage (20%) thinks they should be less strict" (Saad, 2004). If we focused only on this social issue, we would surely be confounded by our attempts to spread democracy and freedom around the world while the rights of our female citizens are in jeopardy and the will of the people is completely polarized.

Women and Men Striding toward Equality; Average 72 percent of Known Sexual Assaults Committed by Lovers, Friends, or Relatives

Women and men believe that contemporary American women's lives are better in many ways than women's lives historically. "A June 2001 Gallup Poll found majority support for affirmative action for women—53 percent" (Robison, 2002).[28] Women in public opinion polls appear rather satisfied with the direction of their lives (Saad, 2001).[29] "Overall, a majority of women say they are at least somewhat satisfied with the way society treats women: 13% are very satisfied and 48% are somewhat satisfied. However, more than one in three women, 37%, say they are dissatisfied with society's treatment of women, including 15% who are very dissatisfied," Saad wrote. Women in the national random representative sample were satisfied with things like family, education, physical health, jobs, and opportunities for success. Men and women appear to feel similarly about most of these aspects of life. It is worth noting, however, that in a 1998 Time/CNN national poll, although 42 percent of self-described nonfeminists agreed that "feminism today is relevant to most women," 43 percent had an "unfavorable impression" of feminists (as cited in Kelly 2004: 145).[30] Women of all races and ethnicities can vote, be employed, travel, hold their own property, have children as single parents; struggle, love, cry, rage, and die . . . just like men. Women and men are equal, right?

You know the answer by now. The contradiction inherent in this real-life possible headline is unsettling, to say the least. Women and men may be equal, except when it comes to sexual violence and predatory behavior. As children, boys and girls are subject to the assaults and violations of adults, usually men who are friends of the family, relatives, or trusted authority figures. According to the Rape, Abuse, and Incest National Network (RAINN) and the U.S. Department of Health and Human Services, of the children identified as survivors of "substantiated or indicated sexual abuse," 75 percent were girls (www. RAINN.net). RAINN cites the 1998 Commonwealth Fund Survey of the Health of Adolescent Boys finding that 3 percent of boys in grades five through eight and 5 percent of boys in grades nine through twelve reported that they had been sexually abused (as children, clearly). About 90 percent of adult survivors of sexual assault, rape, and related crimes are women, while 10 percent are men, although it is projected that two-thirds of all survivors never report crimes. Men are especially likely to keep assaults and rapes secret. U.S. Department of Justice statistics (2003) reveal that about 70 percent of female rape survivors and 74 percent of male rape survivors know their rapist—friend, acquaintance, "intimate" (lover or mate), or relative (less than 1 percent for male survivors).[31] Most of those assaults occur at home or within one mile of the survivor's home. Women and men may have more apparent equality than ever before in the United States, but women around the world are disproportionately affected by all varieties of sex crimes, including rape as a war crime, sexual slavery, sex trafficking, and sex tourism. How can we argue that men and women are equal, sexually and in other ways, when the evidence contradicts this? And what are the implications of such a profound imbalance, especially for heterosexuals?

Youth Say It's 'No Big Deal' to Be Gay; Support for Same-Sex Marriage Falters and Reverend Fred Phelps Protests Murdered Teen's Funeral, Says Matthew Shepard Will 'Rot in Hell with Other Fags'; Spanish Legislature Approves Same-Sex Marriage Bill

Researchers like Steven Seidman (2004) and Ritch Savin-Williams (2005) have recently argued that the "closet"—as in "coming out of the closet" and disclosing being gay or lesbian—may be a metaphor of the past.[32] Seidman cites a *New York* magazine poll of New Yorkers, who overwhelmingly would be comfortable with openly gay police officers, doctors, and elementary school teachers. Savin-Williams asserts that gay and lesbian life for current teens and young adults is very different than it was even 10 years ago, and both scholars cite things like more open, diverse mass media portrayals, shifts in hegemonic heterosexualities, and liberalization of individual perceptions of homosexuality. Teens report feeling like being gay is "no big deal," that they are just "regular people," and that "true friends" accept them for who they are (Wloszczyna, 2003; www.sexetc.org).[33]

But Seidman clarifies that "gay life today is defined by a contradiction: *many individuals can choose to live beyond the closet but they must still live and participate in a world where most institutions maintain heterosexual domination*" (italics original) (2004: 6). That domination is perhaps most visible in the fact that cultural support for same-sex marriage is not broadly supported by heterosexuals, but there is no chance for equal protections under the law *without* this support. In fact, the issue is controversial among those with same-sex partners. The Gay and Lesbian Alliance against Defamation (GLAAD) reported on opinion polls in 2005, by CNN/*USA Today*, CBS/*New York Times*, and NBC News/*Wall St. Journal* (www.glaad.org).[34] Such polls are implemented by polling agencies with expertise in sampling and posing questions, but results appear to be highly dependent on exactly how questions are worded. Although it *appears* that the majority of respondents support "legal recognition" for same-sex couples, the majority of positive attitudes relate to civil unions, not marriage. As a legal, emotional, financial, and sexual status traditionally reserved for heterosexually committed people, "marriage" is heavily symbolic. It has been invested with the dreams, hopes, and love of heterosexuals for at least the last 80 to 90 years (prior to that, marriage was a much less romanticized ideal). When Americans are asked about whether same-sex *marriage* should be "allowed" or legally recognized, fears about the future of heterosexual marriage are activated. In all three of the news agencies' polls, only 29 percent of respondents (on average) supported same-sex "marriage."

The other headline was plucked from the events surrounding one of the most infamous hate crimes of the last decade. Matthew Shepard, a 21-year-old college student, was murdered in Laramie, Wyoming, in 1998. Two young men left a bar with Matthew and after learning that he was gay, drove to a remote field, tied him to a fence, beat him, and left him for dead in near-freezing temperatures (taking his wallet and shoes with them). Reverend Fred Phelps, founder of the Westboro Baptist Church in Topeka, Kansas, targeted the funeral, having staged similar picket lines and protests at political and social events and funerals around the country. His Web site clarifies the extent of his belief in the "Primitive/Old School" interpretations of the

Bible. Phelps and his followers exemplify extremes of homophobic virulence, anger, hatred, and fear.

It should be somewhat confusing, then, to see how religion intersects with homosexuality in another context. In Spain, a country with a long history of Catholicism, there is now no legal distinction between same-sex and other-sex pairings (McLean, 2005).[35] The very liberally worded bill passed in the Spanish parliament with a vote of 187 to 147 and gives same-sex couples the right to marry and adopt children. The Netherlands, Canada, and Belgium have similar laws, though not quite as widely applicable and equalizing as Spain's. As has been true in the United States regarding similar proposed legislation, some prominent global religious leaders, including Vatican City officials, worked to prevent passage, claiming that it would threaten the social status quo and moral order. Although more than 80 percent of Spaniards identify themselves as Catholic, religion apparently does not color point of view the way it does in the United States, and in Phelps's case; opinion polls show that between 55 and 65 percent of Spaniards support same-sex *marriage*.

Carlos Baturim and Emilio Menendez, as the first Spanish couple married under the new equalizing legislation, now have a union that recognizes their 30-year relationship. Their lives will be immeasurably different, compared to U.S. same-sex couples, because they were able to choose to sanctify it legally. Marriage is definitely not for everyone, but the choice should be available to all citizens. It is confusing that while other countries have honored civil and equal rights in this context—even nations with long-held religious traditions—the United States is unable to disconnect Christian traditions from our policies.

Women, Inspired by 'Sex and the City,' Have Sex and Hook-Ups on 'Own Terms'; Pharmacists Deny Women 'Morning-After' Pills, RU–486, and Condoms

It seems as if we can easily find evidence of "the revolution in heterosexual dating," proof that "dating is dead," that women are "happily" hooking-up instead of committing to dead-end relationships that may require compromise, change, and heartache. Everywhere we turn we see that things seem to be different, the 1950s notion of "going steady" is obsolete, and women are "having sex like men" (Kamen, 2002).[36] There are at least *three* guides to teach women how to have better hook-ups—regardless of how hook-up is defined, by the way. (If we asked 20 people to define the term, we might get 17 different interpretations.) Journalist Vanessa Grigoriadis explored the intersection of Internet "dating" and "casual sex" in New York City (2003).[37] One of her interviewees, "Jessica," may exemplify the (white, middle-class) heterosexual woman of the new millennium. She explains, "Look, I would like to make babies, but this is primo genetic material we're dealing with here [meaning, herself]—quality control is a big issue. As much as I hope there's some lurking jewel out there, right now, I'm just lonely, curious, and horny." Another woman posted an Internet personals ad reading: "I have declared December 2002 a morals-free zone, where I do what I want, when I want, with whom I want. I want to fuck you. Offer expires 12/31/02." Grigoriadis describes the results:

> She received responses from 70 men and met 10 of them. "Most of them have been quite surprised that I have a personality and a brain—I guess only dull, stupid women are supposed to be sexual? Whatever. I had the best sex of my life with one of them—he discovered my G spot, which I didn't even know I had, I swear. I was like, '*This* is what they're talking about in *Cosmo*'" (2003).

Speaking of *Cosmopolitan*, the magazine might be the most preferred source of information for the newly sexual, no-strings-attached woman looking to hook up. And what would we learn about this kind of sex? It is "morals free," stereotyped ("only dull, stupid women are . . . sexual"), connected to loneliness in some way, and is not about hard and fast commitments. It appears to be a way for heterosexual women to have sex "like men," and for heterosexual men to finally have sex the way they have always wanted to. We will explore these ideas further in chapter 5, because I do not believe that this simplification of either gender is accurate. But for the moment, let's assume this is an accurate description of some single young people's sex lives.

So why, then, are some women being denied the chance to *really* have sex "on their terms" (Kamen, 2002)? There are numerous reports of pharmacists and other medical professionals interfering with women's sexual and reproductive freedoms on the grounds of religion. Pharmacists opposed to the rights protected by *Roe v. Wade* have refused to fill legal prescriptions for the "morning after pill," unfortunate slang for *emergency contraception* (EC), a regimen of several elevated-dose birth control pills, taken within three days after unprotected intercourse. Global retail giant Wal-Mart, with pharmacies in all but 22 of its several thousand North American stores, refused to sell emergency contraception, starting in 1999 (Robinson, 2005).[38] In many small towns in the United States and Canada, having "out competed" locally owned stores, Wal-Mart is the only pharmacy for tens or hundreds of miles, therefore rendering a prescription for emergency contraception useless. As I write, this news report is circulating:

> New York Catholic Leaders Urge Gov. Pataki to Veto Legislation Making EC Available without Doctor's Prescription
> [Jul 13, 2005]
> Catholic leaders in New York are encouraging state Gov. George Pataki (R) to veto legislation (SB 3661) that would make emergency contraception available to all women in the state without a doctor's prescription, the *Albany Times Union* reports (Benjamin, Albany Times Union, 7/12). The bill—which was approved in January by the state Assembly and last month by the state Senate—would allow pharmacists and nurses to dispense EC to women without a doctor's prescription by using blanket prescriptions issued by physicians, certified nurse midwives or certified nurse practitioners that do not name a specific patient. The measure would allow the pills to be dispensed to patients of any age without parental consent (*Kaiser Daily Reproductive Health Report*, 6/23). In a July 6 letter to the governor, the state's eight Catholic bishops said EC is equivalent to abortion and urged Pataki to veto the measure to return "common sense and time-tested values to the public square." The bishops also expressed concern over the lack of an age restriction or parental consent requirement in the measure, saying in the letter, "It is difficult to imagine why anyone would support restricting parental rights and potentially exposing young girls to harmful and powerful medications on a repeated basis in this way." Pataki spokesperson Andrew Rush said the governor has received the letter and will review it when he receives the legislation in question. The state Assembly has until the end of the first week in August to send the bill to Pataki, but Charles Carrier—spokesperson for Assembly Speaker Sheldon Silver (D)—on Monday said the Assembly has not yet decided when it will do so. Once Pataki receives the legislation, he will have about 10 days to decide whether to sign it, veto it or allow the measure to become law without his signature (*Albany Times Union*, 7/12).[39]

Indeed, "it is difficult to imagine why anyone" would think that the new hookup culture has uncomplicated and uncontradictory sociocultural effects. Realistically, hooking up may include some occasional "oops, the condom broke" encounters, along with some, "Contra-what? Oh no!" follies. But if Wal-Mart is your pharmacy or you live in New York (and Pataki gives in to religious entreaties to "return common sense

and time-tested values to the public square"), heterosexual hook-ups will need an extra dose of care.

I recently heard the story of a 25-year-old woman in Washington, D.C., trying to buy condoms in a CVS pharmacy. The educated, professional woman was Asian American, the pharmacist had a similar ethnic background, and he simply refused to sell them to her (Huberman, 2005).[40] He pushed the package back across the counter, shaking his head and saying "No." He then turned away and refused to speak to her about it. The other circumstances surrounding the event are worth noting. The woman was a radio reporter who had been interviewing an expert on teen sexuality. The reporter had expressed her chagrin and consternation about adolescents—"why can't they just use condoms? Why risk pregnancy and diseases?" In response, the expert asked the reporter to go buy condoms; after about an hour, the reporter summoned her courage and walked to the CVS, where her effort was thwarted. What did she learn? Just because it is now legal for anyone to purchase condoms in the United States (see *Griswold v. Connecticut*) does not mean it is *psychologically* easy, nor is it a morally neutral act, similar to buying aspirin.

Cross-Cultural, Global Differences and Similarities in Sexualities

It should make sense that global differences in sex would be confusing. But why would global *similarities* be confusing? Given that I am taking a perspective that challenges the idea that sexualities are reducible to universal absolutes, how can we explain similarities that transcend culture and history? It might be confusing to consider the handful of things that appear to be similar. Linguistic psychologist Steven Pinker (2002) lists a handful of apparent cross-cultural similarities: attraction, jealousy, sexual modesty, and sexual regulation (i.e., the social control of sexuality, including incest prevention).[41] Evolutionary psychologist David Buss studied 37 cultures in 33 countries, gathering data from 10,047 subjects (1994).[42] With the help of 50 unpaid collaborators, Buss aimed to explore which Darwinian hypotheses of evolution could be applied to "human mating." He found that some elements of "mate selection" appear to be universal (although his focus was therefore solely on heterosexual behavior): men seek younger, fit-for-motherhood women, while women seek older, resource-heavy (whether monetary resources or other) men; men seek and desire more partners than do women; both men and women experience jealousy, though men are more jealous about female partners' sexual infidelities and women are more jealous about male partners' emotional infidelities. Buss and other evolutionary psychologists argue that in *is social / political / relative?*

order to really understand human sexuality, we must account for these "fundamental differences" in (heterosexual) men's and women's sexual psychologies. We will return to evolutionary psychology momentarily, and later in the book.

So it may be confusing to consider the perspective in this book—the social construction of sexualities—alongside the arguments of evolutionary psychology, especially because these arguments make sense to most people. Most of us know some women who focus on only men with financial and material resources; there are even several Internet dating services solely for meeting "millionaire" men. Most of us know what jealousy feels like, and we may even have experienced it in the gendered/sexed way that sexual selection strategies predict. Because men's and women's differences are highlighted in our culture while similarities tend to be glossed over, it is easy to accept arguments and evidence that extend our perceptions of difference.

Given that evolutionary psychology posits several sexual universals, it may then be confusing to note that there are numerous contemporary cross-cultural differences. What Americans probably think of as homosexuality is not necessarily found in all cultures, although anthropologists can document instances of men engaging in "sexual" contact with other men (Herdt, 1999).[43] I say "sexual" because although the behavior may include, for example, genital-mouth contact, it is not necessarily experienced as "sexual." Premarital heterosexual intercourse rates vary widely among teens. Studies report that perhaps 11 percent of women in Asia have had intercourse by age 18, and anywhere from 45 to 52 percent of sub-Saharan African women have had intercourse by age 19 (www.WHO.int, 2001).[44] In Western countries, by age 20 most young women have had intercourse: 67 percent in France, 79 percent in Great Britain, and 71 percent in the United States (Darroch, Singh, and Frost, 2001).[45] For 60 percent of the heterosexually married couples in the world, marriage is arranged, suggesting that the importance placed on love, lust, and chemistry in Western countries is certainly not universal (Mackay, 2001).[46] In the United Kingdom, of the 42,000 babies born to women aged 15–19, 87 percent are born to young women who are not married. In Japan, only 10 percent of babies born to 15–19-year-olds are born to young women who are not married ("Into a New World," 1998).[47]

So what do these and many other differences mean? What is their significance? It is beyond our scope to really delve into the meanings and interpretations global citizens give to their sexualities, but we can explore some of the implications of these differences. For now, we can note that global differences seem to support the argument that culture, society, and subcultural influences shape individuals' sexualities.

Academic and Scholarly Perspectives on Sexualities

There is no doubt that academic and scholarly perspectives promote enormous confusion. Among the major disciplines—including psychology, sociology, biology, anthropology, and history—there is little consensus about most aspects of sex. Are all things sexual attributable to genes, hormones, and evolution? How do sexual orientations develop? What does it mean to say that sexualities come from "nature" or "nurture"? Why do human animals engage in oral, anal, and other forms of nonreproductive sex? Why do all the disciplines seem to have such different ways of asking questions and seeking answers?

The most facile answer to all these questions, and to the question of why the major disciplines discuss sex differently, is that sexualities are far from simple. No one perspective or approach can possibly suffice for such a complex, multifaceted aspect of humanity. The attempt to unify the perspectives and honor the multidisciplinary nature of sex resulted in a hybrid field, *sexology*. Sexology, the systematic study of sexuality patterns and generalizations, combined with theorizing about human sexualities as a way to bridge the gaps in each individual field (Bland and Doan, 1998).[48] In the early 1900s, a German dermatologist, Iwan Bloch, proposed that in order to fully understand human love, we needed to combine the knowledge and perspectives of the natural and social sciences with the humanities.

Due to its interdisciplinary nature, sexology is not recognizable at universities and colleges. You cannot earn a "sexology" bachelor's degree in a regular degree program (and even so, it would not be as fun or naughty as it sounds), although there are several U.S. graduate programs with a focus on human sexuality (and several U.S. undergraduate minors do exist). The graduate programs often focus on anatomy, physiology, and counseling skills, presuming that graduates will use their knowledge to offer sex or marital therapy. This hints at some of the problems with academic and scholarly perspectives. We tend to see relatively disconnected arguments, theories, and empirical methods across the disciplines. Sexology, as Bloch conceived it, has not unified or revolutionized our knowledge. In fact, our thinking about sexualities may be more fragmented than ever, now that women's studies, cultural studies, humanities disciplines, and other epistemologies are contributing to the discourse about sex. You may be taking this course having already taken several other college classes that include sex. But rather than clarifying sex, due to disciplinary contradictions and debates, your academic knowledge and individual experiences may only serve to muddy the waters.

Nature and Nurture

Within the specific context of academic and scholarly perspectives, we find perhaps the most well known debate. People who know little about specific sexuality research may nonetheless know about what is commonly called "nature versus nurture." The word *versus* is meant to connote opposition, the idea that one thing is against the other, and of course, that there is no common ground between the two. When stated this way, it is of course less confusing: sexualities are attributable to either nature (i.e., genes, hormones, the brain) OR nurture (i.e., family of origin, individual psychology, sociocultural factors). But it is misleading to argue that sexualities are the result of either what is natural or innate or how and where we are raised. Everything about sex is simply far too complex to argue for only one influence or contribution. Because humans are constantly and actively shaping the world around us, it may never be possible to know which elements of nature and nurture contribute to which specific aspects of our sexualities. For example, we know that sex hormones, such as testosterone, are highest at dawn and first thing in the morning, yet the most popular time for sex is in the evening, before bed (Margolis, 2004).[49] If nature were solely responsible, we would probably just respond to those hormonal cues. Indeed, there must be some intervening variables of culture or nurture that inspire us to instead be sexual later in the evening. We will address nature and nurture, along with corollary concepts of essentialism and social constructionism, in chapter 2.

THINKING CRITICALLY ABOUT THE BIG PICTURE

What does it mean to be a critical thinker? Does it simply mean that we have to incessantly find fault with everything? Critical thinking is actually deeper than simply criticizing and nitpicking. It is probably relatively easy for most people to just criticize. Instead, let me argue that true critical thinking is both a process and a disciplined cognitive habit. The quality of our lives is directly connected to the quality of our thinking. Scriven and Paul (undated) write that "Critical thinking is the intellectually disciplined process of actively and skillfully conceptualizing, applying, analyzing, synthesizing, and/or evaluating information gathered from, or generated by, observation, experience, reflection, reasoning, or communication, as a guide to belief and action."[50] In describing this as a process, I mean to convey that critical thinking is something you can begin doing. Through trial and error, you will develop facility and skills, and gradually, you will feel more confident about your abilities, but you will probably never stop refining the *process* of reasoned critique. In describing this as a disciplined cognitive habit, I mean to convey that critical thinking involves some mental retraining. Paul and Elder note that "everyone thinks. . . . But much of our thinking, left to itself, is biased, distorted, partial, uninformed or down-right prejudiced" (2001: 1).[51]

So the new habit is based on things like clarity, relevance, sound evidence, and good reasoning. The process of learning how to think critically is characterized by noting the difference between thinking and memorizing and simply gaining a skill and using that skill repeatedly. Paul and Elder's model of critical thinking (2001) encompasses eight *elements of thought* that they argue are universally applicable (though some would argue that they only apply to Western, contemporary thinking and ideas):

1. *purpose of the thinking:* the goal or objective; the writer's aim or intention
2. *question at issue:* the key or most important question(s); not always stated in the interrogative form
3. *point of view:* the writer's frame of reference or perspective relative to the issue; writer's orientation or stance
4. *key concepts:* theories, ideas, principles; broad, vague abstractions; disciplinary axioms
5. *information and/or evidence:* observations and experiences; data and things taken to be facts
6. *assumptions:* presuppositions, ideas taken for granted
7. *interpretation and inference:* examining the evidence and beginning to draw conclusions; exploring leaps of logic or mind
8. *implications and consequences:* potential conclusions; something necessarily following from a set of conditions or from the evidence

These elements of thought are foundational to developing a good, new habit of mind. To understand any creator's ideas, including our own—whether the ideas are in a song, a film, a scholarly article, or a *Cosmopolitan* magazine article—we must apply the elements of thought. We could ask questions about every source we run across, and then we could ask these questions of our work as well (adapted from Paul and Elder, 2001):

1. What is the main purpose of this [article, paper, chapter, film, poem, and so on]? Is it clearly stated or do you need to infer to figure it out?
2. What is the key question or problem at issue in the [article, paper, chapter, film, poem, and so on]? Is the key question directly related to the purpose?

3. What is the author's point of view? What is his or her stance relative to the issue? How does it affect the arguments the author makes? Does s/he consider any alternate points of view?

4. What are the key concepts? What main axioms, principles, abstractions, and so on would the reader need to understand in order to understand the author's reasoning?

5. What is the most important information [e.g., observations and experiences]? What is the most important evidence [e.g., data and facts]? Is the author's information/evidence persuasive and purposive?

6. What assumptions is the author making? What is being taken for granted or as "a given"?

7. What are the main inferences—what leaps of logic does the author make? Are all conclusions well supported by the information and evidence?

8. What are the implications and/or consequences of the author's argument? What might follow from the author's logic? What is the possible significance of the ideas the author presents?

The most vital starting point might be *point of view*. What is yours? Where do you stand relative to any issue? You may be tempted to answer that you don't take a position or develop an opinion until you have all the facts. Or that you don't offer your opinion because you think people should be free to just be themselves. You may say that your point of view is "don't bother me, I won't bother you." In any case, each of these constitutes a stance, and each affects the way that you read, listen, hear, respond, perceive, and think. The fact is that you will read this text with a point of view pretty firmly entrenched and developed; you walk into your classroom with it, and that cannot be overlooked. Your *assumptions* and *inferences*—leaps of logic, maybe unsupported by evidence—also form and contribute to your point of view (or *perspective*). If you acknowledge and examine your point of view, your critical thinking skills will begin to blossom.

Another important element of critical thinking, especially regarding sexualities, is clarification of evidence, data, and facts, compared to personal opinion. What is the difference and why is it important? Personal opinion is naturally subjective, which is not necessarily problematic. But opinion can be limited and limiting, confined only to the experiences and observations of any individual. Evidence, data, and facts afford the critical thinker the chance to assess the method of data collection, to generalize from outside oneself, and to plot patterns of behavior. Like your point of view, you will have opinions—probably developed from your life experiences. But you may be missing data or evidence with which to explore, strengthen, and/or challenge those opinions. Working with data—and making arguments with evidence—enables us to really transcend the basic opinions we may take for granted.

Paul and Elder also caution us to become aware of our *egocentrism*. Egocentric points of view are basically self-centered and certainly uncritical and unreflective. Ego-centrism gives rise to conclusions with unreflective logic at the core, propositions about the world that are wholly unquestioned because there is some benefit to main-taining the status quo. These justifications for beliefs and ideas can be characterized as: "it is true because I have been told it is"; "it is true because my family or friends believe it"; "it is true because my religion, state, and so on have told me so"; "it is true because it is in my best interests to believe it and I will lose something if I disbelieve it"; and "it is true because I directly stand to benefit if I maintain this belief." Here are some examples of egocentric thinking:

- it is true because my family or friends believe it
  EX: Adults who choose to be celibate and not engage in sex, or who are not particu-larly interested in sex, have something wrong with them.
- it is true because my religion and state have told me so
  EX: Homosexuality is wrong. Why? Because my religion argues this.
- it is true because I directly stand to benefit if I maintain this belief
  EX: People who are poor are simply too lazy to work hard and get ahead, and only the smart, hard-working, attractive people get ahead in this world (i.e., people like me).

In this book, you will see many of the elements of thought utilized in discus-sions of research and theorizing about sexualities, especially point of view, assump-tions, and implications. It is important to think in a concerted way about these and the other elements in order to truly understand the social construction of sex, gen-der, and all things sexual. Throughout this book, we will explore context, contradic-tions, variables, and critiques. You are invited to embark on a brief journey into the heart of one of the most intimate things about us, if not *the* most intimate. My hope is that by the time you finish reading this book, your critical and social imagination will be finely tuned, and that you will never forget, as Leonore Tiefer says, that sex is *not* a natural act (2004).[52]

Questions to Ponder

1. What issues besides adultery have been socially constructed? How would you know if some aspect of sexualities had indeed been socially constructed?

2. Which terms do you use to talk about sexualities? Do you favor slang, and if so, a wider or smaller variety? Do you know anyone who uses more clinical, medical, or academic terminologies?

3. What are some of *your* egocentric beliefs, assumptions, and/or points of view about sexualities?

Suggested Projects

1. Find your own newspaper (printed or online version) headlines. Focus on headlines that can be juxtaposed to reveal the confusing, contradictory, or ambivalent aspects of human sexualities. What else can you learn about the issues presented in the accompanying articles? What analysis can you develop?

2. Practice critical thinking by finding an article (magazine, newspaper, or scholarly journal) and work with the elements of thought to discern the author's purpose, key questions, assumptions, and so forth. Use the elements of thoughts to clearly and concisely present your analysis, making your own purpose clear.

2

Studying the Sexual

CLASSIFYING AND THEORIZING

You are standing in a small room. The room is filled with machines tabulating, recording, and beeping. You are looking into a larger, connected room; using a one-way mirror, you can see clearly, as if looking through glass. The man and woman in the other room can only see themselves, reflected in the mirror. The couple knows that you and others are watching and listening, but you think they may be more comfortable if they cannot see the faces and reactions of you and your colleagues. The couple is on an elevated platform—not quite a bed, but similar. They each have electrodes affixed to their temples, the base of their skull, their chests. They have blood pressure cuffs around their arms and pulse meters on a finger. The beeps in your room correspond to heart rate; the machines are recording this and respiration, blood flow, and brain activity. The man in the observation room has an additional device on his penis, a plethysmograph, measuring blood flow and engorgement. The woman has a small probe in her vagina, measuring lubrication and blood flow. The couple is kissing and touching each other. You are keeping track of the couple's body language and movements, the noises they are making, and the monitors beeping in your room. Is this science fiction or a real way to study human sexualities?

Believe it or not, one of the most well known studies of the twentieth century, William Masters and Virginia Johnson's 1950s research into "human sexual response" (orgasm, specifically), took place in a very similar setting. Masters, a physician in St. Louis, Missouri, and Johnson, recruited specifically for the study, wanted to understand men's and women's patterns of orgasm, so they solicited people with previous orgasmic experience. The first step was to interview women and men gathered from the ranks of St. Louis's sex workers; they wanted to understand more about variations in sexuality.

They eventually recruited 694 people (between about 16 and 80 years old) to have intercourse and masturbate in their sex lab, while being observed by Masters and a team. Some of the subjects had vaginal intercourse with a mechanized, thrusting "coition machine." The machine had a transparent, hollow, penis-shaped probe with a movie camera and lights. Women were able to control the machine's thrusts. In all, Masters and Johnson estimated that 10,000 orgasms shuddered and groaned through their labs over the course of the study. They concluded that "the human sexual response" followed a discernible pattern, arbitrarily divided into four phases:

1. excitement: vasocongestion, or flow of blood into genital area, begins
2. plateau: vasocongestion at its peak; penis erect, though subject to waxing and waning; change in tightness of vagina
3. orgasm: rhythmic contractions of pelvic organs, increased breathing and heart rate
4. resolution: after orgasm's release of muscular tension and reversal of genital blood flow, the return of body to pre-excitement levels (includes men's refractory period, when erection is not possible though desire may remain elevated)

The researchers argued that women had three basic patterns that included these four phases, while men had one basic pattern. Their research has had profound effects on the way we view sexualities, and not all those effects have been positive, as we will see later in this chapter.

Although scholars occasionally study sexual acts by observation, it is actually the least frequent way in which we gather information and develop data about patterns in sexualities. A handful of more recent laboratory studies of orgasms have been done, using very small groups of very specific people, or population *samples* (e.g., Ladas, Whipple, and Perry, 1982; Zaviacic et al., 1988; Schubach, 2001[1]). A sample is a smaller segment of a larger population, studied so that we can make inferences or draw conclusions about the larger group. When we refer to the *population*, we are referring to the whole number, or a body of individuals or objects with something in common, such as the U.S. population. But with something as complex as sexualities it is simply not enough to know how many times, how many partners, how many sex acts. We need to know more about how people feel about what they do or don't do, how they learn about sex, and how they come to understand themselves. In this chapter, we will explore some methods of studying and theorizing about sex. Sexual science (*sexology*) is largely concerned with documenting "the truth" of human sexualities. A founding principle of natural science—*positivism*—was imported into social sciences. Positivism is the idea that knowledge is based on natural phenomena and their properties, verifiable by empiricism, or the seeking of evidence to test hypotheses and establish "the truth." But how do we learn about sexualities? Is there a truth that we can find? Is it possible to document the truth of sex? In this chapter, you will learn about specific methodologies, a few theories, and most importantly, you will learn how to be critical of what you read, hear, and see.

MAKING SENSE OF SEX IN THE MEDIA

"What Everyone You Know Is *Really* Doing in Bed: The Sex Survey That'll Shock You"

When we turn to page 198 in the June 2005 *Glamour* to read about what everyone we know is doing in bed, we discover that the article is titled, "What's *Really* Going On in Other People's Sex Lives?" Indeed, a reporter simply stopped people on the streets in Miami and posed questions like, "How often do you have sex?" and "What's your favorite sexual position?" This might grab you; you might buy the magazine, hoping to be shocked and informed about what's happening in other people's bedrooms. You would read for entertainment, picking up sex tips here and there and hoping (against hope) that you might remember the suggestions some night when you're actually in a position to try them out. But we have a different goal—to use this article to learn more about how we study and talk about sex. We will also clarify the distinctions between quantitative and qualitative research.

First, consider that the cover headline advertises a "survey." Loosely speaking, we could say that the article does report the results of a *survey*, a set of questions posed for the purpose of quantifying (counting) data or information. The method of data collection could instead be called an *interview*, which is qualitative, where the researcher is assessing the quality, type, and meaning of respondents' answers. But in order for any research to be useful, from a social scientific point of view, we would need to know more details. So what distinguishes a more scientific survey or interview from the one carried out by *Glamour*? The questions you should ask about surveys and interviews include:

- Who is the population and how was the sample collected? Was it random? Representative?
- How many people were asked to participate, and what percentage (or proportion) refused to participate?
- Who agrees to participate in sex research anyway?
- How representative are the answers offered?
- What is the context in which sex research is undertaken?
- What point of view or perspective does the researcher (or reporter) bring to the study?

Critical Thinking and Research: Asking the Right Questions

Who is the population and how was the sample collected? Was it random? Representative? What does it mean to describe a survey (or poll) as *random* or *representative?* These terms refer to the way in which the sample was derived. Random sampling means that each member of the broader population (from which the smaller sample is drawn) has an equal chance of being selected for the study. A representative sample is one in which all the elements in the sample represent or approximate the broader population. These concerns are relevant in *quantitative research*, a formal, systematic method utilizing data that can be counted. Quantitative researchers want to report findings that are generalizable to other samples and populations; there is an assumption that quantitative research is objective, which we will explore later in this chapter. Let's return to the Gallup public opinion surveys discussed in chapter 1, where researchers were asking a random, representative sample of Americans about their attitudes on adultery.

The Gallup sample. The "adultery" poll reported in chapter 1 was based on a survey of 1,005 adults, over 18 years old, phoned at home over three days (Carroll, 2005).[2] The population of the United States is about 296 million, clearly an unfeasibly large number of people to survey. In order to study "Americans," researchers must sample a smaller group from that broader population. Things like opinion polls are generally done with random, representative samples, thus every American over 18 (with a land line phone number—still more than 90 percent of the population) has an equal chance or probability of being included. Representation is achieved by using known population parameters, or statistics, to ensure that some dominant or important features of the population are found in the sample as well.

Often "representative" refers to racial/ethnic composition. U.S. 2000 Census figures suggest that about 69 percent of Americans are Caucasian, 12 percent are

African American, 12.5 percent are Hispanic American, 3.5 percent are Asian American, about 1 percent are Native American, and about 1.5 percent are multiracial/multiethnic. In the Gallup poll, a representative sample means that the 1,005 respondents are composed of people who essentially represent the racial/ethnic characteristics of the broader population. Sometimes researchers will design a *stratified* sample. This design strives to equalize all the elements in the sample, so if race/ethnicity is our example, we might see a sample that was 25 percent Caucasian, 25 percent African American, 25 percent Asian America, and 25 percent Hispanic American (Schutt, 2004).[3]

If a study's sample is truly random and representative, we can generalize about the findings in terms of the overall population. Public opinion surveys generally use the term *Americans;* this is how we can say, while sounding very confident indeed, that 93 percent of Americans think that adultery is immoral. The benefit of a random, representative sample is clear: greater ability to draw conclusions about behavior, attitudes, or any other arena of social life.

In contrast to public opinion polls, the mid-century research of Kinsey and others did not utilize random, representative sampling. Although the research team was able to gather sexual history interviews from 5,300 men and 5,940 women, the samples were skewed. There were disproportionately high percentages of prisoners and other captive populations (including college students), and those interviewed were Caucasian; many were formally educated, which was rarer in the 1940s. Although the data are flawed by inattention to certain scientific principles, they have been cited for decades partially because of the sheer volume of sexual histories obtained.

Qualitative Research. With qualitative interview studies, we are not concerned with sampling in the same way. But we do need to know who was selected for the study and why. Shari Dworkin and Lucia O'Sullivan (2005) wanted to know whether there are gaps between heterosexual men's patterns of who initiates sex and what they actually desire (e.g., wanted female partners to make the first move).[4] While they undoubtedly could have devised a survey or questionnaire, they wanted to *explore* respondents' experiences and thoughts about sexual desires and initiation. *Qualitative research* is characterized by an emphasis on exploring the individual, subjective meanings and interpretations people make and give to their lives and experiences. Dworkin and O'Sullivan describe their sample in a way that clarifies who was chosen and why:

> The sample included 32 men enrolled [in] a city college in New York City. . . . To be eligible, participants had to be between the ages of 18 and 24 and be in a sexually active, heterosexual romantic relationship of at least two

months' duration. . . . Corresponding to the demographics of residents in the neighborhood, almost one third (30%) described their race as African American/Black, 50% as White, and 20% as Other. In terms of ethnicity, less than one quarter (20%) reported that they were Hispanic or Latino. Less than half were born in the United States (45%), 25% were from Puerto Rico, the Dominican Republic, and Columbia [*sic*], 20% were from Europe, and the remaining men reported other origins (2005: 152).

Although randomness and representation are not vital to qualitative studies, well-designed work will be purposive. The sample described above is purposive, in that the respondents were not selected simply out of *convenience* (e.g., the first 20 men walking down a local street). The parameters for inclusion served a purpose for the research—men in a specific age range, with demographics similar to that of the college's area, involved in relationships of a specific type. Why do you think Dworkin and O'Sullivan wanted those in relationships of at least two months? In order to study the patterns of sexual initiation, they needed respondents with sufficient experiences. And finally, why do you suppose they specified only heterosexual men? That was purposive as well, given that they wished to explore gender(ed) dynamics in who initiates sexual activity, and whether men with female partners like the traditional script of man-as-initiator. In the *Glamour* article, we have no idea how the reporter chose the couples she did.

How many people were asked to participate, and what percentage (or proportion) refused to participate?   The *Glamour* article does not indicate how many people the reporter stopped on the street before she found enough willing participants. In this case, both members of the couple had to be willing to talk and be photographed for the magazine. For more scientific research, it is useful to know the *response rate,* the number or percentage of people who returned mail surveys; or, the percentage of those sampled who agreed to participate. A high response rate is most desirable, naturally. In the National Health and Social Life Survey (NHSLS) referred to in chapter 1, researchers were diligent about obtaining the strongest possible sample (Laumann et al., 1994).[5] Their response rate was about 72 percent, meaning that of all the people contacted for participation, 72 percent agreed to be surveyed. This is a very robust rate for any survey, let alone a lengthy one with page after page of questions about sex and relationships. Overall, 3,432 Americans between 18 and 59 participated; the sample was random and representative.

We always need to know how many people fail to or refuse to respond to any survey. What if you drew a random sample of 500 juniors and seniors at your college and mailed sex surveys to each, but only 85 returned the survey? Would the 85 respondents differ in some meaningful or consequential way, compared to the 415 who did not take the time to reply? Maybe the 85 respondents were more liberal and comfortable talking about sex. Maybe they were actually more conservative and wanted to take the time to express their views. In qualitative studies, response rate is less directly applicable, but we do need to know whether any respondents began interviews that they did not complete.

Who agrees to participate in sex research anyway?   Have you ever participated in academic sex research, perhaps as part of a class? Not surprisingly, many of the studies published in journals utilize college student samples. Professors find that students are essentially a captive, adventurous audience and will accept minimal participation incentives, including course credit and nominal reimbursements of a few dollars. The Internet has made it easier for scholars to, theoretically at least, expand the subject pool. Studies can be posted and publicized via sites like "Online Social Psychology Studies."[6] But even with the potential to gather respondents more widely, a persistent problem in all sex research is *respondent bias*, a problem with several primary elements.

Memory Problems: A young man who is "sexually experienced" has been selected for a psychology professor's study. He is asked to recall the last time he engaged in any kind of sex with a partner. Then he is asked to think back to the last 10, 20, or 50 times he was sexual with a partner. Most likely, he cannot precisely pin down each incident of partnered sex. The fact is that respondents cannot always recall how many times, with whom, when, why, and how. Were drugs and/or alcohol ever involved? This could certainly impede someone's memory for details they never dreamed they would later need to conjure up for a study.

Do some people willfully lie or misrepresent the truth? Undoubtedly, but it is probably more likely that confusing and contradictory statistics about some aspects of sexuality are attributable to poor recall. Michael W. Wiederman, in a text entirely devoted to the specifics of sex research, gives an example of "a respondent who in actuality has experienced vaginal intercourse with 16 partners over a span of 30 years" (2001: 21).[7] It begins to sound like a convoluted math problem. If the person has been married and monogamous since age 29, and is now 47, having first had penile-vaginal intercourse at age 17, that means "this person accumulated 15 of the total 16 partners between the ages of 17 and 29, a period that ended 18 years ago!" (Wiederman,

2001: 21). The likelihood of quickly and accurately remembering every partner and the relevant details is slim.

Downey et al. (1995) report the details of their study with 87 men.[8] Respondents completed "Sexual Activity Records," indicating the number of times during a specified interval they had engaged in 15 types of sexual activity with three types of male partners: primary, occasional, and one time. The men completed the sexual activity records once per week, and after three months were asked to recall their activities from the entire three-month period. The men could remember what kinds of things they had done, but not very much about specific activities with specific kinds of partners. More partners combined with more activities lead to greater recall problems. Another study of the accuracy of self-report data revealed that the ability to accurately remember was linked to time frame and number of partners (Jaccard et al., 2004).[9] In this study, 285 single, heterosexually active adults kept weekly records of sexual partners. At intervals of one month, three months, six months, and twelve months, researchers compared the weekly records to respondents' recall. Those with no shared sexual activities or who claimed monogamy had better recall, while those with multiple partners had worse recall. Jaccard and colleagues also found associations between behavior and other variables; those with less formal education and those who advocated nonrelational sex had worse recall.

The lesson here is therefore simple. Most of us do not record our sex lives in detail contemporaneously with the occurrence of events. So when asked for details in surveys or interviews, we must dig deep into our memories. We may not recall correctly, but the fact is that a lot of what we know about sex, from a research standpoint, is derived solely from self-reported information, most of it retrospective.

This is the case in both quantitative and qualitative studies. The difference is that qualitative research privileges participants' subjective memories, experiences, and impressions. Qualitative studies acknowledge the particular context and issues inherent in self-reported, retrospective data. Well-designed quantitative and qualitative studies attempt to minimize the effects of self-report data by repeating questions throughout a survey and using different questions to assess the same concept (e.g., multiple questions to get at sexual self-esteem, also known as a *scale* or *index*).

Other Forms of Bias. Who would agree to answer questions about their sex lives? What motivates people to participate in revealing intimate details in the name of science or entertainment (as in the case of magazine articles)? We have to wonder whether respondent bias extends to those who actually take part in research. Is it only that people with really interesting, exciting, or unusual sex lives take part? Maybe it is only the most open-minded and liberal among us who participate. Is there a difference between those who *volunteer* for a study, compared to those who are included in a sample and are then contacted by researchers? These questions are among those that have been raised about the Kinsey studies, especially given that many of his findings have not been replicated in any subsequent research (e.g., 70 percent of the men had visited a prostitute at least once, 37 percent at had at least one same-sex sexual encounter).

Is it possible for respondents to be completely honest about something as fraught with cultural baggage as sex? For example, in a study of the frequency of safer sex practices, respondents may imagine that the researcher wants to hear evidence of safer sex. Respondents may inflate the number of behaviors or number of instances, fearing that the researcher would be judgmental if respondents admitted that safer sex practices were not part of their sex lives. The consequences of honesty may differ for men and women. Heterosexual men may exaggerate the number of partners they have had, assuming that masculinity is connected to sexual prowess. Heterosexual women may underreport their partners, assuming that femininity is connected to chastity. Men may be judged by peers and others for not having "enough" partners, while women may be judged for having too many partners. Shame, fear, and guilt are not natural elements of sexuality—they are socially constructed and still function as powerful motivators.

Question Bias. Who asks questions about sexual attitudes and behaviors? Let's review for a moment: most sex research is quantitative or qualitative (although some, though not many, studies employ both approaches). Quantitative research in any field or specialty is thought to be objective, value-neutral, concerned with developing theories, and invested in establishing countable patterns and generalizations. Qualitative research is not as invested in the objectivity of the researcher and is more open to the idea that a researcher may in fact have a subjective perspective on the topic (e.g., a woman who identifies as lesbian may study aspects of lesbian women's sexual identities).

So who asks questions? Who does research? Richard von Krafft-Ebing offered his case studies of "perversion" in the name of educating medical professionals. Kinsey, trained as a zoologist and recognized as an expert on gall wasps, wanted to apply his statistical training and quantitative perspective to sex. Masters and Johnson wanted to generalize about patterns of orgasm. But none of these researchers was objective in the truest sense of the word. Each had an agenda, specific to his or her sociocultural and historical moment and subjective experiences. Even if we might support the ultimate aims—like Kinsey's, whose research was intended to normalize sex by showing that behavior was just a matter of counting who did what to or with whom—it is clear that questions about sex are posed by people subject to specific contexts. Sexology is filled with examples of nonobjective scholars disseminating findings under the guise of objectivity.

Given this, how are questions worded? What specific terms and concepts are employed? Consider this popular question: How often have you and your partner engaged in sex during the past month? Imagine a respondent answering this: She wonders what "sex" means, because she is bisexual and currently has a female partner. She thinks that it must mean penile-vaginal intercourse, because that's *usually* what "sex" means, when the average person refers to it. Three weeks ago she did hook up with a guy while she and her girlfriend were taking a little break—should she count that instance as "sex," even though the actual intercourse was very brief because they both drank too much, and neither had an orgasm? And what about the fact that the guy was not really a "partner" (she considers her partner to be her on-again, off-again girlfriend)?

So she's decided that for her, "partner" equals girlfriend, solving one quandary. But she's back to the question of what "sex" means. She decides to define it according to her experiences . . . but should sex be anything that produces an orgasm with her girlfriend? For both or only one of them? What about the time when her girlfriend fell asleep but she quietly masturbated without waking the girlfriend?

This cumbersome example is not merely theoretical and magnifies the difficulties inherent in querying people about sex. Not all sex researchers are savvy about the slang, concepts, relationships, and activities most meaningful to respondents. This produces humorous but inadequate wording, and potentially, inaccurate measurements. An example of an awkward question can be found in the National Longitudinal Study of Adolescent Health (Add Health), a random, representative sample of 18,924 American students in grade seven through grade twelve: "Have you ever had vaginal intercourse? (Vaginal intercourse is when a man inserts his penis into a woman's vagina.)."[10] This certainly sounds like a researcher's question, and it is not worded in the most user-friendly manner, given the teen population/sample.

Another example of question bias can be found in the ubiquitous items that assume a "romantic relationship" between sex partners. Given that many studies utilize college students, it is far from accurate to assume that college students are sexual only within defined relationships. Manning, Longmore, and Giordano address this in an analysis of Add Health data on teens' sexual experiences outside a relationship (2005).[11] Oddly though, they refer to these experiences as "non-romantic sex" (2005: 385). And finally, many questions are biased by assumptions of heterosexuality. If I ask respondents about "sex" without defining what I mean by "sex," I may actually end up measuring a range of sexual behaviors I had not anticipated.

Researchers must be sensitive to the nuances, connotations, and blind spots in the questions they pose.

How representative are the answers offered?   In the *Glamour* article, the reporter generally provides three or four couples' responses for each question:

> Question: "What's the craziest thing you've done sexually?
> • We had sex in a car on I–95
> • We went to a swingers' club
> • S&M—with handcuffs!" (Anonymous, 2005: 199)

When you read the couple's answer to the last "confession," you learn that the pair has not actually tried SM, or sadomasochistic activities. When I discovered this, I immediately thought, Wow! They can't find three people who have actually done "crazy" sexual things. They had to fudge a little and include a couple who have just been thinking about something "crazy." It made me wonder how many people really had answered the other questions, and whether the published answers accurately represented the range of answers couples provided.

My guess is that the reporter was not necessarily attentive to whether the published answers were representative. But when you assess and evaluate scientific research, you should be alert to this. If the survey includes open-ended answers, where respondents write freely, has the researcher explained how the published examples were chosen? There are two other components of survey research we should briefly explore, pilot testing and researcher bias, or point of view.

Pilot testing is an initial data collection, usually done on a small scale, with the intention of helping the researcher refine procedures and survey (or interview) questions. In pilot testing, a researcher can determine whether she needs to change, reword, or clarify key concepts and questions. For example, imagine a survey or interview question like this: "How often do you usually have sex?" Now imagine all the potential problems with even a short question like this! What does "usually" mean? Is it referring to an average day, week, month, semester, or year? And what does "have sex" mean? Will the respondent interpret it in the way the researcher intends it? Will the respondent assume that "have sex" means engage in penile-vaginal intercourse, simply because that's what it *usually* means? So pilot testing can benefit the researcher, especially for sexuality studies, which can be riddled with confusing, unclear terms and concepts.

Researcher bias is what it sounds like, the usually unintentional skewing of research. This can take the form of a taken-for-granted bias favoring heterosexuality, which would be evident in questions that only apply to heterosexual conduct and/or identity. Or the researcher can embody very distinct perspectives or attitudes that seep into the research, tainting the researcher's claims of *objectivity*. Merriam-Webster OnLine defines this as "expressing or dealing with facts or conditions as perceived without distortion by personal feelings, prejudices, or interpretations." Objectivity has been established as a gold standard for research, certainly in the natural and social sciences. But is it likely that we will find researchers who can study sexuality without any "personal feelings, prejudices, or interpretations"? It is possible, of course, but the history of sex research reveals a long trajectory of biased studies. The researcher set out to prove something—that homosexuality was deviant, or that women were inferior to men, or that people who desired to transition from one gender to another were mentally ill. Someone who wished to demonstrate all these assertions was Richard von Krafft-Ebing (1840–1902), who published a classic work of sexology, *Psychopathia Sexualis,* in 1886. Krafft-Ebing was operating within a context in which it was expected that he document "psychopathological manifestations" (quoted in Szasz, 2000).[12] He did so by listing case after case of "unspeakable [sexual] abominations," describing, among other things, people who had sex with animals and who were aroused by corpses.

The fact that we are still discussing him in the twenty-first century should hint at the general importance of research, but more so at the specific consequences of reading research uncritically. It is naïve to simply assume that all contemporary sex research, whether in *Glamour* magazine or in an academic source, is carefully and objectively undertaken. All research is done by humans, and since we all develop points of view (as outlined in chapter 1 in the discussion on critical thinking), it is a fiction to think that we can be totally objective about something as confusing and contradictory as sex. Becoming aware of our subjective points of view is the first step toward reducing "personal feelings, prejudices, or interpretations," but I do not think they can ever be eliminated.

What is the context in which sex research is undertaken? What point of view or perspective does the researcher (or reporter) bring to the study? What do you think the *Glamour* reporter's bias was? Remember that the cover teaser read, "What Everyone You Know Is *Really* Doing in Bed." The article itself was titled "What's *Really* Going On in Other People's Sex Lives?" Before we speculate on her point of view, let's establish that the main purpose of any magazine is to sell more issues, and for women's magazines, competition for readers is tight. Given that, the reporter may believe that her readers really do want or need to know about other people's sex lives. She herself may be curious about other people's practices and attitudes. Maybe her point of view is that we cannot really know much about sex unless we know what the neighbors, our friends, and total strangers are doing. Maybe she thinks that we (the hypothetical readers) are insecure about sex and need to compare ourselves to others, assess where we are relative to others, and adjust ourselves accordingly.

One thing I *am* sure about is that thinking, studying, and writing about sex in the United States occurs in a society that is conflicted about sex. You are probably shaking your head, disagreeing with me right now. Magazine headlines, movies, and television shows give the impression that this is a highly sexual culture. Indeed, your surroundings (e.g., a dormitory, an apartment in a student neighborhood) and your peers may seem to confirm that impression. And it's no longer just that we can see actors kissing and pretending to make love—with cable, we can see a comedian talking about a famous singer's interest in urinating on women. We can see four single women in Manhattan talking about (and appearing to have) everything from anal sex to oral sex to full Brazilian bikini waxing. The extent of the media's influence can be seen in this quote on an Internet bulletin board about *Sex and the City* (emphasis and typographical errors are original):

> BUT. . . THE EPISODE WHEN HER LOVER WANTS HER TO TALK DIRTY DID GREAT THINGS FOR MY LOVE LIFE. My wife started doing it, and its great. Theres an early episode where Charlottes guy wants her to try anal, she says she 'doesn't want to be the up-the-butt girl'. Fortunatly my wife was interested enought to try it. Who needs porno. Funny, and a chinese menu of positions and sex ideas. I hope there a threesome episode. . . . "Honey, we can't miss tonights show!!!!!!!"
>
> —Anonymous, http://www.jumptheshark.com/s/sexandthecity.htm

It is hard to argue with a man whose sex life improved because of a television show. Doesn't this help to prove that American society is open, free, and nonjudgmental about sex?

Let's return to that 2005 Gallup poll of Americans' attitudes. When asked whether "sex between an unmarried man and woman" is morally acceptable, 39 percent of Americans said that it is not. About 43 percent said that having a baby outside marriage is not morally acceptable. Regarding same-sex relationships, 52 percent said that "homosexual relations" are "morally wrong." And finally, 51 percent said that abortion is morally wrong (Carroll, 2005). Pause here for a moment and consider the implications. Nearly 40 percent of adult Americans appear to think that premarital intercourse is morally wrong. I will wager that you would not have guessed that the proportion would be that high, because your immediate context and experiences— your point of view—may be very different.

There are other aspects of American culture that lead me to suggest that the apparent openness we have about sex is somewhat illusory. You will learn more about the contradictions in gender socialization, in messages for adolescent boys and girls regarding puberty, and in behavioral double standards that follow us into adulthood. For now, let's agree that social, cultural, and historical context has much to do with our collective point of view.

Theorizing about Sex

Much of our theorizing about sexuality reflects our collective confusion about *essentialism* ("nature") and *social constructionism* ("nurture"). It is very seductive to fall into the trap of thinking that sexuality is best explained by *either* one *or* the other, as I suggested in chapter 1. Besides the false dichotomy this constructs, we run the risk of oversimplifying sex. Social critic and feminist sexologist Leonore Tiefer writes,

> Human sexuality is not a biological given and cannot be explained in terms of reproductive biology or instinct. All human actions need a body, but only part of human sexuality has to do with actions. . . . What is done, when, where, by whom, with whom, with what, and why—these things have almost nothing to do with biology (2004: 3).[13]

What all these other things *do* have to do with is the complexity of human sexualities. As I wrote in chapter 1, it is easy to accept arguments and evidence that extend our perceptions of difference. Essentialism allows us to believe that, at our core (in our *essence*), everything sexual represents fundamental, innate distinctions—between men and women, heterosexual and homosexual conduct, normal and pathological. Essentialist arguments seem to correspond with our everyday, lived experiences. But it is difficult to disprove essentialist and sociobiological theories that suggest that human sexualities are attributable to genes, hormones, physiology, and evolutionary history. In evolutionary psychology, for example, genes are thought to exist for every social phenomenon. Social institutions such as marriage and monogamy are products of evolutionary necessity, making evolutionary mandates possible (such as reproduction of the species). Social practices such as breast augmentation, vaginal rejuvenation, and penile enlargement can be explained as ways to maximize the mandate to mate with an attractive, other-sexed partner. We cannot exactly manipulate "evolution" to test the theories offered within evolutionary psychology. And a body of theory predicated on the assumption that heterosexual reproduction is the focus of sexuality therefore cannot fully explain nonreproductive intercourse, oral sex, anal sex, and same-sex relationships.

Other theories that rely heavily on anatomy and physiology attempt to explain sexuality by locating it solely within the body. Neuroscientist Simon LeVay published a highly controversial study in which he argued that there is something called "the gay brain" (1991).[14] Using brains from cadavers, LeVay found differences in the anterior portion of the *hypothalamus*. The hypothalamus is a small but vital region of the brain, responsible for homeostasis, the regulation of body temperature, mood patterns, appetite and thirst, and the body clock (e.g., being a "night person"). The hypothalamus is part of the endocrine system, which you will see (in chapter 3) is implicated in the development of biological sex. In LeVay's study, it appeared as if the cells from the gay men's brains were more similar to cells from women's brains than to supposed heterosexual men's brains. The intention of this and subsequent research was to establish that sexual orientation is hard-wired—that is, essential, something we are born with.

There were problems with LeVay's research, however. First, for obvious reasons the brain tissue was taken from cadavers. The sample consisted of 19 gay men, 16 heterosexual men, and six heterosexual women; all of the gay men died of AIDS, while only six other men and one woman did. There is no way to know how AIDS and opportunistic illnesses affect brain tissues. The subjects' sexual orientations were essentially guessed at—it was assumed that the "gay" men were in fact gay, while no conclusive information was provided for the other subjects. It was merely assumed that the others were heterosexual. Lesbian women were entirely excluded from the study.

If we want to develop critical thinking skills, we should take at least one step back at this juncture. To begin clarifying the distinctions between and among essentialism and social constructionism, we need to briefly establish what constructionist thinking is:

- Being critical about the ideas and information that we have eventually come to take for granted;
- Being aware of culture, society, and history; and

- Being aware of the social processes that sustain our ways of looking at the world around us.

With these concepts, we can clarify the final problem or concern with research like LeVay's. The whole basis for the research is the assumption that sexual orientation is hard-wired into the brain, that it is essential. But the flaw in this and similar research is that neurobiologists (and evolutionary psychologists) do not seem to be wondering what the basis is for heterosexuality. Few ask where heterosexuality "comes from." Is it safe to simply assume that no one asks this research question because heterosexuality is the norm and we do not need to study what is most widespread and most usual? Think about the weather, for example. Lightning and thunder are "normal"—they occur with some frequency even. Meteorologists do not fail to study these things simply because they are not as unusual as, say, a tsunami. So clearly we cannot justify the failure to pose certain questions by saying that we do not need to understand *everything* there is to know about human sexualities. A detriment of most essentialist research is that it rarely interrogates what we believe are the normal or usual features of sex. A virtue of social constructionist research is that critique is integral, especially about the things we tend to take for granted.

Power and Other Key Concepts

There is a growing consensus in this literature that power is best defined as the net ability to cause intended outcomes in a relationship, particularly as this involves the behavior of others. . . . In other words, power is the ability to get what you want and to get another person to do it. This can be distinguished from the concept of control, which involves the actual use of power. Power is, then, a potential, and it is a multi-dimensional construct. Persons in relationships have multiple sources or bases of power and employ a variety of power strategies. . . . This literature does acknowledge the importance of such structural variables as social position, access to opportunity, and social norms in shaping power, but it also examines the role of such interpersonal issues as the willingness to use power, personal expertise and competence, and tactical strategies. Simply stated, power cannot be reduced to its structural components. It is time for sexuality researchers to acknowledge this complexity and to begin to examine the ways in which women, as well as men, exercise power in sexual relationships. Ultimately, we need to examine how various kinds of sexual power are exerted under what specific conditions and the means through which power is exercised in its various forms (Weis, 1998: 106–7).[15]

In order to really understand theories about sexualities, we have to start with the key concept of power. If power involves the ability "to cause intended outcomes," then we must consider power in light of scholars like Krafft-Ebing, Kinsey, and Masters and Johnson. Did any of them have the power to change, influence, or moderate sociocultural views of sexuality? Obviously the answer is yes. Their influence can be seen in the academic field of human sexuality, where a study of 15 leading textbooks revealed that the only citations to appear in all 15 were for Kinsey's research and Masters and Johnson's orgasm study (Hogben, Hartlaub, and Wisely, 1999).[16]

Krafft-Ebing's case studies facilitated the labeling of "sexual pathologies," Kinsey's taxonomies of sexual behaviors (called the Kinsey Scale) facilitated the labeling of "sexual orientation," and Masters and Johnson contributed linear conceptualizations of orgasmic responses, facilitating the labeling of "sexual dysfunctions." But what were the goals of each researcher and theorist? Kinsey argued, or guessed (in other words, theorized!), that human sexual conduct could be counted and measured similarly to animal sexual conduct. Assessments of animals' sex acts were value-neutral, not used to develop social and religious policy and prohibitions. Kinsey wanted to apply this model to human behavior, arguing that simply knowing more about the range of individual conduct would enable us to lead happier, more productive lives. Masters and Johnson wanted to demystify sex as well, suggesting that knowing about "the human sexual response" would lead to better sex lives. While these things absolutely do matter and should, ostensibly, enhance individuals' sex lives, there are other things critical thinkers need to know about:

- Why do we label and classify? What purposes or goals are served?
- Why do we theorize about sex? Why not just accept things as they are?
- What explanations have been developed to explain aspects of sexualities?

There is more to the context of sexuality research than just the perspective and goals of the researcher. The short history of formal sexological studies, including Krafft-Ebing's case studies, Kinsey's thousands of interviews, and Masters and Johnson's orgasm observations, includes work described as "groundbreaking" that we still reference to this day. But this groundbreaking research, and other, lesser-known works, could instead be described as a history of *classification*. Krafft-Ebing set the tone, describing some conduct as "perversion" or "inversion," and coining for the first time the terms *fetishism, masochism, sadism,* and *sexual psychopath* (Storr, 1998).[17] In his initial writings about inversion, Krafft-Ebing argued that "inverts"—those with same-sex attractions—were really suffering from a gender problem, not an issue of sexuality. Male inverts were more like women, and female inverts were more like men. His assertions were debunked at the turn of the twentieth century, and Krafft-Ebing later revised his opinion of inversion. In fact, he was the first sexologist to use the term *homosexual,* concurrent with his changed opinion that same-sex sexuality could be an "object choice" present from birth, and therefore not immoral (Oosterhuis, 2000).[18] But in classifying people on the basis of behaviors, Krafft-Ebing also facilitated the process of sexual *labeling,* reinforced and furthered in subsequent researchers' work.

Labeling theory (in sociology) is a way to explain how individuals come to understand themselves and their behavior as "deviant." Labeling theorists explore the processes by which a culture's particular interpretations of deviance are formalized into official sanctions, rules, and laws. We would then need to ask how these formal codifications of deviance become meaningful for individuals. How do the expectations of a culture inhere in the members of that culture?

The first essential ingredient is power. Who has the power to define deviance? Who has the power to codify expectations *and* the penalties for defying those expectations? The second necessary ingredient is social interaction. Individuals and groups do not operate independently of the broader culture, and thus they learn the expectations (*mores*) of that culture. Without an audience, acts in and of themselves are not "deviant"—they come to be defined that way via social construction and cultural consensus. If enough people—and especially those with power—agree that an act or behavior should be called "deviant," societal expectations will change to reflect that. When we connect labeling theory to sexualities, we can see some obvious applications.

Although Krafft-Ebing used terms (in the 1880s) that only seemed to describe behavior or conduct (e.g., *fetishism, inversion*), those terms quickly changed and expanded to reflect assessments of a person's character or personality (e.g., *fetishist, invert*). The individual became their behavior—someone who exposed themselves to others for sexual gratification became an *exhibitionist.* This is another example of how language is a source of power. Instead of simply referring to patterns of conduct, we began to identify people as little more than their behavior. By the 1920s, terms like *heterosexual* and *homosexual* began to be used. *Heterosexual* had different connotations than it does currently, however (Katz, 1995).[19] As late as 1923, one could still find *heterosexual* defined in the dictionary as a *medical* term (not an identity term) meaning "morbid sexual passion for one of the opposite sex" (Katz, 2004: 44).[20] But both terms were thought to describe the essence, character, and nature of a person. We see similar denotations for *pervert, exhibitionist, voyeur, rapist, pedophile,* and *child molester.*

This shift in language is not incidental or trivial. It coincides with the rise of medicine as a social institution (Pfeiffer, 1985) and the privileging of medical knowledge and physicians.[21] Prior to about the 1860s, physicians were regarded as

& psychologists

quacks or charlatans with limited knowledge and minimal social respect. Subsequent enhanced status of physicians and rising prestige of medicine gave doctors the power to define illness, sanity, and wellness, among other things. Krafft-Ebing's initial goal, as a physician himself, was to create a text for medical and legal professionals that would clarify the range of sexual deviations. He even wrote some passages in Latin to dissuade all but the most erudite readers. His descriptions of sexual "perversions" enabled other powerful people to codify those perversions and develop formal and informal sanctions for "social deviants." The roots of sexological research thus reflect the history and importance of labeling and classifying. And so a new class of people was formed—sexual deviants—in keeping with the age-old privilege of the socially powerful enforcing their definitions and interpretations. By labeling some conduct deviant, those with power ensure that those who deviate will do so knowing that their behavior transgresses sociocultural norms. A contemporary example of this appears in a report about training medical students to be more comfortable speaking with patients about sexualities (Dixon-Woods et al., 2002).[22] Medical students "are asked to reflect on why 'wanker' is a pejorative term" for masturbation (434) and to reflect on "how common use of terms such as 'poofter' can inhibit gay people from admitting their sexuality to doctors" (434).

A more subtle application of labeling theory and concepts of deviance can be found in Masters and Johnson's work on orgasm. Their intention was to explore orgasm by asking, "What physical reactions develop as the human male and female respond to effective sexual stimulation?" (1966: 4).[23] Note the use of the word "the." Masters and Johnson also used "the" to describe "the human sexual response cycle." Why are we nitpicking the terms? Consider the actual difference between the articles "a" and "the." What are the connotations, denotations, and definitions? What is the difference between "a boyfriend" and "the boyfriend"? Or "a lover" and "the lover"? What about the phrase "The One" (as in "Mr. Right")? *The* human sexual response cycle is singular—there is only one, singular, universal cycle describing how human animals respond sexually. Period. *A* human sexual response cycle suggests that it may be one of many, or several; that it is an idea, a hypothesis, a speculation.

So Masters and Johnson offered a theory that they asserted constitutes "the human sexual response cycle." The most significant outcome of their work is that "the HSRC model has had a profound impact on clinical sexology" (Tiefer, 1995: 49).[24] Clinical psychologists, psychiatrists, and other mental health professionals diagnose mental health disturbances using the *Diagnostic and Statistical Manual,* now in its fourth edition (DSM-IV). According to the official Web site of the American Psychiatric Association, "The DSM is a manual that contains a listing of psychiatric disorders and their corresponding diagnostic codes. Each disorder included in the manual is accompanied by a set of diagnostic criteria and text containing information about the disorder, such as associated features, prevalence, familial patterns, age-, culture- and gender-specific features, and differential diagnosis."[25] DSM-IV lists several sexual "dysfunctions," including female orgasmic disorder, female sexual arousal disorder, hypoactive sexual desire disorder, male erectile disorder, male orgasmic disorder, premature ejaculation, and sexual aversion disorder. These classifications are almost entirely based on Masters and Johnson's findings regarding the four "phases" of orgasm.

Female orgasmic disorder includes the symptom of "delay" of orgasm following "normal" sexual excitement. What is "normal" sexual excitement? What is "delay"? What is the normal amount or level, and from what source or input? Premature ejaculation involves ejaculation with "minimal sexual stimulation," before or shortly after (vaginal) penetration, and before the person desires it. By this definition, all people with penises have had at least one instance of premature ejaculation! In this way, physiology is taken to be "the truth" of sexuality, independent of individual, social, cultural, or other context. As a critical thinker, you must ask what are the implications or consequences of labeling and classifying sex in this way. Who has the *power* to apply these labels? Who benefits from developing a linear continuum of normalcy? Is it useful for individuals to utilize and apply the terms of sexual dysfunction to themselves? (We will further address some of the specifics of the medicalization of human sexuality in chapter 9.)

But as one journalist notes, all this research, while important, has "left many fundamental questions unanswered. How does sexual desire affect judgment? Why do people choose to express sexuality that might be destructive to them? Why do some people have high sex drives while others do not? . . . How do people develop sexual identities?" (Lovgren, 2004).[26] Indeed, it is the hope of answering these and other questions that compels sexual theorists and researchers.

Psychoanalytic Theory

Famous psychoanalyst Sigmund Freud (1856–1939) theorized about many aspects of human sexuality. Though there has been enormous controversy about and dissension from his ideas, his ideas have been instrumental for generations of scholars. He was interested in how different practices and parts of the body became eroticized. His concept of *polymorphous perversity*, which will be addressed more in chapter 3, relates to his argument that infants are not born with sexual feelings centralized in the genitalia. He argued, without making particular value judgments, that undifferentiated sexual satisfaction could focus on masturbation, penile-vaginal intercourse, oral sex, or any other sexual act. He argued, however, that part of developing a sexual identity is learning to properly direct, or channel, sexual interests into the genitalia. We also must learn about heterosexuality and gender identity (see chapter 3 for his theory) and direct our interests to the other sex—after watching a same-sex parent for cues about gender roles.

His argument about why people engage in destructive sexual conduct related to his perception, in effect, of the nature of civilization and humanity. In a slim volume called *Civilization and Its Discontents*, published in 1929, Freud argued that individuals have two primary, and often competing, *drives*. *Eros* is the drive to gratify basic needs, especially pleasure. *Thanatos* is the drive for destruction and degradation. In his book, Freud argued that the central purpose of civilization is to (teach us to) repress, or *sublimate* these drives so that some balance can be attained. (This sublimation can create or lead to *neurosis*, he suggested.) Things like heterosexuality, monogamy, and legal marriage are institutions that encompass the social rules of a civilization, deemed necessary for the sublimation of eros and thanatos. These institutions combine with others, such as work, the economy, and the polity, to channel sexual energy into productive, socially acceptable pursuits. So Freud might argue that people express "destructive" sexualities because of a complex mix of unsublimated pleasure-seeking and destruction.

Hence psychoanalytic theory would argue that much of sexuality is essential and as a result, that patterns of behavior can be observed across individuals. Sexual "dysfunctions" and problems would be attributable to issues of sublimation or the failure to move from polymorphous perversity to correctly differentiated sexuality. Identity issues would be explained as part of an individual's pathway in the "proper" development of sexual orientation and/or gender. If we think critically about this body of theory, we have to ask, What are the consequences of viewing individual sexualities as the result of hardwired drives? Does this perspective support or disrupt the status quo? Does this perspective enable us to empirically test any of the basic principles or assumptions? As you will see later in the book, purely psychological approaches to sexualities, along with the belief that gender identity and sexual orientation are linked, have been consequential in the medicalization of sexualities, the pathologizing of certain forms of sex and identities, and the maintenance of expert, powerful discourses about sex.

Social Learning Theory

Most sexuality research and theory prior to the advent of the social learning formulations tended to rely on a psychodynamic conceptualization (see Gagnon, 1975, for a review). Typically, sexuality has been depicted as a biological drive/force in Freudian psychodynamic theory, which is very different from its depiction in the more cogni-tively oriented social learning theories. Gagnon (1975) also pointed out that cognitive social learning, which treats human sexuality as at least partly learned and cognitively oriented, is a relatively new concept of sexuality (Hogben and Byrne, 1998: 59).[27]

So the "new" idea here—that sexuality is at least "partly" learned, is a concept developed only over the last 30 years or so. It was *novel* to think that sexuality tran-scended the biological. Social learning theory is predicated on several assumptions:

- that humans are social creatures who are attentive to their environments;
- that humans are interactive in and with those environments;
- that humans are responsive to stimuli and conditioning.

This paradigm is notable for these presumptions, which pave the way for making arguments and hypothesizing about humans' ability to learn the elements of our sex-ualities and not simply be programmed at birth.

Learning theories argue that the way we learn and repeat behaviors is via several forms of conditioning. *Classical conditioning* involves generating or establishing new behaviors, in response to stimuli; importantly, it also involves making psychological adjustments. *Operant conditioning* is achieved via reinforcement and/or punishment. Being rewarded or punished for behavior would then lead to increase, repetition, or decrease. (If you ever watch the *Dr. Phil* show, this is basically what he's talking about when he tells a guest, "You teach people how to treat you.") Social learning theories (a subset of learning theories) generally assert that gender identity and sexuality are formed through imitation, direct reinforcement for sex-typed activities, and vicarious learning from peer and adult models. The term "role model" comes from social learn-ing theory; they are the people whom we are told embody and who ostensibly exem-plify sociocultural ideals.

Learning theories would posit, therefore, that human sexualities result from fig-uring out what is in our environment, whether in terms of stimuli or examples (mod-els). It certainly may be the case that we learn how to formulate *attitudes* from our sur-roundings and our significant influences, such as peers and family. In terms of actual behaviors, many sex researchers *hope* that learning theory can explain what we do and why we do it. Studies of sexual health and AIDS often apply these theoretical assump-tions, asking, for example, whether operant conditioning can be employed to influ-ence condom use in teenagers (Hogben and Byrne, 1998). Can peer networks teach members of the network ways to incorporate safer sex, whether through modeling or vicarious learning (Laumann et al., 2004)?[28]

Again, you must stop and ask, what are the implications of learning theories? One is that millions of dollars have been spent on peer education programs, hoping to change (mostly youth) sexual attitudes and practices. This is not necessarily a bad thing, but much of the programming is predicated on this one perspective and set of beliefs about how humans enact their sexualities. It can lead to oversimplification and overrationalization of sex, assuming falsely that what motivates us can be outlined on a relatively simple pathway of "stimulus-response." So what are the implications of the ways in which learning theories, in effect, attempt to describe various cultural narratives about sexualities?

Exchange Theory

A social exchange framework, in its various forms, has been applied to a number of topics within sexuality. In particular, because the focus of exchange theories is on interpersonal transactions (Huston & Burgess, 1979), this framework is useful for understanding sexuality within a relational context, including why two people choose each other as sexual partners, which partner has more influence on what sexual activities they do together, sexual satisfaction, and the likelihood that one or both partners seek sexual activity outside the relationship. The exchange approach is applicable to all types of sexual dyads, ranging from the prostitute-client relationship (where exchange is very explicit and salient) to a couple married for many years (where the exchange is more implicit).

> A social exchange framework, very broadly, refers to any conceptual model or theoretical approach that focuses on the exchange of resources (material or symbolic) between or among people and/or refers to one of the major exchange concepts, which are rewards, costs, and reciprocity. Some exchange theorists also consider the fairness or equity of the exchange, which refers to the relative rewards and costs for both partners (Sprecher, 1998: 32).[29]

Social exchange theories presume that human animals interact on the basis of rational, reasoned *exchanges*, giving or taking one thing in return for another. Following loosely from Freud's argument about the drive to seek *eros*, people would strive to maximize benefits (rewards) and minimize costs; sometimes exchange theory is referred to as *cost-benefit analysis*. Reciprocation is a key assumption—theorists expect that if one person receives something good or beneficial from another, they will reciprocate. Clearly this body of theory, along with (social) learning theories, assumes that human animals are rational, capable of applying reasoned analysis to sexuality.

It is sometimes difficult for my students to understand this theory and give it any credence as an explanation for any human sexual behavior. It can seem a bit repulsive to think of sex involving rationalized trades—we might like to think it is more spontaneous, lusty, loving, or intimate. My students will often oversimplify and think very literally about what it means to make exchanges, about what "cost" might entail (e.g., that it is monetary). If we think more broadly about what we exchange or trade in the sexual realm, this theory will make more sense. In older analyses of heterosexual teens' behaviors, it was often written that boys exchanged love for sex while girls exchanged sex for love. What does that mean? Boys would be willing to say "I love you," maybe even insincerely, to convince girls to have sex. Girls would be willing to have sex, maybe even without really desiring to, in the hopes that it would lead to "true love." Give her what she wants, give him what he wants—what each wants is different, but an exchange is made and hopefully the outcome is positive. You may be tempted to dismiss this example by immediately finding examples of young women and men who, respectively, really want to be sexual and really want to be in love. The theory does not describe *all* aspects of sexualities, nor does it purport to apply to every specific circumstance. It, like other theories, is an educated guess about what might explain certain aspects of human experience.

As Sprecher notes, ". . . in many intimate relationships, sexual rewards and costs are sometimes exchanged for other resources in the relationship, such as intimacy, love, favors, and money" (1998: 32). So "rewards" are best conceptualized as both material (e.g., "Pay me $100 and I will clean your house while wearing only a frilly white apron") and/or intangible (e.g., "If you love me you will sleep with me"). Exchange theory could be applied to analyses of relationships, especially when what we are curious about is how people weigh the variables involved in making decisions: Why do heterosexuals marry? Why not just live together? Why do people stay in relationships that make them unhappy? Why would same-sex couples wish to be legally married? Why do people between 16 and 40 engage in hook-ups? Living in a Western culture in which many of our interpersonal interactions are indeed based on the question "what's in it for me?," it should be relatively easy to see how to apply these ideas to sex.

Sexual Script Theory

Sexual script theory was first outlined by sociologists John Gagnon and William H. Simon in 1973.[30] Scripting is a subset of broader (symbolic) interactionist theories, which posit that societies are created by and within the interactions of individuals. Sociologist (and one-time professional football player) Herbert Blumer (1900–1986) argued that

- humans act towards things on the basis of meanings we have for those things;
- meaning is created through interaction between people;
- meanings are modified through an interpretive process.

Sexual scripts are culturally produced, shared, and reinforced social norms that serve as blueprints, in effect, to guide sexual and gender behavior. "The term script might properly be invoked to describe virtually all human behavior in the sense that there is very little that can in a full measure be called spontaneous" (Gagnon and Simon [1973], 2004: 33).[31] This idea may be difficult to accept simply on face value—we value the cultural belief that sexual activities are spontaneous, hot, passionate, and driven. Script theory is based on the argument that biology, anatomy, and the like are insufficient for sex:

> Without the proper elements of a script that defines the situation, names the actors, and plots the behavior, nothing sexual is likely to happen. One can easily conceive of numerous social situations in which all or almost all of the ingredients of a sexual event are present but that remain nonsexual in that not even sexual arousal occurs. Thus, combining such elements as desire, privacy, and a physically attractive person of the appropriate sex, the probability of something sexual happening will, under normal circumstances, remain exceedingly small until either one or both actors organize these behaviors into an appropriate script ([1973] 2004: 33).

So even under what might seem like ideal circumstances, with the proper "characters" and other elements, an interaction cannot become something that participants would call "sexual" unless those elements are *organized* as "sexual." An example would be the gynecological exam. It involves two people, nudity, spread legs, the insertion of fingers into vagina, and the touching (palpation) of breasts. Sexual acts often include one—or all—of these events. Is a gynecological exam "sexual"? It is a safe bet to say that virtually no one considers it such a thing, even if the patient and the practitioner are otherwise attractive, sexy, interesting people. Why is it, in fact, one of the most asexual, unisexual, and frankly unarousing events we could imagine?

Gagnon and Simon would argue that the "doing of sex" (i.e., making events or patterns of events sexual) involves particular strategies, concrete elements of what a culture "agrees" is sexy, sensual, or sexual. One way to think about this is via the history of the heterosexual, feminine erotic. At the turn of the twentieth century, proper femininity necessitated the concealment of all skin, save hands and face. Thus a sliver of skin above the ankle-high boot or below the edge of the knickers was terribly arousing to behold. In Japan at that time, the back (nape) of a woman's neck was defined as the height of erotic, so well-groomed women drew attention to their necks via beautiful upswept hairstyles, combs, and hair jewelry. That these elements of the erotic are subject to historical and cultural variation supports the argument that sexuality has socially constructed elements that supersede biological and hormonal contributions. Thus the script can be thought of as the blueprint or map of cultural consensus about what is defined as sexual in any given community, society, or era.

There are three levels of scripting in Gagnon and Simon's model: *cultural, interpersonal,* and *intrapsychic.* I add a fourth level—*subcultural. Cultural* scripting constitutes the blueprint or expectations on the broadest, most general societal level. Cultural level scenarios direct and influence all of our performances; this is the big picture of how and where we get cues and clues about sexuality. At this level, we are taught that heterosexuality is the expected, taken for granted approach. *Subcultural* scripting would include the messages offered by smaller entities, such as a religious affiliation, ethnic/racial identity, or geography. In a religious subculture, the messages may revolve around developing the sexual self within the context of a legal, adult marriage. Sexual orientation can be thought of as a subculture, especially if it is a minority orientation; certainly the blueprints for sex differ from subculture to subculture. *Interpersonal* scripting occurs at the small group level, such as peer networks, families, intimates, and so on. This is where we might see messages to the effect of "everyone is doing it. . . ." And finally, *intrapsychic* scripting involves the mind, memories, fantasies, desires, wishes, and recollections. It is the most internal and clearly mental; it is where and how we translate broader messages about how to feel, what to do, and what to think about our sexualities. We become the screenwriters or playwrights, directing, adapting, and shaping the cultural-level messages we seem to seamlessly absorb. We incorporate messages from the broader levels of "society" about what to do, with whom to do it, and why to do whatever it is we do. Scripts influence our perceptions and knowledge about appropriate partners, relationships in which sex "should" occur, and sexual emotions. Perhaps the easiest way to understand and consider applying scripting theory is to consider the following example.

When I teach this theory in my class, I start by asking the students, "What is first base?" They usually laugh and then fall silent. I wait, then ask, "Am I talking about baseball in a sex class?" Someone usually jumps in to put me out of my misery and says, "It's kissing, basically. Or French kissing." Then we go around the bases—second base is "up the shirt."

"Up whose shirt?," I ask. "What if I was your best friend and I hooked up with someone last night and then told you, 'I went up Joe's shirt!!'?" Okay, the students tell me—second base is a guy going up a girl's shirt. And we go from there, rounding the bases, sliding into home, debating about what shortstops or midfielders or outfielders do. There is high consensus about what activities are associated with which bases in this timeless example.

There are two points here. First, how do all my students, with their diverse backgrounds and points of view, know what "the bases" are? Did they get the gender- and sexual orientation-appropriate "Bases Memo" in fifth grade? The fact that there is knowledge of, let alone consensus about the bases is suggestive of Gagnon and Simon's claim that sexuality is not purely spontaneous, immune from social context. The trip around the bases is socially constructed, blueprinted—scripted—and it has prescriptive expectations for

- gender roles and gendered activities;
- heterosexuality;
- the progression of "sexual" activities and stimulation;
- how arousal should operate;
- the ganization of what we call "sexual."

How does this operate? The prescription for gender includes the taken for granted notion that sex happens between a man and a woman, and that *he* is the initiator, the person moving sex along from one point to the next. It is meaningful if *he* gets up *her* shirt, because women have been taught to keep breasts private (except in special circumstances, such as during Mardi Gras and in *Girls Gone Wild!* videos). Women are also taught to be the gatekeepers of sex, especially in adolescence and as teens; women *respond* to initiated actions with assent or dissent but have to learn, as adults, when and with whom to initiate (more on this in chapter 5). Sexual scripting provides a blueprint for the *sequence* of activities, the *form* of activities, and *roles* for gendered characters to play.

Scripting theorists would argue that what we do with genitalia, how we feel about what we do, who we do things with, the order in which we do things, what we define as sexual, what we define as erotic—all of that is sociocultural. This is where sexual scripting comes in: how we get cues about order, timing, and what's arousing. The who, what, where, when, how, and why of all aspects of sexualities are delineated and described by the four levels of scripting. *Who* is someone of the other sex, *what* is penile-vaginal intercourse, *where* is somewhere private, *when* is after marriage or at least, once in love, *how* is "normally," and *why* . . . that is the most complex element of the script. There are many other prescriptions in cultural and subcultural scripting for the five W's and the "how."

At this point, it should be obvious that I have devoted more space to this theory than to any others thus far. My point of view, or stance, is that scripting theory has a lot of potential to explain multiple aspects of sexualities and to answer many questions. But similarly to learning and evolutionary theories, it is difficult to tease out exactly how something as broad and abstract as "culture" lodges itself inside individuals. It may be easier to test scripting theories on the intrapsychic and interpersonal levels, posing questions such as, what meaning does a 20-year-old woman give to her sexual behavior? How does she interpret "casual" sex? How does she feel about what she does? What beliefs does she have about her friends' behaviors?

Feminist, Postmodern, and Queer Theories: The Tip of the Iceberg

"Feminist" theory has existed, in various forms, since the late 1700s; the first clearly feminist publication is generally taken to be Mary Wollstonecraft's *A Vindication of the Rights of Woman*, published in 1792. She wrote about girls and education, women and work, and the need for equality. Perhaps the first organized feminist movement was the group of well-off, educated white women—the suffragettes (including Susan B. Anthony)—who fought for the right of white women to vote—headquartered in Seneca Falls, New York. That fight spanned 1858 to 1920 and spawned many other feminist movements, organizations, causes, and bodies of theory. Considering that the word "woman" is derived from *wifmann,* or wife of man, it is not surprising that feminist theorists initially debated the word itself. Subsequent topics included critiques of the binary sex/gender system, biological determinism, and essentialist thinking about gender. Feminist theories have disrupted the notion that positivism and researcher objectivity are possible when studying aspects of social life, arguing first that sex and later, gender, have been made so central to self-concept that human activity is not separable from subjective gendered (and raced and classed) lenses. This kind of critique of the normally taken-for-granted is the hallmark of all varieties of feminist theorizing, making it an obvious subset of social constructionist thinking. Another arena of inquiry relates to the question of how the self is constructed; feminism generally argues that the self (or individual) is not developed in a vacuum, and we are not born with selves. The self is thus created within sociocultural contexts. The other hallmark of feminist theories is the emphasis on exploring cultural power imbalances, oppression, and *sexism* (belief in the superiority of one sex). But there is no one set of questions posed by theorists, and there is no consensus about the best ways to apply feminist thinking.

More recent but classic works of feminism have paved the way for expansions of these original ideas. Poet and writer Adrienne Rich's article "Compulsory Heterosexuality and Lesbian Existence" (1980) drew from historical evidence to argue that heterosexuality had been made imperative and obligatory to support sexism and *patriarchy*, a social system organized around men having power over women and children.[32] Jumping off from a Freudian assertion that infants' primary identification is with mother, she argues that lesbian identification is "natural," perhaps more so than heterosexuality. Rich attempts to establish that heterosexuality is an institution of social control designed to perpetuate men's superiority and privilege.

Anthropologist and social critic Gayle Rubin described the judgments and politics implicated in the social control of sexualities (1984).[33] "Sexuality in western societies has been structured within an extremely punitive social framework, and has been subjected to very real formal and informal controls" (1984: 277). She argues that there is a general intolerance of sexual difference, along with extreme cultural negativity and distaste for sex. A particularly noteworthy concept is her statement that sexual interests or preferences, typically called "kinky" or "deviant," are no different from other preferences, such as those for particular foods or hobbies. But value judgments are made about sex while other things are simply called "different strokes for different folks." Other feminist theorists have interrogated racial-sexual politics (e.g., Allen, 1986; Anzaldua, 1987; Collins, 1990),[34] lesbian identity, history, and politics (e.g., Moraga, 1983; Faderman, 1992; Newton, 1993),[35] and gender identity and construction (e.g., hooks, 1982; Butler, 1990).[36] In the aggregate, feminist theory's contributions to the study of sexualities have been fundamental for critical thinking about both gender and sex.

Postmodern Theories—Focus on Foucault. Postmodern theory owes much to French philosopher Michel Foucault (1926–1984) and is intellectually similar to feminist theory in terms of questioning the taken-for-granted. Postmodern theorists deconstruct, or "unpack," the concepts of constancy, stability, and essentialism. Foucault offered a seemingly infinitely provocative contribution to postmodern theorizing about sexuality in the form of

- constructive criticisms: Foucault wrote that the goal is to "make facile gestures difficult"—to force us to look beneath the surface of our assumptions, the things that have become naturalized and therefore invisible;
- examinations of the socially constructed contours of "sex";
- arguments about how "sex" is constructed through discourse, practices, and social institutions;
- critiques of the cliché that "knowledge is power"; Foucault wrote that power allows *definitions* of knowledge, but simply knowing things does not give individuals power. Instead, knowledge is taken as a form of social regulation and control of sexualities;
- the statement that *resistance* to power (and oppression) is in the interstices of culture, within our interactions and our selves; resistance, or challenges to power, are always there.

Foucault argued that power and knowledge intersect and interact, to create and enforce order, rules, norms, and sanctions. In *Discipline and Punish*, Foucault theorized that our abilities, inclinations, and self-concepts are subtly shaped by "gentle, caring institutions." The refinements of social institutions "not only change us in various ways but . . . legitimate such changes, as the knowledge gained is deemed to be 'true'" (Marshall, 1990: 15).[37] In his (unfinished) work on sexuality, Foucault began to uncover *discursive* and institutional strategies that have contributed to the formation of subjects or individuals (discourse is essentially the abstraction of written and oral communication, through which meaning is transmitted). According to Foucault, the population becomes a "moral subject." Discourses prepare and organize individual members of society into subjects in whom power and ideologies can take hold. Sexuality becomes the instrumental element in the social appropriation of bodies: "Sex is located at the point of intersection of the discipline of the body and the control of the population" (1980: 125).[38]

In Foucault's theory of the *repressive hypothesis*, the social control of sexuality may appear as an invitation (incitement) to conversation (discourse) as well as in the guise of denial and censorship. So we may be called to speak loudly and openly about sex, or we may be prevented from doing so. You should pause here and ask, "how can social control be found in the form of an invitation to conversation, to confession, to speaking about sex?" Isn't social control something negative, repressive, controlling?

And isn't speaking freely about sex liberating—the opposite of controlling? But Foucault says that we have to question both the historical interpretation that the Victorian era (late 1800s) favored sexual repression, along with the assumption that there has been a more recent liberation of sex (heralded by new "openness" about sex). Sexuality in modern societies is a principal instrument for exercising power over bodies and populations; thus, we need to specify and explore the entities with power and their means of employing it. The power to categorize, label, and classify, and therefore engage in social control, is a property of both individuals and institutions. An example of social control in the guise of the new openness is rhetoric about safer sex. The AIDS crisis paved the way for new forms of discourse about sex—the ability to discuss penises and condoms in schools, for example—but the end message is that sex is dangerous and needs to be controlled (made safer).

Sociologist Ken Plummer has also observed that talk about sex ("the new openness") may not simply liberate us from the ostensible restrictions of the past but may also signify the *expansion* and *diffusion* of sexual social controls (Plummer, 1995).[39] Actually, Foucault suggests that in reality, it was necessary to gain mastery and social control over sex by "subjugating it at the level of language." Think back to chapter 1's brief discussion of language and how it structures gender and sexualities. The "confessional impulse" instituted within religion (especially Catholicism) is seen currently in "blogs," online journals that can be read by anyone with Internet access and that can describe things formerly kept "private." The historical confession served two purposes. First, priests were duty-bound to pass everything "through the endless mill of speech," writes Foucault, and sex thus became *discourse* and as such, was sanitized. Second, the confessor could share his "strangest practices, undoubtedly shared by all men"; there have been a handful of famous historical confessions of sexual conduct, notably *My Secret Life*, the diary of an anonymous Victorian man, and books by Rousseau, St. Augustine, and the Marquis de Sade. Sexual behavior thus became the province of all, both to reassure people of the "normality" of their own impulses *and* to cleanse and normalize the confessor. Sexuality became blandly public, devoid of the eroticism of private indulgence (like, for example, when transcripts of Monica Lewinsky's phone sex with President Bill Clinton became public).

Foucault also discusses how the science of sex developed as a form of power. The power differentials built into relationships coalesced with discourses (e.g., technical writings and language) in the form of confessors and confessees: psychiatrist and patient; teacher and student; parent and child; priest and penitent. *Resistance* to these forms of power and social control is not an objective concept that exists independently from systems of power relations. He argued that if resistance did not exist, "there would be no power relations," which must be necessary to keep resistance in check (otherwise it would be "a matter of obedience"). Foucault (1978) thought that resistance was superior and would always prevail. Thus, postmodern theories inspire us to pose questions such as: Whose ideology is institutionalized in discussions of sexuality? Who has power to determine the form and content of the things we call sexual? Can individuals subvert institutionalized sexuality discourses and modes of power?

A Note about Feminist Theories and Foucault.   Foucault's utility to feminist theories has been the source of much debate. His work is marshaled, on one hand, to support the contention that something collectively called "power" has considerable social currency and is particularly responsible for social stratification. Feminists use Foucault's arguments about the social construction of sexuality to combat the claims of essentialists. His ideas also help support the contention that the body is a cultural product and is situated in power relations, epistemologies (forms of knowledge), and culture.

Foucaultian and other postmodern concepts are less useful to feminist (and other) scholars who wish to examine the emancipatory possibilities for humanity and women specifically. Some criticize Foucault by arguing that he reduces people to passive social and cultural constructions, with body, mind, and reason represented as nothing more than shifting cultural properties instead of "real," individual resources. Foucault does little to suggest specifically how individuals or groups might combat the social effects of power. Further, it has been argued that by reducing all social institutions to a broad discussion of "power," Foucault ignores the salient effects and consequences of specific stratifications, by race, class, gender, and so on. He also neglects the subjective experience of how it feels to be subordinated (as in sexism, racism, etc).

Queer Theories.   "Queer theory" refers to propositions about sexualities that are based around the idea that identities are not fixed and are not the determining factors in who we are. In its original meaning, "queer" has a primary meaning of "strange, odd, peculiar, or out of the ordinary." Queer theories are thus concerned with the forms of sexuality that are queer/ed—outside the standard, narrow interpretations. Queer theory's "poststructuralist roots were revealed in its claims that sexual and other identities are 'arbitrary, unstable, and exclusionary,'" write sociologists Joshua Gamson and Dawne Moon (2004: 48).[40] Similarly to feminist and Foucaultian theories, queer theories set out to rock the proverbial boat, to trouble the waters. Queer theories therefore share several basic orientations to empiricism and theorizing:

- power is a key feature organizing social life, utilizing binary assumptions about gender, sex, and sexual orientation to enforce the status quo.
- these categorizations and labels need to be examined and clarified as "problematic."
- simplistic interpretations need to be revised.
- interrogation of areas of study that are normally unaddressed in sexological study is essential. (Stein and Plummer, 1996: 134)[41]

This would suggest, for example, that it is meaningless to speak in the aggregate about "men" or any other grouping or classification of people. If we accept the reasoning of queer theorists, then we would have to accept that "identities" are multifaceted, encompassing cultural, subcultural, interpersonal, and intrapsychic components (to use the language of script theory). Therefore, to assume that people can be viewed collectively, lumped together by virtue of one shared characteristic, such as biological sex or sexual orientation, is erroneous and incomplete. Indeed, it proposes that we deliberately challenge all notions of fixed identity, in varied and nonpredictable ways. This is what Annemarie Jagose means when she writes, "Broadly speaking, queer describes those gestures or analytical models which dramatise incoherencies in the allegedly stable relations between chromosomal sex, gender and sexual desire" (1996).[42] In this way, queer theories can be applied to the critical study of forms of heterosexualities as well.

Queer, postmodern, and feminist theories are applicable to many kinds of inquiries, including examinations of transgender people (e.g., the diversity of gendered portrayals and roles humans enact); intersexuality as individually and culturally experienced (e.g., how intersex people make sense of themselves in the context of medical endeavors to maintain the binary sex/gender system); sexual orientation as a fluid, lifelong development (e.g., how sexual interests, activities, and behaviors change and develop over the life course). A major task for queer theorists is documenting the separation of "identity" from "activity," given that the usual assumption is that you are what you do. Thus, if a person has genital, sexual contact with someone of the same sex, they "are" gay, lesbian, or bisexual. The writing-in-stone of this inferential leap—that behavior = identity—has never been devoid of moral, religious, social, political, and emotional judgments. All these bodies of theory generally acknowledge that *power* is a key concept in the ways in which sexualities and genders are culturally defined and produced. The thinking and critiques developed herein inspire (and require) us to ask, yet again, who benefits from the sociocultural arrangements within which we experience and develop our sexualities.

CONCLUSIONS

Let me offer a final theory, my own, called the "Goldilocks" theory (of everything sexual). Goldilocks was the fairy-tale character who didn't like the porridge, chairs, or beds she tried unless they were "just right." In terms of sexualities, very simply, there is a "just right" amount of anything we should have, be, or desire. A woman with too much interest in sex is called a slut, loose, or easy. If she has too little interest, she is called frigid, cold, weird. A man with too much interest in watching people have sex or undress is called a voyeur or a peeping Tom. If he has the just right amount of interest in watching others have sex, in the just right setting, then he is probably just called a guy who watches people have sex and undress . . . in pornographic movies. The myriad ways in which a "just right" discourse or theory is the foundation of our thinking will be apparent in coming chapters, in which we address everything from orgasms to hooking up to gay and lesbian identities to pornography.

It is crucial to remember that neither theorizing about nor directly studying sexualities is without context. It does not occur within a vacuum. The ways in which scholars have studied and theorized about sexuality have been intimately connected to our social, political, and cultural history. It is impossible for research to be completely objective. Oversimplification is clearly not only the province of sexuality studies. We see similar classification attempts in studies of crime, medicine, health, work, politics, and economies, among others, which does not make it "okay." Earlier in this chapter, I mentioned that Krafft-Ebing's case studies facilitated the labeling of "sexual pathologies," Kinsey's taxonomies of sexual behaviors (called the Kinsey Scale) facilitated the labeling of "sexual orientation," and Masters and Johnson's work developed linear conceptualizations of orgasmic responses, facilitating the labeling of "sexual dysfunctions."

All of these scholars contributed positively to the fund of knowledge about sex, but all, in their own ways, reinforced the power of labels and labeling. None of the work they did, nor any of the subsequent, vast body of sexological studies and thinking, stands alone. For example, when Krafft-Ebing and others classified some conduct and interests as "pathological," they necessarily had to simultaneously classify other conduct as "normal." When Kinsey developed his scale (very simply, of one to seven), which categorized people based on their same-sex conduct and fantasies, it necessarily forced individuals into boxes. It reinforced the idea that behavior = identity = self; people today refer to themselves and others as "a Kinsey six" (primarily same-sex conduct, but occasional other-sex fantasies) or "a Kinsey one" (exclusively heterosexual). Masters and Johnson's work truly established the belief that there was a singular "normal" sexual response, and any deviations from that pattern are "dysfunctional."

When "deviance" is established conceptually, it gives rise to a corresponding and seemingly polar opposite of "normal." The words "deviance," "abnormal," "atypical," and "paraphilia" are not merely words. Remember the discussion in chapter 1 about language? The central argument was that language is not neutral, not merely an interaction of sounds, air, and vocal cords. These words carry moral weight. But who benefits from labeling, categorizations, and classification schemes that attempt to narrowly describe and prescribe the variability of human sexual (and gender) expressions? What are the implications of the ways in which sexualities have been conceptualized over the last 100 years? And what are the implications of the critical and reflective points of view that have arisen particularly in the last 30 years? One consequence is that we have a more nuanced sense of how biological sex and socially constructed gender are connected to sexuality. In chapter 3, we will begin to sketch the landscape of sex, gender, and sexualities.

Questions to Ponder

1. Thinking about the concept of a human sexual response, can you envision circumstances in which a (narrow) standard of response might not apply? What is the value to viewing sexual response as having a narrow pathway or a more broad pathway?

2. Which theories appeal to you most? Is it possible to develop one broad, encompassing sociocultural explanation of sexualities? Or is it more feasible to think about sexualities in terms of multiple explanations?

3. What definition of "sex" do you use in your everyday life? Does the definition change depending on the circumstances?

Suggested Projects

1. Using library databases to search within scholarly articles, find an example of human sexuality from another culture. Your task is to try to apply at least one theory of sexualities. Which do you choose? Why?

2. Design a mini-research project. What topics will you study? How will you carry out your study—questionnaire, interview, observations, or other method(s)? What specific questions will you pose, and whom will you query? Importantly, what would be your purpose for the research you propose?

3

Boys, Girls, Men and Women

VARIABLES OF EXPERIENCE

There has been a great diversity of opinion on the subject, but the generally accepted rule is pink for the boy and blue for the girl. The reason is that pink being a more decided and stronger color is more suitable for the boy, while blue, which is more delicate and dainty, is prettier for the girl (*Ladies Home Journal*, 1918).

Pink, a dilution of red, the color of blood—the life force—was once the preferred hue for baby boys. Baby blue, a dilution of blue, the color of the sky and sea—the ethereal, filmy heavens and watery deep—once the preferred hue for baby girls. The reversal of this clearly arbitrary symbolism—pink for girls, blue for boys—seems to have occurred in the 1950s (Rhode, 1997).[1] Now we take for granted that this and other socially constructed conventions of gender are "natural." In this chapter, we continue thinking critically about gender and biological sex as key variables of human experience.

WHAT IS "SEX"?

Sex is a curious term. In this form, it means "doing it," "making love," or any other synonym for penile-vaginal intercourse (we tend to assume heterosexuality). People also use *sex* to refer to various activities with same-sex partners. Physicians, statisticians, and biologists use *sex* to refer to the biologically based components of organisms. Merriam-Webster OnLine clarifies that it is "either of the two major forms of individuals that occur in many species and that are distinguished respectively as female or male." The wording "two major forms" is a hint that there *are* more than two sexes in many species; "major" can be interpreted as "most prevalent." We will explore variation and diversity in the sexes a bit later in this chapter. So *sex* does double duty, used in a variety of contexts to refer to sexual activities and to refer to biological characteristics, or "the sum of the structural, functional, and behavioral characteristics of living things" (Merriam-Webster OnLine). In this way, sex is connected to what we have been told is in our essence, present at birth. It seems to reveal itself through fetal development, in the form of chromosomes, gonads, genitalia and body sex, and hormones.

Chromosomes (long strands of DNA that contains genetic coding): While in utero, we usually get 23 chromosomes from our mothers and 23 from our fathers, for a total of 46. Forty-four chromosomes are identical in men and women, called autosomes. The remaining two chromosomes are the sex chromosomes, designated X and Y. Females inherit an X chromosome from each parent, whereas males inherit one X chromosome from their mother and one Y chromosome from their father. Females can only pass on X chromosomes, while males can pass on either X or Y. Usually, babies are born with exactly 46 chromosomes and the standard division of sex chromosomes, females with XX and males with XY. XX chromosomal makeup typically indicates that the person is female, and XY chromosomal makeup indicates that the person is male. But this is not always the case, and we can see people with these chromosomal configurations and the "opposite" sexual characteristics. Sometimes babies are born with extra chromosomes. Klinefelter syndrome is when a baby has two X chromosomes along with a Y (47,XXY is the notation, or *karyotype*). Turner syndrome is seen when a baby has only one X chromosome instead of two (45,X). These conditions tend to be accompanied by reduced fertility or infertility. Klinefelter syndrome can result in breast growth at puberty (gynecomastia), which can be confusing for someone used to thinking of himself as male and who has been socialized as a boy. Turner syndrome can lead to reduced or absent breast growth and menstruation, which can be confusing for someone who thinks of herself as female and who has been socialized as a girl.

Gonads (sex and reproductive glands, testes or ovaries, which produce hormones in utero and eventually, sperm or eggs): Regardless of chromosomal composition, embryos develop along the same pathway for about the first eight weeks of gestation. Unsexed gonads, which have the potential to become testes or ovaries, exist along with Mullerian ducts (potential female reproductive structures), Wolffian ducts (potential male reproductive structures), and a genital tubercle, or tube. The default mode of embryonic development is for female differentiation. A series of relatively complex events must occur in utero for male differentiation to result. The Y chromosome carries a gene, called the sex-determining region (SRY), vital for determining whether those ducts will develop into testes or ovaries. The complex and delicate process of sex development in utero can lead to the seemingly straightforward creation of genitalia that resemble the usual "male" or "female" arrangement of skin. More creative adaptations of the sex continuum may result, marked by genitalia arranged in less typical ways.

Genitalia (sex organs; usually penis, testicles, vulva, vagina, clitoris): For the first six weeks or so of life, all fetuses have the same genital structures: phallus, labioscrotal swelling, urogenital fold, and urogenital membrane. By the twelfth week of fetal development, the genital tubercle has differentiated into testes, scrotum, and penis, or clitoris, vulva, and vagina. Androgens (male hormones) must flood the fetus if testes and penis are to develop. (SickKids, a Canadian Web site, has an excellent animation showing the precise processes, from conception to puberty.[2])

The physiological structure of the eventual "male" and "female" genitalia is more similar than different. But the genital structures that develop in utero eventually become the primary visible symbol of maleness or femaleness. Medical professionals look to genitalia to get their first hint about a baby's sex, and indeed the initial attribution paves the way for the start of the gendering process. "Congratulations, you have a healthy baby boy!," the doctor or midwife might announce. In this way, genitalia are taken to be representative of biological sex and social gender. We will explore this further.

What Is Gender?

Gender is multifaceted, complex, always changing, and infinitely sociocultural in nature. Gender differs across cultures and historical eras. The concept encompasses at least four key concepts:

gender assignment: a person's initial designation, usually by medical professionals, usually made at birth

gender identity: a person's internal sense of self; the answer to the question "Who am I?" (Bornstein, 1994)[3] *gender role (or expression)*: the social presentation of that self; this includes clothing, hairstyle, and attitudinal and behavioral traits

gender attribution: the process we all engage in, usually unconsciously, of glancing at someone, interacting with someone, and making a split-second decision about gender; the answer to the question "Who is that?"

Entire textbooks and whole semesters examine gender as a major variable of human experience. We study gender anthropologically by delving deeply into cultures around the world and clarifying how gender operates. Historically, we have uncovered facts, fictions, and experiences to substantiate the argument that gender is socially constructed and constantly changes. Economists, political scientists, psychologists, poets, writers, musicians—all have weighed in on gender in our culture and our world. Clearly there is a lot of territory to cover and we will no doubt miss some of that ground, but gender is our key variable throughout this text. And with any discussion of gender there must be concurrent discussion of power, privilege, and difference.

What does it mean to say that gender is socially constructed? First, let's try to clarify *social constructionism* (Burr, 1995).[4] If you have read chapters 1 and 2, these ideas will not be brand new. Social constructionism entails:

Being critical about the ideas and information that we eventually come to take for granted.   This includes questioning the idea that researchers are objective, that what we call "knowledge" is bona fide and unproblematic, and that our way of thinking about the world is unquestionably correct. The first step in developing a critical stance is becoming aware of your own perspective and point of view. Given what you have just read about sex, and the extent to which becoming "male" or "female" is a complex process that can have more than just two outcomes, the second step would be to question "why this distinction has been given so much importance by human beings that whole categories of personhood (i.e. man/woman) have been built upon it" (Burr, 1995: 3).

Being aware of culture, society, and history.   We have already discussed that many, if not most, aspects of the society we see around us are only relevant to the immediate moments in which we find ourselves. Much of what we understand or know is directly the product of the culture in which that knowledge is produced. Throughout history "knowledge" has changed. The shape of the Earth was debated for centuries— round or flat? Women's bodies were subject to all kinds of discussion—uteruses were thought to wander freely through the body and this was said to cause the sex-stereo-typed condition called *hysteria*. Perry and Whiteside (2000) describe historical think-ing about women: "The apparently *natural* 'objectivity' of biology as evolutionary 'sci-ence,' was therefore applied with a vengeance, to female 'problems' of menstruation, pregnancy, and childbirth. This resulted in the articulation and explication of a spec-tacular range of mental and physical illnesses, which were considered to reflect, *and* to affect the *naturally* vulnerable and more nervous constitution of women."[5]

Being aware of the social processes that sustain our ways of looking at the world around us. What are these social processes? They are as small and "local" as the interactions we have on a daily or regular basis, those we may take for granted, things like flirting, greet-ing friends, meeting strangers, talking on cell phones, and sitting in class. In the worst-case scenario, a college classroom exemplifies broader elements of culture that we have made meaningful. The professor stands while students sit, displaying her power and social status. The professor may be dressed professionally, distinguishing himself from students wearing sweat pants or jeans. The professor is referred to with an earned title, and with her last name only, while students are called by first names only, showing their subordinate position. The course was probably designed by the professor, absent of any student input; the rules and expectations are not negotiable, and students' only power is to drop the course upon learning these one-way rules. Although we proclaim that the United States is a country where everyone is equal, this is not visible in many of our social processes, which reinforce and value power, hierarchies, and superiority. When we take for granted that some people are winners and some are losers, or some people are valedictorians and others are "drop outs," and that these concepts truly describe how we should define people, we squelch our critical imaginations.

The larger social processes that surround us, independent of our own individual whims or wishes, also construct knowledge and our ways of viewing the world. Things like the political structure, democracy, the economy, capitalism, and formal religion constitute these larger processes. The complex ways in which these sociocultural insti-tutions maintain society, and persist and are perpetuated independently of specific individuals, are worth examining.

THE REALITY OF INTERSEXUALITY

"Intersex" is a general term used for a variety of conditions in which a person is born with a reproductive or sexual anatomy that doesn't seem to fit the typical definitions of female or male. For example, a person might be born appearing to be female on the outside, but having mostly male-typical anatomy on the inside. Or a person may be born with genitals that seem to be in-between the usual male and female types—for example, a girl may be born with a noticeably large clitoris, or lacking a vaginal opening, or a boy may be born with a notably small penis, or with a scrotum that is divided so that it has formed more like labia. Or a person may be born with mosaic genetics, so that some of her cells have XX chromosomes and some of them have XY.

> Though we speak of intersex as an inborn condition, intersex anatomy doesn't always show up at birth. Sometimes a person isn't found to have intersex anatomy until she or he reaches the age of puberty, or finds himself [to be] an infertile adult, or dies of old age and is autopsied. Some people live and die with intersex anatomy without anyone (including themselves) ever knowing (www.isna.org).[6]

The Intersex Society of North America (ISNA) was founded in 1993 by Cheryl Chase. Chase and many others have spent the last 12 years working "to end shame, secrecy, and unwanted genital surgeries for people born with an anatomy that someone decided is not standard for male or female" (www.isna.org). There is a range of circumstances in which a person may be defined, usually by medical professionals, as "intersex." Klinefelter and Turner syndromes are only two of a handful of sex variations, which include congenital adrenal hyperplasia (CAH), androgen insensitivity syndrome, and hypospadias. There are estimates that about one in every 2,000 individuals has an intersexed condition.

Sex Variations

A few of the many intersex conditions have physiological or biological aspects that represent what ISNA calls "real medical emergencies," calling for immediate intervention at the time of birth; one of these is congenital adrenal hyperplasia. The other conditions do not require parents and medical professionals to make quick or hasty decisions. CAH creates problems in the adrenal glands, small structures that sit atop the kidneys and are responsible for releasing cortisone, a hormone that helps the body deal with stress. CAH inhibits the production of cortisone and wreaks havoc on the ability to monitor salt levels. Because the adrenals add various hormones to the bloodstream, a "broken genetic recipe" (www.isna.org) can lead to high levels of virilizing hormones, creating larger than average clitoral structures and labia that look like a scrotum (in XX individuals). That "broken recipe" is implicated in virilizing effects that continue into puberty, such as thick body hair, receding hairline, deep voice, and so on.

Androgen insensitivity syndrome (AIS) is a condition where individuals "are chromosomally and gonadally male (that is, XY with testicles), but lack a key androgen receptor that facilitates the ability, fetally and onward, to respond to androgens (male hormones) produced in normal amounts by the testes" (Preves, 2003: 28).[7] So the individual would have no internal "female" organs while also having no epididymis, vas deferens, and seminal vesicles, all of which are responsible for delivering semen from the testes. Babies with AIS will have genitalia that look "female," undescended (internal) testes, and a vagina but no uterus, fallopian tubes, or ovaries. Sometimes AIS is not discovered until puberty, when the girl does not menstruate and may not develop *secondary sexual characteristics*, such as pubic and underarm hair.

Remember that "'Intersex' is a general term used for a variety of conditions in which a person is born with a reproductive or sexual anatomy that doesn't seem to fit the typical definitions of female or male" (www.isna.org). Hypospadias is one such condition and may contribute most to the one in 2,000 estimate cited earlier. It relates to the position of the urethral opening on the penis, which is usually at the tip of the penis. Hypospadias can result in an opening that is anywhere else along the penis, thus creating "non-standard" genitalia. This is not a medical emergency in most circumstances; the most extreme instances may involve a missing urethra (which causes urine to leave the bladder behind the penis).

In and of themselves, genitalia that do not look like the standard "male" and "female" bits of skin are not life-threatening. Yet virtually all intersex conditions have been treated this way, until recently. Activist and educational groups like ISNA, Bodies Like Ours, and Survivor Project have been created by people diagnosed with intersexed conditions. Not all intersexuality awareness groups have the same aims—two organizations focusing on CAH and AIS are oriented for parents (and medical professionals), while Survivor Project and Intersex Initiative Portland are more explicitly aimed at activism. But their broader goals are similar: to draw attention to the involuntary surgeries (intersex genital mutilation), stigmatizing and arbitrary judgments, and narrowness of binary models.

Physicians and scientists, themselves members of a culture with a dualistic gender system, have played a large role in the modern development of intersexuality. Sociologist Sharon Preves, who interviewed 37 intersex individuals in North America, describes what happens when an infant is born: ". . . a common method of handling an ambiguous birth includes telling the parent(s) that their child's genitals are not yet 'fully developed' before quickly whisking the infant away for myriad medical diagnostic procedures with which to ascertain the infant's 'most appropriate' gender assignment" (2003: 54). This treatment perpetuates the myth that there is something *medically* wrong with the child, when it is really more of a *social* emergency (Kessler, 1998).[8] In an examination of the medical aspects of intersexuality, psychologist Suzanne Kessler reviewed the literature describing operative and diagnostic techniques, interviewed physicians, and concluded that doctors respond according to societal conceptualizations of "normal" sex and gender.

"Normal" and "medically acceptable" is a clitoris between 0 and 0.9 centimeters, or 3/8 of an inch (Kessler, 1998, citing physicians Meyers-Seifer and Charest). But to be considered a penis, the organ must be between 2.5 and 4.5 centimeters. (Penile size standards for infants were published in the 1960s, and clitoral size standards were published in the late 1980s.) Without even knowing the metric system, one can still see that there is a gap between 0.9 centimeters and 2.5 centimeters. The marks on the ruler in this gap therefore represent something "unacceptable," a limbo that has traditionally been addressed by involuntary surgeries (what some call intersex genital mutilation) to shorten the clitoral structure. The surgeries often leave the clitoris scarred and with diminished or absent sensation. But medical thinking has been informed by cultural viewpoints that privilege the penis. Many infants are assigned the sex "female" if physicians do not believe that the "micropenis" has the potential to grow more at puberty. Kessler's research made medical logic clear: if an intersex boy would be ostracized in a locker room or public restroom due to the size of his phallus, then the boy should be assigned "female" at birth and undergo "clitoral" reduction.

Medical professionals, as members of the broader culture, react in accord with their socialization into that culture. So the construction of sex as binary and opposite informs physicians' responses, along with our belief that *anatomy is destiny.* This underlies the fear that a clitoris of an unexpected length is unacceptable for a baby assigned female. It underlies the assessment that a penis of an unexpected (smaller) length is unacceptable and must be turned into a clitoris for a baby reassigned to female. How do any of us know what "normal" is, especially when we are discussing genitalia? "Anatomy is destiny" is an expression of our positivist belief that the body tells the truth about who we are—that "true sex" can be ascertained via genitalia. The belief that one body has or should have only one sex in it ("one-body-one-sex") is another way to maintain the binary gender and sexuality status quo (Dreger, 1998).[9] When intersex children are assigned sexes and genders as youth, the physicians' criteria for "success" include ultimately being able to have penile-vaginal intercourse.

One intersex condition, Mayer-Rokitansky-Kuster-Hauser (MRKH) syndrome, involves congenital absence of the vagina and often, internal primary sexual characteristics (e.g., fallopian tubes, cervix, and/or uterus). The vulva, clitoris, and chromosomes are not affected by MRKH, but there may be kidney abnormalities, skeletal problems, and hearing problems. Given that physicians emphasize normalization and heterosexuality in obliterating intersex bodies (via phallic/clitoral reductions, removal of testes, and so on), it is not surprising that doctors' main response to MRKH is to create a vagina:

> My life completely changed when I was 13 and sent home from camp with abdominal pain. When I was examined they discovered an imperforate hymen prohibiting the flow of menstrual fluid. I had my 1st surgery then, to open my hymen so I could bleed. But they found that nothing was there. I had no vagina, just a dimple, and they could detect no uterus. I had secondary sex characteristics, body hair and breasts, so they guessed I had ovaries but no one knew where. The medical profession has known about MRKH since 1838, but I was diagnosed with "congenital absence of vagina" because that's what they cared about. My abdominal pain was quickly forgotten. I was suddenly and shamefully different. Puberty was over for me. I went from selling Girl Scout Cookies to correcting my sexual dysfunction in one afternoon.
>
> My doctors talked to my parents about vaginal reconstruction so I could have a normal sex life with my husband. What husband? And why couldn't he adjust as he would for any other "birth defect"? My parents did the right thing. They took me down the only path available, the path of "corrective" surgery. But I was staggering from the loss of my fertility, the dream of having children. I received sympathy and even pity about that, but the most pressing concern was to create my vagina ASAP (Morris, 2000).[10]

Medical interventions are not benign and often are wholly unnecessary from the standpoint of physical health (Kessler, 1998). The problem with the sex assignment process and "intersex genital mutilation" is that medical professionals have failed to see the human effects of these interventions. Persistent feelings of shame and bodily alienation can combine with feelings of disfigurement and invasion (due to multiple surgeries), inhibition, pain, and the sense of bearing a huge, incomplete secret. The development of healthy self-concept is often hampered by profound sociocultural stigmatization of people born with genitalia that do not conform to expected norms.

Max Beck (2001), assigned female at birth and named Judy, writes about the effects of forced surgeries, secrecy, and silence:

> I grew into a rough-and-tumble tomboy, a precocious, insecure, tree-climbing, dress-hating show-off with a Prince Valiant haircut and razor-sharp wit who was constantly being called "little boy" and "young man."
>
> I quickly came to understand that the tomboy—the gender identity with which I had escaped childhood—was less acceptable in adolescence. Yearly visits to endocrinologists and pediatric urologists, lots of genital poking and prodding, and my mother's unspoken guilt and shame had all served to distance me considerably from my body: I was a walking head. In retrospect, it seems odd that a tomboy should have been so removed from her body. But instead of a daily, muddy, physical celebration of life, my tomboyhood was marked by a reckless disregard for the body and a strong desire to be annihilated. So I reached adolescence with no physical sense of self, and no desire to make that connection. All around me, my peers and former playmates were dating, fooling around, giving and getting hickeys, while I, whose puberty came in pill form, watched aghast from the sidelines.
>
> What *was* I? The doctors and surgeons assured me I was a girl, that I just wasn't yet "finished." I don't think they gave a thought to what that statement would mean to me and my developing gender identity, my developing sense of self. The doctors who told me I was an "unfinished girl" were so focused on the lie—so invested in selling me "girl"—that I doubt they ever considered the effect a word like "unfinished" would have on me. I knew I was incomplete. I could see that compared to—well, compared to everyone!—I was numb from the neck down. When would I be finished? The "finishing" the doctors talked about occurred during my teen years—hormone replacement therapy and a vaginoplasty. Still, the only thing that felt complete was my isolation. Now the numbness below my neck was real—a maze of unfeeling scar tissue. I wandered through that labyrinth for another ten years, with a gender identity and desires born of those medical procedures. I began to experience myself as a sort of sexual Frankenstein's monster.[11]

Beck's experiences highlight how intersexuality has been perceived as a social emergency, the lie of "girlhood" superseding individual needs, feelings, and happiness.

Writer Jim Costich (2003), an "intersexed activist," clarifies the essential problem with surgical interventions:

Forced gender assignment and/or surgical procedures and hormone therapy have never made males or females out of the intersexed. It has only made intersexed people who have been made to look something like males and females. Not all of us were surgically altered. I wasn't. We are all working toward a day when none of us are surgically altered without our informed, mature desire and choice. No child should be mutilated to mollify the gender issues of others.[12]

Intersexuality represents an excellent opportunity for critical thinking. It requires us to explore what it really means to talk about two sexes, and to conceptualize them in the taken-for-granted way, as *opposite* sexes. We must consider how physicians and scientists, as part of the powerful social institution of medicine, have arbitrarily made decisions about what "male" and "female" mean. If we were not as set on promulgating the idea that there are two and only two sexes that are linked directly to the development of two and only two genders, we might have a society that could handle gray areas better. When we persist in seeing biological sex and gender as examples of binary opposites, we perpetuate narrow limitations on individual expression and deny the realities and experiences of many people.

I introduce the concept of intersex here as a way to further the process of critical thinking and to explore social constructionism. The reality of intersexuality forces us to reinterpret what biological sex and social gender are, and to examine the broader social processes underlying our definitions of sex and gender. Most importantly, consider what it means to make intersex people's experiences invisible.

The Binary Approach

As described earlier, biological sex appears to have two and only two categories, male and female. Determination of sex is made superficially, by noting genitalia in utero via ultrasound scans in the second trimester and confirming with a glance at birth (i.e., *primary sexual characteristics,* genitalia). After the initial determination, biological sex is seamlessly and uncritically converted into the socially meaningful categorization system, *gender.* Bodies and biological sex are taken as evidence of indisputable, immutable differences. Activist Riki Wilchins writes:

> Sex is introduced to explain skeletal structure, mental aptitude, posture, emotional disposition, aesthetic preference, body fat, sexual orientation and

responsiveness, athletic ability, social dominance, shape and weight, emotional ability, consumer habits, psychological disposition, and artistic ability.
It is also supposed to explain any number of so-called "instincts," including
the nesting instinct, the maternal instinct, and perhaps even the Budweiser
instinct (2004: 85).[13]

Parents, caregivers, medical professionals, family and friends interact with infants,
who often look very much alike, undistinguished by secondary sexual characteristics,
on the basis of gender. Research confirms that gender stereotypes form our perceptions of newborns. Mothers in one study described baby boys as tall, large, athletic,
and serious (Reid, 1994).[14] They described baby girls as small, pretty, and delicate.
White, middle-class parents speak differently to baby boys and girls, provide more
help to girls while expecting boys to be more independent, and talk about emotions
more with girls than boys, who are taught more about being assertive and stoic (e.g.,
Kuebli et al., 1995; Burns and Homel, 1989; Adams et al., 1995).[15]

In a study of social class, African American and Caucasian parents, and gender
stereotyping, Hoffman and Kloska found some differences in the adoption of stereotypical roles (1995).[16] Race and social class were associated with adoption of more traditional attitudes toward gendered marital roles and attitudes toward gendered child
rearing. Research with single-parent families and two-parent families showed that single-parent families had less traditional gender-role socialization than two-parent families (Leve and Fagot, 1997).[17] Latina mothers do more direct gender socialization with
daughters than Latino fathers do with sons (Raffaelli and Ontai, 2004), but most of
the messages support traditional gender divisions.[18] Daughters reported that their
mothers encouraged them to wear appropriate clothes, play with the correct toys, and
"be ladylike." Sons indicated that fathers encouraged them to be involved in masculine activities, be "manly," and constrain expression of their feelings. Raffaelli and
Ontai cite numerous studies reporting similar findings—gender matters for parents
and caregivers.

Regardless of subcultural parenting styles, we tend to socialize boys and girls on
the basis of differences. The nursery rhyme about the "composition" of boys and girls
hints at this: "What are little boys made of? Snips and snails and puppy dogs' tails.
What are little girls made of? Sugar and spice and everything nice." The ways in which
we teach and interact with children reinforce our belief in the binary sex gender system, and further, that the sexes are opposite to each other. Thus we construct *gender
roles,* behavioral and attitudinal expectations and norms in a given social group or system; these roles are dependent on sex. Gender role *attributes* tend to be assigned in

correspondence—if boys or men are thought to be assertive, for example, girls or women are thought to be more passive. Terman and Miles (1936) created a psychological inventory that was used extensively in schools in the 1940s and beyond.[19] The inventory was designed to assess the level of masculinity or femininity in a boy or girl. Everything from knowledge ("Most of our anthracite coal comes from . . . ") to feelings ("Does seeing boys make fun of old people make you ANGRY?") to occupations, books, character traits, famous people, and individual behaviors carried a gendered significance for Terman and Miles (Kimmel, 2004).[20] If a child "scored too high on the "inappropriate" side of the continuum, intervention strategies might be devised to facilitate the adoption of more appropriate behaviors" (2004: 78). Boys were not expected to know about cooking, household matters, or strong feelings. They were not supposed to read books like *Little Women* or *Rebecca of Sunnybrook Farm*. A pamphlet about adolescence from the 1940s included the idea that puberty gives boys courage: "The fellows who are afraid are called 'sissies' for the reason that they are like the girls when they are in danger or have hard things to do. To be able to fight it out according to the rules of the game and not whine when you are beaten or hurt is to be a man instead of a 'baby'" (Rice, 1948).[21] Possessing the "proper" gender attributes and interests was seen as confirmatory evidence of having attained the proper gender role.

Dichotomized and complementary trait attributions persist well into adulthood and never really diminish. Americans link different traits to each of the two dominant genders (Newport, 2001).[22] "Despite contemporary lip-service to equality, men and women easily associate personality characteristics with the genders. . . . Even today Americans are likely to say that the words 'emotional,' 'affectionate,' 'talkative,' 'patient,' and 'creative' describe women, while associating characteristics such as 'aggressive' and 'courageous' with men. Neither sex is most likely to be described by the terms 'intelligent,' 'easy-going,' and 'ambitious'" (2001). Fully 68 percent of respondents said "aggressive" is more true of men than women (20 percent). The "gap" is pronounced with traits such as "courageous" (50 percent said more true of men, 27 percent said more true of women); "affectionate" (86 percent said it is more true of women); and "emotional" (a whopping 90 percent said it is more true of women). Regarding courage, it is eye-opening to note that, "In 1950 Gallup asked Americans whether they thought men or women were more courageous. Interestingly, 35% of the public said men, 33% said women and 22% said the sexes were equally courageous. It is noteworthy that, 50 years later, the number of people who think men are more courageous than women has increased rather than decreased" (Newport, 2001).

Why do we insist on strict demarcations between the sexes/genders? Sociological theory offers a perspective, *structural-functionalism*, that may shed some light. In this paradigm, society is an orderly, stable system. The system is composed of various *structures* (such as the economy, the polity, religion) that serve particular, defined, and useful *functions*. Each element of a society, including every individual, plays roles that have specific functions (or purposes). Thus strict binary gender divisions can be seen as a small part of a larger whole. Functionalists would say that the natural, inborn differences between males and females—best exemplified by the female ability to give birth and nurture new life—gave rise to dichotomous gender roles. By defining and labeling what constitutes "masculine" or "feminine," we clarify the relation of each set of traits. The two dominant sexes/genders are meant to complement the other. Michael Kimmel (2004) gives an example of this, describing the four basic tenets of being or becoming a man:

1. *No Sissy Stuff.* Masculinity is based on the relentless repudiation of the feminine.
2. *Be a Big Wheel.* Masculinity is measured by the size of your paycheck, and marked by wealth, power and status. As a popular U.S. bumper sticker put it, "He who has the most toys when he dies, wins."
3. *Be a Sturdy Oak.* What makes a man a man is that he is reliable in a crisis. And what makes him reliable in a crisis is that he resembles an inanimate object. A rock, a pillar, a tree.
4. *Give 'Em Hell.* Exude an aura of daring and aggression. Take risks; live life on the edge.[23]

This perspective truly supports the social status quo, in effect asserting that gender roles are constructed as they are because they stem directly from natural, biological realities. The problem is that gender roles, identities, and attributions vary widely from historical era to era, from culture to culture, and from subculture to subculture. Given how much variation we find in the sociocultural construction of gender, is it realistic to assume that gender is a derivative of sex? What are the implications of the binary system and our need to hold fast to it? In fact, intersexuality challenges this assumption. If there are more than two ways for biological sex to be constituted within a single individual, then perhaps there are more than two ways for gender to be socially constructed. If intersexuality shows us that "male" and "female" are *not* opposites—they are just elements of the matrix of sex—then it also challenges the idea that "man" and "woman" are opposites.

Gender Attributions and Schemas

Without even realizing it, the first thing many of us do when we interact with others is guess about gender. We unconsciously make gender attributions all the time, whether speaking with, listening to, or simply watching other people. We may attempt to make other attributions as well, such as nationality, race, ethnicity, and age. Why do we do this? What purpose does it serve?

We live in a complex world where things are not always as they seem, or as simple as they seem. Psychologists suggest that we make sense of complex and multifaceted input by using *schemas*, mental or cognitive structures that we develop through interaction with the world. Schemas help us organize and process information, becoming a template that enables us to discern patterns and develop themes. We initially develop schemas in childhood, though like any other cognitive process, the learning is lifelong. Ultimately, schemas help us explain our interactions, mediate our perceptions, and guide our responses, especially in new situations. Thus schemas can be very useful when managing a lot of new information.

But schemas can be subject to what psychologists call *accessibility*. This refers to how easily a particular schema comes to mind; accessibility is dependent upon subjective interpretations and experiences. Schemas contain "slots" that are filled by specific information gleaned from our environs. So instead of having to develop new schemas for every novel situation, the most common explanation is chosen, or accessed, to make sense of new information. Let's say I go to a bar in a new city, and someone approaches me to make conversation. I do not need to start from scratch to figure out how to interact. I go to my Meet-Someone-in-a-Bar schema, and without even wondering how I got to that schema, I immediately, subconsciously, access everything I have ever learned about how to talk with a stranger in a bar.

The problem is that schemas also exert a great deal of influence over us and sometimes prevent us from integrating new information that does not fit into the template. So when the stranger approaches me in the bar, he has no way to know what my schema is. If I am expecting him to try to flirt with me, and I have my antiflirting schema in place, he may find me to be very unfriendly. But what if he is not flirting with me? What if he simply wants to ask directions to a nearby restaurant? I will certainly be able to interact with him, give him directions, or tell him I don't know where the restaurant is. However, I may not adjust my Meet-Someone-in-a-Bar schema, and I may grumble to myself about how everyone in every bar in every city just wants to flirt.

It seems a little overblown when described in this way. But this example highlights some cognitive close cousins of schemas: stereotypes, social roles, scripts, worldviews, points of view, and archetypes. In developing a schema—a template to help me organize complex input—I may end up narrowing my point of view and *oversimplifying* the complexity of the world around me. My viewpoint is narrowed when I overgeneralize: "all guys in bars in cities just want to flirt." From this I may conclude that all men are only interested in one thing, thereby *stereotyping*, creating an oversimplified and formulaic conception or image.

The process of gender attribution is the act of building a schema. The seemingly simple act of unconsciously guessing at a stranger's gender involves accessing our existing schemas—Who is this person? Who am I dealing with? What cues am I using to give me an idea about gender and/or sex? Several years ago, I was in a restaurant waiting to eat breakfast. A colleague came in with a young child dressed in shorts, a baseball hat, and a simple tee shirt, all in solid dark colors. I quickly attributed the gender "boy" to the child, who had short hair and a matter-of-fact demeanor. When my colleague introduced me to his *niece*, my cognitive schema was so engaged that I actually thought to myself, "No, he's wrong; that's really his nephew." It fascinated me throughout breakfast; I could hardly stop staring at her, trying to "see" her as a girl. What I had done was essentially only observe and recall (or see) the cues that fit my initial gender guess. That a scholar of sexualities and gender could organize her brain in this way is evidence of how entrenched gender classification systems are, and evidence that we have a lot of work to do if we wish to change our schemas.

Schema Challenges: Beyond the Sex/Gender Binary

You receive an invitation to a concert. The top of the invitation reads, "All Genders Welcome." Do you . . .

> Wonder why they phrased it like that.
> Get nervous about who or what might show up.
> Feel defensive.
> Feel included (Bornstein, 1994).[24]

How do we typically determine a person's sex? Their gender? The discussion above suggests that we use genitalia to make a determination. Imagine if we all wore burqa-like cloth covering our entire bodies *except* for an open flap at the genitals! But realistically, how often do we see someone's genitalia prior to attributing to them a sex and a gender? After the initial assignment at birth, we tend to use external symbols, like color, clothing, and hairstyles, to communicate and assess gender/sex. We place so much importance on genitalia, as intersexuality clarifies, but then move to other communication methods, including conversational style, body language and even the way we walk. So what happens in the case of a person whose genitalia are "standard" and "expected" but whose sense of self does not correspond with those genitalia? What happens for someone who experiences cultural gender roles as narrow, and therefore has a gender presentation that differs from the one associated with their sex?

In the United States alone, there are thousands of people born female who transition to become men, and tens of thousands of people born male who transition to become women. It is hard to estimate with great precision because not everyone seeks surgery, hormones, and/or clinical interventions. We can get an estimate of incidence from clinical and medical records, because reassignment surgeries such as *vaginoplasties* (construction of vagina and vulva, using phallic skin and tissues) and *mastectomies* (removal of breast tissues and mammary glands) generally cannot be undertaken without prior psychological counseling, hormone regimens, and a period of living completely in the new gender (e.g., name change, presentation of self via clothing and other outward signs of gender, informing significant others, and so on).

It can be difficult to discuss the issue because of varied language and terms: trans, transgender, transsexual; preoperative, postoperative, sex change, sex reassignment surgery, sex confirmation surgery, sex/gender congruence surgery, gender dysphoria; butch, femme, boi, drag king, drag queen, male-to-female (MTF), female-to-male (FTM), trannyboi, transman, transwoman, genderqueer, transgressively gendered, metagendered. There are undoubtedly other terms, more local or regional, in addition to the fact that some folks do not wish to use any labels or terms. Social institutions like law and medicine have created language and diagnostic categories. Institutions define and label in order to further classify and demarcate individuals. Individuals and small groups transgress and create language to challenge the institutional power of being able to name; the goal is to choose one's own labels or terms. (In this text, it will be easiest and most sensible to use the term "trans.") Here is a brief primer on some of these terms:

Transsexual: A person with persistent and significant discomfort about *natal* (born) sex; a person with the sense that natal sex and natal primary/secondary sexual characteristics are inappropriate, false, or incomplete; may have the desire to remove erroneous genitalia and other characteristics and live as "the other sex"; may have the desire to use hormones to assist transition. Not everyone wishes to have surgeries or hormones or both. This now tends to be mostly a medical term, employed by physicians, researchers, and clinicians.

Transgender: Often used as an umbrella term to describe people who locate themselves somewhere in the broad matrix of socially constructed gender; may not wish to obtain any surgeries or use hormones—may instead focus on changing outward gender presentation or expression. Tends to be more of a social term (i.e., not medical or clinical) and may be more useful for someone transitioning in or challenging the sex/gender system.

Trans: The shortened version of *transgender,* but a term in its own right; works as an umbrella term and an adjective (e.g., transman).

Gender dysphoria: A dysphoria is a difficulty, a state of being or feeling "unwell." It tends to be applied in clinical and medical settings and is therefore an institutional label for a person who feels like their natal sex is inappropriate or incorrect. It is a term of those in power, used to classify people. The *DSM-IV,* described in chapter 2, classifies gender dysphoria, strictly speaking, as a "mental illness."

MTF: Male-to-female, or male-towards-female; see also FTM. Some people prefer the term *transwoman.*

FTM: Female-to-male, or female-towards-male; distinguishes between transpeople who were identified as female at birth from MTF transpeople who were identified as male at birth. Some people dislike the term because it implies they are moving to a set "endpoint" of maleness, while others dislike it because it implies that they were not male to begin with. Others find it a useful description of their experience (www.ftmaustralia.org).[25] Some people prefer the term *transman.*

Genderqueer: This term is not clinical or medical at all and is more individually defined; refers to someone who redefines, plays with, and/or transgresses stereotypical and binary genders and may reject the social construct of "gender" altogether.

Ze, e, and hir: For some people, these words replace the sex-linked pronouns of she, he, his, and her. The dominance of these four pronouns as a form of shorthand in language, obviating the need to repeat a person's name, make it difficult for people to adopt *ze, e,* and *hir.* An example of these terms in a sentence would be: When *ze* was born, *hir* parents were working as farmers; *e* doesn't want to be a farmer *emself.*

Cross-Dressing: Technically, this term may not really fit in this list, but it is worth including to minimize confusion. Historically, it was a pejorative (as in, "cross-dresser") usually applied only to heterosexually oriented men who wore clothing designed for women. There was a misconception that cross-dressing always contained an element of sexual fetish or fascination. Now the term has a broader and far less pejorative spirit and may include the performative elements of *camp, drag queens,* and *drag kings.*

So how do transpeople challenge the typical schemas of people who do not identify as such? Most obviously, a person whose gender expression is transgressive will draw our cultural attention to the fact that we have fairly strict expectations of how men and women should look. Our taken-for-granted schemas are revealed as oversimplifications, drawing our attention to the fact that we normally make (narrow) gender/sex attributions without much thought. On Saturday Night Live in the early 1990s, comedian Julia Sweeney played "Pat," an androgynously dressed, gender-neutrally-named character. Pat had a mid-range, nasal voice, curly short hair, and enacted no specific gender clues or cues. The humor of the Pat skits was based on the other characters, who doggedly attempted to "out" Pat by trying to get Pat to use a restroom or express other preferences that could be gendered (it was sort of like a modern Terman and Miles study). Sweeney was trying to capitalize on and exemplify the discomfort people often feel when confronted with the twin realities of gender bending and stereotyping.

What the Pat skits did not show is the range of feelings, including discomfort, that can accompany individual acknowledgment and development of trans identities. Because of the rigidity of Western sex/gender systems, transpeople may have emotionally, physically, and spiritually difficult experiences. When childhood encompasses gender incongruity, similarly to what Max Beck described, individuals may successfully hide transgressions, but at the potential cost of shame and silence. Puberty can bring a host of challenges, including grappling with the bodily changes wrought by hormones. These changes may magnify the feeling of having a body that diverges from one's internal experience of gender identity:

> Transiting even a garden-variety puberty can be challenging and confusing. Add to that turmoil the bewilderment and panic of gender and sexual nonconformity at a time when sex and conformity are the two most important things in life, and one may find transgender kids acting out conflicts in ways even more bizarre than normal teens. Some flaunt their differentness, some withdraw, some conform to the norms of their peers at great personal cost, some find that drugs and alcohol help ease the pain, some act as extreme versions of their genetic sex, some overachieve, some drop out, some leave home

and become street kids, and some boys act in super-macho and bigoted ways. Most go through a succession of such reactions as they flail about trying to find a safe place to exist (Osborne, 2005).[26]

Individual responses will run the gamut and may include positive, negative, and neutral techniques to accommodate sex/gender identities that differ from typical, hegemonic identities.

The trouble is that individual coping strategies occur within larger cultural contexts that may be quite negative, prejudicial, and painful. One mother describes how her child's individual clarity about gender and sexuality was constrained by the rigidity of her surroundings:

> By mid-adolescence it was clear that Jenny was more than a tomboy. As a 16-year-old "dyke," she was so extreme in appearance that her role model was James Dean. She couldn't use public restrooms without someone calling security. The college kids in the apartment upstairs urinated on her bedroom window. The world was actively discriminating against her. There is no favorite picture [photograph] from these years. Jenny had forgotten how to smile. There was no question that something needed to change so Jenny could have space to navigate in the world (Lantz, 2003: 7).[27]

It is striking that Jenny's mom, Barbara Lantz, perceived these events as "active" discrimination (they were indeed). There was no sense of live and let live or nonjudgmental understanding, and in many ways, it makes sense that "the world" would respond by actively discouraging Jenny's diversity. This is an example of how someone who was perceived as a threat to the dominant sex/gender order was subjected to social control, with no regard for her experiences or needs.

The emphasis on genitalia, evident in the accounts of childhood intersex "mutilation," persists in accounts of trans experiences. It is assumed that all transpeople want different genitalia than those they were born with. In fact, there is really no universality to individual desires and experiences; some folks want some surgeries or cosmetic procedures, and some simply do not (Sullivan and Plante, 2005).[28] Philosopher C. Jacob Hale (2002) explains how central genitalia are, listing a wide range of individuals and social institutions with a singular focus:

> There was the passport agency official who told me that if I want an M on my passport, I should have already had a surgeon cut on my genitals (p. 250).

There are FTMs who tell me that if I want to be one of them, I should be delighted and congratulatory when one of them finds a surgeon to cut on his genitals (p. 250).

There are shrinks who tell me that if I want testosterone, I should get myself diagnosed with a mental disorder and seek a surgeon to cut on my genitals when the shrinks tell me I am ready to have a surgeon cut on my genitals (p. 252).

There are all those nontransexuals [sic] who tell me that if I get some surgeon to cut on my genitals, I will be mutilating myself or sinning or making myself into a monster or a freak (p. 252).[29]

Transpeople of all kinds force our culture to reckon with the fact that we seem to need gender/sex to be binary, as well as oppositional. Why *is* the binary or dichotomous gender system so appealing? Structural-functional theorists would suggest that it enhances social order. Evolutionary psychologists might argue that it is appealing because it is natural and predominant, though sex diversity does exist in nature (Roughgarden, 2004).[30] Anthropologists might say that binary systems are not limited to the Western world, although there are a few cultures that include a third sex, third gender, or the concept of "two-spirit" people. Even for people self-identified in the trans umbrella, there are tensions created and sustained by the hegemonic, dualistic system:

I have issues in general with the queer community and femme-phobia and/or over-valuing masculinity. Whether I am presenting (over-generalizing here) "male" or "female" (or both, or neither, for that matter), on any given day, I am most definitely femme and it's undeniable, you know?! Regardless of internal or external presentation or feelings, it's a constant in my world. Oh, damn. It (femme-phobia) is just EVERYWHERE—maybe magnified more so within the gq [genderqueer] and tg [transgender] communities (and in this case, specifically with female-born or female-bodied genderqueer-identified individuals). Seems like everyone's trying so hard to get away from anything femme and anything stereotypically female—and instead of embracing both sides, the female or femme, depending on how you look at it, and the male or masculine (again, subjective)—the femme/more stereotypically "female" side gets push [sic] down, treated like a lesser than, an old hat—negative. It (femme) *is* an identity label (for me). If you think about it, there are femme boys and femme girls—and me—I'm a femme girlboyboygirl-neithereitheror. But, yes. I came to terms with my femme identity before I came to terms with my/the genderqueer identity—and, regardless, I never felt like one negated (or *had to* negate) the other—or—not even negated; but neither carried higher importance (to me). (www.trans-academics.org)[31]

This contributor to a trans discussion forum highlights some ways in which broader cultural context pervades gender/sex subcultures. She describes her sense that *sexism*, prejudice or discrimination, or the belief that one sex is superior, exists even in the trans community—"everyone's trying so hard to get away from anything femme and anything stereotypically female." She hints at the idea that the binary sex/gender system defines everyone's experience in this culture, whether they are challenging the structure or taking it as a given. Why do we discuss men and women as different creatures? The extent to which our culture privileges difference is evident in the quotes above, when she characterizes "femme" as a "side" of an individual, with butchness or maleness as the other side. So even within one individual there may be a sense of a straight, linear continuum of gender/sex, with characteristics, traits, and feelings aligned.

In working to develop a "sociology of transgendered bodies," Richard Ekins and Dave King described the main elements in the "story" of transitioning and redefining the binary (1999).[32] Not everyone who defines themselves as trans is engaged in the same process, as the Web site post above implies. Some people are "migrating," "oscillating," "erasing," or "transcending." Ekins and King clarify:

> *Migrating* body stories involve moving the body from one side of the binary divide to the other on a permanent basis. *Oscillating* body stories are stories of moving backwards and forwards over the gender border, only temporarily resting on one side or the other. *Erasing* body stories are those in which the gender of the person erasing is expunged. *Transcending* body stories tell of moving beyond gender into a third space.

Clearly, each of these efforts reveals different motivations and perspectives. Some individuals see gender as infinitely fluid and engage in further "subprocesses" such as *redefining*. Redefining can also occur when a person positions the body in a different way. "The male to female transsexual may redefine her beard growth as facial hair. The penis may be redefined as a 'growth between the legs', as in 'I was a woman who had needed some corrective surgery'" (Ekins and King, 1999). *Substituting* involves replacing body parts/characteristics associated with one sex for characteristics associated with the other. *Concealing*, which relates to "the concealing or hiding of parts of the body which are seen to conflict with the intended gender display," is likely to occur for most transpeople, dependent upon the desired gender performance. Finally, *implying* gender may occur. King and Ekins explain, "Because the body is usually apprehended in social interaction in its clothed form, it is possible to imply the gendered form of the body beneath. So, for example, males can wear breast forms inside a bra, or hip pads inside a panty girdle; females may place something in their underpants to imply the possession of a penis."

The body becomes crucial in the presentation of a gendered self for every member of society. If you accept the idea that gender is socially constructed, with its "appropriate" portrayal defined via societal consensus, then you must consider the notion that *all* gender role expressions involve all of the techniques King and Ekins describe. We redefine when we seek cosmetic surgery, substitute when we get Botox injections (though the substitution is something "aging" for something "youthful"), conceal body parts that conflict with the display we wish to present (for example, when women camouflage their hips with control-top panty hose), and imply (think padded bras). But because we take for granted that binary gender is "natural," we often overlook the ways in which all public presentations of gender involve at least some unnatural elements. The overwhelming majority of women in Western countries shave, pluck, wax or otherwise remove naturally growing body hair. Since facial hair is no longer in vogue for men, most shave regularly. We employ products, clothing, and accessories in the attempt to present ourselves as hygienic and (appropriately) gendered creatures.

Because our culture places so much stock in the body as the symbol of biological sex, we respond to schema-challenging bodies in various ways. As Suzanne Kessler described in the case of intersexuality, we place special significance on the genitalia. We assume that male bodies have penises, testicles, and scrotums and female bodies have vaginas, vulvas, clitorises, and breasts. But transpeople may have bodies that are configured in other ways. For example, many transmen do not undergo *phalloplasties*, the construction of a penis from skin grafts and muscle tissues. *Mastectomy*, removal of breast tissues, is more common, but not all transmen have *hysterectomies*, the removal of uterus, ovaries, and fallopian tubes.

A 2005 episode of *The Maury Povich Show* featured people born female who transitioned to become men. Maury seemed obsessed with the question of what the men were like "down below," asking one person, "What's it feel like?" When the man replied that he had full sensation after his phalloplasty, Maury was incredulous, "You have all of the nerves and things . . . ?" What he really wanted to say was, "You have all of the nerves and things that *normal* men have?" With another guest, he asked, "So you're a man?" His guest replied, smiling broadly, "I'm 100% a man." Maury said, "But you're missing something!" Still smiling, the man said, "I'm missing what *you* think is necessary. . . ." Maury trotted out the wives and girlfriends of the men and although this should have reinforced their heterosexuality, it instead acted as a way to reinforce Maury's, and the audience's, confusion. It was clear that they were all wondering how the women partners handled PVI with their trans partners. Without penises, or with a constructed penis, how was "sex" possible? And how could it feel good or pleasurable? Because surgical procedures like vaginoplasty and breast augmentation are more perfected for transwomen, the question of *how* "sex" (meaning PVI) can happen is less salient.

People still wonder what sex is like for transwomen and their partners, but the curiosity never seems to extend to how transfolk feel about their own sex lives:

> Of course, having a sex partner who desires me the way I am (my ex was very conflicted about my transition) makes all the difference in the world. I still feel conflict and sadness about what I call my "genital situation," but what I've got is working better for me now than it ever did in the past. That's major.
>
> In sum, yes: feeling so much better about myself, sharing my bed with a woman who treats my body with reverence, and being on a very powerful sex hormone have all contributed to a vastly improved sex life and to a greater sense of intimacy. The key thing with the intimacy is that my lover truly wants me as a man, respects my boundaries when I'm not up to certain things, and has proved she is worthy of the deep trust necessary for me to give her sexual access to my person. By the way, I'm 38. Just goes to show you're never too old to change! (Berg, 2004)[33]

The key thing for Berg and the men featured on *Maury* is that all had developed meaningful intimate relationships. Acceptance, love, and support are vital regardless of where we are in the sex/gender system.

Other cultures have managed to find ways to incorporate sex and gender diversity. Some Native cultures have always included what are now called *two-spirit people*, a term coined by Native LGBT activists (Thomas and Jacobs, 1999).[34] Two-spirit replaces the highly derogatory *berdache*, made popular in anthropological literature. Berdache has connotations of prostitution, is an Arabic-derived term that is too broad, and does not really reflect the breadth of the sociocultural position occupied by two-spirit people (usually shaman or blessed person). In fact, Navajo conceive of a world in which everything manifests an interconnectedness that the Western conception of gender oversimplifies (Epple, 1998).[35] In some areas of India, there is an institutionalized "third gender," called *Hijra* (Nanda, 1998).[36] Hijras contain elements of what Indian society has labeled masculine and feminine; they adopt women's clothing and dress styles, and some remove their genitalia. They do not get vaginas constructed, rendering them eunuchs (Nanda, 1999).[37] Though some Indians demean Hijras, they are seen by some as having a special place in Indian society, with the power to curse or confer blessings on male infants. In Sa'moa, third-gender people are called *fa'afafine* (a man who is "like a lady") and *fa'afatama* (a woman who is "like a man"). Fa'afafine are treated as women and play the same roles in Samoan culture as other women— caretakers, teachers, and the like. They are not discouraged or condemned but may not be encouraged either (Schmidt, 2001).[38] Less is known about fa'afatama, but what Western culture might call androgynous traits and attitudes are assumed for women who are fa'afatama. I once met a fa'afatama woman who told me that she enjoyed the ocean, fishing, woodworking, and building things, but was considered generous, quiet, and gentle—a mix of the typically gendered traits Sa'moans had assigned to men and women.

Focus on . . . the Scientific Narrative of Conception.   Typically, those whom we call male and female have interdependent reproductive capabilities. For conception to occur, eggs need to be fertilized by sperm, whether in a laboratory petri dish or inside a female's body. No one could logically argue against how conception occurs, not even a social constructionist. But we have given this fact dominant significance in spite of the reality of heterosex in Western cultures. Most instances of penile-vaginal inter- course do not result in conception and are not intended to. On average, most Amer- ican women first menstruate by age 13, complete menopause in their early 50s, and have one or two children. Assuming that most heterosexually active women are sexu- ally experienced and active by age 19, that equals about 30 years (maybe more) of PVI that generally does not lead to pregnancy. So why do we build a sex/gender system on something that can be immaterial in most people's daily lives?

Anthropologist Emily Martin (1991) wrote a classic analysis of how unconscious sexism and the binary sex/gender system have shaped the way in which scientific researchers conceptualize reproductive biology.[39] Biologist Anne Fausto-Sterling writes that "our beliefs about gender affect what kinds of knowledge scientists produce about sex in the first place" (2000: 3).[40] Martin tests this idea, analyzing major scientific text- books' coverage of sperm and egg and what happens when they meet (or not). She starts with menstruation and the monthly cycle, designed to release eggs and develop a uterine environment to grow fertilized eggs. In this light, menstruation is viewed as a failure, with shedding of the uterine lining (bleeding) described as "debris," "dying," "losing," "denuding," and "expelling." Egg production is described as inferior, waste- ful, degenerative, because although female babies have seven million egg germ cells, only about 400 to 500 eggs are released before menopause. But Martin suggests that it is more curious that male overproduction of sperm is "not seen as wasteful," although the testes apparently create 100 million sperm daily, conservatively. That could equal two trillion sperm in the average male's lifetime. Yet Martin found no wording in scientific textbooks implying that these sperm are wasted.

She describes the textbooks she read, laden with unconscious, socially constructed gender attributions:

> How is it that positive images are denied to the bodies of women? A look at language—in this case, scientific language—provides the first clue. Take the egg and the sperm. It is remarkable how "femininely" the egg behaves and how "masculinely" the sperm. The egg is seen as large and passive. It does not *move* or *journey*, but passively "is transported," "is swept," or even "drifts" along the fallopian tube. In utter contrast, sperm are small, "streamlined," and invariably active. They "deliver" their genes to the egg, "activate the developmental program of the egg," and have a "velocity" that is often remarked upon. Their tails are "strong" and efficiently powered. Together with the forces of ejaculation, they can "propel the semen into the deepest recesses of the vagina." For this they need "energy," "fuel," so that with a "whiplashlike motion and strong lurches" they can "burrow through the egg coat," and "penetrate" it (1991: 489).

There is no evidence to support these conceptualizations of egg and sperm. The adjectives cannot be construed as merely words. Martin suggests that we view the descriptions as examples of both sexism and the act of "endowing cellular entities with personhood" (1991: 501).

> At its extreme, the age-old relationship of the egg and the sperm takes on a royal or religious patina. The egg coat, its protective barrier, is sometimes called its "vestments," a term usually reserved for sacred, religious dress. The egg is said to have a "corona," a crown, and to be accompanied by "attendant cells." It is holy, set apart and above, the queen to the sperm's king. The egg is also passive, which means it must depend on sperm for rescue. Gerald Schatten and Helen Schatten liken the egg's role to that of Sleeping Beauty: "a dormant bride awaiting her mate's magic kiss, which instills the spirit that brings her to life." Sperm, by contrast, have a "mission," which is to "move through the female genital tract in quest of the ovum." One popular account

has it that the sperm carry out a "perilous journey" into the "warm darkness," where some fall away "exhausted." "Survivors" "assault" the egg, the successful candidates "surrounding the prize." Part of the urgency of this journey, in more scientific terms, is that "once released from the supportive environment of the ovary, an egg will die within hours unless rescued by a sperm." The wording stresses the fragility and dependency of the egg, even though the same text acknowledges elsewhere that sperm also live for only a few hours (1991: 489).

We can easily see examples of embedded cultural beliefs, feminizing the egg and masculinizing the sperm. Scientists attribute qualities to eggs, seen as uniquely female and therefore feminine, and to sperm, uniquely male and therefore masculine. Thus egg and sperm are constructed as true opposites, essential to the "opposite sexes." Martin says, "At the very least, the imagery keeps alive some of the hoariest old stereotypes about weak damsels in distress and their strong male rescuers. That these stereotypes are now being written in at the level of the *cell* constitutes a powerful move to make them seem so natural as to be beyond alteration" (1991: 500).

The implications should be obvious. If we inscribe a dualistic sex/gender system into cells that we argue are fundamentally different, fundamental to sex differences, then what hope do we have of ever conceiving of sex and gender beyond the binaries? In the essence of femininity is a dormant egg, on a pedestal, waiting to be set in passive motion by the rowdy, active, productive warrior sperm—the essence of masculinity. These metaphors and this cultural narrative are revealed in the gendered, heterosexed differences created throughout our lives. In subsequent chapters, we will see other consequences of this point of view.

It should not be surprising that most of the scientific knowledge Emily Martin critiqued was produced by men in a climate of questionable equality for women. It is not that male scientists are evil—more so that culture strongly influences the way we produce and describe the world around us. So why don't we discuss, focus on, and research gender similarities? Why are arguments about "natural differences" so appealing—men are from Mars, women are from Venus . . . ? One social purpose that may be served by the unrelenting quest to establish sex/gender differences is the ability to delineate, to label those differences. In maintaining structures of difference, whether class, race, ethnicity, sexuality or other, we can label the differences "deviant." Throughout our history, we can find numerous examples of exactly this feature of human existence. Anything that is not the hegemonic norm is classified as "Other." Differences have served the purpose of preserving the status quo by setting a normative standard to which citizens can aspire. If we learn that difference is bad and will be punished with formal and informal sanctions, we will strive to conform.

Gender socialization links with conceptions of "normal" in that it also reinforces socialization into heterosexuality, as Martin's research implies. Because we tend to believe and indeed, are taught explicitly, that heterosexuality is the norm, culturally we view any other forms of sexual expression in that light. Freud theorized about how gender and heterosexuality are linked. He started with the idea that infants are *poly-morphously perverse* (1962).[41] "Perverse" does not just mean sexually kinky. Freud's interpretation of polymorphous perversity was different—"relating to or exhibiting infantile sexual tendencies in which the genitals are not yet identified as the sole or principal sexual organs nor coitus as the goal of erotic activity" (Merriam-Webster OnLine). Defined this way, perversion was a typical feature of usual sexual develop-ment, "an original and universal" aspect of the "human sexual instinct." Polymor-phous refers to "undifferentiated," and Freud argued that infants are capable of receiv-ing pleasure from numerous sources, without judging or negating any. The goal of socialization then is to help infants become gendered children capable of channeling "sexual tendencies" into socially acceptable forms (e.g., nonincestuous heterosexuality based on penile-vaginal intercourse), thus exemplifying social control over sexuality. The primary developmental task, Freud posited, is for girls and boys to learn to devel-op desire for opposite sex people to whom they are unrelated. By the late 1960s, some people were incensed by Freud's idea that, in order to develop properly into adults, girls had to shift out of the phallic/clitoral stage and learn to seek pleasure via the vagi-na, while boys were able to retain the phallus as a source of pleasure.

Children begin life with affection and attachment directed largely at their moth-er, Freud says, because of her usual role as caregiver and nurturer. Proper achievement of heterosexuality and gender are achieved when the boy no longer desires to remove his father (the competition) so he can possess his mother sexually (i.e., the *Oedipal complex*). Instead, the boy must realize that when he grows to adulthood, he can then meet and marry a woman "just like dear old mom." So he achieves gender by identi-fying with dad—first as a rival, then as a literal role model. The girl sees her mother as a rival for father's affections (i.e., the *Electra complex*), and her task then is to real-ize that she can grow up to become her mom (thus achieving gender) and find her own mate, "just like dear old dad." Freud argues that this is tougher for girls, because their experience of mom's body is associated with the first experiences of pleasure—being breast fed, having basic needs met. A boy would just need to shift his attachment from mom to some other female in order to attain adult heterosexuality and gender. More controversy ensued from this theory. Freud asserted that since girls needed to shift identification twice—away from the clitoris and away from mother—there was greater potential for something to go wrong, resulting in *neurosis*. *Penis envy* doesn't help any. Freud argued that girls will eventually notice that they "lack" something boys have; proper gender socialization thus included the recognition that, well, women are inferior (after getting angry at mom for failing to give her a penis). Without a penis of her own, the next best thing is to get as close to a penis as possible (as an adult, of course)—another way of reinforcing heterosexuality and gender. Freud's ideas are not uncritically accepted and have provided a wealth of ideas for scholars and psychoanalysts to interpret, challenge, and dissect.

IMPLICATIONS AND CONCLUSION

Recall that the "modern" era of sex research was ushered in with Krafft-Ebing's attempt to label every instance of nonheterosexual, nonreproductive sexual conduct. The Oscar Wilde trials ushered in an era of labels-as-identities, where persons were classified according to the morality of their sexual behavior. We can see the classifications entrenched in this point of view when we remember public opinion polls, where attitudes are assessed on the basis of what is morally acceptable or not. The power to define sexualities is exemplified by Martin's analysis of scientific narratives. The sex/gender binary reflects cultural power and the need to narrowly define us, even at the cellular level, thereby inhibiting us from questioning the entire system of labels, classifications, and morality. But it is hard to believe that sex and gender *have to be* polarized, made opposites. Social constructionism (nurture) and essentialism/evolutionary psychology (nature) do not need to be polarized either. The problem is that essentialism has been used to justify hierarchies of race, class, gender, and sexuality, among other aspects of human existence. Societies and social institutions have then been built on the logic of superiority and inferiority. But we cannot support final answers with the data we currently have about sexualities.

This chapter represents a very brief foray into the universe of biological sex and socially constructed gender. The rest of the book is organized around central questions and arenas of sexualities in which gender is a major variable, shaping and moderating our experiences. There is certainly one clear, key question before us for the rest of this book: What *is* the "truth" about sex and sexualities? But we also need to address other questions. How does biology—even at the cellular level—intersect and interact with the social, cultural, and contextual? How do puberty-related biological processes impact the development of individual sexualities? What are we taught about sex in this culture, and what are the effects of those messages? In the next chapter, we will explore adolescence, socialization, and gender.

Questions to Ponder

1. What are some implications of the sex and gender binary? How is the either/or division consequential?

2. Why should we study a full range of sex and gender presentations? How does this highlight the aspects of sex and gender that we tend to take for granted?

Suggested Projects

1. Using one of several popular blog Web sites (e.g., Blogger, Journalspace, Live-Journal, and so on), find some blog entries that address gender and sexuality. You will probably need to use inferential thinking to see the ways in which gender is revealed in the entries. What topic have you chosen to focus on? Can you find the same topic addressed in men's and women's blogs?

2. Explore gender and biological sex through children's books. Your local community library will have a selection of children's picture books; ask the librarian for help finding titles that deal with some aspect of gender, sex, and/or sexuality. You could analyze the illustrations for gendered messages, or just focus on the story told in the book. If you look at stories about "where babies come from," how are eggs, sperm, and conception depicted in the books?

SECTION II

Becoming Sexual

4

Birds Do It, Bees Do It

LEARNING ABOUT "IT"

A formally dressed schoolteacher enters the classroom of a very traditional boys' school. He wears a suit and the robe of a British "master"; the pupils are wearing their uniform suits, with ties and messy hair. The teacher runs through a list of bland announcements about school activities, when to take recess, and so forth.

Teacher: Sex, sex, sex. Where were we? [sniffs] Well, had I got as far as the penis entering the vagina? [sniffs]

The pupils slowly answer no.

Teacher: Well, had I done foreplay?

The pupils slowly answer yes. Some have begun looking out the windows, doodling, staring into space.

Teacher: Ahh, well, as we all know all about foreplay, no doubt you can tell me what the purpose of foreplay is . . . Biggs?

Biggs: Uhm . . . don't know. Sorry, sir.

Teacher: Carter?

Carter: Ah. Uhh, was it taking your clothes off, sir?

Teacher: Well, and . . . and after that?

He then reprimands a student for distractedly staring out the window at the soccer game . . .

So *just listen.* Now, did I or did I not . . . do . . . vaginal . . . juices?

Pupils: Mmm. Mmm. Yes, sir. Yes, sir.

Teacher: Name two ways of getting them flowing, Watson.

Watson: Er—rubbing the clitoris, sir?

Teacher: What's wrong with a kiss, boy? Hmm? Why not start her off with a nice kiss? You don't have to go leaping straight for the clitoris like a bull at a gate. Give her a kiss, boy.

After discussing more aspects of foreplay for the woman, the teacher's wife enters the room. The teacher presses a button, causing the chalkboard to disappear as an elaborate, four-poster bed drops down from a compartment in the wall. The classroom now has a fully made full-sized bed at the front, behind the desk. The teacher and his wife undress and discuss their dinner plans. The teacher notices a student sleeping and says, "Wymer! This is for your benefit. Would you kindly wake up? I've no intention of going through this all again." The wife lies on the bed.

Teacher: Uhh, we'll take the foreplay as "rendered" if you don't mind, dear.

Helen: No, of course not, Humphrey.

Teacher: So, the man starts by entering—or mounting—his good lady wife in the standard way. Uh, the penis is now, as you will observe, more or less, fully erect. There we are. Ah, that's better. Now . . . Carter! [*He notices that one of the students is fiddling with a small plastic musical instrument.*]

Carter: Yes, sir?

Teacher: What is it?

Carter: It's an ocarina, sir.

Teacher: Bring it up here. The man now starts making thrusting movements with his pelvic area, moving the penis up and down inside the vagina, so. . . . [*Carter approaches the teacher, atop his wife, with the ocarina.*] Put it there, boy. Put it there on the table. While the wife maximizes her clitoral stimulation by the shaft of the penis by pushing forward [*she does so*]. Thank you, dear. Now, as sexual . . .

Biggs: [chuckling]

Teacher: . . . excitement mounts, uh . . . what's funny, Biggs?

Biggs: Uh . . . Oh, nothing, sir.

Teacher: Oh, do please share your little joke with the rest of us. I mean, obviously something *frightfully* funny's going on.[1]

This is a scene from Monty Python's *Meaning of Life,* a film spoofing the big questions of life—who are we? Why are we here? Is there really a God? This scene is guaranteed to get a lot of laughs in my classroom. Imagine if we really did learn about sex in this way, via direct demonstration from "experienced" adults! Instead, we learn about sex via awkward adult communication, narrow peer socialization, and youthful fumblings. How else and what else do we learn?

SOCIALIZATION: A BRIEF OVERVIEW

How *do* we learn about sex and sexuality? Do we just know what we need to know without knowing how we've learned it? Or do we need to find magazines under rocks in the woods, figuratively speaking? Consider your own sexual self for a moment. Think back to your first crush, your first kiss. Chances are that your *first* kiss was quite nerve-wracking. You probably wondered what to do, when to do it, and for how long. You wondered what to do with your tongue, what to do with your nose, and maybe you even wondered how to breathe if things got hot and heavy.

Now think about the *last* time you kissed someone. Chances are you felt much more confident. You probably didn't overthink it or wonder just when to gently nibble your partner's lip. It probably felt, well, natural. What may be different or what may have changed between that first kiss and the most recent kiss? Did you kiss more than one person between your first kiss and the last? Maybe you kissed someone who really took their time to tell you about how they preferred to be kissed. Maybe you watched 10, 50, or more Hollywood screen kisses in movies or on television. In other words, the difference between the first time—for anything, really—and the most recent time is experience and learning.

Do we "just know" what we need to know without knowing *how* we've learned it? The answer is almost undoubtedly no. We are not born "just knowing" what is culturally important, meaningful, and significant about sex and sexuality. And certainly it is much harder to argue that we "just know" what we individually prefer and enjoy sexually. The tough part is that our sexual learning process is lifelong, subtle, and always in progress, making it hard to see exactly *what* we learn and from whom.

Early Sources of Socialization: Family, Religion, Peers, and Education

As you read in chapter 3, most of us are born into social and cultural systems that describe gender and biological sex in binary, oppositional, and seemingly natural ways.

That binary system is the first brick in the wall, in effect, in building a powerful structure. Gender and biological sex bond with other elements of sexuality, such as sexual orientation, to create the foundation upon which we construct our sexual selves. The primary goal of socialization is to structure and guide people into socioculturally defined, acceptable, and expected roles. This is one form of the social control of sexuality. What does this mean? Well, far from being just an intimate, individual feeling, drive, or impulse, our sexualities are profoundly socially constructed and determined. Without multiple subtle and overt social controls over individual sexual practices and feelings, "society" (namely, all of us) could not guarantee that people would reproduce and care for children. We construct a social function for things like monogamy and fidelity, because heterosexual, marital monogamy ensures that neither partner will doubt the parentage of any offspring.

The confusing and contradictory universe of sex into which adolescents enter is a jumble of social, cultural, institutional, and historical influences. Parents have a very strong influence on the sexual attitudes and behaviors of adolescents, yet do not tend to provide much information about sex (Moore and Rosenthal, 1993).[2] Peers are far more likely to be an influential source of education and ideas. The contradictions become salient when adolescents realize that while media sources are relatively explicit, their parents and caregivers are not as comfortable or forthright. Our families of origin work in various ways to socialize us into gender and sexuality simultaneously. Even in families that are not organized around a biological mother and father with children, parents and caregivers wish to raise children who can grow up and take their place in society. Male children ideally grow up to become men who work industriously, marry one woman, and commit themselves to fathering children whom they then care for. Female children ideally grow up to become women who marry one man, have his children, and commit themselves to bearing children whom they also care for. In this rubric, we literally and figuratively reproduce cultural scripts and social systems, thus maintaining the status quo. Control of sexualities and reinforcement of existing social order, mores, and expectations makes "society" possible. The key questions are: What does the social control of sex entail, and what are the implications of socialization systems?

The first lesson we learn is that heterosexuality is the *hegemonic*, or dominant, most influential, and expected sexual orientation. This is reinforced when little girls are asked by adults if they have any "boyfriends," simply because they may have a male friend they like playing with. Girls who have male friends, play sports, like the outdoors, or do anything else atypical of femininity are called "tomboys." This is a reminder that these interests are thought to constitute a phase, to be grown out of, and exchanged for a teenaged life of boyfriends and romance. Boys are taught that "becoming a man" is not a given, simply resulting from being born male. Rather, manhood is something that must be achieved, via competition, assertiveness, and dominance; this can inspire insecurity and the fear that something could go awry on the way to manhood. That fear is maintained and reinforced through language, when little boys learn that "sissy," "mama's boy," and "fag" are epithets that other boys will not hesitate to use. As a tool of social control, these terms are quite powerful.

Sociologist C. J. Pascoe (2005) studied how adolescents use "fag discourse" as forms of social control.[3] Citing social critic Leo Bersani, Pascoe writes, "The relationship between adolescent masculinity and sexuality is embedded in the specter of the faggot. Faggots represent a penetrated masculinity in which 'to be penetrated is to abdicate power' [Bersani, 1987: 212]. Penetrated men symbolize a masculinity devoid of power, which, in its contradiction, threatens both psychic and social chaos. It is precisely this specter of penetrated masculinity that functions as a regulatory mechanism of gender for contemporary American adolescent boys" (2005: 329). *Fag* or *gay* denotes a man or a boy who appears different from others—a boy who is quieter, or perhaps more gentle, less competitive, less rigid about masculinity. The use of these epithets is predicated on the fear of not belonging, not fitting in, not being like the other boys. Boys learn a lot about sexuality from these terms that are specifically applied to them. What are the implications or consequences of this for all men? How do other sources of socialization teach us?

If we are inculcated into a religion early in life, messages of gender differences and heterosexuality will most likely bolster the socialization our parents attempt. As we grow, our friends become more and more important—sharing with us their conversations with parents ("I asked my mom what 'masturbation' is!"), their own experiences ("So . . . me and Billy made out after school today . . . "), and their own judgments ("That girl is such a slut!"). And once we start school, we are bound to be exposed to systems of gender ("Boys in one line, girls in the other") and sexualities, such as school dances or formal sexuality education in classes. If the structures of society, in the form of these social institutions and *socializing agents* (entities or structures that formally or informally provide instruction about appropriate social behavior), are mostly consistent, then the members of society will get a singular message about the gender roles they are expected to enact.

Focus on the Family as a Socializing Agent

Sexuality and Childhood

"I'm not gay—I'm nothing yet!"
—Martin Prince, fourth grader, *The Simpsons* (Fox-TV)

On *The Simpsons,* bully Nelson Muntz threatens to rid the town of gays, starting with Martin. When Nelson grabs him by the shirt, Martin protests that he's not gay because, in effect, he is only about nine and is "pre-sexual." Is this true? Loretta Haroian described the sexual evolution of children in the context of children's overt physiological and developmental milestones (2000).[4] She writes:

> In *early childhood,* masturbation alone and in groups, leads to exploration and experimentation among children of same and opposite gender. *Late childhood* (prepubescent) is characterized by heterosexual role modeling and attempted intercourse (girls may begin having regular coitus with older boys). In *pubescence* [e.g., starting at about age 10], girls rapidly accelerate into a phase of intense sexual experience, culminating in the acquisition of basic sexual techniques at the adult level. Boys follow a similar pattern, but their learning process is not as rapid or complete because they are usually experimenting with younger girls. Heterosexual patterns replace masturbation and homosexual activities for the majority of both boys and girls. In *adolescence,* there is increased sexual activity with peers and adults for both boys and girls; and it is believed that birth control is facilitated by the practice of multiple partners.

From infancy through about six, children are learning about their entire bodies; we can often see babies placing their feet and hands into their mouths in this period. Young children begin to learn how to coordinate and use their bodies for everything from sitting upright to crawling and walking to using the toilet. In the guise of exploration, young children will touch their bodies, including the genitals. The nervous system pathways that enable orgasm are viable, enabling children to stimulate their genitals and achieve orgasm; little boys can have erections in the womb and certainly as infants. Depending on parental, subcultural, and cultural expectations, children may start to learn that these natural, pleasurable activities "ought" to be repressed. Parents may begin policing children's behavior, depending on their perceptions of the context and meaning of the activities. If two very young children are playing "show me yours, I'll show you mine," parents may decide the game is innocuous. But if two 10-year-old boys are playing the same game, the reaction is likely to be very different. Thus, by ages 6 to 12, most children have begun to learn that they should keep their sexual explorations to themselves. Privacy and autonomy take center stage. Note that this trajectory presumes that childhood explorations are not connected to nonconsensual (i.e., rape, incest, assault) activities.

Psychologist Sharon Lamb interviewed 30 girls, aged 7 to 18, along with 92 adult women, aged 19 to 72, about the sexual tensions, feelings, and interactions in their friendships with other girls (2004).[5] There was some diversity in the sample, with 25 states represented; 29 of the total sample of 122 were African American, 21 were Puerto Rican, and three were Asian American. All social classes were represented. Lamb was especially interested in their friendships from age 6 to 12, so although the adults were doing retrospective analysis, the younger girls did not have to remember very far back and thus we can assume some accuracy to their memories. She was most interested in these key questions:

1. Did they ever practice kissing games?
2. Did they ever play "practice" games with other kids where "sex" was involved?
3. What game was most fun?
4. What game left them feeling most ashamed?

Respondents aged 12 and under talked about other girls who played sexual games but did not admit to any of their own games. The adults spoke more about the tensions in their childhood friendships being due to secrecy about sexual feelings with and for other girls. Tensions also resulted from framing sexualized play as "just pretending" (and thus not "real"), exacerbated by girls enacting both "male" and "female" roles in play. Respondents described keeping games secret from other adults and parents especially, having learned that secrets "needed" to be kept. Simultaneously, they sensed implicitly that it was necessary to keep feelings of physical excitement and eroticism secret from their friends and partners in play.

Adult respondents explained these tensions in part by offering some of the broader cultural narrative about childhood sexuality, which is that "permission" for sex really does not begin until puberty. Women who labeled youthful feelings as "sexual" described those feelings as "bizarre" and "weird." To generalize, the adult respondents reported feeling that as *girls*, they should not have been "as into that stuff" as they were. Lamb concludes that sexualized games reaffirm the cultural belief that adult sex is "real" and not play, while childhood play is not "real," not meaningful to youthful participants, and not significant in later development. Sometimes, though, childhood play is just that—play, a game like any other. Savin-Williams (2005) shows that even those who eventually identify themselves as same-sex oriented separate same-sex play in childhood from teen and adult relationships and activities.[6]

The current view of children's sexuality—involving the diminishment of children's sexual feelings and games—is bolstered by historical trajectories. There is a longstanding tradition of viewing children's sexualities as sinful and in need of external social controls. By the late 1800s, some physicians, scientists, philosophers, and religious leaders had become antimasturbation entrepreneurs, marketing mechanical and physical restraints and dietary cures. Leather corsets with steel penis tubes, spike-lined penis rings, and other painful variations were intended to prevent boys from getting erections, touching themselves, and stimulating themselves to orgasm. Sylvester Graham had invented the graham cracker in 1834 as part of his antimasturbation diet of bland foods, and Dr. John Harvey Kellogg added to the diet by inventing corn flakes in 1884. The focus was narrowly on boys' self-explorations, as the sexism of the times prevented male doctors, ministers, and others from even believing that women were capable of masturbation.

In Victorian times and into the early twentieth century, psychoanalysts, led by Freud, debated the extent of pathology represented by masturbation, with some arguing that it was an example of the struggle between sublimation and sex drive. Wilhelm Stekel, a contemporary of Freud, went out on a limb to assert that masturbation was necessary and healthy for channeling sexual interests and desires (Stekel [1950], 2004).[7]

Historical context like this hints at the primary problem parents have when considering children's sexualities. As John Gagnon argues, "Adults are caught in an impossible situation. On the one hand, it is important that children *should not* do anything sexual before they are supposed to; on the other hand, adults *should* play some positive role in developing children's sexuality" (1977: 79).[8] He points out that very little sexuality outside of legal marriage is *really* supported, making it difficult for parents to truly be positive about children's sexual explorations. Because parents themselves have learned societal rules and expectations (*cultural level* of scripting), they tend to see children in the lens of their own *adult* point of view, and assume that children share the same point of view about what they think is sexual. Thus parents and others who work with children tend to impute adult interpretations to kids' actions. Let's say a mom sees her daughter rubbing her genitals; the child is clearly not just scratching an itch. Mom asks her daughter, "Whatcha doing over there?," and daughter replies, "Nothing." Mom says, "Why are you doing 'nothing' then?" and daughter replies, "Feels good." Children can recognize that touching their genitalia "feels good" without always or immediately naming that good feeling "sex" or "sexual." For most children, this is one of many things done for fun or a pleasant feeling; it is not simply a means to an end (as is the case for many older teens).

This is where social learning and scripting theory really apply. We are not born knowing that our genitalia are sexual, and indeed though we can use them to feel pleasure, we can also experience that pleasure by learning to control urination and defecation. Toilet training is an example of learning theory, when we learn how good it feels—and how rewarded we are by our caregivers—to use the toilet instead of wearing diapers. Basically, all of this entails simply learning about our bodies, and when we are young, that is a significant aspect of our development: learning to eat with utensils, to make faces, to walk, to ride a bike, and so forth. So how do children learn the meanings and symbolism of specific body parts and sexualities more generally? By the time we are in grade school, the majority of us are aware of social control mechanisms and the repression of our sexualities. We are taught that there is a time and a place for everything, and many of us learn directly from our parents that this involves privacy; penile-vaginal intercourse shared with someone of the other sex; if not marriage then at least strong love and commitment; and being old enough to understand the emotional context of sex.

Children also learn, directly and indirectly, from parental reactions to "sex play" and questions. Children can even learn from how parents handle the issue of the "sexual" body. In a *Simpsons* episode, Marge needed to buy an athletic supporter and protective cup so that Bart could play football. She went to a sporting goods store and said, "I want a . . . *hmmmhmmhmm* for my son." When the salesman handed her a helmet, she tried again, "You know, a *mhhhmm* for his *mhmmmh*. Down there . . ." The salesman continued to hand her other pads for other body parts, not understanding her euphemistic noises. Finally, Marge has to be more direct, spelling what she needs: "I want a see-you-pee [C-U-P]." Realizing how this sounds, poor Marge is even more embarrassed.

I have lost count of the number of my students who have reported that they easily discerned exactly how uncomfortable their parents were. "Mom came into the kitchen one day after school—I was maybe 10 at the time—and told me that she'd left a book on my bed and that I should look at it," a 20-year old junior told our class. "I went to my room and found this book, like, something on how puberty comes and makes your body do all these things, and boys go through puberty too. Mom came into my room before bedtime, like always, and asked if I'd read the book and if I had any questions. But I could just tell—I don't know how really—that she really didn't want me to ask anything at all." When I asked the student if she had ever talked to her mom, she said, "No—that's the only time it's ever come up. I guess maybe she'll just think I'm a virgin 'til I get married or something!"

But research has shown that mothers can positively influence the sexual behavior of their children, especially daughters, simply by learning how to communicate about sexuality. Daughters are influenced by other variables as well, including church attendance, having a sense of future expectations, and feeling that parents care about them (Measor, 2004).[9] Having studied adolescents since 1984, Lynda Measor argues that gender is consequential in other ways as well. Boys and girls get different information at home, potentially affecting their adult viewpoints about sex. Many mothers emphasized themes of intimacy for daughters, connecting sex with love, commitment, and sharing. This was not a dominant theme in what boys were told, and more importantly, boys did not learn much at home. Adolescent boys seem to learn about sex most in external settings, not in the home, and not via trusted authorities or adults. The imbalance in message and the implications are clear. Regardless of eventual sexual orientation and interests, men and women reach adult sexuality with many contributions to gendered, *different* sexualities.

In a study of communication between African American mothers and their adolescent daughters, Erika Pluhar and Peter Kuriloff (2004) described the specific ways in which moms talked to their daughters.[10] Going beyond simply ascertaining the topics discussed—where babies normally come from, why men and women usually have different-looking genitalia, and menstruation—Pluhar and Kuriloff observed 30 working- and middle-class mothers talking with their daughters. In analyzing the conversations, two different dimensions of the communication process became clear—the affective and the stylistic. The affective dimension they observed included attempts to connect via empathy, comfort, anger, and being silent. In contrast, mothers who communicated in a more "stylistic" way focused less on feelings and more on delivery via persuasion, body and nonverbal language and cues, and scene setting. These communication *styles* both positively affected the conversations, resulting in and enhancing mother-daughter relationships. Thus the direct and indirect messages these daughters will get are likely to enhance sexuality instead of creating awkward, reinforcing silences.

But parental discomfort in talking about sexuality cannot be seen as solely an individual problem, the failing of a handful of prudish mothers or fathers. The inability to effectively, supportively, and successfully communicate about everything sexual *must* be attributed to the broader culture in which these conversations are (and *are not*) happening. Remember the chapter 1 discussion about contradictory and confusing aspects of American sexual culture? This is another item for the list we started making in that chapter. Most parents want their children to grow up happy, healthy (and heterosexual); find a loving spouse, get married, and have kids of their own. Money and sex are the topics of the most consistent and most intractable fights in marriages. Parents could better equip children to be happily married adults by talking frequently, honestly, and openly about sexuality, enabling their children to grow up and have happier sexual lives. Yet comparatively few parents are able to do this, and even fewer do it consistently. Moreover, most conversations about sex never involve fathers or male caregivers (Lehr et al., 2005).[11] This study of 155 fathers with sons aged 11 to 17 revealed that physical maturity was associated with fathers talking to sons about sex, though extensive or repeated conversations were rare. Fathers with less formal education were far more likely than better educated dads to speak with sons about sex. Indeed, many of my male students report that the extent of their sex education from fathers or adult men was the terse statement, "Don't get anyone pregnant, okay?" (or maybe "You'd better be using condoms!"), usually said before the prom or a few months or weeks into a high school relationship that seemed serious. This may be a bit too late, as one study found that 30 percent of boys aged 12 to 14 had engaged in PVI, along with 14 percent of girls aged 12 to 14 (Paikoff, 2000).[12] So who *is* teaching young men and boys about sex? And what are they learning?

Sexuality in Adolescence and the Teen Years

Perhaps the best example of an uncomfortable conversation about sex can be found in the 1999 film *American Pie* (Universal Pictures). The film depicts the exploits of four male high school seniors as each tries to lose his virginity before graduation. By the time Jim's dad visits him in his bedroom for some admittedly belated sex education, the audience has already seen Jim's friends sharing what they know about sex, along with Jim humping a pie because his friend had told him that women's vaginas feel like warm apple pie.

> **Dad:** Oh, Jim, you're here. Uh, I was just walking by your room and uh—And, you know, I was thinking, "Boy, it's been a long time since we've had a little father-son, uh-uh, chat." Oh! I almost forgot. I, uh, I bought some magazines. [opens bag of magazines he has brought] Do you just want to flip to the center section? Well, this is the—this is the, uh, female form. And they have focused on the breasts, uh, which are used primarily to, uh, feed young infants . . . and, uh—and also, uh, in foreplay.
> **Jim:** Right.
> **Dad:** This is, uh—This is *Hustler*. And this is a much more exotic magazine. Now, they have decided to focus on the, uh, pubic region—
> **Jim:** Right. Uh-huh.
> **Dad:** The whole groin area. Look at the expression on her face. You see that? See what's she's doing? She's kind of looking right into your eyes saying, "Hey, big boy. Hey how ya doin'?" You see?

Jim: Right.

Dad: *Shaved* is a magazine I'm not too familiar with, but, again, if you flip to the center . . . section. . . . Well, you see the detail that, uh, that they go into in this picture here.

Jim: Uh-huh. Yeah.

Dad: It almost looks like a tropical plant or something . . . underwater. . . thing.

Jim: Yeah. Yes.

Dad: Do you know what a clitoris is?

Jim: Oh my God.

Dad: Well, don't say, "Oh—"

Jim: Yes, I know what a clitoris is.

Dad: Oh, you do. Oh, I see. Yes, you do. I forgot you've been there and back. You know everything—

Jim: I learned about it in Sex Ed.

Dad: I'm trying to make this painless . . .

Jim: I really don't need you to talk about clitoris. You know what? I'm sorry. Okay? I'm sorry.

Dad: No-no-no. I'm sorry. I'm sorry. I'm sorry. I shouldn't have got hot there. Well, you know what I'm gonna do, Jim. I'm going to just leave these books here for you to, uh, peruse at your, uh—at your leisure.

We can see *exactly* how awkward this is for both father and son, evidenced by the frequent pauses (shown here as ellipses), Jim's one-word responses, and the quick pressure that builds and culminates with Jim truncating any further discussion. If you have seen *American Pie* it may be easier to understand this scene, but why do you suppose it might be funny? The humor comes from the unbelievable and surreal approach Jim's dad takes, using not just pornography but *Shaved* and *Hustler* (which make *Playboy* look like a tamer "lifestyle" magazine that just happens to have a couple of naked women). It is also funny because of Eugene Levy's characterization of the geeky dad, trying to take such a casual tone, as if he is just teaching Jim about baseball rules or something. The scene exemplifies how hard it is to imagine any white, middle-class parent doing a good job with "The Sex Talk."

But as the Pluhar and Kuriloff research suggests, family context does matter, along with subcultural variables including ethnicity and social class. A study of African American and Latin American male adolescents hints at these intersections (Rucibwa et al., 2003).[13] In trying to understand individuals' sexual conduct, the researchers selected 178 young men from a larger survey of teens. They discovered that for Latin American young men, having a sibling who had become a young parent was associated with being sexually experienced (i.e., having had penile-vaginal intercourse). For African Americans, this link was observed for young men who had fathers who had become a parent as a teen. A more universal finding related to motivations for becoming sexually active. When the researchers asked why teen boys have sex, the responses included enjoyment of sex, curiosity, pressure from friends, and being able to prove one's manhood. Legendary comedian Richard Pryor ([1971] 2001) said that, for guys, having the sexually transmitted disease *gonorrhea*, a bacterial genital infection, was a status symbol: "It meant you were gettin' some!"[14] This research is an excellent example of the consequences or implications of the myriad ways in which families socialize us into sexuality.

While Rucibwa et al. (2003) described the influence of fathers on sons, Doswell et al. (2003) explored the role of mothers in daughters' sexual decision-making processes.[15] Using a sample of 106 African American girls aged 11 to 14, the authors found that mothers were more influential than peers and fathers. The girls' attitudes about sexuality were most consequential in explaining their intentions to become sexually active or abstain, but attitudes and intentions are directly connected to mothers and *their* conversations and attitudes. Other studies support this finding, suggesting that parents and caregivers are highly influential agents of socialization (for example, Smith, 1997; Browning, Leventhal, and Brooks-Gunn, 2004).[16]

All of these influences are especially salient for heterosexual teens, but gay, lesbian, and bisexual teens are also influenced by parents. Those who have a close relationship with parents and caregivers tend to reveal same-sex sexual orientation at a younger age and have a more positive sense of identity (Beaty, 1999).[17] Beaty cites research suggesting that gender may matter—for gay male teens, more traditional families are associated with less disclosure of orientation, though D'Augelli, Grossman, and Starks (2005) noted that teens who were "out" to their families experienced less *internalized homophobia* (negative attitudes and feelings toward self and/or toward other GLB people).[18] Savin-Williams (2005) points out that the variables of ethnicity, racial/ethnic subculture, and social class add layers of difficulty for those growing up gay, lesbian, or bisexual. Teens wonder if their identities will "pose extra ramifications to . . . immediate and extended family members" (p. 77). Unfortunately, the research on adolescents with same-sex orientations is narrowly focused only on "coming out" as gay, lesbian, or bisexual and the development of a same-sex identity. Researchers have not yet begun to ask the same questions about family influences and context independently of orientation.

CONTEXT AND OTHER SOCIALIZING AGENTS

Peers, religion, school, and media are probably the most significant sexual socializing agents for teenagers. Peers are especially influential in teaching, reinforcing, and *challenging* the cultural level of scripting. "During the teen years, gender identities and sexual attitudes move to the forefront of consciousness. This period of transition is marked and inflected by popular culture. Teenagers in the United States are awash in a sea of mediated texts that play a strong symbolic role in constituting their subjectivities and identities" (Durham, 1998).[19] Durham is arguing that mass media plays an important role in essentially telling teens who to be, what to buy to become who they are, and how to feel about who they are.

Much of socialization into sexuality includes *latent* messages about heterosexuality and "proper" gender behavior. Latent messages are the undeveloped, hidden elements or ideas; they are present but not easily evident. Latent content contrasts with *manifest* messages, which are obvious, observable, or shown. In sociological conceptualizations, the added nuance of latent and manifest messages is that manifest messages have "intentional" content. For example, the manifest message of a music video is to sell a song, an artist, and a body of work. This is also the manifest purpose. But the latent messages (and perhaps latent purposes) are far different. The hidden ideas in the average music video revolve around "selling" or reinforcing hegemonic ideas about gender, heterosexuality, and men's and women's bodies. Which latent and manifest ideas appear in what teenagers learn about sexuality? In what ways do elements of socialization (besides parents) contribute to developing sexualities?

Religion

The obvious messages offered by most organized religions relate to abstinence, sexual fidelity, and the "special" nature of sex. These are the desired outcomes or effects of traditional, religiously inflected teachings about sex. But a brief review of the intersections of religiosity and gender, race, and age shows that there are other effects of the messages, some of which are surprising. This research focuses on heterosexually oriented teens. Unfortunately, the point of view of most researchers seems to preclude them from studying religiosity and same-sex oriented teens' "debut" into shared sexual activities.

Using the National Longitudinal Study of Adolescent Health (Add Health), a random sampling of about 20,745 seventh to twelfth graders, scholars have been able to select smaller subsamples to explore key questions. The study used a random sam-

ple of 80 high schools stratified by region, amount of urbanization, school type, ethnic mix, and size. The study design accommodated the fact that data collection
involved sensitive areas, minors who needed parental consent to participate, and interviews in teens' homes. Interviewers collected data on laptop computers, read questions
and entered respondents' answers. For more sensitive sections, respondents heard pre-
recorded questions via earphones attached to the laptop and entered their own answers
without the interviewer (Guilamo-Ramos et al., 2005).[20]

To test how religiosity affects the likelihood of having penile-vaginal intercourse
(PVI), researchers wanted to utilize the *longitudinal* aspect of data collection (repeated observation or data collection of the same respondents, with the same variables,
over time). Sharon Rostosky and her colleagues analyzed data collected from 3,691
youth aged 15 to 21; information on sexual activities was collected at two different
points in time (Rostosky, Regnerus, and Wright, 2003).[21] The central hypothesis, or
key question, related to what effect *religiosity* had for each individual (defined by frequency of engaging various in religious/spiritual activities, such as going somewhere
to worship). We could predict that increased religiosity, along with attitudes about sex,
would predict whether teens had PVI. Religiosity reduced the likelihood of what the
authors call "coital debut" for both young men and young women. Those who anticipated negative feelings and emotions after first-time PVI tended not to engage in
PVI. But one surprising finding was that young women who anticipated positive feelings were more likely to "debut," reported Rostosky et al. Another surprising finding—indeed counterintuitive—related to virginity pledges, wherein teens vow not to
share sexuality with anyone until legally married to someone of the other sex. African
American young men who had pledged or were more religious were significantly more
likely to engage in first-time PVI, compared to white men and African American men
who were less religious and/or who had not signed a pledge. So over time, the
researchers were able to document interactions between religion, gender, and race.

A study focusing on African American teen women examined similar variables
(McCree et al., 2003).[22] Using 522 women drawn from women's health clinics,
school health classes, and adolescent medicine clinics, McCree and her colleagues
found that 64 percent were above average on religiosity scales, a four-item question
to test strength of religiousness. Respondents with higher religiosity scores were significantly more likely to feel confident about communicating with male sex partners
and being able to refuse to have unsafe sex. Again, this is probably a somewhat surprising result, as we may assume that religiosity would be linked only with abstinence
from sexual activity. It may be hard to believe that high levels of religious commitment and feeling could be associated with positive attitudes toward condom use and

greater likelihood of condom use (McCree et al., 2003). Apparently, the respect for body and self that is often taught in formal religions (e.g., a manifest message) can be positively adapted and interpreted by religious, (hetero)sexually active teens.

Subcultures

[handwritten: ① also assoc. with greater cohesion family or school]

Existing research seems to examine subcultural influences largely in terms of whether the teenager is from another culture, or has parents or grandparents who immigrated from another culture. Researchers assume that African American and Caucasian American teens have already *acculturated* to American culture. Acculturation is defined as "cultural modification of an individual, group, or people by adapting to or borrowing traits from another culture; *also* : a merging of cultures as a result of prolonged contact," according to Merriam Webster OnLine. It tends to be assumed that only Asian American and Latin American adolescents have the potential for conflict and adaptation between ethnic subcultures and American societal norms. Scholars study the impact of acculturation on shared sexual activities, with the same kinds of assumptions that pervade research on other aspects of adolescent socialization—examining only PVI and a narrow concept of "sexual risk taking" (e.g., PVI without condoms or contraception). While it is absolutely valid to study these things, without a broader imagination, researchers miss studying things like oral and anal sex "debuts," along with the effects of other kinds of subcultures.

One group of scholars used the Add Health survey to study the intersection of ethnic subculture and PVI (Guilamo-Ramos et al., 2005). The researchers ensured that they would have enough representation from several Latin ethnicities—Cuban, Puerto Rican, and Mexican—in order to successfully statistically analyze differences within and between the groups. Remember that the Add Health study is longitudinal, so after an initial interview, the teens in this group were interviewed again 12 months later. Being a virgin at the time of the initial interview—never having engaged in "the insertion of the penis into the vagina," according to the study's definition—was a predictive factor for subsequent sexual activity. Differences among Latin ethnicities were apparent. Puerto Rican American teens tended to be more acculturated, having lived in the States longer and being more likely to speak English at home compared to Mexican American and Cuban American teens. The impact of broader sociocultural norms and scripts is salient when we consider that Puerto Rican American teens were more sexually active than teens in the other Latin subgroups. This was especially true for those who lived in the States from birth or the majority of their lives. The puzzling finding was that recent immigrants who spoke Spanish at home were more likely to engage in PVI. Guilamo-Ramos et al. suggest that this may be attributable to the tension between more traditional culture at home and more permissive (and certainly more contradictory and confusing) American culture. It may be that the stress of acculturating places teens at greater risk for early sexuality, among other things. Other studies have shown that less acculturation—in other words, more influence of the native culture—is actually a "protective factor," enhancing the likelihood of remaining sexually inactive (Adam et al., 2005).[23]

There is little research on Asian American teens. Generally, any data on Asian Americans is obscured by the fact that ethnic and subcultural variables are not taken into account. We would expect to see variations depending on whether an individual's heritage is Korean, Vietnamese, Japanese, Indian, or Pakistani, for example, representative of home cultures with different religions, economies, and politics. Nonetheless, it seems as if Asian Americans generally have later sexual and romantic debuts. One study of everything from first kiss to first love and everything in between shows that timing and trajectories differ according to ethnicity (Regan et al., 2004).[24] The sample of 683 "ethnically diverse" young adults revealed patterns of behavior *and* the influences of cultural and subcultural scripting. First kisses and first dates occurred before first PVI, serious relationship and experience of falling in love; these events had occurred by the end of high school for most. That first kisses tend to precede first PVI is not "natural"—there is no objective reason why kisses should occur first. But it is encoded in American cultural scripts that a kiss should be the first act of physical intimacy between two people. Incidentally, the standard trajectory for the young women (first kiss, date, love, PVI, and serious relationship) differed from that for young men (first kiss, date, PVI, love, and serious relationship).

The study showed that Asian American respondents tended to have the least sexual and romantic experience, especially compared to Caucasian Americans. While 85 percent of Caucasian Americans had engaged in PVI by the end of high school, only 64 percent of Asian Americans had. First kisses and first serious relationships also happen later for Asian American; the average age of first kiss was 17.6, and the average age for relationships was 19 (Regan et al., 2004). Another study revealed bigger gaps between Asian Americans and others (Miller and Leavitt, 2003).[25] About 16 percent of Asian Americans aged 15 to 19 had engaged in PVI, compared to 79 percent of African Americans, 54 percent of Latin-Americans, and 37 percent of European-Americans. Though there are some discrepancies in exact percentages, these studies reveal the overall patterns similarly: Asian Americans appear to have subcultural influences that enable a slower progression into partnered sexual activities (see also Upchurch et al., 1998).[26]

If we accept the argument that heterosexuality represents the hegemonic cultural sexual orientation, then it is reasonable to suggest that homosexuality represents a sub-culture. Within the domain of "homosexuality," we can identify various subcultures—homosexualities and bisexualities—into which teens can be socialized. These subcultures are also influenced by class, race, ethnicity, nationality, age, and geography. One element of socialization—a feeling of belonging to a larger group—is especially important for same-sex oriented teens (Swann and Spivey, 2004).[27] They note that having an LGBT peer group is essential for the development of self-esteem and self-concept and for facilitating identity choices. Savin-Williams (2005) notes that the cultural context of homosexuality is itself an element of GLB teens' identity choices and sexual activities. The narrow societal focus on homosexuality as only a sexual behavior while ignoring emotional, relational, and affective dimensions creates an expectation that same-sex oriented teens are therefore sexually active. Savin-Williams quotes young men talking about why they remain virgins:

> "I'm looking for someone very special, but it is really hard to meet such a guy. They all just want sex. I need to know the person; ideally we would be friends for a while. This I know is an elusive goal but I want to hold onto it."
>
> "I knew I was attracted to boys in my class but I couldn't be gay because of all the horrible stuff that was associated with it. Me, a good kid, just could not be all of that. To stick it up someone's ass . . . " (2005: 137–138).

These respondents may be part of what college sophomore Michael Amico (2005) calls a "gay youth culture" that includes the rejection of "the idea of being whores," along with a reclaiming of virginity. The problem is that sex is culturally defined as PVI, so what does it virginity mean for those who may not ever have PVI? Amico asks, "How does a gay person lose his or her virginity? What bodily orifices must be penetrated? Is it the giver, receiver, or both who lose their virginity? Do lesbians need a strap-on to get the job done? Do gay men require a penis?" (p. 34).[28] The confusion over terms and activities may be attributable to the larger sex-negative culture that includes ambivalence and discomfort with youth sexualities. Amico writes that "Gay youths . . . often use the concept of virginity to explain away an endless amount of wonderful, exciting, and sometimes confusing physical contact. . . . Gay youths internalize heterosexual relationships and their rules and modes of conduct because that's what they see in the media and experience firsthand with policing adults" (p. 36).

Our socialization is only as good as the messages, rules, and expectations transmitted to us. Narrowly focused mores about homosexuality combine with mores about heterosexuality to create a potentially stressful mix. Strong peer networks, self-concept, and desire to choose one's own identity and behavior are features of positive sexual socialization for all American youth. The ability to develop these elements of the self can, however, be confounded by gender socialization.

Masculinity and Subcultural Norms

> So now I'm walkin' and I'm trying to figure out what to do. And when I get there, the most embarrassing thing is gonna be when I have to take my pants down. See, right away then, I'm buck naked . . . buck naked in front of this girl. Now what happens then? Do . . . do you just . . . I don't even know what to do . . . I'm gonna just stand there and she's gonna say, "You don't know how to do it." And I'm gonna say, "Yes I do, but I forgot." I never thought of her showing me, because I'm a man. I don't want her to show me. I don't want nobody to show me, but I wish somebody would kinda slip me a note.
>
> —*comedian Bill Cosby*

Becoming a man in Western cultures carries with it the burden of proof, in a sense. Young men are generally expected to attain masculinity via expressions of heterosexuality, assertiveness, control of the body, and competitiveness. Mairtin Mac an Ghaill (1994) further describes the work of masculinity—regardless of orientation—as learning that the masculine code involves splitting sexual practices from emotional feelings.[29] Men train each other and socialize each other with both positive reinforcement and negative reinforcement, in the form of sanctions and appeals to group norms. This is true of the most hegemonic versions of masculinity, but it would be inaccurate to ignore the fact there are other versions of masculinities—multiple forms that "do not sit side-by-side like dishes on a smorgasbord. There are definite social relations between them. Especially, there are relations of hierarchy, for some masculinities are dominant while others are subordinated or marginalized" (Connell, 2000: 10).[30]

A British interview study demonstrates the most hegemonic forms of youthful masculinity (Walker and Kushner, 1999).[31] Using female interviewers and offering a choice of one-on-one talks or small focus groups, Walker and Kushner talked with 39 white, heterosexually active males, aged 11 to 21, in a working-class city in

Britain. Respondents were united in denying the utility of school sex education and confirmed their "emotional isolation from each other and from older males" (1999: 48). Initiation into hegemonic masculinity began early; for the 11- to 12-year-olds, girls existed in a sort of mysterious, hidden world. There was not a lot of mixing or mingling of sexes; hardly anyone had kissed a girl. Socialization into profound gender differentiation revealed itself in subtle ways. The youngest boys described the passive activity of television watching, rendering it as nonetheless a way to demonstrate masculinity, through programming choices (e.g., action and adventure). At school, gender was described in this way: "Boys' naughtiness is jumping round the classroom, from table to table, hitting people, dropping things, getting severely angry with the teacher" while girls' naughtiness involved talking too much, being "rude" or "uppity" (1999: 49).

The older boys in Walker and Kushner's study described high school as stressful, where, with adulthood looming, "mutual support is rare" and "problems are not to be shared" (1999: 50). An "adult" man was defined as someone who needed no support from anyone else. The interviewers described the later teen years as a time when masculinity was organized around working to build a public self (or selves) and working to build a private self. The public selves included public bravado, bragging about conquests, and generally reinforcing heterosexuality and conformity to group norms. "So the group he chooses to relate to, and its rules of engagement, can help to define the individual—I'm the sort of guy who's a good laugh, likes a drink with my mates, bunks off [skips] school . . . " (1999: 51). Although the young men clearly acknowledged public norms and expectations, often in conflict with private selves (which include "messy" feelings and insecurities), they could not challenge the public norms. One example related to relationships: "Having a girlfriend seems to confer no great status in group terms—being successful in getting off with lots of girls is of more use there" (1999: 53). So those with (steady) girlfriends instead of "lots of girls" ran the risk of enacting the wrong version of heterosexuality.

A different example of problematic heterosexuality in a masculine subculture can be found in research on gender and sexuality in a working-class job training program in the United Kingdom (Mac an Ghaill, 1999).[32] He characterized the two dominant groups of young men (late teens to early twenties) as "Explicit Heterosexuals" and "Fashionable Heterosexuals" (a third group, "Sexual Outsiders," is discussed later in the chapter). "Explicit Heterosexuals" enacted a version of "heterosexuality that tended to be based on a demonstration of extreme perversity, violent misogyny and a racialised sexuality. These characteristics served to emphasise their projected sexual competence." The "Fashionable Heterosexuals" interpreted sexuality as "displaying competence in forming heterosexual relationships based upon being attractive to females. This attractiveness was achieved by writing ascribed female definitions of desirable masculinity onto their bodies." Mac an Ghaill described a young man, James, who had longer hair and a quiet demeanor. The men in the "Explicit Heterosexuals" group ostracized James, calling him "gay." To their surprise, James was, of course, not gay:

> **Paul:** The other day Gary came in at 8:30 in the morning to tell us James had found someone. He couldn't believe it.
> **Simon:** When the lesson started, we couldn't shut him up.
> **Phillip:** It was best at dinnertime though. James was in here (the cafe) having his dinner when Gary came in and in the middle of everyone.
> **Simon:** It was full as well.
> **Phillip:** . . . shouted pervert, pervert, pervert, pointing down at him like. Because he had found a girlfriend.

James, by publicly forming a heterosexual relationship, shifts Gary's representation of him as gay. As a result, Gary desperately tries to reposition James by reconstructing James's heterosexuality as a perversion. As a result Gary disconnects heterosexual practice from a sign of straightness, reworking it as a sign of his inherent homosexuality.

There are other examples of masculinity subcultures that are far more supportive and enable young men's "private selves" to have more public expression. Niobe Way has been conducting a longitudinal interview study of same-sex friendship patterns among working-class youth of color since 1989 (2004).[33] She notes that what boys learn from each other differs depending on race, ethnicity, and social class, citing numerous studies positing that African American young men felt that they had close friendships with more intimacy, compared to young Caucasian American men. In Way's own research—interviews of 200 boys, every year for three to five years—she found that even in the face of betrayals and distrust, male adolescents desired to have close friendships with other males.

In many films (and on television), when male friends of any age talk about sexuality, it is treated solely with humor, mixed with a sort of reverent fear of failing to perform and satisfy female partners. Young men's sexual (mis)adventures are the subject of countless "coming-of-age" films. An example of white, middle-class teen men's exploits can be found in the film *American Pie*. In one scene, high school senior Kevin is on the phone with his older brother, asking for some advice about how to help his girlfriend have an orgasm.

> **Brother:** . . . Listen, pay attention. Is that all that you're interested in, tryin' to get your girl into bed?
>
> **Kevin:** No, it'd be good to be able to, you know, return the favor. Be nice to know she enjoys things as much as I do.
>
> **Brother:** See that? That's good. That's what I wanted to hear. Now you qualify.
>
> **Kevin:** Qualify for what?
>
> **Brother:** My man, you've just inherited "The Bible." It originally started as a sex manual, this book that some guys brought back from Amsterdam. And each year it got passed on to one East student who was worthy. Now, it's full of all sorts of stuff that guys have added over the years. But you have to keep it a secret and return it at the end of the year. All right. So now you know. Good luck.

Kevin's brother has to ascertain Kevin's motives, positing women's pleasure as more important than men's desire to get women into bed. In this example, Kevin *is* able to be a bit vulnerable, admitting that he doesn't have all the answers about sex. Of course, it is a nice fantasy to think that young men would have this kind of open, straightforward access to sexual information. Instead, what many experience is a realm of bravado and bragging, overly focused only on accumulating partners.

An interview study of 15 urban, heterosexually active African American teens shows the more precise effects of peers as sexual socializers (Harper et al., 2004).[34] Peers affect both young men's and women's conceptualizations of sexuality, the success or failure of dating relationships, and perceptions of the other sex. Harper and his colleagues did see gender differences in respondents' comfort when disclosing sexual activity to friends; girls would need to be coaxed while boys would speak openly without needing encouragement. The boys learned that the content of discussion had to follow a certain, scripted formula and talked about sex "in terms of competition for who had the most sexual conquests and bragged about the types and frequency of their sexual activity." Respondents describe the way they talk to friends about sex:

> . . . they might feel like they might get embarrassed out, they'd be like, they'd let us know there is more, but they're not going to tell us, like. And then sometimes they let us push it out of them. (Jasmine)

Then we'll start talking about how many females we got. How many times we did it to them. We'll start having a competition, like who did the most girls. Who had the most sex. (Keith)

First word would be, probably, did you get some last night? Did you fuck her? Was it good? That's the first thing that they want to know. Did you get some and was it good? The conversation would pick up from there. (Greg)

Not surprisingly, boys and girls had different ways of describing dating and sex; girls spoke relationally, using euphemisms that implied "the dyadic nature of the union," such as "had sex" or "we did it." Female friends would ask if it was enjoyable, exactly what happened, if the encounter was "fun." Harper et al. (2004) described young men in this way:

In contrast to the females, males sometimes shared information with their close friends regarding females whom the friends wanted to pursue for sex. These comments often focused on the likelihood that particular females would agree to have sex with them. They used a variety of terms when talking about sexual activity, all of which were egocentrically based and focused on the male either receiving something (e.g., "getting some ass," "get some") or doing something to a female (e.g., "hit them," "screw her"). There was no obvious acknowledgement that the sexual activity involved two people who were engaging in a mutual activity.

I just hit [have sex with] them. Then it would be like, you just hit them for real? I be like, yup. (Terrance)

We talk about how many girls we did it to. We talk about when the last time you had some or whatever. Are you still a virgin or not? Do you want us to help you get some? (Keith)

This research hints at the complexity of differences in peer socialization for heterosexual men and women. What are the implications of these differences? What are young men and women learning about sex and the other gender? Women learn that sex is, ideally, relational, fun, enjoyable, and private enough that it takes a little coaxing (and well-placed questioning) to discuss it. Men learn that sex is about competition, conquest, and is de-individuated and impersonal. Sex becomes an external experience, an accomplishment independent of a partner.

The worst, and most extreme example of these oppositional, gendered points of view is the "Spur Posse." Naming themselves after a favorite NBA basketball player signed to the San Antonio Spurs, the Lakewood, California, male teenagers used a point system for their sexual conquests, making comparisons easy. The police arrested some of the members in early 1993 for various sexual crimes after a number of young women came forward, but prosecutors later dropped all but one of the charges after finding that most of the encounters were consensual. In a book about California, writer Joan Didion observed one of the Spur Posse members on a television talk show (2003):

> One of the ugliest and most revelatory of the many ugly and revelatory moments that characterized the 1993 television appearances of Lakewood's Spur Posse members occurred on the Jane Whitney talk show, when a nineteen-year-old Lakewood High School graduate named Chris Albert ("Boasts He has 44 'Points' for Having Sex With Girls") turned mean with a member of the audience, a young black woman who had tried to suggest that the Spurs on view were not exhibiting what she considered native intelligence.
>
> "What education does she have?" Chris Albert had then demanded, and crouched forward toward the young woman, as if trying to shake himself alert. "Where do you work at? McDonald's?" And then, there it was, the piton, driven in this case not into granite but into shale, already disintegrating: "*I go to college.*" Two years later Chris Albert would be dead, shot in the chest and killed during a Fourth of July celebration on the Pacific Coast Highway in Huntington Beach.[35]

This young man clearly displays his heterosexuality, sense of privilege, social class, racism, and *misogyny* (hatred of women), but the coda to the story—Albert's violent death—hints at the underlying foundations of American masculinity (Messerschmidt, 2000).[36] Years after the Spur Posse captured the nation's attention, sparking debates about whether the "boys" were "just being boys," a thread on a Web site's bulletin board sprang up, saying, "A new website has appeared featuring, so far, [pictures of] at least one of the testosterone-brimming jock studs of the early 90s who shocked the world by being into looking good, pumping up, and enjoying sex" (www.atkol.com).[37] Responses ranged from surprise that women had any interest in him, to noting that "the guys reek of testosterone, of male attitude," to commenting favorably on his physique, to "That guy may be a 'chick magnet', but he's a 'gay magnet' too. I wonder if he expanded his sexual repertoire in prison as much as he did his body?" Three days after the initial post, someone finally wrote, "Why would a rapist be appealing to anyone of either sex?"

This message thread suggests that the construction and maintenance of heterosexual masculinities are inextricably linked to *homophobia* (fear of anyone or anything "gay," fear of being or appearing "gay"). Mairtin Mac an Ghaill studied a work training site (like an apprenticeship in the trades) in the United Kingdom (1999).[38] He observed three versions of young men's heterosexuality. The "Fashionable Heterosexuals" defined their attractiveness based on consumerism, ascribing interpretations of what they thought women would desire. This was demonstrated through consumer choices and identification with pop culture labeling of what was attractive to women. Think "metrosexual" and think hairstyles, brands of clothing, and accessories like cars and technology. The "Explicit Heterosexuals" resembled the Spur Posse. "This group's heterosexuality tended to be based on a demonstration of extreme perversity, violent misogyny and a racialised sexuality. These characteristics served to emphasise their projected sexual competence" (1999: 437). These were the guys who made sure that everyone knew, unequivocally, that they were heterosexual. Tools, machines, techniques of the trade, blackboards, and double entendres were employed, with great fanfare and attention, to disrupt the occupational training the men were undergoing.

The last group Mac an Ghaill observed were the "Sexual Outsiders." They were the youngest men in the program, still in their late teens, and they did not hinge their public presentations of self on heterosexuality. They were less experienced with women and more interested in quietly learning and were thus subject to harassment from the other guys. "The dynamics of sexual harassment in this educational course, within and between different groups of students, could be located by recognising sexual harassment as a highly visible technique of consolidating heterosexuality" (Mac an Ghaill, 1999: 440). This means that sexual harassment within same-sex groups acts as a form of social control, a way of reminding everyone that straying from hegemonic interpretations (in this case, of masculinity) is subject to penalties and sanctions. A conversation excerpt from the study demonstrates how important it is for these men to regiment the display of heterosexuality, restrict it to be either "fashionable" or "explicit":

> **Richard:** Oi gayboy, what you sitting here for?
> **James:** Why not?
> **Gareth:** Look we can't have longhaired people sitting with us.
> **James:** So?
> **Richard:** OK long greasy hair.

Jeremy: Why can't you get your hair cut? Why don't you have short hair and be a bit fashionable?

James: Why should I? You lot are mad. You only follow what's fashion, like with your clothes and with your hair and your music.

Jeremy: Look, I have always listened to Oasis and Blur ever since they came out. See you do it all the time, why can't you take a joke?

James: I can take a joke but you go on about it all the time.

Richard: That's because you get wound up all the time. Why can't you just laugh along with us, and we wouldn't take the piss so much.

James: Well, I don't want to. I don't give a damn what you think either, you're all the same, you can't be different.

In this example, heterosexual masculinity seems to depend upon consensus, that all the players use the same rules for the same goals.

There are also contradictions in the multiple versions of masculinities offered in North America. Michael Kimmel writes that masculinity is "a constantly changing collection of meanings that we construct through our relationships with ourselves, with each other, and with our world. . . . We come to know what it means to be a man in our culture by setting our definitions in opposition to a set of 'other'—racial minorities, sexual minorities, and, above all, women" (1994: 120).[39] In this way, African American, Asian American, Latin American, and Native American men are constructed as the Other, as subordinate, and as flawed. As long as white middle- and upper-class masculinity maintains its distance from working-class men, men of color, and women, men are safe.

Femininity and Subcultural Norms

> Guys! Come on. You're ruining my moment here. This is our very man-hood at stake. We must make a stand, here and now. No longer will our penises remain flaccid and unused! We will fight for every man out there who isn't getting laid and should be. This is our day. This is our time. And, by God, we will not stand by and watch history condemn us into celibacy.
>
> —Kevin in the film *American Pie*

Imagine this speech done by a female lead in a movie about high school seniors trying to lose their virginity . . . : "No longer will our clitorises remain hidden and unused, our vulvas unstimulated! We will fight for every woman out there who isn't getting laid and should be." It should make you laugh, because the idea of young women saying things like this is a nice fantasy perhaps, but unfortunately still fairly far from reality.

The reality is that socialization into white, middle-class heterosexual femininity is marked by an emphasis on the creation of the "proper" kind of girl or young woman: someone who purchases the accoutrements of femininity, develops herself as sexually appealing to men, and who accepts a cultural discourse privileging individuality and "girl power" (Harris, 2004).[40] Like boys, girls learn about sexuality from their peers, families, and the formal educational system. Teens also learn from mass media; combining and averaging exposure to all forms of media results in the estimate that teens spend half of their waking hours with some form of media (Brown, Steele, and Walsh-Childers, 2002).[41] Individuals choose different media forms depending on their gender, race, and ethnicity. Studies show that African American women are less susceptible to narrow media images and messages about femininity (e.g., David et al., 2002; Schooler et al., 2004).[42] Latin American women seem to fall somewhere between African American women and Caucasian American women, who are consistently affected by media messages (e.g., Goodman, 2002; Pompper and Koenig, 2004; Van-der Wal and Thomas, 2004).[43]

Young women of all ethnicities do get sexuality and gender socialization messages from a specific source that seems to have no corollary for men—magazines. Teen women can choose from at least 10 magazines specifically for them, with several publishers creating teen versions from existing adult magazines (e.g., *Vogue* spun off *Teen Vogue*, *Elle* spun off *Elle Girl*). Media for young women constitute "field guides" and training manuals for femininity, narrowly defining heterosexuality, teaching women to be and become sex objects, and ultimately, subordinate some aspects of the self. The messages about gender and sexuality are uniform and narrow. Note that lesbian relationships, sexualities, and sexual health issues really do not appear in mainstream women's magazines, and my informal survey of magazines for lesbians (i.e., *Curve*, *Girlfriends*, *Advocate*, *Pride*) revealed no similar emphases on femininity and objectification.

In a study of sexual etiquette offered in the advice columns of five women's magazines, the authors found that advice for women had changed very little from 1974 to 1994 (Garner, Sterk, and Adams, 1998).[44] The five magazines each had circulations of over 1.5 million copies and included three specifically for teens—*YM*, *Seventeen*, and *Teen*. The authors analyzed the April and October issues from 1974, 1984, 1994, ending up with a sample of 175 issues. Their key question was, what messages do popular teen magazines have for young women about social and cultural norms for sex and sexual relationships?

Readers were given a picture of sexuality as mainly a matter of "meeting or dealing with his constant sexual desire and readiness." In magazines for teens, young women were warned—expect to be pressured into sex and "experience painful emotional and sexual scars" from heterosexual relationships (1998: 66). Young men were presented as "guys" who were self-centered, simplistic, "thickheaded," and pushy about sex. Rules for relationships included: don't be pushy or bossy; give guys space; don't be demanding; and fight the urge to push for commitments. Women who read magazines specifically for their advice about sex and relationships held stronger beliefs that men are driven by sexual urges and are fearful of commitment (Kim and Ward, 2004).[45] Consequently, these women held stronger beliefs that women needed to be sexually assertive and direct to attract men's interest, with the goal of developing a relationship. The message for women seems to be "know thy enemy," with heterosexual men constructed as enemy combatants with very different goals. Girls succeed ". . . by being better informed than guys about male and female physiology and psychology; by attracting guys through good-looking hair, beautiful clothes, and thin bodies; and by developing sex and relationship skills" (Garner, Sterk, and Adams, 1998: 66).

Messages in adult women's magazines, such as *Cosmo* and *Glamour*, argue that a woman's goal is to meet a man's needs (Garner, Sterk, and Adams, 1998). She should present herself as desirable (but not as desiring sex independently of a man); develop sex therapist or counselor skills (to enhance his pleasure and skills); become a linguist (learning "communication" skills to help him become a better verbalizer). So taking matters "into her own hands," for a woman, was about mastering him before he mastered her. Meeting her own needs appeared in the guise of standing up to "guys," avoiding men's pressure, and *gatekeeping*, or slowing down sex or foreplay and preventing him from going further (e.g., Durham, 1996).[46] Unfortunately, these messages have changed very little since the 1950s heyday of training manuals for girls and young women. Journalist Lynn Peril (2002) discusses expert commentaries on sex, which still include the idea that girls who get into sexual scenarios with boys are giving boys the message that wanting sex is okay; that boys only respond sexually if girls lead them on; and that boys' drives are so strong that to remain chaste, a girl has to stay away from any remotely sexual scenarios.[47]

Messages about sex for teen women still include the idea that virginity (chastity) is a valuable resource that should be not frittered away. Similarly to GLBT youth, it has grown difficult to know exactly what "virginity" means. Does it refer to specific physical, partnered acts? Is it more about "an irreversible transition from innocence (and virtue) to experience (and corruption)," a moral concept (Carpenter, citing Nathanson, 2001a)?[48] By the time women are in college, their perception of what "sex" means is established. A random sampling of 599 Midwestern university students, surveyed before President Bill Clinton had oral sex with Monica Lewinsky, shed some light on the subject (Sanders and Reinisch, 1999).[49] When asked, "Would you say you 'had sex' with someone if the most intimate behavior you engaged in was . . . ," respondents overwhelmingly indicated that penile-vaginal intercourse (99.5 percent) and penile-anal intercourse would be "having sex" (81 percent). Giving or receiving oral sex (40 percent) and manual genital stimulation (14 percent) did not have as much support. This study implies that, for heterosexually active people, "sex" is generally defined as penile penetration of an orifice below the belly button.

Besides this conceptualization, what does it mean subjectively to "lose your virginity" if you are a woman? How do women feel about this? Sociologist Laura Carpenter (2001a) interviewed 33 women (and 28 men) about virginity; most had engaged in first-time PVI during adolescence (at age 16, on average). "Regardless of when I spoke with them, most heterosexual respondents initially defined virginity loss with a simple statement such as "[Virginity loss is] the first time having sex" (Lavinia, 30, heterosexual), by which they meant vaginal intercourse. In contrast, virtually every lesbian, gay, or bisexual participant responded by raising the issue of sex between same-sex partners, often referring more generally to the existence of different ways of defining sex (Carpenter, 2001a). It is especially easy for heterosexual women to envision virginity as a "treasured gift." One respondent, Kelly (age 24), said it is ". . . supposed to be something special and cherished and wonderful and something to keep and you give to someone who is . . . I don't know if lose is the right word . . . I'll say you give to someone, whenever you find the right person." Carpenter's female respondents were more likely than male respondents to consider virginity a gift (61 percent vs. 36 percent). Men were much more likely than women to have ever viewed virginity as a stigma, an unfortunate status to be modified quickly (57 percent vs. 21 percent). The virginity-as-gift concept was much more prevalent for heterosexually oriented respondents, while GLB respondents were more likely to see virginity as part of a process (of growing, learning, and so on).

Young women may get mixed messages about virginity. One study of 20 immigrant Mexican fathers revealed that virginity status was not directly the men's concern (Gonzalez-Lopez, 2004).[50] Fathers were actually focused on ensuring that their daughters were protected from what was perceived to be sexually dangerous U.S. culture. Content analysis of German and U.S. teen magazines suggests that, for white girls, virginity surpasses all other sexuality topics (Carpenter, 2001b).[51] In the

German magazine (*Bravo!*) Carpenter analyzed, there was a weekly column, "My First Time," that detailed a teen's story, often considering virginity loss with a current partner. Most of the virginity stories in the U.S. magazine (*Seventeen*) focused on "hypothetical or medical scenarios" (p. 42). But both sources roundly emphasized virginity loss within the context of a "close, caring relationship." While *Bravo!*'s editors highlighted the pleasures of sex within these relationships, *Seventeen*'s editors "did not mention the potential for enhanced pleasure, physical or otherwise" (p. 43). This omission is glaring, with clear implications, but sadly, the omission is unsurprising.   *German - Pleasure ; Us. No*

Many scholars have addressed the idea that for young women there is a missing or, at best, ambivalent discourse of desire (Fine, 1988; Tolman, 1994; Thompson, 1995).[52] This may be reflected in the emphasis on women's sexuality existing in the shadow of and in light of men's sexual interests and attractions. This could be called the "it just happened" narrative. Young women learn to describe, and more importantly, to actually conceptualize their sexualities in terms of "it" just happening. Psychologist Deborah Tolman writes, "Having sex 'just happen' is one of the few acceptable ways available to adolescent girls for making sense of and describing their sexual experiences; and, given the power of such stories to shape our experiences of our bodies, it may tell us what their sexual experiences are actually like" (2002: 2).[53] When sex "just happens," or when "one thing leads to another," and lived experiences are characterized in fuzzy and ambiguous ways, it protects young women from the confusing social discourses about desire and sex. These discourses are perfect examples of the Goldilocks theory of sex: heterosexual women should be sexually interested, but not slutty; appealing, but not slutty; sexually active . . . but not slutty; and adventurous, but not kinky (or slutty!).

The experience of desire can be muted, absent, confusing, awkward, unpredictable, frustrating, and/or constrained (Holland, Ramazanoglu, and Sharpe, 1994).[54] This is especially true if love and romance, or at least, a sense that the sex partner "cares," are also absent or confusing. Young women are still offered a relatively narrow cultural context for sexual activity that privileges love as the justification for becoming sexually active. Historically, there was no doubt about when a woman would "say yes" to sex—it was supposed to be on her wedding night. About 90 percent of women born between 1933 and 1942 were (PVI) virgins when they married or had had premarital PVI with their fiancés (Moore, Driscoll, and Lindberg, 1998).[55] But in a nod to the reality that more than 50 percent of today's teen girls have had PVI by age 17, the message about love has had to change. This may explain teen magazine and teen sex Web site emphases on "how to tell if you're ready to say yes" (Bay-Cheng, 2001).[56]

Instead of assuming that love is part of the decision or the moment, we have to find some other clarity (e.g., ability to discern readiness) within the confusion that defines socialization messages for young women. In a focus-group study of 11- to 16-year-old heterosexual teens in Britain, Rachel Thomson (2004) heard distinct differences in the ways that girls and boys understood "readiness."[57] For the girls, it had to do it with the quality of their relationships. Sandra said, "You should be—you can't just go doing it with any lad you see when you're 14—if you love him or if you're in a relationship and you know it's going to last and he's not gonna go round school saying, 'oh, I've done this with her'" (p. 143). Imagine if young men were constantly advised on how to figure it out. They probably need this help too, but the assumption is that only women *need* help figuring out what they desire and when. Men's desires are thought to be as obvious and seemingly simple as an erection; an erection is taken as the only necessary evidence that a man is turned on.

Heterosexual women's experiences are not necessarily representative of all women's. Though the confusing and Goldilocks-esque construction of desire appears to be an element of cultural scripting, subcultural differences are salient. Interviews with 31 young Latinas (Puerto Rican, Dominican, and Cuban) showed that women understand their sexualities in light of U.S. culture, Latin subcultures, and interpersonal scripting (Faulkner, 2003).[58] The scripted expectation that men's sexuality is an incontrollable force inspired the women to strategize about ways to avoid men they called "players" and to avoid being called a "flirty girl." Though women adapted their sexual expressions to perceived norms, the expression of individual desires was still muted.

For young lesbian women, it is clear that "desire" is learned, but the learning process has different implications depending on sexual orientation (Tolman, 1994; Diamond, 2003; Ussher, 2005).[59] Jane Ussher's interviews with 8 lesbian women and 12 heterosexual women (aged 17 to 24) in southern England revealed that interpreting a feeling as "desire" is complex. Once named, what should be done about it? One heterosexual woman said, "I have to let him make the first move, not appear too keen, so that he can feel as if he's in control" (p. 29). Another said, "I don't want to seem easy, so I keep my sexual feelings to myself" (p. 29). The lesbian women did not feel they had to role play femininity in this way—they did not have to "do girl," "knowingly taking up a position of archetypal femininity, of acquiescence and coquettishness, yet doing so as an act" (Ussher, 1997: 450).[60] She argues that sexual desire is a learned phenomenon:

One young lesbian described feelings she would now categorize as desire as initially being experienced as nervousness, or as a feeling of being impressed by another woman. "I don't think I had a crush on her or something, it was just like I was really impressed by her whole personality. I think that was really the first time when a woman made me really nervous" (Ussher, 2005: 28).

There are some implications to the approach described by this respondent, reflecting Adrienne Rich's arguments that compulsory heterosexuality renders lesbian expression invisible. It is difficult for women to imagine sex with another woman— what would it be? How would it feel (Thompson, 1995; Tolman, 2002)? Ussher's interviewees stated that it was only in an unequivocally sexual encounter that they could label their feelings as sexual desire: "I was probably really aware of kind of perv feelings or sexual feelings when we kissed which was completely a big surprise, completely out of the blue" (2005: 28).

The compromises that white, middle-class women have to make to fulfill hegemonic expectations of femininity may be, at best, confusing. At worst, these women may never fully clarify what desire, arousal, and lust feels like. Lesbian women, who may feel as if they are already challenging the hegemony and therefore have little to lose, may ultimately feel empowered: "I feel I can take the initiative, and be dominant, and be active, whereas in straight relationships I've had, ah, I never felt that was allowed, or was okay, or I would be seen as masculine if I did" (Ussher, 2005: 30). Heterosexual women who challenge gender role expectations may also be able to challenge ambivalent cultural discourses of desire (Wilkins, 2004).[61] Sociologist Amy Wilkins did an *ethnographic* study (in-depth research, includes immersion in a study site) of a Goth scene. She found that young women were able to resist, to a certain extent, mainstream ideas about women's sexualities. In describing themselves, young women used concepts of active choice and empowerment, reflecting some who explored bisexuality and openly nonmonogamous sexuality. This was an attempt, perhaps, to sidestep the stigma of "slut" and the dangers of rape and coercive sex. The women experienced themselves as having control over their sexualities and a sense that their desires were their own.

As we will see in subsequent chapters, there are significant consequences of masculine socialization into homophobia, competition, aggression, and sex-partner-as-object. There are significant consequences of feminine socialization into subordinated desires and becoming identified as objects more than as subjects or active agents. Regardless of sexual orientation, men *and* women eventually have to deal with the repercussions of scripting that positions men and women as total opposites. Socialization messages, latent and manifest, are the first brick in the wall built between us. These messages can be detrimental and limiting for men and women. What are the consequences of such fully institutionalized and divergent gender trajectories? How are adult sexualities affected? What can we learn about ourselves by focusing on these and other questions? This is our central focus in the next section, where we will explore several contemporary aspects of sex—masturbation, fantasies, hooking up, and how sex intersects with social context.

Questions to Ponder

1. Do you know anyone who uses the terms "fag" and "slut"? In what contexts or circumstances could you argue that they have neutral (e.g., not negative) meanings? What are the (gendered) implications of using these terms?

2. Why is it so difficult for adults to talk to children about sex? What barriers would confront you if you were a parent? What barriers would confront you if you were a teacher?

Suggested Projects

1. Interview several people about their socialization into gender and sexualities. From whom did they learn? What messages did they get, latent and manifest? Did they have subcultural influences as well? When you analyze the answers, think about patterns, themes, and trends across the lifespan (instead of focusing on the specifics of one person's life).

2. Using magazines intended for women and/or men, select some articles about sex. Analyze the articles with critical thinking in mind—what purpose do they serve, what information and evidence do they offer, and what are the implications of the author's argument? How do magazine articles (and media more generally) act as agents of socialization, and what do they teach us?

5

Finding a <u>Playboy</u> under a Rock in the Woods

SEX IN THE MIND

When I was in high school, one of my friends told me about his first exposure to pornography. He was out in the woods behind his house, with his best friend, poking around with a big stick he had found. They were doing what eight- or nine-year-old boys like to do—searching for adventure, something fun, something to do. He poked his stick into a pile of leaves at the base of a rock and was surprised to feel something give. When he investigated further, he realized that the leaves were covering a hole that had been dug out below the rock. As he bent to the ground and began digging out the leaves, he wondered what was under the rock. Maybe it was money or a secret treasure. He yelled to his friend, "Hey, I found something."

Under the rock was a stash of pornographic magazines—*Playboy* and *Penthouse*. It wasn't money, but it was almost as good. When he opened the magazine, he was amazed. There were naked girls, staring at him, so pretty and sexy. He told me that as the boys stood looking at the magazines, in awed silence of the breasts and legs that seemed to fill every page, his first thought was, "Wow! I sure hope I meet a girl like this some day."

It is tough to know exactly how this discovery affected my high school friend. Did he become heterosexual as an adult? Did he ever meet a woman who resembled a Playmate? If not, did he accept that? Did he start masturbating after finding the stash? Did he masturbate with magazines to help define his fantasies and enhance his arousal? In this chapter, we will continue exploring how culture, gender, and socialization impact individual sexualities. By studying the intrapsychic realm of sexual fantasies, we can gain a better understanding of how sexual expectations, rules, and proscriptions take root and affect us.

THE EXAMPLE OF MENARCHE, SEMENARCHE, AND MASTURBATION

By the time hormones and physiological changes have an established foothold—age 16 or so—and act as an apparent mandate for sharing and exploring sexuality, most individuals have learned myriad elements of the social construction of sex. Any of the "shoulds" and "should nots" that our caregivers may have missed will be inculcated by our peers, friends, the formal educational system, religion, and mass media. By the end of high school, the average U.S. teen has had penile-vaginal intercourse—about 80 percent (Haffner, 1995).[1] At the start of high school, about half of heterosexual 14-year-olds have played above the waist, while about a quarter have explored below the waist (*Teens Talk about Sex,* 1994).[2] Conduct and cultural expectations merge with the body, further developing the sexual self for many teens.

Puberty is in some ways the great democratizer of humans. For most males and females, independent of race, class, and nationality, hormones and biochemical processes kick in, promoting hair growth in the armpit, pubic region, and other places. External genitalia begin to change slowly, with the penis gradually lengthening and thickening; secondary sex characteristics, such as breasts, develop. Girls tend to experience menarche, the onset of the menstrual cycle that may persist from about 12 until 50, or older. Boys tend to experience semenarche, the technical term for first ejaculation. What happens before the first time? What happens subsequently?

The body is seen as the starting point of gender (and sex) difference, as discussed in chapter 3. By puberty, it seems as obvious as whether the sun is up or down: boys and girls are different—just look at their bodies for proof. But beneath the often overt physiological changes are two issues that characterize exactly how differently boys and girls are taught about sexualities. We will first examine *menarche,* or onset of first menstruation, and *semenarche,* onset of first ejaculation, and then discuss masturbation and sexual fantasies. Our purpose is ultimately to understand the implications and consequences of socialization and gender messages.

By the time the solstice announces the arrival of summer, American homes may be witness to a dramatic upsurge in the population of 10-year-olds who find themselves suddenly versed in the language of endocrinology. For decades now, during late May and June, fifth graders in many parts of the country have been herded into dark classrooms and auditoriums to squeamishly watch the movie for which no companion Xbox game is made—the video that seeks to explain why 12-year-old Sam now speaks in a pitch resembling Donald Sutherland's and why his friend Emma is suddenly finding herself ill-tempered for reasons that have nothing to do with Kevin Federline's marital status (Bellafante, 2005).[3]

In this article about sex education films, Ginia Bellafante suggests that the staple of sex education in schools—the sex education classroom film—has changed very little since you saw it 10 or more years ago, and very little since your parents saw it decades ago. Filmmakers and educators argue that this is due to two constants of sexuality. First, children know little about their bodies and sexual anatomies. Second, parents still struggle to find the right words, the right setting, and the right time. Many simply relinquish responsibility to school-based sex ed; hence the rather stable genre of the sex ed film. In fact, Bellafante points out, 30 states mandate that sex education be provided in schools, hinting at the importance parents and others place on the school as the desirable setting for such education.

In this setting, boys and girls are often separated for an hour, an afternoon, or sometimes more. Each group is shown different films, and chances are, the boys hear (from a coach or another adult man) a lot about what's "normal," including the potentially frightening "hair in strange places," nocturnal emissions, and masturbation. The girls probably hear a lot about fallopian tubes, hormones, and sanitary napkins. The gendered message is obvious: boyhood is about becoming a man, while girlhood is about reproduction.

The opportunity to merge marketing and message has not been lost on those who manufacture the euphemistically named "feminine hygiene products." Bellafante reports that Procter and Gamble, maker of the Always brand of panty liners and napkins, offers a film, "Always Changing: About You." Versions can be shown to girls, boys, or boys and girls together. A corporate spokesperson claims that the film and its educational materials are used in 85 percent of the schools in the country.

Flaake (2005) studied the meaning of physical, pubertal changes for girls.[4] She argues that adults—parents, particularly—can react to their daughters in ways that subtly communicate and can negatively affect daughters' perceptions and self-concepts.

Indeed, adolescents are sensitive to what is said, and perhaps more importantly, to what is not said. The following statement is representative of what most of my female students have experienced: "My mom left a book on my bed one day and told me to ask if I had any questions. It was just obvious to me that she didn't really mean it, didn't want me to ask her anything. So I never did."

Boys and the Body

One thing that has not changed about sex is the existence of a taboo around boys' first ejaculations. Though Kinsey and his colleagues asked men about ejaculation and *nocturnal emissions*, the first study specifically focusing on the topic was done in 1971 (Shipman).[5] Sexuality.org defines nocturnal emissions as "an involuntary seminal discharge in the male during REM sleep which may or may not be accompanied by a dream of erotic content; night visitor; sex dream; polluting dream; wet dream." The synonyms are telling—"polluting" and "sex" dream hint at the taboos associated with the event. First ejaculations, whether as nocturnal emissions or via masturbation, are surely a pivotal, fundamental aspect of young men's sexual selves, yet unfortunately very little research has been undertaken.

Shipman reported that boys had a lot of interest but not much conversation or communication about the meaning and mechanics of semenarche. This may be attributable to parents. He had found that 90 percent of the boys in his study had not spoken with *either* parent, nor gotten any information from a parent. You may be thinking, well, that was 1971, so it makes sense. Things were different then. The parents who might have done the talking would be your grandparents, and it was a different time in 1971. Your grandparents would not have been talking so openly about sex, certainly unlike today. You may be thinking that a more recent study would *surely* have different results.

Except that, unfortunately, very little has changed. Loren Frankel reviewed all the research on or related to semenarche, scant though it is (2002).[6] The most consistent finding in all the research was this: men were highly intrigued and curious about first ejaculation, whether it happened due to *masturbation* (self-stimulation of the genitals) or nocturnal emission. But, Frankel reports, "For the vast majority of American adolescent males, their response to the experience—whether they felt surprised, prepared, fearful, curious, or happy—is cloaked in silence." So men were curious and kept in the dark. In fact, when Frankel interviewed 28 parents with sons between 10 and 13, he found that the taboo about discussing semenarche persisted. Though 92 percent of the parents (and 13 of them were fathers) intended to talk with their sons about the general changes of puberty, 54 percent indicated that they "had never thought about" specifically discussing first ejaculation. The vast majority did not know if they would eventually discuss it, taking a wait-and-see attitude. At the same time, Frankel asked the parents if they would discuss *menarche*, or the start of menstruation, with female children. He also found that, in studies of disclosure, generally about 85 percent of girls would or had told their mothers about menarche. Further, these parents did not see any correlation between menarche and semenarche, asserting that they were not at all the same thing. What would explain the parents' differences in approach and attitude? For many boys, the first nocturnal emission is a moment of confusion but also the start of an important realization that has implications for adult sexuality. This is even more profound if first ejaculation is the result of the boy's efforts, via masturbation.

A study of Nigerian boys revealed that although semenarche was not viewed as a negative event, there were some cultural differences in interpretation (Adegoke, 1993).[7] Researchers gave 188 surveys to schoolboys aged 12 to 18, convinced that the anonymity of the method would inspire honest answers. The majority of the boys said that they had gotten some information about first ejaculation prior to it (68 percent, n = 129). Of these, 62 percent (n = 89) were informed by other men, older authority figures, and only 17 of the respondents were informed by women. But 60 percent (n = 118) felt unprepared for the experience. When asked "How did you experience your first ejaculation?" only 26 (or 13 percent) of the boys had experienced ejaculation through masturbation, and 104 (or 53 percent) said they had had a nocturnal emission. Adegoke's finding that 38 (20 percent) of the respondents reported first ejaculation during (heterosexual) intercourse clarifies an assumption made about semenarche—that it is either nocturnal or self-generated. Most of the boys in the study told someone about their first ejaculation (57 percent), though few told anyone besides friends. The respondents primarily felt excited, proud, adult, and grown up.

Menstruation

This journey of discovery led me to my infamous questions—Do you brush your teeth with shampoo? Wash your hair with toothpaste? Of course not. But you use WHAT? On your WHERE? Why would any woman cleanse any part of her body with products not designed for that specific use. Could many women unknowingly suffer physiological consequences from the products they were using that didn't complement their *sweet spot* needs? Could we do more to optimize the health and well-being of their *sweet spot?* Of course we could. Were there products out there? NO! The only products that addressed intimate grooming were relegated to the bottom shelf of stores, had graceless names, and were associated with yeast infections and other medicinal and clinical products. Is intimate grooming not intimately connected to a woman's sense of beauty? Must intimate grooming be a source of embarrassment? Why not a source of splendor? (http://sweetspotlabs.com)

"Mom, do you ever have that not-so-fresh feeling?" (television commercial for feminine hygiene product, 1980s)

What do girls and women learn about their bodies? Diorio and Munro (2000)[8] report that sex education in New Zealand is still characterized by overt gender differences. Girls are taught about puberty as a function of reproduction, hygiene, and the body. Boys are taught about the "exciting" and "powerful" bodily changes they can look forward to and enjoy. They write, "Though sexual desire is excluded from sex education, puberty fits readily into the "facts and dangers" motif; it is a relatively safe topic which teaches pupils—but especially girls—to understand their bodies essentially as gender differentiated reproductive vehicles" (p. 348). The main emphases of puberty education for girls include: teaching about menstruation so that girls can arm themselves against teen pregnancy; teaching that menstruation is something to learn to cope with; and teaching that menstruation is problematic.

The issues Diorio and Munro raise hint at the adult consequences of this approach. Girls can easily come to view their bodies as enemy territory, a landscape of pain, discomfort, and at the least, monthly annoyance. Boys can come to view their bodies as "exciting," though also unpredictable terrains of (self) exploration (Martin, 1996).[9] Women's bodies are constructed as a site of trouble and danger, because of unplanned pregnancies and the increased risk of sexually transmitted infections. Further, the authors argue that the "trouble and danger" take on menstruation becomes part of young men's (emerging) power over women. Diorio and Munro reveal that puberty education includes the perspective that menstruation can make girls and women moody, irritable, and capricious. Casually, this belief is supported by slang such as *on the rag, ragging, female trouble, that time of the month,* and my favorite (obscure) term, *serving Menstruada, the bitch goddess.*

How Do Girls Feel When Menarche Happens?

In Western cultures, menstruation seems to bring with it discomfort, embarrassment, anxiety, and some ambivalence about growing up (Moore, 1995).[10] Lovering interviewed 40 girls, all 12 years old, and found that most did not see menarche as something positive (1995).[11] The girls did not conceive of it as a developmental marker, nor did they connect menarche to fertility and sexuality. In this way, the gap between the body and self is exacerbated. The body is seen as disengaged from the girls' developing self-concept, contributing to negative feelings about the body (Martin, 1996). Menarche can be associated with shame, fear, disgust, and the feeling that the body is out of control.

Koff and Rierdan (1995)[12] asked 157 racially diverse ninth-grade girls, all of whom had been menstruating for one to three years, what preparatory advice they would offer to younger girls and to parents. They were asked to consider their own experiences and their own conversations with parents. Not surprisingly, most of the parental discussion occurred with mothers (77 percent of the girls); only 8 percent of the girls reported speaking to a father or other male caregiver. The good news is that most of the girls found their discussions at least "somewhat helpful." The girls reported feeling a disconnect, in effect, between the relatively abstract and impersonal facts of menstruation and their individual, lived experiences.

The disconnect extends further. In an attempt to erase the history of shame, embarrassment, and secrecy attached to menstruation, current menarchal education focuses on normalizing and naturalizing the experience. This is laudable, in the abstract, but many young women experience a different reality, Koff and Rierdan suggest: pain, discomfort, disgust, annoyance. But mothers face a "daunting responsibility," because these girls wanted their moms to be calm, reassuring, supportive, aware, knowledgeable, and able to provide the products associated with menstruation (except tampons, which the girls wanted to learn about from friends). Most of the respondents (69 percent) suggested unequivocally that fathers should "stay out of it." Family context *is* important. An in-depth interview study of 22 ethnically and racially diverse girls, aged 14 to 18, suggested that when parents emphasized the positive aspects of menarche, girls benefited (Teitelman, 2004).[13] Describing menstruation as a creative process was a better approach than primarily referencing reproduction, because girls were more likely to have negative feelings and interpretations of puberty and reproduction.

To understand the eventual implications of how these issues are generally handled, we have to go back to basics for a moment. Menstruation can be viewed as a health issue, a sign of impending womanhood or maturity, and therefore as something that needs to be discussed. We can easily imagine that girls need to consult with mothers or female caregivers to ensure that there's a regular supply of what we euphemistically call *feminine hygiene products*. Even this term hints at the way we may view menstruation: it's a simple matter of hygiene.

Stop for a moment and think about the dictionary definition of *menstruation*: "a discharging of blood, secretions, and tissue debris from the uterus that recurs in nonpregnant breeding-age primate females at approximately monthly intervals and that is considered to represent a readjustment of the uterus to the nonpregnant state following proliferative changes accompanying the preceding ovulation" (Merriam-Webster OnLine).

How might semenarche be viewed? Is it a matter of hygiene or pubertal health? Do boys need help obtaining "masculine hygiene products"? Remember the definition of nocturnal emission—"erotic content," "sex dream," and the idea of pollution, which has the connotation of contamination? So the main difference between semenarche and menarche is that one is associated very directly with sex, and the other is associated with discharge, "Aunt Flo," and reproduction. Boys' first ejaculations, whether the result of REM sleep or conscious, awake actions, are often associated with masturbation, which is often joked about but rarely seriously discussed, especially by or with parents. Ejaculation is associated with sex, sexual desire, arousal, and orgasm. In short, it is a highly sexual event, and as Frankel clarifies, there is no equivalent event for girls or young women.

Does semenarche mark the start of differing sexualities for men and women? Kinsey, Pomeroy, and Martin (1948)[14] remarked that males who went through puberty earlier were, overall, more sexual. Compared to men who went through puberty later, they masturbated earlier and more frequently engaged in heterosexual intercourse and same-sex activities. Kinsey et al. (1953)[15] did not find similar correlations for women—age at puberty had no association with any of these sexual behaviors. Men generally seemed more sexual than women in Kinsey's studies. What about sexual desire, which is not the same as behavior? Ostovich and Sabini (2005) surveyed 277 students to test whether Kinsey's results could be replicated, and whether there were any links in terms of puberty, arousal, and desire.[16] The researchers asked when respondents had experienced various signs of puberty; their first memory of experiencing "sexual desire"; and their current behavior, including desire, number of lifetime sex partners, and average frequency of intercourse. For the most part, Ostovich and Sabini discovered that Kinsey's findings held true for their contemporary sample: men were more sexual, on every measured dimension, than women, in spite of the fact that women experienced puberty earlier than did men (2005).

What is intriguing about menarche compared to semenarche is the collective shift from public to private in terms of how the issues are addressed. Boys in Western cultures appear to be told very little about first ejaculation (and masturbation, for that matter). The event is private, potentially causing fear and shame, along with hiding the sheets or wet pajamas. But most boys (especially white, middle-class boys) quickly learn that it is okay to joke with friends about ejaculations, random erections, and masturbation. While masturbation itself may not become a public, shared event, it enters the conversations and laughter of many young men. It is probably safe to assume that most of the more colorful slang for masturbation—*jerk the gherkin, choke the chicken, flog the bishop,* for example—is primarily used in groups of friends. Have you ever heard a guy say something like, "About 90 percent of men masturbate . . . and the other 10 percent are liars"? Masturbation may not start as a normalized, neutralized event in many boys' lives, but it quickly and easily can become a topic of boasting and humor.

For girls, menarche can be a much more public rite of passage—(female) relatives may celebrate the advent of "womanhood," and caregivers may initiate more conversation about its implications than about any other pubertal event. Girlfriends may giggle their way into the "feminine hygiene" aisle at the drugstore and select tampons in a small group. I remember a ring of girls in junior high who were essentially the "Period Police," watching out for impending embarrassments. The group was formed after one girl had unknowingly started her first period in math class . . . while wearing white Capri pants, of course. We were mortified and offended and confused and determined that no one else would ever suffer that kind of shame again. At any time during the school day, any day of the week, a girl could go into any bathroom and find another girl willing to lend a panty liner or check for leakage ("Am I showing anything?," we'd ask, and turn around for a "stain check"). We collectively knew which girls had their periods because those girls would come to school with shirts or jackets tied around their waists—for a week!

While menstruation can remain a "public" topic—going from "stain checks" to simply venting about cramps and cravings—masturbation does not always become the public, jocular topic that it often is for young men. Consider how few slang terms there are, and how even fewer are widely used—*fiddling the bean, fingerbating, fingerpainting, getting to know yourself, getting a stinky pinky* (pleasant, eh?), *polishing the pearl, jilling off, rowing the man in the boat.* It may be generational, but although I have been studying sex for almost two decades, I have never heard a woman refer to masturbation with any slang besides "do it" or "touch myself." This is precisely why Samantha on *Sex and the City* was so noteworthy for her frank discussions of her desires and habits. In one episode, "The Agony and the 'Ex'-tasy," Samantha *really* explored a taboo, spending all day masturbating to fantasies of a "hot priest" who later explained to her that (gasp) there was more to life than sex. We will discuss fantasies later in this chapter.

In just 10 years or so, we have come *some* distance at least in terms of how masturbation is discussed in the media, if not in cultural attitudes. President Bill Clinton's surgeon general, Joycelyn Elders, was immediately dismissed in 1994 after she stated that masturbation "is something that is part of human sexuality and it's part of something that perhaps should be taught." Actor Paul Reubens (a.k.a. Pee-Wee Herman) was caught masturbating to a pornographic film featuring heterosexual men and women, "Nancy's Nurse," in an adult movie theater in 1991. He was arrested, his career fell apart, and his hand prints and star were removed from Hollywood's Walk of Fame (Cornog, 2003: 286).[17] Because he had become famous for a children's television show, parents were instructed to tell their children that people touch themselves "privately, not publicly." There was a sense of deep shame about what he had done—that he had disgraced himself, whether because he was in an adult theatre or because he was actually masturbating was unclear. It is clear that he never again had a career as a children's entertainer. The responses to both of these events indicate the deep ambivalence U.S. culture has about masturbation and pleasure.

Masturbation

Manhood, and adult men's sexuality, often has its roots in young men's self-explorations. Most importantly, when sexuality is associated with ejaculation (and masturbation), young men can begin to see that some measure of their sexuality is within their control. When womanhood is associated with menstruation, the monthly, uncontrollable discharge associated with unfulfilled fertilization of an egg, what young women learn is quite different. Women learn that what happens "down there" can be painful and unpleasant at the worst. At best, menarche can be associated with becoming a woman, maturing, and growing. But menstruation is infrequently associated with anything sexual, and even less so with the concept that sexuality is within a girl's hands. Boys can learn about their sexual selves via masturbation, experiencing their genitalia as a source of pleasure and autonomy. Girls do not typically learn that menstruation has any relationship to pleasure or orgasm.

Empirically, we see that men's and women's masturbatory habits differ, in frequency, level of desire, and motivation. Over the course of the 20th century, these differences have remained constant in spite of vast sociocultural changes. Men masturbate more than women, in the aggregate, and individually, more men masturbate regularly and with frequency. Most Caucasian American boys experience orgasm, ejaculation, and pleasure via masturbation *before* experiencing these things with a partner (DeLamater, 1987).[18] There are differences in frequency for African Americans; both men and women reported masturbating less overall than Caucasian Americans (Laumann et al., 1994). Religiosity, social class, and ethnicity affect frequency for men and women.

Since most women do not masturbate for the first time prior to age 16, when partnered activities tend to begin, it is likely that most women's experiences of sexuality are very partner-focused, regardless of race (Cornog, 2003). Women are more likely than men to begin masturbating later in life, and tend to learn about it through media and peers, and less so via self-exploration. The majority of men of all races, classes, and sexual orientations masturbate at least occasionally but less than half of all women do so occasionally (Smith, Rosenthal, and Reichler, 1996).[19] In the National Health and Social Life Survey (NHSLS), 60 percent of men between 18 and 59 had masturbated at least once in the preceding 12 months; 40 percent of women had done so (Laumann et al., 1994).[20] But while 25 percent of the men masturbated once a week or more, only 10 percent of the women did so. This may be due to blind spots in women's knowledge of their bodies, arousal, and desires. One young woman described knowing everything about her breasts, because they are so "public"—ogled, depicted in magazines, and spilling out of Wonderbras (Hex, 1999).[21] Yet she "had no idea what a clitoris looked like, let alone what one was" (p. 94). While discussions of masturbation have begun to appear in adult women's magazines, the message focuses on "how to"—learning how to masturbate, feel comfortable with one's body, and reach orgasm. What are the implications of the fact that women may not know their bodies, may not have comfortable language to describe their bodies, and may not know their desires?

There is a belief that solo sex is a poor substitute for sex with someone else, that it is not as good as "the real thing." People with partners who are having regular partnered sex tend to masturbate more than those without partners. It may be that thinking about sex and being sexual inspires *more* desire, leading to higher rates of both solo sex and partnered sex. In my sex classes I show two video clips that really put the issue in perspective. In one video, *Private Dicks,* diverse men talk about all aspects of sex. One man describes how sometimes he likes to make a date with himself—light candles, play mood music, get some oil, and make masturbation an event. The young women in my class laugh and laugh; the men say nothing at all. Women can pick up any women's magazine and find tips on how to learn to masturbate, how to improve orgasms, and how to discover what pleasure feels like (e.g., run a bath, make sure you're alone, light candles, buy a vibrator). Although it is a humorous image, and the guy telling the anecdote hams it up a bit, women may be better able to appreciate his mood-setting efforts because it sounds like something from an issue of *Cosmo* or

Glamour. But there is a perception, and the laughter hints at this, that masturbation should _not_ be a seduction of the self—should not be an event orchestrated and planned for in the same way that many people plan partnered sex.

The other video clip is from an episode of the *Rikki Lake* talk show broadcast in the early 2000s, "Help! My Man's Obsessed with Pornography!" Women describe their disdain for male partners who masturbate, saying things like "if he really loved me, he wouldn't do that." One woman described her husband masturbating to porn films in the other room while she slept—"he shouldn't do it—he should just do it with me, I mean, I'm real and I'm there!" Now an obvious part of the issue is the use of pornography, and we will further explore the link between masturbation and pornography later in the book. My white female students respond to this quite differently than my white male students, who claim that sometimes men just "need" to masturbate, independently of a partner. Most of the female students do not understand this logic, seeing masturbation as a poor substitute for a partner at worst, and at best, something to be shared (e.g., with a male partner, for his pleasure). I suspect that this line of reasoning is at least partly, if not wholly, due to reading those articles in *Cosmo* and other magazines. One of my particularly talkative female students said, "If I'm horny, yeah sure, I'll touch myself, but what's the point? I would rather just save it for a guy."

Men experience semenarche, a physically pleasant (i.e., not painful) sensation that they quickly associate with ejaculation and orgasm. Many boys do the addition and learn that masturbation enables them to fantasize and figure out the stimulation and sensations they enjoy. Although little boys often stroke their penises prior to being able to ejaculate, for young men genitalia can become associated with pleasure, desire, control, and autonomy. The possibility of pleasure is literally in their own hands. Women experience menarche, a sometimes physically and emotionally painful event that recurs every month or so regardless of an individual's desires. (This is one reason why some women were excited to hear that the contraceptive pill Alesse could be used to skip periods altogether.) Although little girls often rub themselves (not necessarily masturbating) prior to menarche, for young women, genitalia can become associated with pain, discomfort, blood, and reproduction—not with pleasure or sexuality. Indeed, men have more positive perceptions of their genitals and their partners' genitals (Reinholtz and Muehlenhard, 1995).[22]

What are the implications for men's and women's adult experiences of pleasure and orgasm? Are there special consequences for heterosexually oriented men and women? Does it matter that women tend to learn about their bodies and orgasm from partners, while men tend to have more diverse pathways to pleasure? What about the route to masturbation in the first place? How does gendered sexual socialization affect the ways in which we are sexual, the forms and formats of sex, and the way we see ourselves and develop sexual identities?

Having established some of the contours of cultural context, the importance of sex/gender, and the ways in which we begin to learn about sex, let's focus on one aspect of sexual behavior: fantasies—the most intrapsychic, "private" realm of sex. In this arena we continue learning about individual sexualities and the social context within which we develop. Be prepared to critically engage and think further about other forms of sex.

Sexual Fantasies: The Intrapsychic Realm

Sexual fantasies are an element that we touched upon briefly; it is safe to say that they are fundamental to masturbation. Given that fantasies are mental and internal, how can we define them and how do we study them? Fantasies are mental images of people (known or not), objects, or scenarios; the images can be entirely invented or inspired by an interaction, a memory, an experience, or some combination of these. Fantasies can be triggered by a fragrance, a feeling, or a glance from a stranger. The film *Unfaithful,* starring Diane Lane, has an excellent example of this. Constance remembers her rendezvous with her lover, vividly fantasizing while on the train after their first sexcapade. Later, she recalls their time together while she relaxes in the bathtub. Some people would love to have their fantasies come true while others have no desire to ever realize their fantasies. Sometimes, a memorable experience is combined with a hope or desire for a future experience, creating a collage of "real" and "unreal" sensations.

In terms of gender and desire, men seem to express theirs more than women do. In terms of thinking about sex, having sexual fantasies, and feeling sexually aroused, men score higher than women on frequency of and level, kind, and type of desires and thoughts. Men rate the strength of their desire (broadly defined) higher than do peer women (Baumeister, Catanese, and Vohs, 2001).[23] For women especially, in the Western world most of us believe that "being in love" goes hand in hand with feelings of sexual desire (Regan, Kocan, and Whitlock, 1998).[24] We have also been told that sexual desire is best and most appropriately felt only in the context of romantic, committed love. This can be contradictory and confusing for women who may feel desire or have fantasies involving people with whom they are not in committed relationships (see chapter 6 for more). In terms of actual activity, men outperform women. Behavior for heterosexually oriented people seems to involve behavioral compromises, with men tending to have less sexual contact than they might desire. In one study comparing straight married couples, straight cohabitors, gay couples, and lesbian couples, lesbians tended to have the lowest amount of sexual activity (Blumstein and Schwartz, 1983).[25] Men masturbate more (e.g., Smith et al., 1995) and consume more sexually explicit materials, along with paying for more sexual services (e.g. Monto, 2001).[26]

These differences in sexual interest and activities reveal themselves in the intrapsychic, where we script fantasies from our hopes and memories. Some fantasies have a lot of sensual depth, with sights, smells, sounds, and tastes that the fantasizer could explain to someone in a story form. Some fantasies have a lot of sexual depth, with very clear, singular images of positions, actions, and partners. It is a rich area for study, including a wide range of activities, partners, settings, feelings, and interpretations. Most men and women do fantasize during heterosexual, partnered sex, according to a research review by psychologists Harold Leitenberg and Kris Henning (1995).[27]

But how can scholars possibly study something that is so completely self-contained and internal (unless a person decides to divulge the details)? With Michael Kimmel, I studied the sociological nature of sexual fantasies (2002).[28] We were interested in gender, of course, and how, precisely, people expressed their mental images and sensations. What words did they use? How did they describe the setting, participants, actions, and feelings? What inferences could we draw from men's and women's expressions of their desires, especially heterosexually active men and women? Before we could answer these questions, though, we had to look at existing studies and theories about fantasies.

Research on Gender in Fantasies

Contrary to Freudian-era studies of sexuality, researchers believe fantasy is a "normal" component of sexual experience (Masters and Johnson, 1966, 1970; Kaplan, 1974).[29] Sexual fantasies have developed a role in sexual research, inspiring psychologists David Chick and Steven Gold to write,

> Sexual fantasy is hypothesized to have links to the cognitive, affective, and behavioral systems as erotic fantasies can contain factual information, affective reactions, and lead to overt responses. Sexual fantasies can also serve as the stimulus leading to physiological arousal, the subsequent cognitive and

affective. In short sexual fantasies may be the driving force for human sexuality (1987–1988: 62).[30]

It is a big claim to make—that fantasies are "the driving force" of sex. Chick and Gold are saying that they may be the underlying impetus for sex, the "motion" in the proverbial "ocean." Certainly, without fantasies and imagery, it seems unlikely that much else could happen sexually. Some researchers go as far as claiming that sexual fantasy "provides a clearer picture of male and female sexual natures than does the study of sexual action" (Ellis and Symons, 1990: 551).[31] "Sexual action" essentially refers to shared activities, partnered conduct. Ellis and Symons are suggesting that fantasy might be a more direct way to understand men and women as individuals. Partnered sexuality does involve the potential, and often the reality, of compromises, adjustments, and changes. Fantasies, by definition, are exactly and precisely tailored to the fantasizer's wishes. But Ellis and Symons also use a key concept—"male and female sexual natures"—in advancing an analysis rooted in evolutionary psychology. The idea is that fantasies reveal something about the essential character (and differences) of "males and females."

Arguments about gender and biological sex differences are central to fantasies research. Freud understood the centrality of fantasy to individual sexualities when he wrote that "the motive forces of phantasies are unsatisfied wishes . . . [and further] these motivating wishes vary according to . . . sex" (Freud, [1949]1975: 146).[32] Other researchers have explored fantasies during partnered sexual activity, during masturbation, and during solo sex (masturbation) and have consistently found gender differences. Kinsey et al. (1953) found that women's masturbation fantasies were similar to actual sexual behaviors, e.g., women who were coitally inactive rarely had fantasies of intercourse. Men's fantasies were less dependent on their actual experiences, instead relating as much to desired future experiences or taboos (Kinsey, Pomeroy, and Martin, 1948). More recent research confirms that gender differences persist. Men's fantasies detail many more sexual activities and more visual content than do women's (Follingstad and Kimbrell, 1986).[33]

Men tend to pay more attention to the minutiae of partners' physical appearance and are far more likely to include multiple and/or anonymous partners (Barclay, 1973; Iwawaki and Wilson, 1983; Knafo and Jaffe, 1984).[34] By contrast, women's sexual fantasies are more likely to contain familiar partners and to include descriptions of context, setting, and feelings associated with the sexual encounter (Barclay, 1973). Women are more likely to be *emotionally* aroused by their fantasies, which contain more themes of affection and commitment than do men's (Zurbriggen and Yost, 2004).[35] Men's sexual fantasies tend to be "more ubiquitous, frequent, visual, specifically sexual, promiscuous, and active." Women's sexual fantasies tend to be more "contextual, emotive, intimate, and passive" (Ellis and Symons, 1990: 529). One could say that women's fantasies are feminized while men's are masculinized, and that each can use the fantasy realm to confirm gender identity (Chick and Gold, 1987–1988).

Women are more likely to imagine themselves as the recipients of sexual activities from fantasized partners, while men are more likely to imagine themselves as sexual actors and their imagined partners as the recipients of sexual activities (Barclay, 1973; Mednick, 1977; Iwawaki and Wilson, 1983; Knafo and Jaffe, 1984).[36] More recent research revealed that, in written fantasies, heterosexually active men mentioned their own desire and the desire of their partners, while heterosexually active women tended to mention only their own desire and pleasure (Zurbriggen and Yost, 2004).

Thinking Critically

That was a relatively exhaustive list of differences. But what key questions arise from this information and evidence? First, what does it mean that there are so many differences, and that they seem so consistent over the last 25 years or so? What might explain that? Second, what *difference* does it make that men's and women's fantasies are so different? What are the implications? Other scholars pose other relevant questions:

> One of the central questions regarding fantasy concerns its relationship to attitudes and behaviors. Is fantasy distinct from reality, with what one imagines completely unrelated to what one actually does? Or are there connections between the frequency or content of fantasies and real-world behaviors and relevant attitudes? (Zurbriggen and Yost, 2004).

Indeed, the connection between fantasy and reality is a valid one, especially if we reconsider the intrapsychic level in sexual script theory. We invoke the distinction between fantasy and reality in other kinds of discussions, such as referring to life after college as "the real world" and disparaging people by saying they are "in fantasy land." Let's address all these questions by focusing on issues in data collection; "deviance"; explanations for gendered differences; and gender in heterosexual fantasies.

Issues in Data Collection

Fantasies studies have primarily been divided between research in which respondents answered a questionnaire (e.g., Mednick, 1977; Knafo and Jaffe, 1984; Ellis and Symons, 1990) or were presented with a "fantasy checklist" and asked how many or how often various items appeared in their own fantasies (Wilson and Lang, 1981; Iwawaki and Wilson, 1983; Knafo and Jaffe, 1984).[37] Virtually all research uses the terms "male" and "female" instead of "men's" and "women's" to describe the genders' fantasies. Mednick (1977) combined respondent-generated fantasies with a "Sexual Fantasy Questionnaire" and found that men were much more likely than women to imagine themselves as the sexual initiators. Women fantasized themselves as "the recipients of sexual activity from fantasized sexual objects." In other studies, respondents were given sexual fantasies to read and then were measured for levels of arousal, either by self-reporting or by measuring blood flow to the genitals (Stock and Geer, 1982; Follingstad and Kimbrell, 1986).[38] Follingstad and Kimbrell had women read 112 fantasies, rate how arousing they were, and then report how often *they* had had such fantasies in the past year.

Such methods could skew or bias the data. By providing the answers and asking how many of these scenes had been fantasized, the respondents' answers were limited to the choices on the questionnaire. If they had had fantasies that fell outside the list, they were unable to code them, and respondents who were unable (or unwilling) to think of one of their own fantasies could have had one suggested by the list. Such methods also tend to minimize affective, or feeling/emotional dimensions of fantasy and maximize overt conduct, by primarily asking about activities and orgasms (outlets). Reducing such a complex intrapsychic activity to a simplified checklist does not really add to our knowledge of how individuals really imagine, remember, and create mental representations of sex and relationships.

Several studies have attempted to address these limitations by asking respondents to write their own fantasies, either once or over time, in a "diary," recording fantasies during, say, two weeks or over the course of a month (Leitenberg and Henning, 1995; Dubois, 1997; Zurbriggen and Yost, 2004).[39] In one study, respondents were instructed to write about the most recent or favorite fantasy, in as specific detail as possible (Zurbriggen and Yost, 2004). Psychologist Stephanie Dubois instructed respondents to "Narratively describe, in as specific, comprehensive, and complete detail as possible, a sexual fantasy you like most." The benefit to asking respondents to write fantasies is that more than just themes or partner choices can be examined. Handwritten fantasies contain words, language, slang, nuance; scene-setting and details; sexual activities and images; and hints of romantic, affective, and emotional content.

There are also problems with this approach—most obviously the *respondent bias* discussed in chapter 2. A respondent may be too self-conscious about his favorite fantasy, worry that he may be judged for it, and elect to provide a "clean" version. Or she may think she knows what the researcher is studying and either try to provide him with a fantasy that will help the research *or* try to throw off his results by providing something "kinky" or beyond the pale. In the data collection for my study with Michael Kimmel (2002), respondents wrote things like, "I'm sure you wouldn't be interested in mine. They're just really simple, about me and my boyfriend." More than one woman in our study presumed that her thoughts were not interesting or kinky enough and self-censored, trying to guess at what we, the researchers, wanted to hear. Another fantasy was about me (!) at first, and then the respondent changed gears, writing, "But you wanted to hear about a favorite, and that one I just made up when you walked in, so . . . "

The other rather glaring flaw of almost all fantasy research is *who* is studied—the sample. Nearly all the cited research utilized college student populations, and most of the students were drawn from psychology subject pools or were given psychology course credit for participation. Kimmel and I were able to gather students from other kinds of classes, from multiple universities, and with some racial/ethnic diversity in the sample. But generally, what we know about gender differences in fantasies is actually gender differences in the intrapsychic imaginations of 18- to 22-year-old, middle-class Caucasian American college students. Additionally, many of the studies, ours included, are gender-skewed—more women than men enroll in college now, and psychology majors are more likely to be women. To their credit, Zurbriggen and Yost gathered a community sample of 85 men and 77 women, aged 21 to 45, for their study of themes of dominance and pleasure in written fantasies. In fantasy research off-campus, work like journalist Nancy Friday's *My Secret Garden* (1973) and *Men in Love* (1980), respondent and sampling bias are also germane.[40] These books collected fantasies of hundreds of American men and women who saw Friday's advertisements and solicitations and mailed their fantasies. In fact, these kinds of books made it difficult for social scientists to justify research on fantasies. The attitude was that the topic had been covered in a titillating way (assuming that people read books like Friday's solely for arousal), rendering them "too silly" for academic inquiries.

We know very little about men and women of color, anyone outside the middle class, and little (from a scholarly perspective) about anyone over age 22. A scholar of American Studies, Tricia Rose, interviewed African American women (2003) from around the United States, asking about sexuality, intimacy, and relationships.[41] Not everyone talked about fantasies, but those who did said things like, "I don't have fantasies—I actually did it [instead]" (2003: 166) or described fantasies of love, intimacies, and memories similar to those of white student women. Independent of race and ethnicity, we know that as people have diverse sexual experiences, their fantasies seem to expand and change. For a heterosexual guy of 14, the most exciting thing in the world might be the thought of a breast, or two, up close and personal. Once that particular event has occurred 10, 50, or 200 times, he might expand his range of fantasy material. So it would be worthwhile to have more scholarship on fantasies throughout the life course, for more diverse citizens, and for people with diverse sexualities.

Going beyond Heterosexualities

The studies cited above tend to separate fantasies according to respondent sexual orientation, ultimately focusing only on fantasies describing "heterosexual" fantasy content. Note that this includes cases of a man fantasizing about multiple women sexually involved with both him and each other. But a man fantasizing about himself with multiple men would be discarded from the study. The only time that sexual orientation is overtly acknowledged is in studies of same-sex orientation/identity development, when respondents are asked to recall their first arousing or sexual thoughts of others of the same sex. In that context, researchers are looking at adolescent and teenaged fantasies for clues, like crime scene investigators, hoping to decipher a path to sexual identity (e.g., Lehne, 1978; Billingham and Hockenberry, 1987).[42] The fantasies of self-identified gay, lesbian, bisexual people—or anyone else who is not heterosexual—are really not examined simply as narratives of sexual imagination, sensual details, and intrapsychic desires.

There is a subset of studies that I have not addressed yet, those focused on people involved in criminal, socially unacceptable, and controversial sexual behaviors (see Leitenberg and Henning, 1995; Dean and Malamuth, 1997).[43] Researchers studying adults who are sexually interested in children (a condition commonly called *pedophilia*) and the sexualities of those convicted of rape often explore sexual fantasies in this context. The key questions in these studies relate to fantasizing and the commission of crime(s)—what were the fantasies? Did the accused/convicted person fantasize about the sex implicated in the crime? Is there a link between fantasies and realities? Although research on college students does not tend to assume a given or direct relationship between fantasies and actual sex lives, much of the literature on "deviant fantasies" assumes that to think about something is akin to acting it out. Can we call a fantasy "deviant" even if the events never actually get brought to light—if the fantasy never becomes real (Leitenberg and Henning,

1995)? The criminal offender populations that seem to show the largest connection between fantasizing and then committing crimes are chronic child sex abusers, rapists who also have sadistic qualities (i.e., also torturing or physically abusing), and those who expose their genitalia in public.

What Explains Gender Differences?

We want to shed some light on the question I posed earlier, "What does it mean that there are so many differences, and that they seem so consistent over the last 25 years or so?" The forms of explanation differ depending on *who* is attempting to explain, of course. Evolutionary psychologists like Ellis and Symons (1990) would say that the differences reflect hard-wired reproductive strategies. Heterosexual women would therefore desire sex in the context of a committed relationship with one man, in hopes that he would then be a good provider and father. Heterosexual men would desire a lot of sex with a United Nations–inspired array of women, in hopes of maximizing the "spread" of his genes. For Ellis and Symons, it is predictable and logical to see women fantasizing about known partners, not strangers, and prioritizing love and romance. That men are far more likely to fantasize about multiple partners, strangers, and taboo experiences is also predictable and logical.

In order for this to really be the cause of and explanation for gender differences, we would need to completely disregard any fantasies depicting same-sex activities (regardless of the fantasizer's sexual orientation). Heterosexually identified people do imagine themselves in scenarios with people of the same sex, and these fantasies may have little to no bearing on lived experiences or "real world" desires. It would also help to have global, comparative data on fantasies. If our sexual and sensual imaginations are the result of hard-wiring and thousands of years of evolution, then we would expect to see the same results in the world's cultures.

Social psychologists, sociologists, and feminist scholars would explain gender differences with a different point of view. The differences that we observe are attributable to social, cultural, and historical factors. Women have typically been constructed as the *objects* of men's desires, where their sexuality is dependent on being viewed as sexy, desirable, and "do-able." How might this affect the way women fantasize?

Gender in Heterosexual Fantasies

Let's focus on the study I did with Michael Kimmel. Our research differed from others because of the method used and our distinctly sociological interpretation. Similarly to other studies, we had a sex-skewed college sample of 340 respondents (249 women and 91 men). We asked respondents to write the sexual fantasy that they *consistently* found arousing—the one they thought about most often. We did not specify what kind of fantasies we wanted, so respondents may ultimately have provided masturbatory or coital fantasies, or daydreams. Content could involve any partners, same-sex or other. The open-ended response format enabled us to obtain fantasies expressed in the language, tone, and descriptive depth that each respondent chose. The only independent variable we requested was sex. Respondents were assured of the anonymity and confidentiality of their responses. If respondents did not wish to participate for any reason, we asked them to state that; some did so and explained why. These were collected along with the fantasies. In all, 9 men and 46 women did not wish to participate. We were looking at four primary dimensions of the written fantasies:

1. narrative description: the use of language, linguistic explicitness vs. vagueness, use of slang
2. emotional description: relationship of affective behaviors to sexual behaviors, explicitness of emotional/intimate feelings
3. sensual imagery: scene setting, use of props, level of nonsexual detail, geographical and temporal settings
4. sexual imagery: elaborateness, specificity, and vagueness of sexual activities

Based on what we knew from prior research, we had some expectations of what we might find. In men's fantasies, we expected to find:

- more explicit discussion of sexual conduct
- more slang for activities and genitalia
- little connection between partner choice and feelings
- vague or nonexistent emotional content
- little sensual imagery and romance
- diverse sexual imaginations

In women's fantasies, we expected to find:

- vague or nonexistent descriptions of sexual conduct
- more formal terminology, when used, for activities and genitalia
- detailed emotional connections with partners
- rich sensual imagery and romantic content
- narrow or minimal sexual imagination

So how did it end up? Of course we saw differences, which is the least interesting finding, really. More intriguing are the contours of the differences—what was written, how it was said, the feelings and actions described.

What Is Said and How It's Said

Narrative strategies differed significantly between women and men. Take, for example, these fantasies:

"Menage-a-trois."
"2 hot babes and myself going at it."
"To have sex [crossed out, with "make love" substituted] with an older woman 10 or so years older."
"Have sex on the beach."

These are not excerpts from fantasies—they are the entire fantasies! Overall, we found that men's fantasies were shorter than women's, word for word, largely due to the amount of emotional and sensual scenery women tended to provide. Notice that we have no idea who the hot babes are, who is having sex on the beach, or where the threesome occurs (hopefully somewhere they can spread out). We also learned a lot of new slang from the men in the sample. Though men and women both used words you would expect, like *make love, have intercourse, have sex, do it,* and the always-popular *fuck,* men were just a bit more creative than women. Men's terms included: *going at it, having her way with me, sexual encounter, sexual acts, sleep with, knocks my socks off, collect my banks, involve myself, have, perform, beautiful event, inflict extreme pleasure on* (my personal favorite), *knocking boots, satisfying them, penetration, thrusting.* Women's terms were softer, more euphemistic and indirect: *get intimate, doing his dishes, jumping him, have me, be together, become one, impalement, sexual experience/situation, rolling and thrusting, it goes from there, you can guess the rest, pelvic thrust, inside me.* Men's descriptions of sexual activities were direct:

"The women would wipe my cum all over themselves and lick it off one another."
"She says, 'Put your cock in my ass.'"
"I'll be more interest[ed] if she started playing with those beautiful tits she has & starts fingering herself."
"She falls down, slowly landing directly on my penis, moving in a motion I have never witnessed before. She makes me have orgasms I never had before."

Women tended to be more evasive and vague:

"We do not make love genitally, but whole bodily."
"We begin to have intercourse."
"One thing leads to another."
"Use your imagination."
"Having my partner soap and massage my body, then carrying me into the bedroom . . . and then holding each other all night long."

It is hard to know whether women were picturing or imagining the things they omitted. Were the specifics and details clear to our respondents though they wrote in such euphemistic ways? Or were the intrapsychic images similarly vague? We do know that the emotional details of men's and women's fantasies differed. On this dimension, women were much more clear about exactly who their partners were.

The Who (to "Do It" with) and the How (to Feel about "It")

Women were far more likely to specify that the fantasy partner was a significant other, and typically used the words "boyfriend" or "husband." Women described opposite sex partners whom they called "Mr. Right," the "man of my dreams," and "wonderful in every way." Men were more likely to specify that their fantasies involved a famous person (generally models, singers, or actresses), a taboo partner (e.g., teacher, employer), or multiple partners. Typical women's fantasies were:

"He would hold me close and cater to my every need. He would treat me like a princess."
"I want this to be my honeymoon. I want this to be the first time that I make love."
"Finally he comes right out and says really sensitively and emotionally how he needs me as more than a friend and we get into this huge fight and then he suddenly pins me against the wall, and starts kissing me and then stops and says he's sorry but he couldn't help it."

Women's fantasies narrated love stories with affection, intimacy, and romance. Men's fantasies were less likely to be so richly emotional or romantic. A few men's fantasies included gender-transgressive storylines, where the man described a loving, committed relationship with a significant other or "the woman of [his] dreams."

Gender-transgressive tales written by women included sexually active, ardent, assertive women, searching for multiple partners, multiple orgasms, moods and contexts for sexual expression.

We noted interesting connections between who the fantasy partner was and whether they were described physically. When a respondent elaborated on the physical attributes of the fantasy partner, they included less emotional and romantic content. Men were much more likely to mention the appearance of the partner(s) and specifically describe the partner(s). This may be due to the partner choice. Since men were less likely to fantasize about a significant other, spouse, or lover, they may have felt more compelled to specify the distinct "pieces and parts" of the fantasy partner. Men were far more likely than women to fantasize about multiple partners, at a statistically significant level (41 percent vs. 9 percent). Men also learn, via socialization, to link their sexual attraction to specific parts or attributes—"I'm a leg man" or "I'm a butt man" are common expressions. By contrast, have you ever heard a heterosexual woman say, "I'm a penis woman"? So men's fantasies included explicit physical characteristics:

"They must be thin with nice bubble asses and medium, upturned breasts (with nipples like pencil erasers)."

"Elle McPherson type, gorgeous looking, hot woman, straight long hair, with lots of great hot looking clothes on."

"These women are of course slim, trim & tan and obviously incredibly sexy."

". . . entire Swedish bikini team—big breasts, blond, unbelievably curvy asses."

"One of the women would be blonde, the other dark haired, about 5'7"—5'10", knock-out bodies."

Women's fantasies were a bit more general:

"I'm out on a date with a nicely built man . . . "

"tall, built, and unbelievably gorgeous . . . "

"really good looking."

"Someone so gorgeous I have to have him."

Men described exactly what their female partners looked like, and even mentioned celebrities as visual templates for their affinities, in case the reader was unclear about exactly how gorgeous or firm the fantasy partner should be. Women simply conveyed that their male partners were attractive and fit.

Setting the Scene: Where, When, and How "It" Should Happen

Descriptions of fantasy location were more common among women, who described the moment with rich "sensual props." In longer fantasies, women's *sensual* descriptions were more elaborate, while men's *sexual* descriptions were more elaborate. Women tended to emphasize romantic and aesthetic elements. Some of their fantasies include very detailed settings, with colors, textures, and fabrics . . . but no mention of anything sexual! More often than expected, men did tell us where their fantasies were taking place, but *rarely* with the extensive description found in women's fantasies. About 64 percent of the men specified some location, while about 74 percent of the women did so. But this surface statistical similarity does not fully reveal the divergence in scene setting. While many men mentioned that their fantasies occurred near water or on a beach, this was all they said. Most women not only mentioned the place, but also things like the air and water temperature, the ocean surrounding the fantasy island, the number of other people in the area (if any), and a variety of sensual props (e.g., dinner, a picnic, wine, rain). Men offered these descriptions of the fantasy setting:

"If I had to pick a location, I guess I would choose a place a little out of the ordinary."

"My sexual fantasy involves being on an island with only sexually attractive and available females."

"I like to think of dogs barking and being in an industrial setting, during love-making that is. Fear and discomfort are integral parts of my fantasy."

"As far as the setting goes it makes no difference, only important factor is that we are both with her at the same time."

Women offered lush, sensual settings straight out of Hollywood, in effect:

". . . A tropical island. I've always dreamed about making love in a crystal blue sea, with a waterfall in the background, then moving on shore to a white, sandy beach."

"It's evening time, the sun is setting, I'm on a tropical island, a light breeze is blowing into my balcony doors and the curtains (white) are fluttering lightly in the wind. The room is spacious and there is white everywhere, even the bed. There are flowers of all kinds and the light fragrance fills the room."

"The room would be filled with candles and soft music would fill the air, he would feed me strawberries, which we'd share, and in the morning we'd wake, bathe one another, and . . . ”

"We are out in the country. There is no one for miles around. There is an open yard in the back of the house surrounded by woods. All we can hear is the chirping of birds and the rustling of leaves. It is raining. Not a monsoon, not a drizzle, but a warm summer afternoon shower. There is a big, beautiful, white gazebo in the middle of the yard."

Although women seemed to have more elaborate sensual imaginations than men, we noted that many women skimped on the sexual details.

So What Really Happens . . . ?

When it came to the actual "sex" part of these sexual fantasies, men really got their swerve on, so to speak. Women may have more highly developed sensual imaginations, but men have more highly developed sexual imaginations. Men were more likely to mention intercourse, giving/getting fellatio, masturbatory activities, lesbian activities, and "woman as aggressor"—the woman making the first move and/or orchestrating the encounter. Women were more likely to mention "man as aggressor." We got the sense that men felt empowered enough to play with sex via their creative, nuanced use of language. Women's language was more proper, in effect, more restrained. At the conclusion of the average woman's fantasy, a reader has little idea of exactly what transpired. She might say they "made love," but it is unclear whether there was oral sex of any kind, who caressed whom, whether each coupling was punctuated by his orgasm, whether they changed positions. We were left thinking that if the specifics of heterosex were left solely up to women, there certainly would be a lot of romantic picnics on the beach (in the rain) culminating in . . . (something—perhaps a nap, but maybe nothing sexual!). Men's descriptions of sex were clear and explicitly sexual:

"The fantasy reaches a second high point during the longest and most powerful orgasm/ejaculation ever."

"Totally uninhibited sexual activity."

"All out, no holds barred, continuous sex with someone who obviously knows what she's doing."

"Her voice will be sincere, yet playful. She will suggest that I take a good look at her breasts. In her attitude I would find no inhibitions whatsoever."

Women wrote things like:

"He tells me I mean more to him than anything else in the world and that he's never been happier in his entire life. . . . I then look into his gorgeous eyes and say—'I do want this more than anything in the world—I love you.'"

". . . It's our secret, not even knowing each others' name. Like a mystery, and I'll never see him again."

"He'd get so excited that he wouldn't be able to control himself and he would grab me and make passionate love to me."

"Have my ideal man & myself together for the whole day. While we are together, we would play sports and then go home & take a shower together. Have no one else to bother us from the outside world and have it feel like eternity and never wanting to leave."

Men envisioned sexual moments of wild abandon, no inhibitions, with sexually inventive, assertive women. Women *rarely* imagined themselves as sexual actors, more so as subjects or the objects of men's desires. There was an obvious discrepancy between how much men imagined women as sexual actors and how much women saw themselves that way.

I should note that we did get fantasies that described same-sex encounters. We could not see any differences within men and women based on the sex of the fantasy partner. When women wrote about female partners, the fantasies were sensually rich, clear about the setting and the fact that the partner was someone special, and vague and euphemistic about anything overtly sexual. When men wrote about male partners, they were sexually imaginative, savvy with slang, and clear about who did what to whom and in what order. So it seemed that gender trumped sexual orientation.

Fantasies are different based on gender—you get that by now. So what? What difference does it make that these fantasies diverge on so many levels? Aren't fantasies often kept private anyway, not shared and not acted on or acted out? Earlier, I quoted Zurbriggen and Yost: "More recent research revealed that, in written fantasies, heterosexually-active men mentioned their own desire and the desire and pleasure of their partners, while heterosexually-active women tended to mention only their own desire and pleasure" (2004). If you are a heterosexually interested man, you may not have wanted to read this again. What does this suggest about heterosexual women? Does this finding mean that women are selfish, at least in the coziness of their own minds?

This may be explained not by innate selfishness but by the ways that sexual scripts take root in individuals at the intrapsychic, mental level. This gets at the question of how "society" gets inside us—how do we come to believe and reproduce broader cultural messages and socialization? Let me argue that by the time we get to the point of having sexual fantasies (late childhood)—and then reproducing them for academic studies—we are well aware of sociocultural gender and sexuality scripts. The socialization that we explored in chapter 4 is suggestive of how we slowly and incrementally learn, via interactions with parents, peers, teachers, and larger social institutions. By the time women and men are divulging their fantasies for researchers to analyze, respondents already know what our cultural blueprints are.

Both women and men fantasized themselves as sexually irresistible objects of desire, and both fantasized themselves as the recipients of sexual activities. But women were more passive when describing penile-vaginal intercourse—they wrote about things being done to them, about being on the receiving end (like philosopher Robert Baker suggested in chapter 1). Men used more active language, even when fantasizing themselves as the recipients of these activities, like being tied up! Even when outnumbered, as in multiple partner fantasies, men still used language depicting themselves as active, assertive partners.

In heterosexual conduct, men and women often interpret the same behaviors from different sides of a power equation. In our study, men seemed to experience both fellatio and cunnilingus as expressions of power—"I'm so powerful that I get her to suck me," and "When I go down on her I'm in complete control and make her come"—regardless of whether the man was "actually" active or passive, giving or receiving. Symmetrically, women described both fellatio and cunnilingus as expressions of their *lack* of power—"He forces my mouth onto his penis," and "He goes down on me and I'm helpless"—regardless of whether the woman was "actually" passive or active. Tellingly, only 4 percent of women clearly described themselves as the initiators in their fantasies, while 21 percent of men described women as initiators. Perhaps measures of activity and passivity may more accurately be cast as measures of interpersonal sexual power.

Socialization is powerful enough to subtly seep into what we think are the most intimate, private, and individual aspects of ourselves. All of this may explain Zerbriggen and Yost's finding that women did not write about male partners' pleasure and desire. To fantasize about men's pleasure would be a rather big leap given what women have been taught about sex—the goal is to be sexy, desirable, alluring. In short, be or become the object of *others'* desires.

Since our social structures also have inequities built in, we would expect to see these inequities reproduced in even the most intimate realms of individuals—the intrapsychic level. Structural gender inequalities have consequences. By casting themselves as the objects of desire, with less apparent sexual agency, heterosexual women may ultimately be less able to express sexual desires in social interactions. Meanwhile men, who cast themselves as sexual actors, filled with sexual agency, may ultimately enact a wider range of sexual behaviors without quandaries. If we connect this with the discussion of menarche, semenarche, and masturbation, we can start seeing the thread, the bread crumb trail that connects adolescence with young adulthood. We can start to see how socialization and early lessons about our bodies have subsequent effects on how we think about sex, even to the seemingly individual level of our fantasies. Kimmel and I observed that the fantasies even referenced the basic progression of the sexual script (going around the bases, discussed in chapter 2), namely kissing and touching, then oral sex, then PVI. Often this progression was merely hinted at when women wrote "guess the rest." Recall that Zurbriggen and Yost (2004) asked whether there are "connections between the frequency or content of fantasies and real-world behaviors and relevant attitudes." One way to explore this is to examine the real-world behavior of heterosexual "hooking up."

Questions to Ponder

1. Imagine a culture with no television, no printed or visual pornography, no Hollywood movies, and no magazines. What kind of sexual fantasies would the citizens of this culture have? Would they have any? Explain your logic.

2. How can men and women learn to be comfortable with their bodies? Is there a connection between acceptance of one's body and their sexuality?

3. What could be done to equalize the way that men and women approach masturbation? Is it really true that people can learn about their sexualities through masturbation?

Suggested Projects

1. Do your own fantasies research. Ask people to write "their old standby, the one that always does the trick." Analyze themes, patterns, and trends. How do your results compare to those described here? If you were so inclined, you could tabulate your findings quantitatively as well, doing a simple content analysis to indicate how many times various fantasy elements (e.g., language, activities, and settings) appear.

2. Look for references to masturbation in pop culture—in films and novels, on television, and in magazines. Do a simple content analysis. How is masturbation described? How is humor used? What kinds of emotions are mentioned in connection to masturbation (e.g., guilt, pleasure, shame, embarrassment, arousal, and so on)? What assumptions are made about masturbation?

3. Go to a drugstore and head for the hygiene row. How are menstrual and related products displayed? Compare this to the way that products for "jock itch" are displayed.

6

Hooking It Up

SEX IN THE BEDROOM

Chances are that you know a lot more about *hooking up* than I do. Researchers are definitely on the slow end of the learning curve here, and few studies have explored what hooking up means to people between 15 and 39. It is difficult to even define the concept because people tend to have at least slightly different definitions. If we asked 25 people what "hooking up" means, we would be likely to hear 22 distinctly different ideas. Consider the following exchange from an online message forum for teen women (typographical and spelling errors are original):[1]

> *citrusfancy*
> **Hooking up. What's your definition?**
> Posted: Oct 13, 2003 9:32 PM
> What is your definition of "hooking up." Does it mean having sex, fooling around, or like starting a relationship? I'm a little confused about this, so could someone please help? I like this guy and one of his friends told me I should hook up with him, but I want to know what i'm getting into.
> Thanks.

> *_lady_temper*
> **Re: Hooking up. What's your definition?**
> Posted: Oct 13, 2003 9:36 PM in response to: citrusfancy

Reply
hooking up is when you start a relationship and talk to him
example: hook me up with your number = giving the guy or girl your number

china3
Re: Hooking up. What's your definition?
Posted: Oct 13, 2003 9:44 PM in response to: citrusfancy
Reply
um *cough* that's funy. hooking up is basically when you make out iwht osmeone you don't really know at a party. from there you might start a relationship or you might not. so it's basically a fling.

citrusfancy
Re: Hooking up. What's your definition?
Posted: Oct 13, 2003 9:50 PM in response to: china3
Reply
See, that's funny. I'm getting totally oppostie answers. Would anyone else like to give me their opinion?

amandadanielle2008
Re: Hooking up. What's your definition?
Posted: Oct 13, 2003 10:05 PM in response to: citrusfancy
Reply
i agree with ladytemper

Combining brainstorming, logic, and a process of elimination, I will try to clarify how I am using the term. Hooking up is *not*: dating, going steady (in the 1950s and 1960s usage), having a boyfriend or girlfriend, being engaged to be married. Hooking up *may* be any of the following: committed, casual, regular, habitual, a fling of brief duration, emotionally intense, physically intense, sporadic, irregular, intoxicating, drunken, late night/early morning, embarrassing, a point of pride.

Synonymous terms might include: being "involved," one night stand, having/being a fuckbuddy, friends with benefits/privileges, booty calls (which may involve drunk dialing), getting lucky, scoring. Potential elements of hooking up include: making out, snogging, relatively unrestrained groping, various tricks with hands and tongues, nudity, oral and anal exploits, and of course, PVI (perhaps even in this order!). Regardless of your own experiences, you are likely to be familiar with this concept in its multifaceted complexity, given your environment. A feature article in the Swarthmore College newspaper highlights the confusion over definitions (Dunn, 2004):[2]

> This fall, Bella Liu '07 found herself laughing and embarrassed after she stumbled into tricky linguistic territory. Her mistake: failing to agree on a definition of the term "hooking up."
>
> "I was talking to another freshman I had been getting to know during the first month or so of school, and she mentioned that she had hooked up with the guy she was currently dating during orientation," Liu said. "It kind of surprised me that she'd slept with someone she'd only known for four days, and I didn't judge, but I did make some assumptions about her attitude towards sex and all that."
>
> The girl told Liu she had encountered a much more casual attitude toward sex at Swarthmore than at her high school.
>
> "'Yeah, I mean, you slept with your boyfriend after being here four days?'" Liu said she responded. "She just looked horrified and then started laughing. All she'd meant was that they'd kissed once or twice during orientation. She still makes fun of me for that."

Many people appear to start college with some familiarity with hooking up, whether via their own or through friends. Analyses of national, random, representative samples of adolescents suggest that about 23 percent of girls have significant sexual experiences with people who were "just friends," whom they had just met, or whom they had gone out with "once in a while" (Manning, Longmore, and Giordano, 2000).[3]

"Ambiguity is key to hooking up," write journalists Andrea Lavinthal and Jessica Rozler (2005: 3).[4] The concept is not meant to be clarified, just as each potential hookup is meant to bring with it a sense of infinite possibility—will it be kissing? Oral sex? Rolling around in bed? Intercourse? Will it ever happen again? Will it be fun and worthwhile? Will someone develop more romantic feelings? Will it become something more? If we think logically, it is not really surprising that ambiguity is appealing. Think back to the discussion of sexual slang and language (chapter 1). Ambiguity and euphemism are hallmarks of the first way in which we learn to communicate about sex—via words. Slang represents the diversity and playfulness that can be associated with sex, and we see this in the breadth of definitions for *hooking up*. We also have broader cultural narratives that argue for the spontaneity of sex, that sex is best seen as "mysterious" or something "magical" (Kleinplatz, 1992).[5] So the ambiguity of "hooking up," evident in its shifty definitions, seemingly spontaneous (non)planning, and its adherence to cultural scripting, is fundamental. But apparently the ambiguity of hooking up is not quite "natural":

> Who knew it could be so complicated? After all, the word "casual" carries with it an implication of carelessness and simplicity—but perhaps that's where the problems begin. As much as no-strings-attached action may be a spur of the moment experience, we've come to realize that being careless can make casual sex a lot less fun for a girl, both physically and emotionally (Sherman and Tocantins, 2004: ix).[6]

There are three heterosexual hook-up handbooks on the shelves of chain bookstores, all designed to give "the single girl" the new nonrules of how to (a) squeeze sex into a lifestyle too busy to include a boyfriend; (b) "get some" without risking emotions; (c) ensure that "a drunken kiss is entertainment for all of your friends" (Lavinthal and Rozler, 2005: 12). The books read like any other how-to sex manual on the bookshelf, except that each has a chapter for the reader to determine if she is "the casual sex type." One author admonishes women to forget about love, always use condoms, and "never put meat before mates" (Dubberley, 2005: 20).[7]

Dubberley discusses the myriad reasons why women tend to have "casual" sex and poses questions to ponder: Do you enjoy sex? Are you happy with your body? Do you want to? Are you underage? Are you chained to your phone waiting for his call? Do you fall in love with every guy you have sex with? Can you insist on safe sex no matter how drunk you are? If a guy doesn't cuddle, can you deal with it?

> But not everyone you have sex with will necessarily be affectionate. Deal with it. You got laid, didn't you? If you can't live without cuddles, get a dog. Sure, it needs walking and feeding, but it's way more likely to give you affection than some random guy you've pulled (2005: 7).

There are a lot of seemingly rational choices women seem to have to make in order to make hooking up worthwhile. The costs apparently should be outweighed by the simple benefit of "you got laid, didn't you?" For straight women, hooking up obviously requires some intrapsychic and interpersonal rescripting. For gay men, it is presented as an entirely different story. One how-to book promised its readers ways to have "hot sex":

You think you know how to get laid? Sure, gay men can have sex on demand—it's our defining stereotype! You're confident enough, hot enough, and sexy enough to hook up whenever and wherever the mood strikes you, right? Well, honey, I'm calling your bluff. You've played the field, made your conquests, and had one-night hookups—maybe even a regular fuckbuddy, a few threesomes, or an anonymous boy-bang at the local sex club. You're a walking, talking encyclopedia of homo sex info, and you don't need no stinking book to score. Right? (Bass, 2005).[8]

That is quite a departure from the books for straight women! Imagine if these words *were* directed to women . . . "an anonymous boy-bang at the local sex club." Or imagine this book for straight men (it should be a little less amusing in this context). . . ! Another how-to book for gay men advised that "trick sex" (i.e., hook-ups) is as ubiquitous as fast food—it is also that unnutritious (Brass, 1999).[9] It is worth noting that in the handful of how-to sex books for lesbians, hooking up was barely addressed. *The Lesbian Sex Book* (Caster, 2003) indicated that "casual sex can be warm, enjoyable, and hot" (p. 32).[10] An encyclopedia-style sex book had nothing in the index and no encyclopedic entries on "casual" sex, friends with benefits, or hooking up (Newman, 2004).[11] In the *On Our Backs Guide to Lesbian Sex* (Cage, 2004), a short chapter on "cruising the Web" included a woman saying, "Dykes like one night stands just as much as the next guy or girl. . . . One night I even scheduled two dates by accident and all three of us got lucky!" (p. 16).[12]

Now while it would be flattering for contemporary heterosexual students (and 20-somethings) to think that they had somehow invented a totally new mode of sexual interaction, it would be historically inaccurate as well. Sociologists Barbara Risman and Pepper Schwartz suggest that the "sexual revolution" of the late 1960s to early 1970s changed the current landscape. ". . . It has revised the entire framework of how American society thinks about sex. Premarital, unmarried, and post-divorce sex are now seen as individual choices for both women and men. The revolutionary principle that divorced the right to sexual pleasure from marriage (at least for adults) is no longer controversial" (Risman and Schwartz, 2002: 22).[13] Historical context gives us a bridge to contemporary practices, in effect answering the question of how we have gotten to the point where (apparently) the majority of college students are hooking up. But it is not necessarily a straight line from the late 1960s sexual revolution to the early 2000s "hook up revolution."

Every year for the last 33, the Higher Education Research Institute at the University of California at Los Angeles has surveyed entering college freshmen at two- and four-year schools. In the fall of 1998, of the 275,811 freshmen, only 51 percent believed that abortion should be legal, a decline from 65 percent at the start of the 1990s (Reisberg, 1999).[14] Only 40 percent of the freshmen indicated that "it's all right" for "two people who really like each other to have sex even if they've known each other for a very short time." This represented the smallest proportion of students agreeing with the statement over a 10-year period. Both findings, about abortion and "casual sex," imply that there is not necessarily a consensus on exactly how far our society should go in terms of "individual choices" about sex. Let's examine how much of hooking up is an individual choice and how much is contextualized by broader forces.

Um . . . So What!? Who Cares about Hooking Up? (or, Don't Ruin It by Studying It)

(A Brief Digression?)   So far I have quoted from an online teen bulletin board, a college newspaper, and three paperback guides to hooking up with style. Since I haven't yet discussed any academic research on hooking up, maybe it means that hooking up is just not worth studying. Let me answer the "so what?" question now, and we can retrace my analytical steps together. We want to explore this issue for several reasons. The most obvious is that it vividly highlights some gender issues. Hooking up also gives us an opportunity to see how subcultural and interpersonal scripting combine with the intrapsychic. Does "everyone" do it? How does it feel? What meaning do people give to the act of hooking up? And finally, looking at this aspect of sexuality enables us to place it all in a broader context, as *Newsweek* did recently:

> The early research confirms just how widespread the behavior has become. In 2000 [Dr. Elizabeth] Paul published what colleagues credit as the first academic article that explored college hookups in depth. Her survey of 555 undergrads found that 78 percent of students had hooked up, that they usually did so after consuming alcohol and that the average student had accumulated 10.8 hookup partners during college. Studies on other campuses produced similar numbers. Researchers at James Madison University found that 77.7 percent of women and 84.2 percent of men had hooked up, a process they said routinely involving "petting below the waist, oral sex or intercourse." At the University of Michigan, more than 60 percent of students reported hooking up; they said that a typical hookup more often included "genital touching" than "a meaningful conversation" (McGinn, 2004).[15]

Hello, casual sex—how nice to see you in the family-friendly news magazine, *Newsweek*, striking (moral) panic in the hearts of parents and teen health experts, all with amnesia about their own college years.

Remember that in chapter 1 I sketched out some things that contribute to our cultural, interpersonal, and individual sexual quandaries. *Newsweek*'s summary of relevant scholarly research nicely captures exactly what is confusing and contradictory about the current sexual landscape. The language the author uses reflects the problems of trying to discuss sexualities generally, and hooking up specifically:

- "usually did so after consuming alcohol"

How do scholars get information about sex? Generally, we ask people to honestly recall their experiences, whether in "diary" form or years or months later, on a questionnaire or in an interview (see chapter 2). If we want to understand something about hook-ups, and hook-ups normally occur at the end of an outing involving alcohol consumption . . . you do the math! Are we likely to get (a) the truth, (b) a clear recollection, (c) any useful data? (There are bigger questions about the connection between sex and alcohol that we will address later.)

- "the average student had accumulated 10.8 hookup partners"

You may agree with me that "hook-up partners" hints at the awkwardness inherent in this discussion. For the journalist, the solution is this clinical-sounding, businesslike phrasing; he could easily be talking about accumulating money, or shot glasses, or poker partners. Although it may appear as if *everyone* at colleges around the United States is "accumulating," the experience may not be common enough for new concepts, like *fuckbuddy* or *friends with benefits* (FWB), to have infiltrated other adults' thinking. Later in the article, the journalist used *hookee,* more family-friendly than *boytoy* or *FWB*, but still awkward. Imagine it: "Sally, me, and my hookee snogged like mad last night in the bathroom at the party!"

- "petting below the waist"

Hands down, I suspect you will all agree that college students do not "pet below the waist." (They engage in the behavior, but they do not use this language.) Clearly there is a gap between how non–college students and college students view sex. If researchers are asking about things like "petting," it is a dead giveaway of a particular point of view (perhaps more conservative?), and student respondents may guess that the researcher does not really want to hear about the details of hook-ups—whether sordid, sexy, exciting, or blacked out.

- "typical hookup more often included 'genital touching'"

See "petting." This makes it sound like a cross between an accident—"Oops, I think I ended up doing some genital touching!"—and something terribly clinical, like what is described in the Monty Python classroom scene.

Why examine the article in this depth? First, your future knowledge about sex is unlikely to be gained from more textbook reading—you will get it from reading *Newsweek*, or *Cosmo*, or the celebrity gossip page. Thus it makes sense to apply critical thinking to the kinds of sources you will be exposed to throughout your life. Looking a little more deeply at the article shows us exactly what is difficult about cultural-level conversations about sexuality. Finally, we get some ideas we need to explore further—hook-ups and alcohol, who is doing it, and what is actually happening.

Scholarly Research on Hooking Up

There is very little scholarship on this subject, though it is difficult to understand precisely why. Certainly it would make sense for researchers to study hooking up, friends with benefits relationships, and other permutations. It would be a case where having a college student sample was not a liability. Furthermore, researchers are interested in how people form relationships, the dynamics of dating, and the particulars of sexual conduct. The few studies that have been done address "campus" hook-ups, spring break and vacation or travel sex, and FWB as distinct from hook-ups (e.g., Maticka-Tyndale, Herold, and Mewhinney, 1998; Paul, McManus, and Hayes, 2000; Hughes, Morrison, and Asada, 2005).[16]

Thus far, studies tend to be quantitative, offering indexes and questionnaires, and testing theories and hypotheses to attempt to explain why heterosexual men and women engage in these behaviors. The underlying presumption is that sex without a clearly structured, more socially acceptable relationship is unusual, and therefore must be explained.

The other assumptions researchers make about hooking up should not surprise you at this point. Women are the majority in the samples of college students, and the samples are overwhelmingly white and middle-class. No one appears to have studied hook-ups for people aged 22 to 40, although post-college "casual" sex has been described in the *New York Times* and *New York* magazine. There is no equivalent, scholarly research about lesbian, gay, and bisexual people of any age. The *Journal of Lesbian Studies* (1999) did do a special issue on lesbian *polyamorous* (many loves) and "open" relationships, but the emphasis was more on relationships than flings or hook-ups.[17] Studies of gay men and hook-ups are singularly organized around questions of safer sex and HIV risk. This singular focus on lesbians' relationships and gay men's risk narrows the scholarly body of knowledge and perpetuates a heterocentric research bias. The emphasis on risk when studying gay men's nonrelational sex is not wholly illogical in light of HIV transmission rates. But there are about 19 million cases of other sexually transmitted infection (STI) in the United States annually (www.cdc.gov), about 50 percent of them among 15- to 24-year-olds.[18] Scientists estimate that there are 2.8 million cases of chlamydia in the United States; it is a bacterial infection that primarily affects heterosexually active people. Most STIs occur via opposite-sex sexual contact, yet assumptions of risk do not *automatically* underlie research on heterosexual hook ups.

The first research specifically about hooking up was done by a team of psychologists (Paul, McManus, and Hayes, 2000). Key questions focused on what differentiates college students who have hook-ups from those who don't and what differentiates those who had intercourse on a hook-up from those who had not.

> This study focused on a specific risky practice common among contemporary college students: the hookup. Hookups are defined as a sexual encounter which may or may not include sexual intercourse, usually occurring on only one occasion between two people who are strangers or brief acquaintances (Paul, McManus, and Hayes, 2000).

The researchers' point of view is evident in their use of "risky" to describe hooking up. They focus on a number of risks—PVI without condoms, being intoxicated, and damage to self-esteem. Researchers are approaching the issues as outsiders and thus look at hooking up mainly from the perspective of "concerned adults."

In this particular study, Paul, McManus, and Hayes drew a random sample of 600 undergraduate students from a roster of those living on campus. Questionnaires were delivered to campus mailboxes and 555 returned the survey (response rate of 93 percent). Given the gender imbalance in those attending college (i.e., more women than men), unsurprisingly, their sample was 38 percent male and 63 percent female with more juniors (35 percent) and seniors (39 percent); 86 percent were white. Sexual orientation did not matter for the survey but 98 percent of the sample were heterosexual. Respondents were given a definition of hook-up: "A sexual encounter, usually only lasting one night, between two people who are strangers or brief acquaintances. Some physical interaction is typical but may or may not include sexual intercourse" (Paul et al., 2000). Defined this way, the researchers were not necessarily able to capture experiences of continuing flings or FWB, though they did ask whether "a relationship" had ever come from hooking up.

They found that 120 respondents had never hooked up, 266 had hooked up without PVI, and 169 had hooked up with PVI. Hook-ups averaged almost 11 each school year, with a high of 65. Paul McManus, and Hayes found that those in a romantic relationship at the time of the study were less likely to have ever had any hook-ups and had maintained all their romantic relationships on average longer than those who had ever hooked up. This suggests that there may be a different point of view or orientation to love, romance, and relationships, distinguishing those who hook up from those who do not. The majority of men and women had hooked up (78 percent), but more men than women had hook-ups that included PVI (48 percent vs. 33 percent), implying that there is a small(er) number of heterosexual women hooking up with the men. It may also be that the questions did not accurately capture hook-ups between men who may not have identified themselves as gay.

The problem of discrepant reporting of heterosexual men and women is pervasive in sexuality research, by the way (Wiederman, 1997).[19] Numerous studies have found differences in reported number of partners for self-identified heterosexuals. It may be due to the ways in which researchers define sex acts and sex partners, with the same ambiguity and lack of clarity that underlies definitions of hooking up. Does it count if it was just one night? What about if it was supposed to be a fling but someone fell asleep or passed out before anything really happened? Men may have wider parameters for deciding what constitutes a sex "partner." Discrepancy in figures may be due to respondent bias, wherein women develop self-consciousness about the number of partners they have had and shave a few numbers from the total. There may be a small number of women who are more sexually active and have more partners, and a large number of women with fewer partners.

Some of the discrepancy may be due to situational factors, including alcohol and drug use—14 percent of those who had ever had PVI during a hook-up needed friends to piece together the events, and 22 percent of those who had hook-up PVI reported that they had "felt out of control" during such a hook-up (Paul, McManus, and Hayes, 2000). Other situational factors seem to influence hook-ups, including fraternity or sorority parties/events, where 44 percent of the respondents had engaged in hook-ups. Based on this study, it seems fairly clear that the goal of a hook-up, especially if PVI is involved, is very momentary. Almost half of those who had ever had PVI during a hook-up (49 percent) never saw the hook-up partner again, and only 12 percent of all the respondents who had hooked up developed relationships from such events.

These findings are not completely specific to the United States. A study of "casual sex" (defined as "engaging in sexual intercourse with a new partner within 24 hours of initial meeting") among Australian high school seniors reveals that peers, alcohol, and expectations also influence decisions about hooking up (Maticka-Tyndale, Herold, and Oppermann, 2003).[20] Researchers surveyed 570 male and 776 female Australian high school students ("schoolies") on a weeklong vacation, similar to American college students' spring break weeks. Peers influenced whether men and women schoolies hooked up. For men, what mattered was what peers ended up doing while on vacation—men took their cues from each other. For women, specifically entering into agreements with friends about not hooking up had more of an influence. Were women worried about friends' judgments, or was it more a case of mutual support—friends looking out for each other?

Do people behave differently when on vacation, compared to their everyday lives? Most of the schoolies had engaged in PVI prior to their vacation (64 percent of men, 59.8 percent of women), and 66 percent of these men and 33 percent of these women had had hook-ups before the vacation. There was a difference in expectations for having sex while on break though; 58 percent of men (vs. 18 percent of women) intended to do so. Here again, peers were consequential: men's friends were more likely to make agreements to have sex on vacation while women's friends were more likely to have agreed *not* to. More gender discrepancies about actual conduct were observed, with 60 percent of men saying they had "fooled around" (vs. 45 percent of women) and 34.5 percent saying they had engaged in PVI (vs. 23.6 percent of women). Most of the men—60 percent—were with "casual" partners on vacation, and the same proportion were with more than one. About 40 percent of the women were with casual partners, and the same proportion were with more than one. Both men and women had similar experiences with alcohol, with most having drunk alcohol every day during their vacation.

Peers, Alcohol, and Perceptions

Peer networks are a major part of what makes hook-ups possible, along with alcohol. We guess at what our best friends will think, we guess at who will approve or disapprove of what, and we guess at what "everyone else" is doing, including strangers. In sociology, this called *significant others*, specific and important members of a person's network, and *generalized others,* typical members of society, exemplified by the concern, "but what would *people* think?" A handful of research has been done on friends (significant others) and sexual choices. Unsurprisingly, students tend to rate their own decision-making processes as least permissive and most responsible (Agostinelli and Seal, 1998).[21] They think their friends are almost as responsible and discerning as they think themselves to be. It is all those other people—the generalized other of "other students"—to whom students attribute more permissive sexual decisions and the kind of irresponsibility that can have emotional or physical consequences. This is important because of the way in which perceptions can lead to action.

A group of Canadian researchers has studied Canadian college students' intentions to "engage in casual sex" on spring break (Herold, Maticka-Tyndale, and Mewhinney, 1998).[22] What explained whether students had sex on spring break? What Maticka-Tyndale, Herold, and Oppermann (2003) found when studying Australian schoolies was also true for the Canadian students, which tells us something about Western cultures and sexual scripting. The Canadian students were surveyed before break and on the bus going home. Previous experience with hook-ups, expectations of what spring break is supposed to be like, and personal standards strongly influenced the intention to hook up during spring break. Though more men than women intended to hook up, similar percentages actually did (15 percent of men, 13 percent of women).

Besides vacations that are associated with hooking up and being in college, there are other contexts in which people hook up. A study of 504 backpackers and summer travelers supported some of the themes we have already discussed (Egan, 2001).[23] Twenty-six percent of the respondents had hooked up at some point on the trip. They were most likely to be men who had a history of hook-ups and who expected to hook up during their backpacking stint. Again, we can see how attitudes and perceptions combine with individual approaches to sex (e.g., recreational or relational) (see also Conner and Flesch, 2001).[24] What explained any particular scenario going from a potential hook-up to an actual hook-up of some sort? Sexual desire, picking someone up (or being picked up)—but only for men in the study—and alcohol use, combined with being in a "fun" mood.

Alcohol: The Pink Elephant in the Room

It would be impossible to estimate what proportion of hook-ups, booty calls, or FWB rendezvous occur in a context lubricated by alcohol for at least one of the participants. College students' alcohol use contributes to an estimated annual 1,700 student deaths; 600,000 injuries; about 700,000 assaults; more than 90,000 sexual assaults; and countless acts of unprotected (i.e., no condoms) sex (Hingson et al., 2005).[25] Knowing these statistics probably makes little, if any, difference to most people. The knowledge alone would be unlikely to change someone's behavior. But to ignore that there is a very real connection between sex and alcohol would be naïve. Alcohol and sex are a couple with nearly unbreakable bonds—it's almost as if they were made for each other. Alcohol and keeping your pants on? Sex and sobriety? They don't really seem to have the appeal that sex and alcohol do. But what does it mean that we see the two so intertwined so often, so faithful to each other, through good times and bad?

A broad review of studies on the sex and alcohol link reveals that alcohol use and consumption predict levels of sexual conduct—as alcohol consumption increases, so does sexual activity (Cooper, 2002).[26] Alcohol consumption is associated with PVI in scenarios that are *already* scripted as "potential sexual situations"—so alcohol lubricates and facilitates in situations that could, without alcohol, not go all the way to PVI. Drinking before sex is linked with reduced reasoning about partners and reduced likelihood of discussing things like contraception or safer sex. What elements of alcohol consumption are linked with sex?

- "beer goggles"

Also known as "everyone is cuter at closing time." Why might that be the case? Evolutionary psychologists have studied how heterosexual men and women choose partners, theoretically at least (e.g., Buunk et al., 2002).[27] Although similar studies have revealed that men value partners' looks more than women do, this is true mainly for long-term relationships (see also Buss, 1994).[28] In choosing partners for short-term pairings or hook-ups, Buunk and his colleagues found that men were less selective—a much lower level of attractiveness was acceptable. "As relationship involvement *decreases*, men find it more important that a potential mate is physically attractive, but less important that she is intelligent" (Buunk et al., 2002: 272). Considering that evolutionary psychology argues that women look for good husbands and fathers, it is unsurprising that researchers found that women were also less selective in short-term pairings. Other researchers call this "alcohol myopia" (or nearsightedness), the inability to consider implications and consequences due to the way in which alcohol chemically impairs cognitive abilities (Steele and Josephs, 1990).[29] There is also a theory of alcohol expectancy, what you and I might call "association"—the *learned* belief that alcohol and sex make good mates, that it makes sense to get a drink and then get it on. This may indeed be based on a truism. A little alcohol can lower self-consciousness and inhibitions, but too often, people do not stop at just one or two "relaxing" cocktails.

Psychologist Barry Jones and his colleagues (2003) did some experiments in the United Kingdom to test whether alcohol does promote beer goggles (although they did not refer to it this way).[30] They selected a student sample from several campus-area pubs, specifically looking for those who had consumed no alcohol or some alcohol within the preceding three hours. The researchers showed photographs to the respondents and asked for assessments of how attractive the pictured individuals were. They found a link between alcohol consumption and ratings of attractiveness. The more alcohol someone had consumed, the higher their ratings of the attractiveness of the people in the photographs.

- self-consciousness about the body may dissipate
- disinhibition for women that enables ability to be sexual, have desires

In U.S. culture women are objectified, reduced to pieces and parts and valued as much for appearance as for anything else (Fredrickson and Roberts, 1997).[31] When internalized, this can be problematic, resulting in profound self-consciousness. Psychologist Michael Wiederman (2000) developed a multiquestion scale to assess women's body self-consciousness during sex.[32] About 35 percent of the college women he surveyed reported experiencing self-consciousness during sex at least some of the time. This can affect sexual satisfaction, leading to difficulties with orgasm and muted experiences of pleasure (Dove and Wiederman, 2000).[33] Some research has found that college students who do not like their bodies are more likely than others to avoid sexual activities (Faith and Schare, 1993)[34] and see themselves as unskilled partners (Holmes, Chamberlin, and Young, 1994).[35]

Discussions of body satisfaction and sexuality across the lifespan reveal that self-esteem and body image are related regardless of age (Davison and McCabe, 2005).[36] Surveys were distributed to 211 men and 226 women randomly chosen from the phone book in Melbourne and Victoria, Australia, and ranging in age from 18 to 86. The women in the sample had lower levels of body image satisfaction, more anxiety about the way others saw their bodies, and were more likely than men to conceal their bodies. We know less about men and body self-consciousness, but some researchers have explored the connection. Louisa Allen (2002) studied 183 New Zealand men, aged 17 to 19, looking to discover how young heterosexual men experienced their bodies and sexualities.[37] The men tended to reference their girlfriends when discussing their bodies:

Tim: How I feel about my body?. . . no I feel . . . she's fine with my body and that's all that really matters. I'm like not having sex with myself so I don't really care about how I look (laughs), so I mean if she is happy with my body then there is no problem.

Neil: No, no, I don't feel, I just don't feel anything about it, sort of over cocky you know "Oh I've got a good body" so I just don't care. My body's just there and it doesn't worry me you know.

Chris: I don't think that it matters. I mean I don't really care what my body looks like. I do care what Cam [girlfriend] thinks my body looks like. . . .

There seems to be no connection between selves and bodies for these men, but for gay men there appears to be a link between assessment of body and sexual satisfaction (Conner, Johnson, and Grogan, 2004).[38] Their study of 120 people led to the conclusion that heterosexual women and gay men were most concerned with how their bodies looked, compared to heterosexual men.

A study of hooking up used in-person interviews with 62 women at 11 colleges and nationally chosen, representative telephone interviews with another 1,000 to assess women's current experiences and future hopes (Glenn and Marquardt, 2001).[39] It is worth noting that the 18-month study was carried out by a self-proclaimed "non-partisan, non-ideological" think-tank and policy-making organization, the Institute for American Values. There is certainly a point of view orienting the researchers (Norval Glenn is also a sociologist), but the report is worth discussing because for the most part, the findings correspond with those in research done by researchers with no affiliation to any think-tanks. Glenn and Marquardt document the link between women's desire and alcohol consumption:

> Other women observed that being drunk gives a woman license to act sexually interested in public in ways that would not be tolerated if she were sober. For instance, a University of Michigan student said, "Girls are actually allowed to be a lot more sexual when they are drunk . . . ." A University of Chicago junior observed, "One of my best friends . . . sometimes that's her goal when we go out. Like she wants to get drunk so I guess she doesn't have to feel guilty about [hooking up]."

Other women remarked on the idea that hooking up confers "sexual power" on women, that the idea of hooking up, regardless of how far it goes in actual behaviors, is to feel "like a woman." There is no doubt that "feeling sexual" is also a motivator for heterosexual men who hook up. Hooking up is a way of confirming both gender identity *and* heterosexuality for both men and women.

It is an *inference*—a leap of logic or thought, based on evidence—to suggest that body consciousness is one reason why some people drink. But consider the finding that sometimes, people start the evening knowing that they want to go out and hook up with someone (Paul and Hayes, 2002).[40] The hook-up is planned or hoped for, though the partner is unknown. One female respondent wrote that "many situations involve alcohol and drugs because people lose inhibition and wear beer goggles, increasing the likelihood of hooking up" (646). A male respondent indicated that "alcohol is almost always involved. This helps the guy with his confidence to initiate the hookup" (p. 646). Combine the desire to hook up with a touch of self-consciousness, body or otherwise, and this helps to explain why the bond between sex and alcohol seems so unbreakable.

But quantitative instruments cannot adequately capture the complexity of hooking up, so it makes sense to pose open-ended questions to document emotional, phenomenological reactions and processes. How do participants actually feel about hooking up? How do they feel beforehand, and how do they feel afterwards? These questions shed light on the *phenomenology*, or subjective, internal perceptions, of sexuality. Unfortunately, research is biased in favor of quantitative studies, and there is a paucity of evidence and information about men's experiences with hook-ups. I believe this represents unspoken researcher bias that for men, hooking up is somehow a more "natural" way to be sexual (along the lines of the fact that there are no how-to books to teach men how to do so successfully). So researchers have tended to focus on women, believing that the emotional repercussions and context of hooking up are more significant for them. As I noted earlier, whether qualitative or quantitative, there is a dearth of research on people of color and those self-identified as gay, lesbian, bisexual, trans, and so on. There is a little anecdotal evidence about people of color, though Chng and Moore (1994) did find less sexual risk-taking among non-white college students.[41] African American students at predominantly white colleges reported less anonymity with hook-ups (with strangers), likely by virtue of being in the statistical minority. Relationships that began as FWB progressed to romantic, committed relationships.

Psychologists Elizabeth Paul and Kristen Hayes (2002) had 155 women and 32 men give open-ended responses to questions about every aspect of hooking up. Gender differences in expectation and perhaps in the reality of hook-ups are salient in the open-ended responses. An example of this is a typical response to the question, "How do females/males feel during a hookup?"(p. 647):

(woman) Sexually aroused, enjoyed, oblivious to others around, driven only by physical forces, not thinking much—just doing. The feelings are overwhelming sexual desire or lust.

(man) I haven't got a clue as to how females feel during a hookup. I think they probably believe that this is not going to be just a hookup but that something else will come about. The guy feels a sense of pride and accomplishment during almost every hookup (p. 647).

The typical response to the question, "How does it end?" is equally revealing:

(woman) Someone walks in, the party ends, the phone rings, it is time to go, both fall asleep, one passes out, or one just stops. It ends when both have satisfied each other and realize the hookup is complete.

(man) It generally ends when both partners have been satisfied, usually ending with the male. At this time comes an awkward moment when the two put their clothes back on and realize they have nothing to talk about.

Your point of view will influence your response to these respondents' answers. From my point of view, the woman is offering a hook-up that can meet a man's fantasy, in a sense. Recall that heterosexual women's fantasies are far more likely to include elements of romance, caring (known) partners, perfect scenarios and scripting, and overpowering sexual desire and feelings. The hook-ups that the woman describes sound like nice fantasies. What the man describes sounds closer to what probably happens more regularly—the guy and his partner meet only physically, not emotionally, leaving both clueless about how the other really feels; the guy is more likely to have an orgasm (or lose his erection due to exhaustion or alcohol), effectively rendering the hook-up over; and the awkwardness of the still unscripted "afterwards" is probably more salient than any pleasure. The typical responses Paul and Hayes focused on also included men's and women's joint assessments that afterwards, women may "feel cheap or used" while men "brag" or "hope that another pure hookup . . . can occur" (p. 647). And while the aftermath for men may include wanting another "pure" hook-up, free of turmoil and strife, women need to be taught how to facilitate this.

How-to authors Lavinthal and Rozler write that, in order to "ensure that any hookup from this day forward will remain free of unnecessary drama (meaning the kind that makes a guy refer to me as 'the psycho')" (2005: 55), women should commit to a "hookup contract." The advice they give is for women to vow to themselves, "I will not define myself by how often I hook up. I will remember that quality over quantity is a good thing" (p. 57). This is echoed by a female respondent in Paul and Hayes's study who wrote, "I was pretty happy, a little drunk, enjoying the fact that the hottest guy at the party was kissing me. I felt like I had just won a game or something. I felt very confident in myself" (2002: 653). The hottest guy represented "quality," but this woman's experience further captures the complex dynamic inherent in hetero-sexual hook-ups; she seems to be experiencing herself passively, through his interest in her. Because *he* was kissing her, because "the hottest guy" was attracted to her, and because it happened in a public setting, it validated her as woman, as the object of someone's desire. His kisses were proof of her femininity, her desirability, her irre-sistibility. Her confidence came from his desire and her physical appeal.

The respondents in Paul and Hayes's study were also asked to describe their best and worst hook-up experiences (respondents provided more than one answer, so totals do not add to 100 percent). The women's "best" experiences had elements of the fan-tasies other women had provided in my study with Michael Kimmel. While most of the women in Paul and Hayes's study (33 percent) indicated that a "best experience" included "interest, attraction" and a good-looking partner, similarly to most of the men (42 percent), enjoyment of sexual behavior and partner's body was a distant choice for women (24 percent vs. 37 percent of men). Most tellingly, a good experi-ence for women was one that included a relationship evolving (27 percent vs. 16 per-cent of men); feeling "wanting and cared about" (23 percent of women vs. 16 percent of men); feeling "comfort, security, trust" (14 percent of women vs. 5 percent of men). One woman wrote that the best experience was "because he made me feel beautiful as a person and not as a body. I could tell he cared about me" (2002: 653). Now it seems much clearer why women might need to choose one of those three how-to hook up books! Similarly to the fantasies, where the actual sex is muted in favor of the sensu-al, emotional details, the "fantasy" best hook-up for women has a real emphasis on the emotional, subverting the sexual and physical.

The respondents' impressions of the "worst" experience showed some differ-ences as well. Alcohol was the overwhelming factor, indicated by 63 percent of the women and 58 percent of the men. But 43 percent of the women indicated that "forced sexual behavior against own will" constituted a "worst experience," while only 11 percent of the men indicated this. The difference was statistically significant, meaning that this indeed represents a real difference, not one due to chance, coinci-dence, or sampling. Feeling "used as an object for partner's physical pleasure" was a choice for 29 percent of the women, compared to 11 percent of the men, another statistically significant finding. Women also chose things like regret or embarrass-ment (27 percent vs. 16 percent of men) and partner was too aggressive (17 percent vs. 0 percent of the men). When women described their worst experiences due to aggression or coercion, they wrote things like, "I was obviously disinterested . . . I didn't want to cause a scene," "I was disgusted. I said to my friends . . . why didn't you help me! I didn't want to do it," "He just mauled me in my drunken stupor . . . the guy was gross," and "I just had low self-esteem . . . I felt dirty . . . I didn't tell anyone because I was very ashamed" (2002: 655). It sounds as if the women are implicating alcohol and assuming that their male partners should have seen their overintoxication and lack of interest. The problem is that the men are also intoxicated, maybe more so even than their female partners, disabling everyone's judgments and ability to pay attention to partners' cues.

On the other hand men chose "no interest in partner" or partner was unattractive (42 percent vs. 16 percent of women); "promiscuous partner" (10.5 percent vs. 0 percent of the women); and "sexually frustrated, partner teased" (21 percent vs. 0 percent of women). The last two responses were statistically significant as well. Regarding the sexual behavior of women, one man wrote, "I got oral sex without putting much effort forth. It felt good but I'm glad that I'm not going out with a girl who is slutty like that" (2002: 653).

While these findings clearly reflect the depth of gender differences, it is important to dissect them a bit. There is a relatively large gulf between men's and women's visions of hooking up—what it is and what it should be. There also appear to be differences in motivations to seek this form of sex. The worst experiences seem to represent the ultimately different realities heterosexual men and women experience and are socialized into throughout the life course, prior to ever attempting to end up together in a sexual scenario. What makes it bad for women? Being drunk, being forced, being used, feeling regret, and being subject to aggression. What makes it bad for men? Being drunk, realizing that the beer goggles were on and she's "not attractive," having a "promiscuous" partner, and feeling like she was a tease. The latter two reference the Goldilocks theory described in chapter 2. There is apparently a "just right" amount of sex and sexual partners a woman should have, a just right amount of coy seduction she should engage in, and a just right amount of giving in and providing some sexual satisfaction. One woman wrote that her best experience occurred when "We were drinking and got carried away. I stopped it. I felt elated and proud, good about myself" (2002: 653). The flip side of this woman's pride is, of course, a man's response: "The girl teased me. She stopped me and said she didn't want me to continue. Why did she kiss me in the first place then?" (p. 654). Men would tell friends about experiences like this, but seemed more circumspect about "picking a dog because of beer goggles." Women were uniformly *unlikely* to tell their friends about the worst experiences that included feeling/being coerced, unsafe PVI, and feeling overwhelmed.

(Social) Learning and Exchange Theory

So what do people get from hooking up? Why do it? On the face of it, it seems like a potentially frustrating way to meet sexual needs, and it seems to require a lot of emotional training (for women), with the potential for awkward fallout afterward. In chapter 2, I described social learning and exchange theories. This school of thought argues that we do cost/benefit analyses when making decisions, and that we prefer to maximize benefits. Even the term "friends-with-benefits" seems to suggest that this is the case—if the relationships were (or became) FWC—friends-with-costs—the rendezvous would be likely to end! Learning theories would argue that we repeat behaviors that have been socially rewarded. So if a person were to consider a FWB relationship, he might assess the costs and benefits of doing so, along with the perceptions of friends and the "rewards" from his peer networks.

Benefits

- ego boost: feeling sexually desirable and desired by others; experiencing one's own desire, released from constraint
- emotional boost: feeling as if interest is reciprocated; being able to feel "close" to someone
- experimentation: a FWB or fuckbuddy situation could afford the opportunity to experiment sexually; a hook-up may be seen as having "little to lose," freeing participants to experiment
- empowerment: probably more likely to be cited or believed by women than men, accompanied by the statement that women are "entitled" to sexual pleasure, too
- the feeling of belonging: it feels good to feel similar, to feel like we fit in with the friends we have chosen (if our friends are hooking up)
- sex without emotions, without the risk of getting "involved" or of getting hurt emotionally
- pleasure
- feeling like an adult, feeling autonomous and in charge of one's life
- the excitement of the various risks and the danger of hook-ups
- fun

Journalist Pamela Johnson, writing in *Essence* magazine (2002) about postcollege hook-ups, addresses the idea of the ego boost.[42] She describes a friend's motivations:

My homeboy, whom I'll call Kenny, is a handsome, successful banker, and much in demand with women, but somewhere inside he sees himself as the ugly duckling he believed himself to be in childhood. Now that he's in his late thirties, it's my sense that these days when he meets a woman who will sleep with him, at some level the little boy inside him is giving that old Sally Field Oscar acceptance speech: "You like me! You really like me!" "I've slept with tons of women, and I've been accused of being a slut," Kenny reveals, a tiny flash of pride in his voice. "Sometimes it bothers me, but mostly it doesn't. People can think whatever they want" (p. 128).

For someone like Kenny, the costs of hooking up—being called a slut—do not appear to outweigh the benefits—self-esteem boosts, feeling desired, and challenging people's expectations of him. How do we make these assessments? How-to book authors Sherman and Tocantins (2004) provide a quiz so that women can determine their readiness for hooking up, at the end of which they summarize:

> Are you in the right head-space for a good, hard roll in the hay, or do you need to work on a few of the finer points before doing the deed? Hopefully, what you're coming to realize is that to successfully enjoy casual sex, you've got to make sure that you're approaching it with the optimum attitude and perspective, that you're having it because it's what you want—and *all* that you want. You've got to do it for good, noncommittal fun—not because you're hoping that sleeping with the guy will make him want you more; not because you're seeking a quick cure for painfully low self-esteem; not because you're looking for Mr. Right (p. 17).

This makes it sound as if women need to get into training, like training for the Olympic Trials of Sex—work on feelings, develop the right attitude, and talk themselves into the right reasons. Women must talk themselves into both being able to and wanting to have "successful casual sex." What are the implications and consequences of constructing masculinity and femininity as so different that, in order to engage in an apparently popular form of intimacy, women need to be taught how to do it well? This leads nicely to the potential "costs" of hook-ups and FWB.

Costs. Even in a well-reasoned state, free from the interference of alcohol, drugs, or feelings, it may not be possible to always anticipate the potential costs of hook-ups and FWB relationships. A scenario can start as mutually beneficial and grow more "costly" for both, inspiring questions such as, "Is it worth it?" and "What are you getting out of this?" Both questions reference a cost/benefit analysis with language of *worth* and *value*. So what are some immediately obvious or eventually apparent costs?

- may not *actually* have chance to experiment sexually, especially in more erratic hook-ups, because there may not be the chance to develop a context in which both are comfortable
- emotional let down because someone may "catch feelings" that are not reciprocated
- may feel as if there are too many compromises: hook-ups may be more convenient for one partner
- may realize that desires and hopes are configured differently: one wants a relationship, wants to fall in love, wants to date; or one doesn't want the commitment of a FWB, doesn't want the risks (whatever they are)
- may not actually be all that fun: one may feel too guilty, ashamed, or used; alcohol or drugs may make the sex unpleasant or unsatisfying
- may require too many rationalizations and grasping at straws to find the benefits
- sex without emotions, without the risk of getting "involved" or of getting hurt emotionally (note: this is also a benefit)

Preg, STIs ?

How-to authors Lavinthal and Rozler (2005) address some potential costs this in their "hookup contract:"

> I will not wait in obsessive agony for him to call me. Instead, I will give myself permission to call him. However, I must not do so in a passive-aggressive manner that will put the ball back in his court (i.e., leaving a message on his cell phone while he is at work . . .) (p. 57).

A qualitative study of hook-up sex and alcohol use among 33 Norwegian young adults (14 women, 19 men) revealed that similar assessments of costs and benefits exist (Traæen and Sørensen, 2000).[43] There are some differences, though. Norwegians may be circumspect about their conduct, with 72 percent of Norwegians reporting no new partners in any average year (meaning they are not sexually active or, more likely, maintaining relationships characterized as "serially monogamous"). Only 2 percent of Norwegians reported having more than three new partners in a year (Stigum et al., 1997).[44] For those with multiple PVI partners in the preceding year, benefits and motives for hooking up included "for the sake of love, for pleasure, or because of strong social expectations and/or sexual abuse" (Traæen and Sørensen, 2000: 289). One 26-year-old woman was looking for the benefit of a relationship but found that the cost was far greater: "[Sex] is something which should be shared between two who love each other. When I think of my short-term relationships it does not leave me with good feelings. I hoped it would develop into something more" (p. 290). She had had five PVI partners in the preceding year.

Another female respondent (31 years old) said, "I want him to invite me for dinner, so that I can get to know him. I want to work out during the course of events whether I feel like having sex. I want some good old-fashioned flirtation, so things are allowed to develop. If it doesn't develop into something more, one may still have an OK feeling" (p. 290). The benefit may be a short-term FWB relationship, sex, and the fleeting intimacy that accompanies a hook-up. But the cost for her, and probably for many other men and women, is that the *process* of desire, arousal, and attraction is accelerated, truncated, and short-circuited. Hooking up can be simply about (quickly) following the steps of a standard script for hook-ups and FWB relationships. As a 28-year-old man described it:

> Sex feels very different when you have feelings for your partner. If you don't have feelings for the partner, it's just a physical thing. I often get a touch of anxiety afterwards. Except feelings of guilt, I'm not getting anything out of it. You're really hurting yourself, plus you may hurt the partner. I think I'm being self-destructive (Traæen and Sørensen, 2000: 291).

But Wait . . . What about FWB Relationships?

In heterosexual friends-with-benefits (FWB) relationships, there may be some differences compared to more typical hook-ups (Hughes, Morrison, and Asada, 2005). Although FWB relationships are not initiated with the goal of establishing "committed" romantic or emotionally deep relationships, they can have a stability that hook-ups lack. Peers are paramount in FWB relationships, similarly to hook-ups—79 of 143 respondents (who were mostly female and white) had had an FWB relationship. When they told their friends about these relationships, 38 percent of respondents indicated that their closest friends "approved," while 36 percent indicated that friends "disapproved." The continuation of FWB scenarios was related to the perceived support of respondents' same-sex friendship network. FWB relationships seem to have rules that both facilitate and limit. Rules address expectations for sex (e.g., condom use); communication (no calls next day); secrecy—for 30 percent of those in first-time FWB relationships; permanence (e.g., it is not going to last forever); emotional (don't "catch feelings"); and friendship (do something besides just have sex if a friendship predated the sexual involvement). Researchers found that 56 percent of respondents had emotional rules, 40 percent had communication rules, and 33 percent had sex rules. Motivations for FWBs appear to be similar to hook-up motivations, including not wanting to be "tied down" in a relationship, wanting (simple) sex without the "hassles" of a relationship, and simply being single and having the opportunity (Hughes, Morrison, and Asada, 2005).

One of the large and obvious ironies about hook ups and FWB relationships is precisely these "rules" and the scripted expectations highlighted in Paul and Hayes's study. Although the ambiguity of definitions is thrilling, and the uncertainty of hooking up on any given day or evening is exciting, even these "casual" scenarios are socially and (sub)culturally scripted. They are intended to deliver a feeling of being sexual, being a man or a woman (e.g., being an adult), being autonomous, being empowered, especially for women. Yet these outcomes, and the path of any particular hook-up, are predictably scripted. They also reflect different socialization patterns into sexuality that accompany the experience of growing up in the binary sex/gender system. All of this is nicely summarized by an anonymous writer (typos and spelling as written):

> [The FWB] somewhat redeemed himself by messaging me later in the night telling me to stop by after my dinner. I messaged him back but am guessing he was already asleep. but for whatever reason that made me feel better. I do not have any idea why I am doing any of this with him in the first place. . . . . sure he's hot. very hot, in fact. super hot, really. but the sex, technically speaking, is no where near as good as with the [other FWB]. and the bother of trying to work out our schedules is really quite prohibitive of any spontaneity. and having even protected sex is of course somewhat dangerous, particularly with someone who I suspect does this exact thing with several other people. so why do I choose to forget all that and continue with this? is it loneliness? my ego? the challenge?[45]

So What Are the Implications and Consequences?

We don't know when the first heterosexual hook-up happened. Who realized that it was possible to have sex outside of the confines of a socially defined relationship? Did this kind of sex become more popular after the sexual revolution, as Risman and Schwartz suggested? Or was it the result of the intersection of a number of cultural changes—development of the Pill and its eventual easy availability, more teens going away to college and living on their own? Was it second-wave feminism of the 1970s giving women the idea that sexuality and desire belong to both men and women? It is too complex to isolate the "path" of FWB and hook-up scenarios, but it is clear that, for heterosexually active men and women, gender roles, socialization and peers mix with flexible subcultural norms and larger cultural shifts. Even so, the hook-up paths of women and men differ, along with costs, benefits, and consequences.

> **Jim:** Dude, why are you doing this?
>
> **Joe:** Doing what?
>
> **Jim:** Letting her just booty call you whenever, show up late and drunk, screw you, and then leave.
>
> **Joe:** But I like her. And I don't want to pressure her so I figure I'll just let her do what she's comfortable with. Maybe she'll start to fall in love with me.
>
> **Jim:** I hate to see you like this. You're always insecure about her, waiting for her to call, blowing off your friends if she does, trying to analyze her feelings.
>
> *Jim gives Joe a hug as Joe sniffles and tries not to cry.*

This hypothetical exchange might make you laugh because it probably does not sound like something a man would say. What does it mean that there are no books called *Hook-Ups for Straight Players: A Single Guy's Guide to Getting Some?* The heterosexual how-to books I analyzed implied that, besides alcohol, the other big thing that no one really wants to address is *feelings*. There are no how-to guides for heterosexual men because the assumption is that men already know how to have "casual" sex. The term "catch feelings" implies that hook-ups should somehow be *devoid* of feelings, that perhaps hook-ups should just be simple transactions in a sense. Maybe there are no books for men because U.S. culture socializes men into a form of disembodiment, a separation of self from body and self from emotions. Gender scholar Annie Potts (2002) suggests that the convention of assigning agency to the penis (as in, "the little head thinks for the big head") enables men to see sexuality as something *merely* physical.[46] Michael Kimmel referred to this as "no sissy stuff"—nothing that might make a guy seem remotely feminine (see chapter 3). (There may also be an element of "give 'em hell" as well—take risks, be daring, spontaneous.) If the average man has already learned the rule of "no sissy stuff," then he might not need any more training to understand how to successfully hook up—meaning, without catching feelings and therefore seeming feminine.

What does it mean that this apparently popular form of sex requires such a mind-body separation for men and women (and this is probably true regardless of sexual orientation)? What happens to the capacity to learn about oneself in an intimate relation-ship? What about the ability to learn about oneself sexually? I read an Internet commentary on this very subject that could be paraphrased like this:

> Since ships only stop into my port for one rendezvous at a time, I haven't exactly had time to figure out what being good in bed would be like, let alone determine whether I'm like that or not. And then a vicious circle starts. A ship visits my port and I don't know whether my port was adequately hospitable or not. The ship never comes again but easily finds a new port which it might well visit more than once, and I assume that my port was not good enough. Except I don't actually know whether my port was good or bad or in between, because I don't have time to adjust to each new ship.[47]

It does not seem as if hooking up is "pure," or clean, or easy. In spite of all the negotiations ("This is just sex, right? Are you cool with that?"), the intentionality of starting a night out by assuming it will end with a hook-up (Glenn and Marquardt, 2001), and in spite of the how-to books offering help and rules—hooking up seems fraught with uncertainty. Heterosexual women seem to think that men who hook up are doing it better than they are, as if the men set the terms and the rules and then "play the game" much better. It is very poignant when a man who hooks up says, "I haven't got a clue as to how females feel during a hookup" (Paul and Hayes, 2002). How do we get inside the minds and feelings of our sexual partners, and in this case, how would a man like this get a better perspective on how "females feel"?

We can make some inferences by exploring some of what we know about sex, particularly for heterosexual women. It is true that the sexual landscape for such women has changed dramatically in the last 25 years, therefore changing heterosexually active men's lives as well. Age of first experience of PVI has decreased, total number of (life-time) sexual partners has increased, and average age at first marriage has increased (Mackay, 2001). These simple figures and averages do not tell the full story though, and may mislead us into thinking that perhaps men's and women's experiences are becoming more similar, that things like being able to "drink like a guy" and hooking up are leveling the playing field. But looking more deeply, we see that in study after study, heterosexual men are more assertive, take more initiative, and are far more like-ly to take the lead in sexual interactions (Impett and Peplau, 2003).[48]

The consequences for men are equally as meaningful as those for women. Because we expect that heterosexual men will make the first move and then continue to move (or push) further at each juncture in a hook-up, we place men in a serious bind. We require a Goldilocks amount of men's assertiveness, sexual interest, and desire. Too much and he becomes threatening, coercive, pushy, or worse. Too little and he is, at best, "weird" and "asexual," and at worst, he has his sexuality and gender maligned (e.g., called "gay"). Men who follow the belief that they must initiate and press for more have no shortage of ambivalence about this. Indeed, 20 percent of the men in my fantasies study specifically indicated that their fantasy partners were assertive women (Kimmel and Plante, 2002).[49] Men are subject to enormous performance pressure to get an erection, maintain it, and successfully orgasm, even under less-than-ideal conditions of alcohol and drug use, hook-ups, and uncertainties. Remember one of the rules of masculinity—"no sissy stuff"? This includes accepting, uncritically perhaps, the narrow and rigid expectations of hook-up subcultures, male peers, and female sex partners.

What else do we know about heterosexually interested women's sexualities at the moment? There is a cultural double standard that persists, in spite of other changes in sexual behavior and attitudes, according to Deborah Tolman, an expert on teen women's sexuality (quoted in Lewin, 2005).[50] How does the double standard operate? "The sexual double standard is regulated through the tool of sexual reputation, that is the negative labeling of an active, desiring female sexuality and positive labeling of active male sexuality" (Jackson and Cram, 2003: 114).[51] It is evident in our casual and uncritical use of the word "slut." *Slut* is a sex-linked and sex-typed word, like "actress" or "wife," not mitigated by the occasional added adjective "male." The practice of saying "male slut" makes it crystal clear that, unadorned, the word refers to women and is a negative judgment on women's sexualities. On one MTV series, *Laguna Beach: The Real Orange County,* I heard "slut" about 20 times in one episode. In one scene, some guys called the female main characters *sluts,* so the young women's boyfriends "defend[ed their] honor." In another scene, one of the young men who had "defended" his girlfriend called her a slut because she was dancing with other guys in a club. As a pejorative, *slut* is an excellent way for both men and women to control women's actions. On campuses across the country, women who hooked up "too much" were also labeled with other synonyms (Glenn and Marquardt, 2001):

slut	couch	trash	trick	tease
whore	skanky	easy	hooch	ho

What does it mean to hook up "too much?" The Goldilocks theory of sex makes it clear that there is a "just right" amount of sex a heterosexual woman should want to have and should seek out. What is just right for gay men or lesbians or bisexuals? What is just right for heterosexual men?

The fear of being called a slut or any synonym can inhibit women, especially young women, in recognizing, developing, and expressing sexuality. For some women, it is not simply the fear of a word but what that word may *symbolize* or represent; it is the fear of fundamentally, at her core, *being* a "slut." Some women appear to acknowledge this fear by giving in to the sex/gender system that perpetuates the double standards and judgments for sexually active women (Williams, 2005).[52] "Can one plus nine ever equal just nine?" is the question for many single young women, apparently:

> "I know a lot of people who will go home with the same guy they have before just because it's not going to raise their number," explained Jennifer Babbit, 26, a publicist.

> "A lot of my friends will say: 'I started having sex with this guy, but it only lasted a minute. I don't know if it counted,'" offered Beth Whiffen, a former associate editor at *Cosmopolitan*.

Apparently, there should be hook-ups, emotion-free liaisons, and FWB relationships, but *not* too many of them. "Few women would want to go over 20, or even 15," Ms. Babbit said, because they would "think of themselves as big sluts" (Williams, 2005). Traæen and Sørensen's study of Norwegians and hook-ups (2002) showed similar double standards and the power of social disapproval. One 25-year-old woman had had 10 PVI partners in the preceding year, which she said was too many compared to her friends. So the fear of really being a slut, whatever that means, is part of how women "calculate" the costs and benefits of hooking up. Women have been calculating the costs of their behavior for decades in the United States—this has not changed, unfortunately. The difference is simply that the stakes for heterosexual women appear to be higher now. In the 1950s, the rule was "don't call a boy" or it would seem too aggressive. In the new millennium, the rule may instead be "don't booty call a boy" (or it will seem too desperate, aggressive, and so on).

These fears are part of the current sexual landscape, along with other salient realities that also have not changed in the last 50 (or more) years: fear of pregnancy; need for safe, tolerable contraception; fear of contracting sexually transmitted infections (STIs); fear of coercion and assault. All of this can combine to create the "missing discourse of desire," or "the ambivalent discourse of desire" described in chapter 4. This may be because in everyday life, there are sociocultural barriers to women's full expression of the sexual desires or feelings they may have. Generally, women think about sex less, masturbate less, have fewer orgasms with partners, and fantasize less (e.g., Laumann et al., 1994; Sprecher and Regan, 1996; Baumeister and Tice, 2001).[53]

Contrast this with one account of young men's sexualities (Izugbara, 2004).[54] The researcher interviewed men aged 17 to 23, asking about sexualities and gender scripts. He found that men's sexual desires were viewed as "natural," and occasionally, "the desire comes by itself." It was acceptable for young men to listen to sexual stories and watch sexually provocative movies and pornography. "Good sex skills" lead to reactions from female partners; "girls were expected to scream, and beg, and call boys great during intercourse as is usually the case in [porn] films." The young men had clear, unequivocal ideas about desire and sex:

> Infrequent sex can make a boy become impotent or unable to satisfy girls sexually. To keep your penis working you need to be using it constantly. (18-year-old)

> It is not improper for boys to have many sexual partners. It is like that's how nature made it. (20-year-old)

> Boys and men are free to have several sexual partners, it is a symbol of virility. They just can't do without it—having several partners. (18-year-old)

There is no Goldilocks theory operating here, no "just right" amount of desire or number of partners. Instead, the masculine body is an unequivocal source of pleasure. In this construction, masculinity itself—the simple act of being a man—is the epitome of sexual.

CONCLUSIONS

Based on what you now know about gender and sexualities, what conclusions can you draw about hooking up in all its various permutations? Researchers express concern that because "patterns of sexual and intimate interactions are largely learned within the context of adolescent experiences, and these are likely to be extended into adulthood" (Weis, 1998: 122), people may develop a relational style that lacks intimacy and commitment.[55] How would we recognize this, document it as a pattern, and understand it? Is this a reasonable fear?

Let's return to where this section began, with the chapter on sexual fantasies. There is undoubtedly a gap between what we imagine sexually and what actually happens sexually. In fantasies, we tend to omit social context, peer (dis)approval, negative consequences, labeling, and the ways in which social controls constrain our behavior. Women imagine themselves with committed, loving partners, in lovely settings, and, well, you can guess the rest. . . . Men imagine themselves with (loving) partners who are active, interested, and skilled . . . and sometimes there just happen to be multiple partners who fit this description. Heterosexual hookups and FWB relationships seem like a noble attempt to compromise somewhere in the middle, but the compass points and the navigation somehow ends up off-course. Partners do not seem to end up in the same place—in a middle ground that closes the gaps between fantasies and realities. Who seems further from what they may really desire, if fantasies are any indication?

We will address questions of identity and desire in chapter 7. We have spent a lot of time outlining the contours of heterosexual desire, and in the process, beginning to establish what heterosexual identities are composed of. So in chapter 7, we will focus on the contemporary "alphabet soup" of same-sex identities and sexual orientations and explore other ways in which we configure our sexualities.

Questions to Ponder

1. What is the role of alcohol and drugs in hook-ups, and in sexual encounters and relationships more generally? Why do sex and substances seem to go hand-in-hand, like peanut butter and jelly or milk and cookies?

2. In heterosexual hook-ups, do men and women enter the "moment" from equal places? How does socialization into gender affect the possibilities and realities of hook-ups?

Suggested Projects

1. Write the introduction to a book proposal for a book on hooking up . . . for men. Decide whether you wish to write a general book or one more specific in terms of sexual orientation. How would you justify the book? What would be the purpose of your book?

2. If you were going to do research on hooking up, what would you do? What questions would you explore and what method would you use?

SECTION III

Outside Ourselves:
Sex in Social Context

7

LGBTQQPA (H), BDSM

THE ALPHABET SOUP OF SEXUALITIES

They shed their clothes, leaving them where they fell, and dropped into Kirk's bunk together. Spock slid his hands around Kirk's back and down to his buttocks, pulling Kirk against him. He could not wait for the sensation of Kirk's naked body against his; when he finally felt it, it was ecstasy. Kirk was warm in some places and cool in others, his arms and chest and thighs like sculpted marble. The pulse in his throat thrilled against Spock's lips. Spock's hands shook as he caressed the curves of Kirk's backside.

Kirk's hands were not particularly steady, either, as he stroked Spock's chest, carding his fingers through the curling black hair. "You're beautiful," Kirk whispered, "and all of a sudden I'm as nervous as a teenager."

—J. S. Cavalcante, "The Word Withheld"[1]

This is an excerpt of slash fiction, a form of fanfiction, and yes, it features Captain Kirk and Mr. Spock of *Star Trek* fame. Fanfiction writers extend and create stories about fictional characters from mass media. Slash writers specialize in transgressive, homoerotic stories about same-sex characters who may or may not be "buddies" in a television show, film, or book. The stories generally have a sexual element, if not actual sex scenes between well-known, presumably heterosexual male characters. Slash is an intriguing genre, as most of the writers and fans are female, the characters are male, and the sex can be hot and graphic. In a very real way, slash writers may represent the future of sexual identities—fluidity, liberation from labels, and individual sexual determinism.

In this chapter, we will explore some aspects of sexual identities. The title should provide a clue that a lot is simmering in the "alphabet soup" of sex. Let's start by briefly noting what each letter stands for:

L = lesbian

G = gay

B = bisexual

T = trans

Q = queer: is intended to be an inclusive term for lesbigay people; has social and political connotations. Historically, queer meant strange, out of alignment, or unusual. The derogatory connotation of queer as "deviant" was employed in the late nineteenth century by the Marquess of Queensberry, father of Alfred Douglas—the man embroiled in the trials of Oscar Wilde (see chapter 1)

Q = questioning: a person exploring and/or wondering about the contours of their feelings, interests, arousals, desires, and behaviors

P = pansexual: a person attracted to all sexes; occasionally applied to a person also attracted to objects, feelings, ideas, and concepts—a person who sees the sexuality and sensuality of many things and people

A = asexual: a person who "does not experience any sexual attraction" (www.asexual.org); may reject any other sexual orientation labeling, or may not

(H) = heterosexual

BD = bondage and domination, or bondage and discipline

DS = domination and submission

SM = sadomasochism, or sadism and masochism

"Bondage means tying, binding or restricting someone's movement. Discipline means corporal punishment, from spanking to paddling to caning. Domination is the act of looking like you're in control of the scene, of issuing the orders and 'running the show.' Submission is the act of lending your power of decision-making to another person for a pre-determined time, for spiritual, recreational, or sexual purposes. Sadism refers to enjoyment of inflicting pain, whether real or playful, and masochism refers to enjoyment of receiving pain, whether real or playful" (Miller, 2004).[2]

There are a lot of labels and a number of alphabetic tongue-twisters here; you may be most familiar with the terms *LGBT* and *BDSM*. Why do we have so many labels and letters, acting as shorthand for such a variety of sexual concepts? At their best and in their most neutral guise, labels serve a purpose, enabling us to communicate and share ideas. But labels also become the basis of and intertwine with expert and powerful diagnoses—think *DSM IV*—used to further define and normalize. Terms can quickly become overarching, used as shorthand to ostensibly explain and describe everything about a person: *lesbian, gay, submissive, dominant.* At their worst, labels become insults, derogatory terms to classify people as "normal" or "abnormal"—*kink, freak, pervert, fag, dyke, queer.* As we construct attributes for the people who are labeled in these ways, schemas take over, enabling us to narrow our perceptions and thus fail to see *individuals.* Instead we see types or stereotypes, and we fall back on schemas to organize our beliefs about the who, what, why, and how of people. Think about the stereotypical traits we attribute to people on the basis of knowing or assuming something about their sexuality. Schemas are implicated in the assumption that all "gay" men are effeminate hairdressers, all "lesbian" women fix cars and have short hair, and all "bisexual" people are indecisive commitment-phobes who are going through a "phase."

You may have noticed the (H) in the chapter title, which stands for "heterosexual." Why is it in parentheses? Why is it included in the alphabet soup? Is it normally in that long list? The letter is in parentheses because of course, *heterosexual* is not generally included when we talk about sexualities that we otherwise reduce to alphabet soup. It is included here because it would be erroneous to leave it out. All too often, discussions of sexualities *presume* heterosexuality without ever making that presumption clear. This presumption normally renders all other forms of sexuality completely invisible and therefore "Other." The other major reason why it is included in this list is a bit more complex.

THE INVENTION OF SEXUAL ORIENTATION

By this point in the text, you may have noticed that I often use the word *heterosexual* to clarify what is normally taken for granted. But you may also have noticed that I have discussed aspects of sexuality that include little research on anyone who is not heterosexual. Researchers will often exclude anyone who is not heterosexually identified, throwing out these respondents' questionnaires because the sample has too few nonheterosexual respondents. Instead of actively working to get more representation, researchers will simply ignore the data. When researchers do focus on LGBT or other-identified people, the studies may start with a research question that presumes that oceans of difference separate LGBT folk from heterosexually identified people. Examples would be questions about gay men's sexual behavior and HIV risks, or questions about identity issues and "coming out." General questions about sexuality are rarely posed—how do (all) sexually active young people feel about hook-ups? What elements characterize everyone's sexual fantasies? How do (all) people feel about their sex lives?

It is true that sexuality has been socially constructed to magnify differences between other-sex orientations and same-sex orientations. We have made orientation meaningful. Philosopher Michel Foucault wrote that sex has become the truth of our being, in effect (1978).[3] We believe that the most important thing we can know about a person, after establishing his or her sex/gender, is sexual orientation. In chapter 2, we briefly discussed how the term *heterosexual* had a different connotation at the turn of the twentieth century. It referred to someone with a "morbid sexual interest in the opposite sex" (Katz, 1995).[4] From its earliest usage in the late 1890s, *heterosexual* was associated with perversion; "normal" sex was procreative or reproductive desire and behavior. Anything else was abnormal or perverse. Remember the example of *The Scarlet Letter*, from chapter 1? In Puritan America, the setting for Hawthorne's novel, sexuality was singular and organized around marital reproduction, period. Anything else, whether adultery, onanism (masturbation), or sodomy (oral and/or anal sex), interfered with procreation and thus was punished. Krafft-Ebing, Freud, and sexologist Havelock Ellis (1859–1939) facilitated the discussion and labeling of individuals based on behavior and the sex of the preferred partner.

The evolution of *heterosexual* from perversion to taken-for-granted and "normal" occurred slowly throughout the first half of the twentieth century (Katz, 1995). For *heterosexual* to make sense as an identity, society had to develop an understanding of the term *homosexual* as its polar opposite. If one was normal, the other had to be abnormal. If one was usual, the other had to be unusual, if one typical, the other atypical. As society refined the terms, attaching behaviors, context, and judgments to *heterosexuality* and *homosexuality*, we also began to attach identities to people. In the abstract, we have to ask why it matters so much who our sexual, romantic, and affectionate partners are. Noted sociologist John Gagnon (1977) wrote:

It is a common, but false, belief that if we know that persons choose same-gender sex partners, we can successfully make inferences about the kinds of families they come from; the kinds of sex lives they lead; their tastes in clothing, art, music, interior decoration; the way they talk; the kinds of work they prefer; and their religious or leisure orientations. We do not believe we can make such inferences about persons who choose opposite-gender sex partners. Homosexuality (unlike heterosexuality) is a significant label, since it elicits a sequence of interlocked beliefs or judgments which organize our responses to ourselves and to other people. Our responses to the word "homosexual" or "homosexuality" (or persons so labeled) are part of a culturally acquired pattern of beliefs about a cultural stereotype, and constitute what we mean by homosexual and homosexuality (p. 235).[5]

People *are* different—we are individuals, after all—and some of that difference *does* relate to our sexualities. In this discussion, I am not denying that there are male individuals who really want to and like to be sexual with female individuals. Nor am I am denying that there are male individuals who really want to be sexual with other male individuals, and female individuals who want to be sexual with other females. There are of course a number of other permutations as well. What I am questioning is why all of this is so important in U.S. culture. Unfortunately, this is a relatively unanswerable question, but it is a worthy question for social constructionists and critical thinkers. Let's examine the question of identities and behaviors, with a focus on the ways in which we have socially constructed same-sex identities.

What Is Sexual Orientation?

One of Alfred Kinsey's enduring contributions to our conceptualization of orientation was the *Kinsey Scale* (discussed in chapter 2), a seven-point continuum from zero to six. Zero represented "exclusively heterosexual" (exclusive contact with and erotic attraction to the other sex) and six represented "exclusively homosexual" (exclusive contact with and attraction to the same sex). To develop the scale, Kinsey counted *outlets*, or orgasms, using data about how many men had (*ever*) had an orgasm via contact with another man. He concluded that since 37 percent of men had done so, most of the population was therefore bisexual, somewhere between one and five on his scale (1948).[6] The benefit to this conceptualization was that it appeared to be scientific and nonjudgmental, making no particular orientation superior. But his work has been challenged because that statistic has never been reported in other studies. Large, more representative samplings of populations in several Western countries indicate that about 5 percent of men and women have (had) same-sex experiences or attractions (e.g., Laumann et al., 1994).[7] Also, Kinsey's scale implies that people locate themselves on the continuum and then stay put. His iteration of the model did not seem to accommodate the reality that people can move throughout attractions, desires, behaviors, and self-conceptions during their lives. Finally, his scale did not include the reality that not everyone is either male or female, same or "opposite" sex, and most importantly, orgasms do not equal "orientation."

So how do we define the key concept of sexual orientation? It is the "cumulative experience and interaction of erotic fantasy, romantic-emotional feelings, and sexual behavior directed toward one or both [sexes]" (Kauth and Kalichman, 1995: 82).[8] Although the authors assume there are only two sexes, this definition does capture three major elements of how we orient ourselves sexually:

fantasies = the intrapsychic or mental realm; arousal and desires

feelings = our affective responses, interests, and inclinations

behavior = what we actually do and/or desire to do

It is also missing another crucial element, one that we have made salient in this culture in a way that other cultures have not—*sexual identity*. How do people understand themselves, how do they think of themselves; do they label themselves, and do they announce or enact that identity to an audience or in a social setting?

But the most enduring question posed in this culture is where does same-sex attraction and orientation come from? This is the umbrella under which the other aspects of orientation are sheltered, in a sense. We rarely hear anyone asking where heterosexualities come from, and that omission is not simply because it is the statistically dominant orientation. In fact, we rarely ask any questions about the societal status quo and the accepted order of things. And when we do ask questions, conflict normally ensues. Questions about slavery, racial inequalities, and the oppression of women promoted slow and subtle changes in culture, followed by strife, violence, and upheaval. In accepting "the way things are" and the belief that they make sense as they are, we are acknowledging that social order is beneficial, and in a way, social order makes "society" possible. However, in simply accepting that (only) same-sex sexuality needs to be questioned, we limit our understanding of all sexualities.

Psychologist Daryl Bem told members of the American Psychological Association, "The question 'What causes homosexuality?' is both politically suspect and scientifically misconceived. Politically suspect because it is so frequently motivated by an agenda of prevention and cure. Scientifically misconceived because it presumes that heterosexuality is so well understood, so obviously the 'natural' evolutionary consequence of reproductive advantage, that only deviations from it are theoretically problematic" (1997).[9] We do tend to presume that we know a lot about heterosexualities, but we really do not. And when we assume that the major element of heterosexualities is reproductive behavior, we really do a disservice to our understanding of sex, given that most heterosexual conduct ultimately prevents conception (whether via contracepted PVI or by choice of behavior, such as oral sex).

The fact that we do not ask certain questions may be a feature of the dichotomizing debate described in the first few chapters: essentialism and social constructionism, or nature and nurture. Recall that essentialism (the nature perspective) would posit that sexual orientation is in our genes, in our biological makeup—in our essence. Essentialists would argue that whom we are attracted to is in fact essential to who we *are*. This would be posited as the answer to my earlier question: Why does it matter so much who our sexual, romantic, and affectionate partners are? Social constructionism (the nurture perspective) would argue that society has constructed dichotomized, binary sexualities and constructed the whole concept of sexual orientation in the first place. As established in chapter 4, we learn about ourselves and others through a process of inference and filling in the blanks. For example, If I am female, and I am told that females are nurturing and caring, then by inference, males must be other things. I learn the rules and expectations from my culture. In constructing myself as *female*, and then as *woman*, I develop an identity. Sexual orientation works similarly, though we rarely hear heterosexually oriented people referring to themselves as "heterosexual," because the identity is taken for granted.

How Does Sexual Orientation Develop?

Essentialist perspectives are organized around the proposition that sexual orientation develops from birth, that we are "born this way." *The Advocate*, a GLBT newsmagazine, published a 2005 chronology called "106 Years of 'Born That Way,'" a report of the science behind essentialism—studies of twins, brains of dead men, genetically altered fruit flies, inner ears, eye-blinks, and gay genes. There are studies arguing that the length of the fingers is related to sexual orientation, and that the pornographic images that arouse us *define* our sexual orientation.[10] Most of these studies are flawed, whether by sampling problems, small sample sizes, poor definitions and key concepts, or exclusion of lesbians and bisexual women. One problem with brain studies is that we do not know how interactions and life experiences change the structure of the brain, but we know that they do. The NBC television show *Fear Factor* often poses a challenge to contestants—can a person actually eat bugs? People can and do (and do so on the television show), but experience convinces most Americans not to do so, or that it is "gross." So our brains may respond to a plate of bugs with the learned cognition of "yuck—that is not edible." We simply do not know exactly how experiences interact with cognitive pathways and brain structures, and we do not have any scientific studies that are able, thus far, to establish cause and effect for sexual orientation.

These studies are also conducted with the belief that identity is fixed. Sociologist Jeffrey Weeks (2003) writes, "Biological determinism insists on the fixity of our sexualities, on their resilience in the face of all efforts at modification. Social and historical explanations, on the other hand, assume a high degree of fluidity and flexibility in 'human nature,' in its potentiality for change—not overnight, not by individual acts of will, but in the long grind of history and through the complexities and agencies of social interaction" (p. 53).[11] Clearly Weeks is more persuaded by social and historical explanations. But as a cultural discourse or narrative, essentialism is seductive. It may feel good to say, as Popeye did in his comic strip and cartoons, "I yam what I yam . . . and that's all what I yam." People with minority sexual and gender orientations can employ this discourse to answer to the inevitable question of "where does a person like you come from?" Essentialism provides a reassuring answer to this question—I can't help who I am, I was born this way, it is natural for me to feel the way that I do, and so on.

Recall that Freud suggested that we are born polymorphously perverse, with the ability to respond to pleasurable feelings and sensations from anyone. He argued that our major developmental tasks include differentiating these sensations and "correctly" labeling them as appropriate or inappropriate, as homosexual or heterosexual. Sociologist Ken Plummer (1975) argues, like Weeks, that people *learn* same-sex orientations, and especially, learn what it means to consider it a crucial piece of self-identity.[12] In chapter 4, Sharon Lamb described how adolescent girls often have sexual interactions with other girls. They had to make sense of this but most developed (adult) identities as heterosexuals. We may feel attracted to and fantasize about a range of people but we must learn to coalesce these feelings into a meaningful orientation, via social

Lemert - labeling
Goffman - stigma

processes and interactions. This is probably facilitated by two social processes: labeling and *stigmatizing.* Labeling, as already described, is the process of naming behaviors, people, and phenomena. Sociologist Edwin Lemert (1912–1996) outlined the social forces behind labeling, which is a necessary element of the social construction of *deviance.*[13] Lemert argued that deviance is not objectively defined—it results from a powerful person or entity labeling, or naming, an act or actor as "deviant."

From the intersection of labeling and power, *stigma* develops. Originally developed by sociologist Erving Goffman (1922–1982), he defined the concept as an "attribute that is deeply discrediting" and that reduces the actor "from a whole and usual person to a tainted, discounted one" (Goffman, 1963: 3).[14] In socially stigmatizing an individual, we overemphasize an attribute, such as a minority sexual orientation, at the expense of seeing the whole person. For example, we employ language like "ex-con" to describe those who have served jail time for crimes (especially serious crimes). We believe that being a convicted criminal is deeply discrediting and allow it to overshadow everything else about the person. A recent example of the stigma's pervasiveness is the case of education professor Paul Krueger. As a juvenile, Krueger was convicted of homicide in Texas in 1965. He earned degrees in prison, was a model prisoner, and had fully complied with his parole. He was an excellent example of "rehabilitation." Though he had never committed any other crimes and had served his time, the Pennsylvania State University system dismissed him. The stigma of being an "ex-con" so discredited Krueger that even his two doctoral degrees and exemplary teaching record could not remove the taint. One thing we see is that a stigmatized individual is believed to possess an attribute that is devalued.

I have stated that we each must learn to develop a meaningful sexual orientation, via social processes and interactions. How do labeling and stigmatization facilitate the creation of sexual orientations? When we label, or name things, we give definition to attributes and identities. We begin the process of marking people because they seem different. The Freudian belief that homosexuality is connected to gender is pervasive. We decide that "gay" consists of things like feminized gestures or voice, interests that are typically attributed to women or girls, and in effect, doing anything that is the opposite of what men are supposed to do. Little boys call other boys "fags" or "queer" because they do not fit in to the hegemonic definition of masculinity. A boy may learn that the awkwardness he feels, or the difference he presents to an audience of peers and others, is called "gay." In chapter 4 I described Mairtin Mac an Ghaill's research with young men in an occupational training program. The men had labeled another man as a "gayboy" and were stunned to hear that he had a girlfriend. It was as if he had not properly embodied his labeling, the labels they had designated. Other boys might be labeled nerd, dweeb, geek, loser. They may view themselves in this light and grow up to be adult nerds, or contestants on the FOX television "reality" show *Average Joe.*

The process of stigmatization helps shape the development and trajectory of individuals' sexual orientation. Culturally, we have discredited and devalued homosexualities. So why would someone gay or lesbian assert that sexual orientation is a choice? Who would choose a profoundly socially stigmatized attribute? Sociologist Vera Whisman (1996) studied the cultural narrative or story of choice versus biology.[15] Via interviews, she found that lesbian women tended to explore the notion of choice more than gay men, who tended to assert a biological inevitability to their sexualities. The difference is exemplified by these respondents:

(Noel) I started to realize I was gay in high school, but I kept denying it and saying, "No, I can't be like that; this is the most horrible thing." I was very frightened and scared by it. That I could be like this, that I'm no good, that I'm not a normal person. Basically, I think as I get older, I've been empowered by knowing that I am gay, and even sometimes a faggot. I'm empowered by it; I'm not frightened by it. Initially, I felt so bad, but then I said, "I just feel it's something innate. I don't think of it as a choice." I really don't (1996: 13).

(Diane) This choice, 'cause it really truly has been a choice, it just feels like I made the choice [that's best for me]. . . . And also there's been something about being involved this way, like I really feel like I can identify myself as a lesbian, it's very much more powerful than I felt before, as a person (p. 33).

Seeing same-sex orientations as essential, or innate, seems like a sensible thing to do. It certainly fits with our cultural predilection for explaining human behavior by seeking biological causes. But perhaps more importantly, it seems less dangerous than advocating for choice (Whisman, 1996). If a minority sexual orientation is a matter of hard wiring, then it is above politics, above discrimination, above policies and regulation and moralizing. The explanation invokes science, which has a hold on the cultural imagination but also has a storied history, as we saw in the first few chapters of the book. If "sexuality" is solely a matter of biology, genetics, brain structure, hormones, and so on, then we could argue that we cannot condemn anything about a person's sexuality. If we are all born into our orientations, then we should not discriminate against

people who are not in the majority. This line of reasoning loosely follows that offered by the women's rights movement and the civil rights movement: do not deny us equality, because we cannot help how we were born.

But this kind of explanation returns us, in a very circular (or *tautological*) way, to the fact that we only require explanations for people with sexual interests, practices, or identities that are in the minority. Plummer (1995) refers to this as *sexual story-telling*, asking why we "turn what was not so long ago a private, secret world into a public one?" (p. 13).[16]

Why do we? The Oscar Wilde trials (see chapter 1) highlighted the public spectacle of someone being called to account for himself, for his interests and practices, his unchosen label of "sodomite." Plummer writes:

> But for many . . . who feel their sexual lives have become a source of suffering and anguish, the telling of a story is literally a "coming to terms." It is sensed as a necessary way of dealing with a sexual and gendered life. Commonly, such stories are taken to be signs of The Truth. . . . Sexual stories are assumed to be an approximation [of] the truth of the sexual (p. 34).

In coming to terms with sexuality, we literally name what we do and who we are. We develop the narrative, or story, of essentialism ("The Truth"), because it contributes to a broader cultural narrative that implores us to explore every last inch of ourselves and explain or account for who we are. The idea of The Truth is seductive. It underlies historical sex research and the search for the "gay gene." The Truth seems stable, scientific, objective—not subject to the whims of culture or individuality.

In contrast to essentialism, the narrative of choice is thought to be personally, individually empowering. It satisfies the cultural belief in individual destiny, the idea that we each have an American Dream (whatever it may be) that we can achieve as the result of our own hard work, efforts, desires, and imaginations. Within this narrative, we make choices, especially about our sexualities, which we think are the most intimate and unique aspects of ourselves. Sociologist Bob Connell (2000) describes an interviewee in his study of men and masculinities.[17] Adam told his sexual story, about which Connell reflected:

> It is easy to find pointers in [Adam's] childhood to why he might develop a sense of difference. They include an early willingness to be "eccentric," a history of pre-pubescent and adolescent erotic play with boys, being warned off "exploring" with a little girl by an angry parent, and feeling "smothered"

when he kissed a bigger girl. But it is interesting that Adam does not himself present this as a pre-history of gayness, and he is surely right. There is nothing here outside the experience of many boys who become exclusively heterosexual (p. 89).

Connell further explains that "we should not too much individualize this choosing. It was vital for Adam that 'being gay' was an identity that was ready and waiting for him. It was already defined by the cultural dynamics and sexual politics of the previous twenty years" (1995: 89). This is what Plummer was getting at with the concept of *sexual stories*. Adam was not interpreting himself, his interests, and his behavior in a vacuum. Within the context of social and institutional definitions and conceptualizations of biological sex, gender, and sexualities, we come to understand ourselves (Gagnon and Simon, 1973)[18] and indeed, are *compelled* to explain and confess these aspects of ourselves (Foucault, 1978).

To do this, we often go back to childhood, to our pasts, to reconstruct from possibly fading memories and experiences—especially if we have minority sexual interests. Note that this is the case for all of the letters in our alphabet soup, and any I have accidentally omitted. People interested in BDSM are expected to explain themselves, to answer the question "how did you get that way?" People who are asexual are expected to account for themselves, especially in the face of a sexualized culture in which we assume that everyone is at least *somewhat* sexual, especially men. In asking people to dissect their lives for clues, we can see the height of self-report bias. It represents a clear problem with asking people to "come to terms" and find language to describe experiences and feelings that only *they* can validate.

It is worth including a somewhat long excerpt from activist Leslie Feinberg's 1998 book on (trans)gender.[19] Feinberg lucidly captures the experience of being expected to account for one's self, sparked by a question about gender identity and "dysphoria":

"When did you first know you were different?" the counselor at the L.A. Free Clinic asked.

"Well," I said, "I knew I was poor and on welfare, and that was different from lots of kids at school, and I had a single mom, which was really uncommon there, and we weren't Christian, which is terribly noticeable in the South. Then later I knew I was a foster child, and in high school, I knew I was a feminist and that caused me all kinds of trouble, so I guess I always knew I was different." His facial expression tells me this isn't what he wanted to hear, but why should I engage this idea that my gender performance has been my most important difference in my life? It hasn't, and I can't separate it from the class, race, and parentage variables through which it was mediated. Does this mean I'm not real enough for [sex change] surgery?

I've worked hard to not engage the gay childhood narrative—I never talk about tomboyish behavior as an antecedent to my lesbian identity, I don't tell stories about cross-dressing or crushes on girls, and I intentionally fuck with the assumption of it by telling people how I used to be straight and have sex with boys like any sweet trashy rural girl and some of it was fun. I see these narratives as strategic, and I've always rejected the strategy that adopts some theory of innate sexuality and forecloses the possibility that anyone, gender troubled childhood or not, could transgress sexual and gender norms at any time. I don't want to participate in an idea that only some people have to engage a struggle of learning gender norms in childhood either. So now, faced with these questions, how do I decide whether to look back on my life through the tranny childhood lens, tell the stories about being a boy for Halloween, not playing with dolls? What is the cost of participation in this selective recitation? What is the cost of not participating? (p. 32)

In Feinberg's explanation, we see what Whisman uncovered in her interviews—a sense of the ways in which individual sexuality may have a chosen element to it. The argument is that we can make choices about how we engage with, interact with, and interpret the powerful cultural concepts surrounding sexual difference. Feinberg's decisions and choices are radical. They disrupt the taken-for-granted notions that, for example, "only some people have to engage a struggle of learning gender norms in childhood." As Connell's interviewee, Adam, demonstrates, the struggle to learn gender norms and interpret hegemonic scripts is a task for most, if not all, of us. Consider the terms *sissy, mama's boy,* and *tomboy.* They are nudges, reminders that gender norms have been subverted. Maybe these terms represent the hope that *tomboy* or *mama's boy* are phases, short-lived stages on the way to more "appropriate" adult gender presentations.

Imagine if heterosexually oriented people were asked to explain every aspect of their sexualities. In the 1970s, Martin Rochlin developed the "Heterosexual Questionnaire."[20] Every question remains relevant today, for example:

1. What do you think caused your heterosexuality?
3. Is it possible your heterosexuality is just a phase you may grow out of?
5. If you've never slept with a person of the same sex, how can you be sure you wouldn't prefer that?

7. Why do heterosexuals feel compelled to seduce others into their lifestyle?

10. A disproportionate majority of child molesters are heterosexual men. Do you consider it safe to expose children to heterosexual male teachers, pediatricians, priests, or scoutmasters?

11. With all the societal support for marriage, the divorce rate is spiraling. Why are there so few stable relationships among heterosexuals?

12. Why do heterosexuals place so much emphasis on sex?

19. Why are heterosexuals so promiscuous?

This questionnaire has been reprinted in its entirety in numerous anthologies, books, and on the Internet because it elegantly and concisely makes the point. We *never* ask these questions of heterosexually oriented people because we assume that heterosexual forms constitute the norm by which everything else is judged. As a result, most heterosexual people do not develop an identity of "heterosexual" that must be explored internally, given a culturally meaningful narrative, and perhaps overtly announced to others.

This is the *social* aspect of the alphabet soup that Feinberg refers to. Because we have, as John Gagnon argued, given terms and labels to make the concept of sexual orientation meaningful, we must socially construct or organize our interpretations. Younger generations may be more likely than older generations to say that they disdain labels altogether, that they are just individuals who love and sleep with other individuals. This may seem an individual, intimate aspect of the self, but is it really?

GENDER AND ORIENTATION

Gay men will often say their sexuality is hard-wired, while lesbians will often say their sexuality is a choice. Bisexual men and women seem more inclined to advocate for choice. Researchers suggest that bisexuality may be "less strongly tied to pre-adult sexual feelings" (Bell, Weinberg, and Hammersmith, 1981: 200–201),[21] implying that identification comes after "adult" experiences and feelings. Why would there be such a gulf in experience and explanation? Why don't all gay men and lesbian women interpret themselves similarly? (We'll address the many facets of bisexuality momentarily.)

One problem with the argument that orientation is hard-wired is that it could be seen as ignoring *desire*, "to want something very strongly." Women in Whisman's study (1996) who argued for choice also argued that in saying that we choose our sexualities, we are affirming what we desire. A respondent in Diamond's longitudinal study (2005) of identity change and stability said:[22]

[C]ertainly being with a woman feels the most comfortable for me . . . but I guess I can also see how if things were different and I felt that I couldn't for some reason be comfortable with a woman that it's certainly possible that I could be with a man. So, I don't know, I do feel like I've been able to make a choice for myself even though these feelings are here anyway (127).

Though this respondent saw herself as innately lesbian, she still maintained that her relationships with women were a feature of her choice—her desire. Thus part of the narrative of choice, for women, is the sense that it is empowering to actively choose how one's sexuality is to be configured. It confers a sense of agency, action, and desire, unfettered by social conventions, fear (including homophobia), and typical gender roles. It could be disturbing to the status quo, given the disenfranchisement of women's desire, to say, "I chose and I choose women. I choose not to sleep with men." Women seem to be more flexible and variable when "coming to terms" with their sexualities (e.g., Stein, 1989; Golden, 2003).[23] Recall that Jane Ussher (1997) did research on how lesbian girls and heterosexual girls experienced desire.[24] For the lesbian girls, the feeling was far more diffuse, less clearly connected to sexual fantasies or ideas independent of a particular partner. When a GLBT magazine asked its readers, "How did you meet your partner?," one respondent replied:

When I met my partner, Ana Maria, I lived with my parents. I was only 16 and about to start my senior year in high school. She was 12 years older. We met in a mall where we were both working. At that time I didn't even think of myself as a lesbian. But from the moment she asked me if I was, I started questioning myself, and after three months of friendship we became a couple. We kept our relationship a secret for about a year until my family started questioning my friendship with her.[25]

In the case above, there was no thought of being a lesbian until the option presented itself in the form of a woman, a friend, an open-ended situation. Adrienne Rich's 1980 treatise on compulsory heterosexuality is particularly salient here.[26] Rich argued that men's power over women and oppression of women has six main components (she references history and global practices in addition to contemporary practices):

1. *denying women's sexuality*
     via genital mutilation, chastity belts; punishment for lesbian sexuality and adultery; denial of the clitoris; denial of older women's sexualities;

pseudolesbian images in media and literature; control of images and ideas or forcing it [male sexuality] upon women

via forms of rape; incest; the socialization of women to feel that men have powerful sex "drives" that demand satisfaction; sex work; propagation of the "rape fantasy"

2. *commanding or exploiting women's labor and production*

via unpaid labors of marriage and motherhood; the "glass ceiling" in corporate structures; controlling access to abortion; sex work (pimping)

3. *controlling or robbing women of children*

via enforced sterilization; infanticide; not allowing lesbian parenting or adoptions; forced hysterectomies

4. *confining women physically and preventing movement*

via threat of and actual rape-as-terrorism; burqas, foot-binding, and so forth; haute couture, "feminine" dress codes; the veil; sexual harassment on the streets, enforced economic dependence of wives who do not work for pay

5. *using women as objects in male transactions*

via women as "gifts," bride-price, dowries; pimping; arranged marriage; women as entertainers to facilitate men's deals, for example, wife-hostess, cocktail waitresses (think the restaurant Hooters, and strippers), call girls, geisha; global sex trafficking, global sex tourism, especially in developing countries

and things like restraining women's creativity and self-knowledge, keeping women illiterate; making women's lives and herstories invisible; excluding women from "masculine" pursuits.

Like the "Heterosexual Questionnaire," "Compulsory Heterosexuality and Lesbian Existence" has been reprinted in numerous books and on the Internet. It represents a fundamental argument about the ways in which "the power of choice" has been constrained by the powerful social and institutional arrangements in cultures around the world. Rich suggests that women end up "trapped, trying to fit mind, spirit, and sexuality into a prescribed script." We need to consider the ways in which cultural and subcultural socialization operate to disable the range of sexual choices we all have. First, we must question the role of heterosexuality in defining itself as normative and anything else therefore as "Other." Then we must, as Rich has done, question the ways in which heterosexuality is "systematically male dominated" (Jackson, 1999: 163).[27]

In Japan, the question of choice is null. Ayako Hattori (1999) wrote that if a woman in Japan was asked what *heterosexual* means, "She probably wouldn't understand the question, because she won't understand the word 'heterosexual.' If she is attracted to men sexually, it is too fundamental for her to need a name for her sexuality."[28] In Japan, she writes, "heterosexuality is so natural, fundamental and common that heterosexual people don't need identity and the word 'heterosexuality.'" This is a common belief—heterosexuality is the fundamental, unnamed orientation. It is similar to other adjectives of power. Writer Beverly Yuen Thompson (2000) observed that sexual orientation relates to the social construction of race, with "white" as the unspoken adjective, the norm within which all other races are referenced:[29]

> Heterosexuality and homosexuality need each other to exist in a way that bisexuality needs neither. Ethnic communities and dominant white society need each other in order to explain their own racial identity. Stating that one is white implies that one is *not* non-white. If everyone were white, then no one would use this as an identity. We can see this played out in daily life. When mainstream white people are discussing another person, they will not point out that person's race unless that person is of color. White people would not state, "my white friend Mark," but they would say "my friend Mark—who's black."

Yuen Thompson's perspective makes sense. Without each term, label, idea, and discourse defining itself against the things that it is *not*, the whole classification system would fall apart. A consequence of societally applied classifications is the entire debate about "cause." If we were not so bent on classifying so that we could establish "normality," we would not need to establish the "cause" of (minority) sexual orientations. Julie Bindel (2004) writes about the distinctions between "choice" and "born that way":

> While understandable that, as a response to horrific homophobia that still prevails in most cultures and societies, some in the gay community wish to pass the buck for their choice of sexual identity to a rogue gene, it plays into the hands of reactionary geneticists whose agenda is terrifying. They are seeking to prove that those outside of the white, able-bodied heterosexual norm are inferior. We must not collude.
>
>   Being gay or lesbian is obviously not a choice like which sauce to have with your pasta, but more a mix of opportunity, luck, chance and, quite frankly, bravery. It is a positive choice, and we do not need anyone with a test

tube telling us otherwise. Heterosexuals? Some of them are OK, but I wouldn't want my daughter marrying one.[30]

This is in contrast to compulsory heterosexuality, which could be seen as a "survival strategy" and thus not a fully consensual choice (e.g., Rich, 1980; Pharr, 1988).[31] When Bindel writes that "it is a positive choice," she is saying that it is both a certain, unequivocal choice and that it is a confident, optimistic, innately beneficial choice. What inhibits everyone from seeing it this way?

Focus on Homophobia

The power of heterosexuality can reveal itself in *homophobia*, most simplistically defined as the fear of being, appearing, or seeming gay; fear of anyone or "anything" gay. It is tempting, especially in a climate in which *Will & Grace*, "gay proms," and queer 12-year olds exist, to dismiss homophobia as the irrational, closed-minded fears of a few people. Homophobia is used as a weapon of sexism in microinteractions, small group interactions, in broader socialization, and culturally (Pharr, 1988). Activist and feminist Suzanne Pharr eloquently describes how homophobia transcends the individual. Homophobia is a profound part of socialization into hegemonic masculinity; it is also at least a subtle aspect of femininities as well. At its most virulent, homophobia inspires hate crimes, murders, assaults (sexual, physical, and emotional), rapes, batteries, and other forms of violence.

Linda Eyre (1993) writes about teaching her prospective health education teachers about compulsory heterosexuality, heterosexism, and homophobia. She invited a queer speakers' panel to visit her course.[32] Afterward, the students had a heated discussion, assailing the event as "promoting homosexuality," among other things. When Eyre later realized that a few students had dominated the class, she asked everyone to write about their reactions to the panel and the class discussions. Two women students shared their thoughts:

I felt intimidated to speak up against the strong opinions raised by some. It is still hard for many of us to speak freely about homosexuality; our silence did not mean we agreed with the negative responses, we are still a little uncomfortable (p. 280).

> I didn't ask many questions because I had an irrational feeling that if I did people in the class might wonder if I was gay. That sounds crazy but I feel that this might be the reason why others didn't speak (p. 280).

These reflections clarify how homophobia works, how it inheres in individuals but has distinctly socio-institutional roots. Why would the first woman be uncomfortable speaking up, voicing her dissent from the loud voices speaking against homosexuality? The second woman provides the answer: people might wonder if she was gay. This fear reveals itself in my classes all the time, when people say things prefaced or concluded with "I'm not gay myself . . ." or "As a heterosexual . . ." Pharr calls this "lesbian baiting," where homophobia keeps women separate. If a woman speaks in support of other women who are lesbians, then she may be labeled or worse. So she keeps her silence, meaning that a woman is not coming to the aid of other women.

It is worse for men. Sociologist C. J. Pascoe (2005) argues that "fag talk and fag imitations serve as a discourse with which boys discipline themselves and each other through joking relationships" (p. 330).[33] Eighteen months of fieldwork in a diverse high school enabled Pascoe to get a sense of the ways in which "fag talk" insinuated itself into and throughout young men's interactions. Pascoe describes the specially masculine nature of this: ". . . Becoming a fag has as much to do with failing at the masculine tasks of competence, heterosexual prowess and strength or in any way revealing weakness or femininity, as it does with a sexual identity" (p. 330). Students told her that homophobia only applied to men, but lesbians were "cool." Pascoe only heard young women use the word "fag" three times, and "dyke" was not employed systematically. Even "slut" (or "ho") only occurred one time for every eight times that someone used "fag."

Hegemonic masculinity requires that anything remotely feminine be renounced (e.g., Herek, 1986; Kimmel, 1994).[34] But this conflicts with the fact that masculinity requires men to *like* women. So homophobia—the fear of anything at all "gay"—requires men to root out any femininity in each other, using insults like "you throw like a girl" and "you pussy." Meanwhile, proving manhood (e.g., heterosexuality) also means that men must be on an unrelenting quest to "get pussy." Contempt for anything "feminine" can unfortunately provoke contempt of women, leading to *sexism*, discrimination against one sex (and belief in the superiority of one sex). "The term *heterosexual* manufactured a new sex-differentiated ideal of the erotically correct, a norm that worked to affirm the superiority of men over women and heterosexuals over homosexuals" (Katz, 1995: 112). Katz is describing the evolution of *heterosexism*, discrimination against other orientations, and belief in the superiority of heterosexuality. There is also a connection between homophobia and violence against women:

> Homophobia and heterosexism are directly implicated for example in boys' and men's bashings and abuse towards other boys and men, in the young male recreational sport of "poofter [gay]-bashing" and in other hate crimes directed at those who are non-heterosexual or who are perceived to be non-heterosexual, and in some forms of violence directed at women (such as abuse of lesbians). The strong relationship between homophobia and masculinity is also a factor in boys' and men's practice of date or acquaintance rape and other forms of sexual violence. Boys and men may seek to have sex with women to prove to themselves and to others that they are heterosexual, to prove their manhood and to gain status among their peers (Flood, 1997).[35]

Flood refers to the use of violence, against women and other men, to embody the tenets of hegemonic masculinity. In an address to psychoanalysts, noted analyst Nancy Chodorow (1999) said, "Masculinity then ties together gender and heterosexuality—a gender defined around active and even aggressive maleness and a heterosexuality that is by definition male dominant and active. I want to emphasize here that there is nothing innate in being male that requires this and it is not universal. It is a joint outcome of cultural and interpersonal and family processes that masculinity must be different and dominant."[36] Chodorow is referring to white, middle-class masculinity. How does homophobia intersect with race, ethnicity, and class?

Race and ethnicity are implicated in the particular ways in which "fag discourse" is deployed (Pascoe, 2005). In the high school Pascoe studied, the standard markers of "fag" included things deemed *effeminate*, such as attentiveness to cleanliness, wearing neat clothing, and dancing. But urban hip-hop culture requires clean, oversized, precisely and carefully put together clothing. Hip hop and dancing were important elements of the high school culture. The best dancers were lauded, not vilified as "fags." Though different standards were applied in this context, it would be inaccurate to say that homophobia does not exist in American subcultures.

Sociologist Paula Rodriguez Rust studied race and class, finding the attitude that "lesbian or gay identity is a white thing among African Americans and Hispanics . . . and homosexuality is a 'Western' behavior among Asian Americans (Chan 1989; Espin 1987; Icard 1986; Matteson 1994; Morales 1989)" (Rust, 1996: 57).[37] A black bisexual woman in Rust's study said, "Homosexuality is frowned upon in the black community more than in the white community. It's as if I'm shaming the community that is trying so hard to be accepted by the white community." If same-sex sexuality is seen as acquiescing to whiteness, or assimilating to a structure that may be seen as valid, then queer people of color will ultimately feel torn in at least two directions (e.g., Delany, 2004).[38] The cultural context of racism means that men of color may "strike a hegemonic bargain" (Chen, 1999).[39] So a Chinese American man may think that "real men" are rich, and if he is rich, he will think he is real (American) man. ". . . His class privilege . . . is exchanged for 'true' manhood" (p. 601). Some gay Asian American men may feel as if they have little to trade in the hegemonic bargain, nothing that can get them closer to the ideal of white, middle-class masculinity. Chen described a man who spent over 10 years trying, mostly unsuccessfully, to date white men because he thought it would increase his status.

Homophobia is a rigid system, devoid of the kind of flexibility and fluidity that many people crave and engage in individually. It requires heterosexually oriented people to either acquiesce and silence themselves, as in the case of the college student in Eyre's classroom, or "come out" as allies to other people in the alphabet soup. The fear and social control in homophobia brings out the worst in all of us, leading to things like internalized homophobia in LGBT people. It can disable us from expressing care and affection for people of the same sex and lead us into sexual activities we are unsure about but engage in to "prove" heterosexuality. Homophobia is disabling and limiting. Hand in hand with compulsory heterosexuality and heterosexism, homophobia is a formidable social obstacle. A young woman's blog describes it this way:

> I am 24. I led a restricted life . . . until I left home at 18. The first week away . . . I met [him]. We had sex several months later, and believed if we did so we must stay together for life and get married. We have been together ever since.
>
> If I was a lesbian, how would I know?
>
> These things . . . are still more complicated than yes or no. These things are not just a matter of individual preference. They are a matter of intense socialization and peer pressure, a matter of rebellion and opportunity to rebel, or lack thereof. . . . Society is still misogynist, sexist, homophobic, and heterosexist. It's still almost impossible for a woman to just stumble onto her authentic self on the path to adulthood. . . . She has to have a certain amount of dumb luck and a great deal of determination. And it still might escape her.[40]

CONTEMPORARY ISSUES

Focus on Bisexualities: Gender, Age, and Race

Have you ever heard anyone say, "I'm not myself today—I must have gotten up on the wrong side of the bed?" This disclaimer is a way of saying "don't mind me today—tomorrow I should be back to normal." We like to think that we possess *stable selves*, that from day to day we are basically the same person, across settings and interactions. Similarly, we like to believe that our sexualities are stable as well. For many people, it is the case that our sexual identities are pretty solidly rooted by the time we are 18. But we can have fantasies and experiences that make us wonder. There may be a sexual encounter that inspires some questioning. When I was in college, the woman who lived across the hall knocked on my door one night. As a peer sexuality educator, I was known as a source for condoms and information. She wanted to talk about what had happened two nights earlier, when she and a friend had gotten tipsy. They ended up in bed together, and though they'd woken up together, they had not talked about the evening, the future, or their friendship. She wanted to know if I thought she was a lesbian, or maybe bisexual.

One masturbatory experience between two 11-year old boys or a tipsy make-out session between two 19-year-old young women does not necessarily have anything to do with sexual identity. It may suggest more about the fluidity of sexualities or people's experimental abilities than anything else. Nonetheless, unexpected attractions, fantasies, desires, and interactions can cause us to question the stable selves that we otherwise like to take for granted. The concept of the stable self, in this case, is also connected to the dichotomization of sexual orientation into same-sex and opposite-sex. Because of this narrow construction, we are expected to box ourselves into one or the other; if it is same-sex, we are also expected to adopt the appropriate labels and identities. So *bisexuality*, being attracted romantically, sexually, relationally, to men and women, is not really culturally or subculturally scripted (Gagnon, 1977). Bisexuality is very hard to define and is most accurately described in the plural as bisexualities, because if we asked 10 self-identified people to describe what being *bi* means, we would get 10 different definitions (e.g., Hutchins and Kaʻahumanu, 1991).[41] One person may be intensely sexually attracted to and involved with one sex, but mostly romantically involved with another. Another person may be infrequently sexually interested in anyone but feel very emotionally drawn to more than one sex. Still another person may like certain sex acts and feelings with one sex and like other acts and feelings with another sex.

As we grow into adulthood we often feel as if our sexual orientations become solidified, but this is certainly not the case for everyone. Have you ever heard the expression *lesbian-until-graduation,* or *l.u.g.*? Or *b.u.g., bisexual-until-graduation*? The slang comes from the observation that some women appear to have same-sex partners mainly while in college and then appear to have only opposite-sex partners afterwards. It is contentious for several reasons. First, the slang implies that women's same-sex attraction is a phase, a transitory interest. This is certainly the case for some women, but clearly not for all. It reinforces the erroneous perception that bisexuality is invisible, that it is not a real way in which some people identify themselves. A woman who has female partners in college and male partners afterward may never have conceived of herself as a lesbian. If she thought of herself as bisexual all along, then l.u.g. is an inaccurate characterization that makes her bisexuality invisible. As activist Robyn Ochs has said, a bisexual woman can walk down the street, affectionately arm-in-arm with her female partner and people will assume that she is a lesbian. If the same woman walks down the same street with her male partner, people will assume that she is heterosexual. Unless a person wears a shirt like "Wanna Know What Bisexuality Looks Like? Then Stop Staring at My Chest and Look at My Face!," bisexuality is hard to convey to social audiences. How many famous bisexuals, living or dead, can you name? Singer Ani DiFranco may be the only person who readily comes to mind, and that is probably because she has sung about it and spoken about it in interviews. So someone who has multisexed partners in college who then becomes *monosexual* (oriented to only one sex) may still consider herself bisexual. But why are these labels almost exclusively applied to women?

Communication professor Michaela Meyer (2005) described a day of impromptu speeches in her public speaking class.[42] Several students drew a card with the subject "Bisexuals"—the first few to draw it kept returning it to the hat. Finally, a student who drew the card toward the end was flustered, but explained the difference between gays and lesbians (who "have a biological deficiency") and bisexuals (who "have a choice"). The evidence to support this, according to the student, was that "most of her friends had experimented with same-sex kissing, or making out, which she considered an act of bisexuality . . . the behavior was experimental" (p. 4). A student in the class commented that "it's a college phase people go through." This myth, misperception, or misinformation is pervasive. Let's explore it a bit further, addressing gender and age issues regarding bisexualities.

Psychologist Lisa Diamond has been doing longitudinal (long-term) studies on sexual identities (e.g., 2003; 2005).[43] Diamond's purpose is to describe and explain patterns in sexual attractions, behaviors, and identities. Her sample consists of 89 young sexual-minority women, all initially interviewed in 1994, when they were between 16 and 23 years old (2003). She has been re-interviewing them at intervals since then, producing solid data about how these women construct their sexualities.

One of Diamond's findings is that women who identify as lesbian or bisexual at ages 18 to 25 may not completely lose their feelings of attraction to other women. Only 25 percent of the 89 interviewees no longer identified as lesbian or bisexual five years later. Only one of these women said that her interest in women was a phase; the others indicated that they were still attracted to women, at least in the abstract. Half of the 25 percent who did not call themselves lesbian or bisexual adopted "heterosexual," while the other half had abandoned labels completely.

While it is appealing to think that sexuality is inborn, and that our interests and attractions are thus stable throughout life, this may not be the case. Psychiatrist Fritz Klein (2003) developed the *Klein Orientation Grid,* inspired by Kinsey's scale.[44] He recognized that, as an unscripted orientation, bisexualities may have multiple dimensions: attraction, behavior, fantasies, emotional/romantic/love preference, social preference, lifestyle/community identification, and self-identification. Klein suggested that questions about these dimensions be posed about respondents' immediate experiences, entire histories, and future ideals. This model hints at the complexity and fluidity of bisexual orientations, which we will explore more later.

The (White, Blond, College) Girls Have Gone Wild . . . : Questions of Identity and Age

You know those videos . . . where "college girls" get a little tipsy, talk to the cameraman, and then flash their breasts or thongs. One day while I was writing this book, a late-night infomercial appeared on a cable channel advertising the "Girls Gone Wild Games":

> "Girls Gone Wild Games/Girls Gone Wild Co-ed Tryouts"
> Ever dream of having your own private island full of hot young girls battling each other for your viewing pleasure? . . . absolutely anything goes with the hottest, sexiest young girls you've ever seen! . . . The Girls Gone Wild Games—no rules, no parents, and of course, no clothes!

> Co-Ed Tryouts . . . looking for the sexiest young girls you've ever seen. These hot, innocent college girls are willing to do ANYTHING. . . .[45] What does this have to with bisexuality? Apparently, the girls have gone so incredibly wild that they are hooking up with each other . . . on film (spelling and typo errors original).

"Girls Gone Wild Island Orgy and Daddy Little Girls!" You'll witness sexy 18-year-old Amber loose her virginity to another girl. . . . And If you like cute, young, innocent blonds—and who doesn't—you're going to love "Daddy's Little Girls" when sweet young things corrupt each other when Daddy's not around . . .

They even have a "Girls Who Like Girls" video with "the hottest girl on girl action." Now, in just this chapter alone, we have seen evidence that culture's perception of women who have sex with women differs compared to culture's perception of men who have sex with men. Women do not seem to control each other's sexual behavior with taunts of "dyke," though societally, women's behavior has been constrained. Research has found that heterosexual men's attitudes about homosexuality differ depending on gender. They are more negative about gay and bisexual men than about bisexual and lesbian women (e.g., Herek, 1988; Horn and Nucci, 2003).[46]

Heterosexual men fantasize about multiple female partners who have sex with each other while including him (e.g., Kimmel and Plante, 2002).[47] Pascoe (2005) also noted this among the male high school students she studied, and Meyer (2005) described a college student who said that "most of her friends had experimented with same-sex kissing, or making out." Are these women and the video girls who went wild (hereafter, "wild girls") all lesbians? Are they bisexual? Are they heterosexual? Are they beyond labeling?

Recall that sexual orientation has four central components: fantasies, feelings, behavior, and identity. Without asking each and every individual about these four things, we cannot really know how sexual orientation is configured.

Fantasies. What do we really know about fantasies? Not enough and not much. Most sexuality research ignores them entirely, as you have read. When they *are* addressed, research is normally quantitative, which may be an incomplete way to understand something that is mental, usually private, and occasionally embarrassing. Do the wild girls fantasize about baring themselves for cameras, audiences, and late-night infomercials? Do other college-aged women fantasize about making out with their female friends and acquaintances? Are they aroused by being sexual with other women?

Feelings. How do women feel about these being sexual with women? Glad, indifferent, embarrassed, thrilled, exposed, happy? Are there feelings of love, romance, desire, and *intrinsic* interest (defined in the dictionary as "by or in itself, rather than because of its associations of consequences")?

Behavior. In U.S. culture, we often make the mistake of assuming that behavior tells the truth about a person—that we are (only) what we do. This is part of how labeling comes about; a person commits a serious crime (behavior) and that becomes all that we see or "know" about them (as in "felon" or "ex-con"). When I was in third grade, I clogged all the toilets in the girls' bathroom at school, unloading all the toilet paper into each bowl. In seventh-grade, I sat on the deserted bleachers behind the middle school holding a marker and trying to think of pithy graffiti that would be eye-catching and provocative but that would not get me caught. Why did I do these things? I was bored, plain and simple. If someone had labeled me a bad kid, a juvenile delinquent, I probably would not be writing this book. I might have become my behavior, in effect. But my childhood behavior says very little about who I am today, trust me.

"Behavior = truth" is connected to the modern invention of *heterosexual* and *homosexual* as designated identities (e.g., Katz, 1995). Prior to the 1880s or so, some people engaged in occasional same-sex activities without being labeled homosexual (Chauncey, 1994; Valocchi, 1999).[48] Women had "Boston marriages," which we might call lesbian relationships, but that were devoid of the stigma and the benefits of current labeling and identities (Faderman, 1981).[49]

There are other cultures where the concept of behavior = truth does not exist in this way. Anthropologist Gilbert Herdt (1981) studied the Sambia, in the Eastern Highlands Province of New Guinea.[50] Sex textbooks almost always mention Herdt's fieldwork because Sambian culture is organized around some very clear gender and sexuality ritual expectations for both men and women. Females are thought to be born possessing everything they need to reproduce, save what a penis can provide (i.e., semen). Reproduction in a marital, heterosexual relationship is the most important adult goal for Sambians, so the problem is that males are not *born* able to reproduce. They need to be "cleansed of pollution from their mothers, followed by insemination by the older boys in order for them to grow big and strong" (Herdt, 1997: xii).[51] "Normal and natural" is for boys to be inseminated by other men, and then do the inseminating, to younger boys and their wives. There is literally no conceptualization of what Westerners would call "homosexuality" or "bisexuality." For Sambians, the same sex rituals are not about "sexuality"—they are about gender role attainment and the ability of a boy to grow up and become a man who fathers children. In fact, Herdt is gay, and his Sambian friends thought he would be lonely without a wife (and tried to set him up with a Sambian woman). To them, it was bizarre that he could be an adult man and not be married and reproducing. So it is a very culture-specific and historically specific concept that same-sex behavior = the truth of an individual's sexuality.

Identity. Identity development in modern Western cultures is dependent on many social variables. Who interacts with us? What are their perceptions of us? How are we labeled by others? How do we see ourselves (self-concept)? What do we call ourselves internally? How do we think about ourselves internally? What do we call ourselves when we speak to others? How do we explain ourselves to others? Once we develop a sense of our sexual selves, we tend to begin sharing aspects of that self with others, our audience of specific and generalized others. This enables us to confirm elements of that self. We will begin to associate with people who confirm our interpretation of ourselves. So a heterosexual teen will probably associate with mostly other heterosexual teens, and interactions will reinforce self-concept.

Having learned through socialization that heterosexual is "normal" and that gender is culturally associated with sexuality, we will begin presenting our identities in gendered ways. One way to know who we are is by establishing who we are *not*. A heterosexual teen may resolve to change her tomboy presentation of self to a more *Cosmopolitan*-inspired presentation of a heterosexual woman. A gay or lesbian teen may resolve to present the self in a way that communicates their sexual orientation—or the total opposite. The risk is that orientation and labels can become a person's *master status*, a status that dominates all of the individual's other statuses (age, race, and so forth) and is the overriding ingredient for determining how that person is viewed and often, how he is treated. The point is that identity, in this culture, is meaningless without an audience confirming it or otherwise weighing in on it. We do not live, develop, or think in a vacuum devoid of any social influence.

The process of identity development is theoretically similar for all eventual permutations, except that anything outside the narrow permutations of hegemonic heterosexuality is fraught with potential problems (e.g., Rubin, 1984).[52] Developing a sense of oneself as outside the narrow boundaries, regardless of whether that self-concept is ever made public in any way, can lead to self-doubt, depression, and confusion (e.g., Halpin and Allen, 2004; Cross and Epting, 2005).[53] Individual determinations of labeling and revelations are probably subject to cost-benefit analyses: what do I have to lose by coming out? What do I have to gain? What do I gain by "being myself" and being sexual in the ways that make the most sense to me? What do I lose? The answers to these questions will differ individually but are subject to broader variables, such as age, class, race, ethnicity, and the like (e.g., Valentine, 2003).[54] Fieldwork with an "alternative lifestyles" group for tenants in low-income housing, mostly African American and Latin American, enabled anthropologist David Valentine to see how complex self-determination can be. As multiply disenfranchised people, by virtue of class, race, ethnicity, and "non-normative genders/sexualities," the group members spoke of themselves in terms that conflicted with the interpretations of social workers and others with power. Nora, a Latina self-identified "heterosexual transsexual woman [and] former drug user," was told in effect to "enlighten her identity" to *transgender*.

So what about all the wild girls and those making out and hooking up in their dorms and at parties? One of my female students wrote a very honest paper addressing this:

> I have kissed a girl—more than one and more than once, in fact. Does this mean that I am bisexual? I don't think so. I consider myself heterosexual, partially because my boyfriend was watching me kiss those other girls. I did it for him, in a way. Being drunk didn't hurt either, but truthfully, I mainly did it because I knew he would like it. I thought it would make me seem more sexy, more of the kind of girl I thought he would like. When I was doing it, I had my eyes closed but I was wondering how many guys were watching me. The kisses didn't turn me on but knowing that guys were looking did, a little bit anyway.

So what is my student's sexual orientation? Is she heterosexual? That's what she calls herself, but if someone else burst onto the scene, lacking context, they might think she was a lesbian. Kissing other women did not arouse her, but the idea of being watched, being gazed upon and deemed "sexy" did. Maybe she is sexually oriented to exhibiting her sexuality? Maybe it could best be described as oriented to being the object of men's desires. Maybe she is oriented to partner dominance and personal submission? She was doing what her boyfriend seemed to want or desire and she wanted to please him. Maybe she has a cost-benefit (social exchange) orientation to sex, trying to do what benefits and rewards her the most. We do not yet live in a sex-positive culture in which we provide ourselves with the tools to easily and successfully pose these questions, let alone answer them.

This could describe all the girls who went wild. The video company markets their products by highlighting "young girls" subject to "no rules, no parents." They are "sweet innocent Daddy's girls" whose "corruption" occurs for your viewing pleasure. The women who engage in "girl on girl" sex are constructed as simultaneously sexually wild and innocent, coaxed into performing for the cameras "for the first time," outside the bounds of social conventions like heterosexuality, sex with men, and Daddy's implicit expectations that a girl like his daughter would never do such a thing! We are led to believe that these innocent, white, "blond," college i.e., middle-class or upper-middle-class) girls are reluctantly showing the camera things they do anyway, but normally in the privacy of their own fantasies and (dorm) rooms.

It is no wonder that we might wonder how women's bisexuality is configured, and really no surprise that anyone would coin the terms *l.u.g.* or *b.u.g.* We are shown behavior devoid of individual interpretations or processes of identity. We do not see the women considering why having a huge audience is more arousing than what they are actually doing sexually. We may not hear friends or acquaintances dissecting fantasies, feelings, and identities after their "experimental" same-sex make-out sessions. Valentine (2003) suggests that we listen to what people say about their desires, "whether in the intimacy of a particular encounter, reports of past experiences, or fantasies spoken out loud" so that "the contradictions . . . of self-identity can become evident" (p. 126). Women who identify as bisexual use, on average, 2.6 terms to describe themselves but some choose 10 or more (Rodriguez Rust, 2001).[55] We also must consider the costs and benefits/rewards for individual enactments of sexuality.

Women's sexualities (regardless of sexual orientation, actually), tend to be more easily shaped by sociocultural and situational factors (Baumeister, 2000).[56] An example of how situational factors influence sexuality is something a friend shared with me in college. She told me that because she had a boyfriend, she found herself being more interested in sex, thinking about it more, and even masturbating. He was interested in regular sex—at least once a day—so she was as well. But without a boyfriend, she found herself relatively uninterested, falling asleep while masturbating (from boredom) and going weeks without even thinking anything sexual. "If I'm not having it, I don't even notice it, and I certainly don't miss it," she told me. It seems as if women's desires are harder to pin down because they are more variable, more contextual.

This can be good and bad. The benefit to this—what Baumeister calls *plasticity*—is that women may be easily able to adapt to changing *cultural* scripts and expectations, along with making adaptations in the context of particular partners. Women may benefit by being more open to trying new things that partners suggest, seeking and taking advice about sex, and developing their sexual selves. But the detriment is that women may be more susceptible to pressure and coercion and more prone to confusion and discontinuity in their sexual lives. Increased plasticity may explain why many women who develop lesbian identifications have had prior other-sex experiences, and why we hear about being a *l.u.g.* but not a *g.u.g.* (gay until graduation). This context can lead to conflict within lesbian communities, debates about whether bisexuality is "real," and claims that lesbian identity is "morally pure" while bisexuality is deviant (Ault, 1994; Stein, 1997).[57] Social pressure and control (Rich's *compulsory heterosexuality* concept) may explain a lot. Historically, it has been easier to present a heterosexual façade than to be lesbian. And why do we not use the term *gay until graduation?* Because, as we have established, there is much more pressure on men to be heterosexual, and there is potentially a much greater cost to men who are attracted to and have sex with other men.

The problem is that women's sexualities and desires have been muted culturally, by fear, repression, and the perception that women's sexualities are too mysterious to be fathomed. If women are more plastic, as in the case of those who appear on *Girls Gone Wild!* and women at parties kissing other women, it may be because women have much less cultural foundation for certainty. It is harder for women to know what they want, what turns them on, what they like or need sexually. We do not have a large and diverse body of touchstones, in a sense. Men's sexualities seem more culturally script-ed and detailed. Men are encouraged to think of themselves in relation to the body parts that turn them on, the body types, the attributes of a partner, and the activities that arouse. They are encouraged to master their sexualities, act on their desires, and satisfy themselves. If we actually enabled this across our culture for everyone—if we de-gendered desire, arousal, and fantasies—who knows what sexualities would be like? What are the costs and benefits? Are the rewards of experimentation, exploration, and potential bisexual identity greater for women than for men?

"Does Men's Bisexuality Really Exist?": *Debates and Context*

While I was writing this book, the *New York Times* reported on a study that compared self-identified bisexual, heterosexual, and gay men.[58] Benedict Carey's article, "Straight, Gay or Lying? Bisexuality Revisited" ignited commentary and controversy all over the Internet; my friends rushed to email me the article before I finished the book. The article described psychologist J. Michael Bailey's and colleagues' ongoing research on arousal and sexual orientation (Rieger, Chivers, and Bailey, 2005).[59] The newspaper article's title referenced something that people will occasionally say—evinc-ing the idea that there is no one who is *really* bisexual (especially not men). Many read-ers and bloggers responded negatively, feeling that the article's title was biased. Some readers objected because the article did not mention that Bailey had previously done some controversial research on trans and gender issues (e.g., Bailey, Bechtold, and Berenbaum, 2002; Bailey, 2003).[60]

It is worthwhile to spend some time really examining the Rieger, Chivers, and Bailey research on which the *Times* reported. First, this is exactly the kind of sexological science you will hear about and be exposed to throughout your life, outside of and beyond college. Second, the *Times* is a very reputable news source, but it is necessary to learn how to analyze even venerable sources of information. Let's use the critical thinking template (see chapter 1) to explore the study that sparked the *Times* article.

Purpose of the Research.   Rieger, Chivers, and Bailey start by saying "there has long been skepticism that [bisexuality] is motivated by strong sexual arousal and attraction to both sexes" (p. 579). They wished to explore arousal without relying solely on self-report data, requiring them to use penile strain gauges to test genital arousal. These gauges reflect even subtle changes in penile girth during erection.

Key Questions/Issues and Hypotheses.
- "Bisexual men are substantially aroused by both male and female stimuli" (p. 580).
- "Bisexual men, like homosexual men, are much more aroused by male than by female stimuli" (p. 580).
- "Bisexual men show a mixture of homosexual and heterosexual patterns of sexual arousal, with some having much more arousal to male stimuli and others having much more arousal to female stimuli" (p. 580).

The authors reported research showing that gay men are more genitally aroused by "sexual stimuli" showing men (e.g., pornographic images), while straight men have the opposite pattern (e.g., Chivers et al., 2004).[61] So the key question really is, do bisexual men show a mixture of gay and straight arousal patterns, based on penile strain gauges?

Key Concepts.   Bisexual, homosexual, heterosexual; arousal; penile strain gauge; sexual orientation.

Point of View.   The researchers are psychologists. Rieger is a graduate student in Bailey's lab; Bailey's research has focused on sexuality, gender, and sexual orientation, with an evolutionary psychology emphasis. Chivers works at a treatment center that studies addictions and mental health.

Evidence and Information.   There is a very brief literature review, citing the work of everyone from Krafft-Ebing in the 1880s to Magnus Hirschfeld in the early 1900s to the NHSL survey (Laumann et al., 1994). We can also see how the authors define the key concepts by looking at this initial evidence. Men who "adopt a bisexual identity . . . may have intense sexual attraction to both men and women, or they might have sex partners of both sexes" (p. 579). So *bisexual* is clearly being defined solely in terms of sex, not romanticism, relationships, feelings, or fantasies.

The other evidence is in the form of specific procedures and findings from the authors' research. They placed advertisements in gay-oriented magazines and one "alternative" newspaper, ending up with a sample of 101 men. Of the sample, 33 men identified themselves as bisexual, 30 as straight, and 38 as homosexual. The authors asked them to locate themselves on the Kinsey Scale; those who were between one and five were classified as bisexual (where zero = straight and six = gay). On average, they were about 30 years old, and about 50 percent were people of color. The respondents watched an 11-minute neutral film of landscapes, followed by two-minute clips of different sexual films, one depicting two men having sex and the other showing two women having sex. The men were hooked up to the penile strain gauges and were asked to indicate "subjective" arousal. After excluding those who did not seem aroused enough, the sample was trimmed to 21 straight men, 22 bisexual men, and 25 gay men (for genital arousal analysis); there were 24 straight men, 24 bisexual men, and 31 gay men in the analyses of subjective arousal.

The authors found that bisexual men did *not* have a "distinctly bisexual pattern of genital sexual arousal, although they did report a distinctly bisexual pattern of subjective sexual arousal" (p. 581). However, arousal connected to the sexual films was greater for *all* men than arousal connected to the neutral, nonsexual film. The divergence between subjective—self-reported arousal—and genital arousal was explained as due to either "exaggeration" of subjective arousal (lying about it) or suppression of genital arousal. The authors conclude that "it remains to be shown that male bisexuality exists" (p. 582).

Inferences the Authors Make.   There may be some leaps in logic, notably that bisexual orientation is solely about sex; that genital arousal is the gold standard with which to determine everything about individual sexuality; that there is a distinctly bisexual arousal pattern that exists, waiting to be documented (but undocumented in this study). One obvious inference is that people who are "Kinsey ones" (mostly heterosexual with incidental homosexual interest) all the way up to "Kinsey fives" (mostly homosexual with incidental heterosexual interest) could logically be lumped together as they were in this study. "I'm not denying that bisexual behavior exists," said Dr. Bailey, "but I am saying that in men there's no hint that true bisexual arousal exists, and that for men arousal is orientation" (Carey, 2005). Bailey is inferring that "for men arousal is orientation." Bailey writes in a letter replying to a critique of some of his earlier work, ". . . men's true sexual orientations can often be discerned using equipment to measure genital arousal" (2002).[62] Can we really know that this is the case, unequivocally, when there is still so much unknown about sexualities?

Assumptions.   Some of the authors' assumptions are essentially the same as their inferences (or, leaps of logic and reasoning): that there is a "distinctly bisexual" arousal pattern; that bisexuality is about sexual attraction and behavior; that penile strain gauges accurately capture genital arousal. There are other assumptions below the surface.

1. The authors assume that the Kinsey Scale *is* an accurate way to assess sexual orientation. If so, then how can the researchers account for the fact that everyone showed at least a little arousal to both sex films, compared to the neutral (landscape) film, which generated no real arousal? If heterosexual men—Kinsey Scale "zeros"—showed a little arousal to the films of men having sex, then perhaps there is no such thing as a "pure" heterosexual! Or maybe it's just that the Kinsey Scale is not necessarily the best measure of orientation.

2. The authors assume that the sample size—approximately 68 valid measurements for genital arousal and 79 for subjective arousal—is sufficient to make the kinds of inferential conclusions the authors offer. The sample lost men because they did not show measurable genital and/or subjective arousal. "Although about a third of the men in each group showed no significant arousal watching the movies, their lack of response did not change the overall findings, Mr. Rieger said" (Carey, 2005). How do we know that the excluded men are the same as those who were aroused enough to be included?

3. The authors assume that the sample is actually in some way representative of bisexual men, in Chicago or anywhere else. There are no real caveats or limitations listed in the study. But the recruitment involved placing ads in gay magazines and an alternative newspaper. It can hardly be said that a representative swath of bisexually-oriented men read these publications. Further, the respondents self-identified as bisexual, but not all bisexually-active men do so. Men who have sex with men but identify as heterosexual would be unlikely to respond to a study like this. Also, people who are not really interested in mass-market pornography cannot be included in the study.

4. The authors assume that things like race, ethnicity, nationality, social class and other (subcultural) variables have no impact on men's genital arousal and subjective arousal. The assumption that arousal=orientation is the dominant, overriding force. Bailey hints at this in a commentary posted on his Web site: "Sexual arousal is as important and fundamental a phenomenon as hunger, fear, or pain. Sexual orientation is a fundamental aspect of who we are" (Bailey, 2002).

5. The authors assume that bisexuality is simplistically understandable as a function of arousal and sex, period. "But other researchers—and some self-identified bisex-

uals—say that the technique used in the study to measure genital arousal is too crude to capture the richness—erotic sensations, affection, admiration—that constitutes sexual attraction" (Carey, 2005). Maybe this study is *really* evidence of diversity in bisexual orientations—that some self-identified bisexuals are sexually more attracted to one sex, but drawn to other things (romantic, emotional, and so on) about the sex that is less sexually captivating. Researchers have found evidence that bisexual orientations have multiple dimensions and complexity (Rust, 2001; Weinrich and Klein, 2002).[63]

6. The authors assume that sexual stimuli, in the form of the two-minute clips, are "pure" for the respondents. What I mean is that the researchers were assuming that arousal is a feature of simply watching two men or two women engaged in a brief sex act. Since we do not have a lot of good research on fantasies, which are crucial to understanding arousal, how can we know what turns people on or off about the films they watched? Respondents simply indicated that they were aroused, and the penile strain gauges measured blood in the penis, but none of this indicated *why* men were aroused or not aroused.

Maybe the bisexual men did not respond as much to the clips of women because the women were actors, presumably heterosexual. Maybe the men would have responded more to images of a man having sex with a woman. Maybe the greater arousal to men having sex was due to the fact that those images are more taboo, more rare. (We rarely see two men kissing in any media, let alone having sex.) A *New York Times* reader suggested, "If our sexual preferences were best detected by who we look at in pornography, wouldn't pretty much everyone be attracted to mildly unattractive people who live on the West Coast and lack acting talent?" (Gaffney, 2005).[64]

Because the respondents were looking at the sexual films using (their) brains that have already engaged with countless other elements of sexual scripts, how can we always know what people are responding to? Is it just the image? Is it a story they are telling to themselves about what the people in the film are doing? Does the image evoke a memory or a fantasy (and these things are probably different from each other, in any event)? We don't know enough about the other elements of sexual orientation to know—are people turned on by the film clip's setting, scenario, verbal communication, and so on, or is it just the actual sex depicted? Couldn't we ask the questions we asked about the "wild girls"? What *are* the bisexual men reacting to when they see the video of men having sex with men? What we end up with is a study of the subjective and genital arousal only of those men who get aroused (enough) by two-minute porn films and are willing to demonstrate this in a laboratory setting. And who live in Chicago and read the gay magazines and alternative newspapers. . . .

7. The authors assume that sexual arousal is only generated by one of the two dominant sexes, male or female. This assumption ignores the possibility of attraction to people with other sex/gender configurations and presentations of self.

Implications of the Research.   If we *accept* the authors' reasoning, then we simply accept the conclusions, inferences, and assumptions as offered. Nothing changes culturally in our approach to sex research. Nothing changes individually if we already believed that bisexual men are really "straight, gay, or lying." If we accept the conclusions, then we accept the idea that there is no "distinctly bisexual arousal." If we *reject* the authors' reasoning, then we open ourselves to the ability to think critically about research and ideas. We open ourselves to the most important concept of all: does it matter whether bisexuality in men "really exists"? What would change if we discovered that it does not exist? What difference would it make?

Because of the enormity of homophobia (directed by men at other men) and the intensity of the social control of masculinity, we must ask if men are truly free to enact bisexual identities. The National Health and Social Life Survey (NHSLS) found that only 0.8 percent of American men self-identified as bisexual, compared to about 1.5 percent of American women (Laumann et al., 1994). Some studies have noted sizable numbers of men transitioning from bisexual identities to gay identities (Lever, 1994; Stokes, Damon, and McKirnan, 1997).[65] Perhaps this is due to early and continuing socialization pressures to be heterosexual. Maybe these men never really felt hetero- or bisexually oriented but recognized the rewards of bowing to social pressure and scripts. The costs of simply identifying as gay may have been too great. This can be taken as evidence of how self-identification intersects with social scripting. Sometimes we identify in alignment with dominant expectations, which are of course heterosexual (but within the homo vs. hetero binary)—so we choose one or the other.

Sociologists Philip Blumstein and Pepper Schwartz (1976) observed that there is "little coherent relationship between the amount and 'mix' of homosexual behavior in a person's biography and that person's choice to label themselves as bisexual, homosexual, or heterosexual" (p. 339).[66] We see this apparent discrepancy in many other forms of socially stigmatized, discrediting behavior. There can be little relationship between the amount of alcohol one drinks in a sitting, the number of black-outs one has from alcohol abuse, and that person's choice to label herself "alcoholic." But rest assured, if a person earned $995,000 one year, she would probably call herself "millionaire."

Unless our culture moves to a radical destigmatization of all consensual forms of sexualities, we are unlikely to see a lot of sense or logic in terms, labels, behaviors, and identities. We cannot discount that there is an element of opportunism for some men that allows them to have sex with people of a nonpreferred sex without specifically "desiring" them. Male-male sexual contact will occur for apparently heterosexual men when there are no available female partners, as in the case of incarceration or in other monosexed environments (e.g., Eigenberg, 1992; Hensley, Tewksbury, and Wright, 2001).[67] But in less extreme circumstances, it is possible that we could find men who strongly prefer women but still occasionally *cruise* for men as an alternative (to masturbation, to opposite sex experiences, and so on). We certainly have seen in the case of hook-ups that some heterosexual men will occasionally cruise for women they otherwise would not be terribly attracted to (see recent films like *Dogfight* and *In the Company of Men*).

Discovering and developing our "real" sexual selves can be a long, agonizing process. Sometimes we never do settle the question of "who" we are, and this process is never free from cultural scripting. The social construction of reality, adulthood, and aging, along with individual desires for families, children, and stable lives can lead to changes for some people with decades of identifying themselves as bisexual. In a longitudinal interview study spanning two decades, researchers found that some people minimize their same-sex relationships and maximize their opposite-sex relationships, while some minimize sex in their lives altogether (Weinberg, Williams, and Pryor, 2001).[68] After marrying and raising children, some began exploring other aspects of their sexualities (including BDSM) in middle age and beyond. Even a highly complex quantitative analysis of orientation yielded the conclusion that "bisexuality [may] not adequately [be] captured by the homosexuality-heterosexuality continuum" (Haslam, 1997.)[69]

The "Down-Low": Race and Bisexualities

Among those contradictions in self-identity is one way in which race and ethnicity intersect with sexual orientation—bisexuality in African American men. Novelist E. Lynn Harris (e.g., *Invisible Life*, 1991) began writing about bisexual black men in the early 1990s, but recent interest was sparked by several books on the subject and Oprah Winfrey addressing the topic on her popular afternoon television show. Another novelist, Terry McMillan (e.g., *How Stella Got Her Groove Back*, 1996), brought the issue to the mass media when she revealed that her husband, Jonathan

Plummer, had come out as gay six years into their marriage. She said, "'It was devastating to discover that a relationship I had publicized to the world as life-affirming and built on mutual love was actually based on deceit,' McMillan says in court papers. 'I was humiliated'" ("'Stella' Inspiration Breaks Silence," 2005).[70] The divorce proceedings grew ugly as she accused him of knowing from the start that he was gay, of tricking her to get residency in the United States (he is Jamaican), and exposing her to HIV risk (Wellington, 2005).[71] Both have filed legal motions—he wants to restrain her from slander and verbal attacks at his dog-grooming business, and she wants to restrain him from coming within 100 feet of her. "Does McMillan blame herself for marrying him and not seeing that he was gay sooner? 'What? Blame myself for what? I did what I wanted to do because I wanted to do it. I'm woman enough to take the responsibility for what I did. But you don't expect someone to lie to you about *everything*'" (Wellington, 2005). The personal elements of a couple's relationship notwithstanding, the McMillan case seems to encapsulate the emotions, fears, anxieties, misinformation, and labeling issues of bisexualities. But there is a particular subcultural context provided by race and ethnicity (Laumann et al., 2004).[72]

African Americans do not start the game on a level playing field; they do not enter the discourse and debate about sexualities from the same place where white, middle-class people enter. Feminist sociologist Patricia Hill Collins (2000) describes how black sexuality was made singular, reduced to the most pathological "essence" white culture could devise, "constructed as an abnormal or pathologized heterosexuality."[73] Stereotypical and narrow images of black women as exoticized, lusty, animalistic "Jezebels," capable of seducing and perverting white men, proliferated. Black men were animals of a different sort—predatory rapists who threatened the purity and sanctity of white women. This ideology was pervasive and deadly. In 1955 Emmett Till, a 14-year-old Chicagoan visiting relatives in Mississippi, allegedly whistled at a white woman. The pathological racism of a handful of white men led to Emmett's kidnapping and lynching. The admitted perpetrators were later acquitted of the crime. Black sexualities were narrowed to "abnormal" and "pathological," with black women subjected to further oppression by virtue of prostitution, rape, and pornography (Hill Collins, 2000). Black men are oppressed by contemporary pornographic (and other) depictions of them as thugs, roughnecks, and "mandingos."

The social constructions of race and sexuality impact the way people of color interpret and develop sexual selves. American and global history has institutionalized hegemonic and narrow visions of sex; laws, mores, taboos, and stereotypes of "ethnicized sexuality and sexualized ethnicity" contextualize black sexualities (e.g., Battle and Lemelle, 2002; Nagel, 2003).[74] We can see numerous historical instances of social control, from preventing slaves from marrying at all, to antimiscegenation laws denying the right to marry anyone of another race. The latter laws were only declared fully unconstitutional in 1967, in the Supreme Court case of *Loving v. Virginia,* when an "interracial" couple sued Virginia in order to have their marriage recognized. The implications of institutionalized inequalities of the most intimate variety are larger than what I can address here, but they are profound. One consequence is the creation of "black sexualities" that have developed with an awareness of the fact that to be black is, in effect, to be continually surveilled, scrutinized for signs of "immorality" and deviation from hegemonic, white sexuality. If we apply sociologist Pierre Bourdieu's (1930–2002) concept of *cultural capital* (nonmaterial advantages, such as knowledge, "good breeding," and access to dominant forms of power), we can argue that "dominated groups engage in more behavioral self-surveillance" and appear to willingly restrict their sexualities accordingly (Gonzales and Rolison, 2005).[75] I say "appear to" because given all of the intersecting variables, we cannot really know how African American men and women would configure their sexualities if there really was freedom to choose, design, respond to, and enact individual approaches.

Author Keith Boykin (2005) describes the effects of reduced cultural capital, especially for black men.[76] When he was 18, he was summarily dismissed from his job at Sears, accused of having stolen money but given no other details. He had a perfect record in seven months of employment and more importantly, "a sense of pride" from his job. Though Boykin later graduated from Dartmouth College and Harvard Law School, being wrongly terminated from Sears was possibly more instrumental:

> I had never thought of myself as a problem before, but from that day forward I realized that I was. Over the following years, I would be blamed for many more crimes that I had not committed. I made white women nervous and white men anxious. They created an image of me that even black people started to believe. I was responsible for murder, rape, drugs, guns, poverty, homelessness, welfare, illiteracy, teen pregnancy, and AIDS. And all because I am a black man. . . . I live in a world that has already been trained to fear and despise me. It is not because of what I have done. I have never murdered anyone. I have never smoked crack. I have never been in prison. And I have never passed a deadly disease to anyone. But none of that matters. I am still guilty, and I will be held accountable for the rest of my life (2005: 4).

Boykin is describing reverse-tokenism, also known as, "you're going to ruin it for the rest of us." When Gonzales and Rolison talk about how social control and racism operate to constrain individual sexual expression, this is what they are referring to. The idea is that since black men and women are so closely scrutinized, the actions of a few—or of only one—get overgeneralized to represent the character and soul of the many.

Undoubtedly this is operating for black men "on the down low." Author J. L. King (2004) garnered a lot of media attention as "the face of 'Down Low' men" (p. ix).[77] He sums up the stereotypes—for example, RuPaul is what comes to mind when people think of black and gay in the same sentence—and points out that white people have been able develop some neutral gay or lesbian media images (think Ellen Degeneres). In asking, "Could a famous, popular black athlete ever come out like the Olympic diver Greg Louganis did and get the same treatment?" (2004: 22), King is implicitly referring to the fact that black "bisexual" men are subject to at least two strata of oppression, race and sexual orientation. When people have less cultural capital with which to construct forms of heterosexuality, let alone forms of same-sex sexuality, they also have less ability to control how they are perceived:

> If you're gay, people don't want to leave their sons around you, because they're afraid you might molest them. People think gay men want sex all the time, wherever they can get it. . . . If I admit I'm gay, my son's friends will look at him differently. If I'm gay or bisexual, every time they talk about some gay thing on television, some gay bashing, or some gay issues, you'll think about me. I don't want that. If I say I'm gay, every time I'm in your presence, you'll make those stupid comments, "Isn't he cute?" Or something stupid like "I saw you looking at his ass" (p. 23).

The cultural apparatus of homophobia and internalized homophobia seem especially evident here, sparking fear and misconceptions.

I once worked as an evaluator of HIV/AIDS prevention and education efforts in a mid-Southern state. Part of my job was to go to gay bars in some of the cities where state-hired educators had been doing programs. I had to get patrons to complete surveys about the programming, their knowledge of AIDS and sexually transmitted infections, and their behavior and sexual practices. I set up my table with surveys, scratch-off lottery tickets (a good incentive for participation, by the way), pencils, and a large drop box for completed surveys. An African American man walked in and warily skirted my table. He glanced at the drop box on another table, looked at me, and approached; he flipped through a survey. He was very smooth and charming. He smiled a lot, made prolonged eye contact. He asked me what I was doing, why, and for whom. At the end of my explanation, I said, "Would you like to complete a survey?"

"Now why would you ask me to do that?" he replied. "Do I look 'gay'? What makes you think I am not interested in attractive ladies . . . ?" He leaned in and made eye contact. He began to press me to explain why I had asked him to fill out the survey, since it was obviously for gay men. Why was I assuming that he was gay? We went around and around—I was assuming nothing, I was just doing my job, I was just asking every man to do a survey. He did not fill out a survey. He did invite me to join him for a drink, though.

So What's the Issue Here?

Of course, we are not simply talking about men who may refuse to call themselves *gay* because of stigma, prejudice, and the desire to remain unlabeled. The men described by the "down low" are attracted to, interested in, involved with, in love with, married to . . . women. King points out that it would be easier if we could just argue that all black men who have sex with men are just gay, because while at least doubly oppressed, "gay" is safe. It's understandable because it fits into cultural binaries. It ostensibly means "man who does not also sleep with women." But the fact is that, similarly to white bisexual identities, we see here fluidity, complexity, disdain of being limited and typecast by labels, and an interest in self-determination.

Unfortunately, the women involved with men who also have sex with men may not see it this way (regardless of the race, class, and other characteristics of those women). Feelings of betrayal, sadness, fear, anger, confusion, and worry about sexually transmitted diseases and HIV infection may overwhelm any other feelings. Bisexual men of all races and classes have been vilified as "vectors of disease" since the early days of the AIDS epidemic in the United States. When I was in college years ago, my activist sex group wrote *Cosmopolitan* a letter, taking them to task for a misleading and homophobic article on "the threat of bisexual men" (they never published it). Boykin (2005) notes that in the black community on the whole, there has been a reluctance to address the issues raised by "the down low," precisely because of the inferential leap to the misperception that black men are "disease vectors" and "HIV spreaders."

There is another issue that is entangled with all of this—the pink elephant in the room—the issue of monogamy. Most Americans presume their relationships are monogamous, and (marital) infidelity is decisively deemed "morally unacceptable" (recall chapter 1). Wrapped up in secret sexual lives is the potentiality or actuality of lying and deceiving, along with "cheating." It is difficult to disentangle feelings of betrayal from those of homophobia and shame. The concept of the black man "on the creep" or the "sneak" dovetails with the existing hegemonic discourses about black men's sexualities and furthers a racist, race-centered discussion. We do not speak about white men who are involved with women and men as "on the down low." We just have scientific discourses asserting that such men do not exist, that they are "straight, gay, or lying!" It is not merely that whites are not cool enough to come up with quaint, in-group slang like "down low." The white men whom writer David Leddick (2003)[78] interviewed were not universally condemned because of their sex lives. Keith Boykin (2005) reminds readers of the very public recent dissolution of New Jersey governor Jim McGreevey's career. With his wife at his side, he announced that not only was he gay, he had had an affair with a (male) state government employee who was trying to extort money in exchange for silence ("New Jersey Governor Quits, Comes Out as Gay," 2004).[79] We did not witness the creation of new labels and the stoking of new fears after this revelation.

David Leddick interviewed 40 men of diverse backgrounds, aged 30 to 60-plus, to talk about having been married to women while also being interested in men. Some were sexual with men while married, others were not, and they married for different sociocultural reasons—wanting to have children, family pressures, social expectations, falling in love. Some were genuinely invested in and attracted to their wives at first and had sex with other men but never developed romantic feelings for anyone else. Many reported that sexual attraction to men came first, while emotions and feelings developed later, sometimes after many years. A study comparing 43 never-married gay men and 26 gay men who had once been married revealed similarly diverse reasons for marrying (Higgins, 2004).[80] The majority of the men in Leddick's sample were white; there was only one black man, a handful of Latinos. He noted that he had talked to many black men off the record but only one agreed to an interview.

Black women are presented in the media as afraid, confused, and worried about "the down low," wondering how to sleuth enough to force their men out of the closet. There is a fear that these men are somehow "getting over" or getting away with something by having sex with men and women. The way that much of the media has covered author Terry McMillan's story is representative:

> So how could this happen to Terry? Weren't there any signs? As she talks, you find yourself getting mad right along with her. This is not fair. It's not that Plummer, 30, is gay that burns her up, she says. The point is that he with-held information. He betrayed her! He risked her life! "I was dealing with a

sociopath . . ." she said. "People want to know how I got tricked. . . . I have to admit, he's good. . . . I'm a hard bitch to fool" (Wellington, 2005).

Because he "tricked" her about his sexuality, she deems him a "sociopath," and the image of her husband as a lying disease vector is furthered. There is also an implicit question of *why* McMillan's husband—or any man—would do this. What can a man possibly get from sex with another man (that he cannot get from a woman)? The cultural discourses of essentialism, origins, and causes are reinvoked. But casting black women as angry and homophobic is in contrast with research showing that black women, like white women, on average are more positive (than are heterosexual black men) about gay men (Whitley, 2001; Battle and Lemelle, 2002).[81] Gender was a more powerful predictor of positive attitudes than variables like age, church attendance, and income.

Generally speaking, ". . . bisexuality, by its very 'existence,' unsettles ideas about priority, singularity, truthfulness, and identity . . . " (Garber, 1995: 140).[82] This certainly is operating in the case of "the down low." What is the antidote to fears and misperceptions among blacks? One solution is to recognize the weight of multiple social inequalities for black men who are attracted to other men. Psychologists who have studied black men self-identified as gay or bisexual say that:

> . . . The more [they] are able to integrate and hold positive self-attitudes toward their racial-ethnic and sexual identities, the more likely they are to value themselves, protect their health, and experience greater levels of personal contentment. . . . Overcoming the social pressure to view identity as a singular construct that requires the renunciation or devaluation of one's race/ethnicity or sexuality appears to be associated with the most psychological benefit for [these men]. This requires the fusion of both African-American and gay subcultures (Crawford et al., 2002).[83]

IMPLICATIONS AND CONCLUSIONS

In order to really transcend the idea that "identity [is] a singular construct"—to see the diversity and complexity—many things would need to change in our culture. How far have we really come from sexologist Havelock Ellis's conceptualization of gays and lesbians as biological "inverts," men with minds of women and women with minds of men? What are the implications of the continued usage of Kinsey's 1948 scale, a way of thinking that perpetuates the idea that heterosexual and homosexual are "opposite" anchors of an otherwise incomplete spectrum? To expand the spectrum of orientation, society would do well to *really* question our taken-for-granted notions (in no particular order):

1. What evidence do we have that the sex of our sexual partners really matters, societally? It matters individually—if you are drawn to light-haired, athletic men who are sort of sweet and shy, it would certainly benefit *you* if those men also happened to be attracted (or could be persuaded to be) to people like you, whoever you are. But if you are also a light-haired, athletic, sweet guy . . . why should it matter to any culture? As long you know what "no thanks" means and move on gracefully if he likes dark-haired, willowy people who light up the room, the gender/sex/bodily aspects of each person *should not be consequential*. Ahh, the crazy fantasies I have! This is a fond desire of mine but as you know by now, it has been made so consequential that it constitutes a master status, a potentially stigmatizing attribute, a basis for criminalizing behavior, and a cornucopia of labels and categories. *Heterosexual privilege* operates to ensure that institutional, social, and interpersonal benefits accrue to those identified as heterosexual, and pervades scientific and everyday thinking about sex.

2. (Bi)Sexualities are way too fluid and individually experienced and defined to be easily measurable by penile strain gauges, vaginal probes, and two-minute porn film clips. Perhaps the fluidity is obscured by narrow-minded interpretations of all the members of our alphabet soup. For example, if heterosexual men's arousal is so narrowly experienced (not very plastic), as some suggest, why are some turned on by pornographic (and fantasized) depictions of two or more women (who may or not actually be sexually attracted to women)? Why are some heterosexual women turned on by pornographic depictions of men having sex with other men? Most of the fans of *Queer as Folk*, a Showtime program showing lusty men's kisses and a bit of foreplay, are straight women (e.g., Baker, 2004).[84] Valentine (2003) suggests that *we listen to what people say* about their desires, whether in particular encounters, in reports of past experiences, or in fantasies so that the contradictions of self-identity can become clear (p. 126).

3. So what *do* people say? My ongoing research with Braeden L. Sullivan on 250 transpeople's experiences of their desires and approaches to sex makes it clear that many transpeople are on the leading edge of sexual truth-seeking.[85] The process of "coming to terms" with issues of gender and biological sex inspires some transfolk to really explore how the sexual self is configured. Our respondents say they are pansexual, omnisexual, hetero, homo, queer, bi, asexual, celibate, undefined, unlabeled—in any combination of these. Some are attracted to women, some to men; some are attracted

to other transfolk; some are attracted to gendered attributes, like a *person* who is sweet and goofy, or a person who is assertive and masterful. Some identify with BDSM and feelings of dominance, submission, control, power, surrender, and so forth. Some learn about their sexualities and evolve in response to interactions with others (interpersonal level of scripting). Transpeople provide an excellent model of how individuals can interpret, give meaning to, and construct the sexual self. And if we think inferentially, we can easily see that *most people* are engaging in this process, whether determining if we're "ass men" or "leg men," if we're more turned on in the dark or at sunset, if we like muscles or curves, if we like to be "taken" or do the "taking."

4. We need to be more willing to enter a new, norm-less frontier of potentially cumbersome, awkward, slow communication, wherein terms and labels are fuzzy, shifting, or absent. Not everyone wishes to identify with a label, a subculture, a sexual community (Savin-Williams, 2005).[86]

5. We may lose the salience of "coming out of the closet," and the concept of "coming out" as an element of same-sex sexualities (Seidman, 2004).[87] As anthropologist Bill Leap told a journalist, *gay* and *lesbian* may have political connotations and therefore baggage. "Some [students] are not political," Leap says. "They're saying '[I] like to party. I don't see anything political in sucking dick'" (Spillane, 2005).[88]

6. We need to accept that our society's contradictory and confusing emphases on sex, characterized by slogans and marketing campaigns—just say no, true love waits, if you're going to do it at least use condoms, learn how to hook up—renders individuality invisible. Who is usually invisible? People who identify as asexual, who choose celibacy, or who are not oriented to active, interpersonal sexualities; people who are not monogamous, by choice, conscious design, or circumstance; people who are LGBT. In order to really understand sexualities in a way that privileges self-report, that makes self-report a strength and not a liability or a "bias," we can choose instead to listen to what all people say. Individual *phenomenologies, or subjective* feelings and experiences, of sex reveal far more about how we "do" our sexualities than Kinsey Scales and machines ever can. As long as we believe that the body represents "the truth" of sexuality, we will continue to omit the phenomenologies—the minds, brains, and humanities—of far too many people.

Questions to Ponder

1. Why do we tend to link gender roles, presentation, and attributes to sexual orientation? Is there any way to document a connection between gender and sexual orientation?

2.   Why is sexual orientation defined in ways that make the sex of the partner central? In other words, is there any other way to define sexual orientation?

Suggested Projects

1. Do a content analysis of a television show that depicts same-sex sexualities (e.g., *Queer Eye for the Straight Guy, Will & Grace, The L-Word,* or *Queer as Folk*). How is the gay or lesbian character depicted? Can you see stereotypes in the portrayal? How do heterosexually oriented characters interact with same-sex oriented characters?

2. Using a library database, find a journal article that deals with some aspect of sexual orientation. Analyze it using critical thinking—what is the author's purpose? What are the key questions and assumptions? What evidence and information does the author use?

8

Bunnies, Bytes,
and Beaches

REPRESENTATIONS OF SEX

The 8 Worst Things You Can to Say to a Man
The Sexiest Hair Trick This Summer
Be Gutsy in Bed
Sex, Men & Your Body
Three Kinds of Sex Guys Crave
The Male G-Spot (Your Sexiest Search Ever!)
Special Touches That Bring You Two Closer

A ll of these are magazine cover "teasers," hinting at the sex information within the pages. If you have ever spent even five minutes at a magazine stand then you are probably familiar with headlines like these. What you may not realize is that each one is from a magazine aimed at a heterosexual female readership. In fact, a quick perusal of magazines aimed at heterosexual men reveals few cover teaser lines about sex, although the cover models are sexy women, usually celebrities, posed and (un)dressed similarly to those on the covers of women's magazines. Sex sells, to be sure, but if you were an alien from another galaxy trying to learn something about Western cultures, you would probably conclude that sex is far more important to women. "Alien you" would think that Earth women do not seem to have many clothes and enjoy roaming around mostly nude. You would wonder why the men are mostly pictured fully clothed, in suits or very baggy pants and polo shirts. You would think that Earth men are interested in all kinds of things—automobiles, large televisions, electronics, sports . . . and a little sex. But Alien You would probably think that Earth women do little besides preen, primp, and prime themselves for the touches, words, and desires of Earth men. How do we sell with sex in this culture? Let us try to count the ways:

Magazines, (nonpornographic or otherwise), advertising and editorial copy; television shows and ads; movies; music—lyrics and marketing of artist, and music videos; cosmetic plastic surgeries such as vaginal rejuvenation and labial shaping, breast implants, penis enlargements, and nearly every other procedure you can name; clothing—"fuck me" shoes, push-up bras, and $50 La Perla thongs; hygiene products, from feminine deodorant spray to toothpaste; lighting (to create "mood . . . "), furniture (to build a "love den"); beauty products; alcohol; automobiles.

Even Bob Dole and people over the age of 50 sell with sex via Viagra and Levitra commercials (gasp!).

RATED "X"

Since earliest recorded history, people have been depicting and representing sex. The *Kama Sutra,* an ancient Indian text for the upper castes, describing everything from types of "love bites" to how partners should pair up based on the size of their genitals, dates from about AD 400. There are Japanese and Chinese erotic paintings depicting all kinds of sexual congress. Ancient Greek and Roman cultures produced ceramics with explicit scenes of intercourse between men. In the South Pacific, people carved statues to honor the phallus—wooden figures of small men with enormous, out of proportion penises can still be found around people's homes. Pre-Columbian pottery from Mexico and Peru shows men masturbating and engaging in oral sex. *Pornography* comes from the ancient Greek word *pornographos,* or writings (the *graph* part) about prostitutes (*porne,* related to "harlot," a type of prostitute). *Pornography* is currently defined as material that is sexually explicit and intended to arouse. This is distinguished from *erotica,* literary or artistic material with an erotic quality.

The technology and tools of every era have been employed to produce and distribute *sexually explicit material* (SEM), whether in fine art or as part of pop culture. The printing presses of the 1500s made their share of Bibles but were also employed for short pornographic stories. Women have exchanged, sold, and traded for sex for a long time—there is a claim that prostitution is the world's oldest profession. The tradition of the "dirty book" may have been ushered in by John Cleland, who published the explicit (and then-shocking) *Fanny Hill* in the mid-1740s in England. The book represented heterosexual men's fantasies in an unblemished light—the idea "that almost anything a man does will have the ladies simpering in delight" was a staple of the stories (Margolis, 2004: 267).[1] The invention of photography in the mid-1800s, later facilitated by the development of more portable cameras, enabled the distribution of "dirty pictures." And then there were moving pictures. . . .

By the middle of the twentieth century, the motion picture industry—centered in Hollywood—had made it possible for people to see films of people engaged in various sex acts. "Stag films," so named because they were often shown in small groups of men, had the mystique of being "underground" and not in general circulation. Mainstream Hollywood films were subject to strict "producers' codes" (e.g., the rating system) of what could be shown and to whom; it was not until 1965 that a woman's breasts first appeared in a regular film, *The Pawnbroker* (Kelly, 2004).[2] Cities large and small had "X-rated movie theaters," showing films day and night, stigmatized as places for "creepy guys" who didn't mind sticky floors. The development of the Betamax videocassette recorder and video technology meant that, instead of slinking off to a movie theater or having to crash a bachelor party's stag film screening, more people could see pornographic movies in the privacy of their own homes. The U.S. pornography industry, centered in Southern California, makes about 11,000 films a year; mainstream Hollywood makes 400 features (Slade, 2001; Paul, 2004).[3] In 1953 the first issue of *Playboy* was printed—Marilyn Monroe was on the cover. (Publisher Hugh Hefner's "Bunnies," his mansion, multiple "girlfriends," and signature smoking jacket have become iconic of what mixing money with sex can accomplish. His three current girlfriends are featured on E! Entertainment Television in the 2005–2006 season series, *The Girls Next Door.*) Books and other printed materials became more widely available, sold in adult bookshops in cities and towns across the country.

Cable television, personal computers, the World Wide Web, and DVD technologies have really changed the marketplace for explicit sexual material. People who never would have gone to an adult theater or bookstore have been able to find whatever materials they like from the privacy of their homes. Rentals of X-rated videos have increased 850 percent, from 79 million in 1985 to 759 million in 2001. Cooper, McLoughlin, and Campbell (2000) reported that in one year, 10 million people visited the 10 most popular cybersex Web sites.[4] The growth and availability of the Internet is truly astonishing. It is hard to verify, but "adult entertainment" could be pulling in anywhere from $8 billion to $11 billion a year, which, at the high end, would make it bigger than Hollywood's feature film business. Trade magazine *Adult Video News* reported that sales and rentals of adult videos alone racked up $4 billion last year (Stanley, 2004).[5] With so many sex sites available, the need to get the "traffic" crucial for earning money inspires site owners to send millions of SPAM email messages. Everyone with an email address has the potential to get unwanted, sexually explicit advertising for everything from penis enlargement pills ("RPlante, have you ever wished you had a little more where it really counts . . . ?") to Web sites depicting "hot, young girls who can't enough" of animals, ejaculate ("cum"), each other, public sex, and enormous sex toys.

This very brief history of the ways in which sex has been represented cannot be divorced from the cultures that produce these representations. Legal and moral battles have been fought over content, production, and distribution. Popes have condemned the distribution of sexually explicit materials starting in the mid-1500s, politicians have legislated to make such materials illegal, and social scientists have questioned the effects of pornographic imagery. Prejudice about social class and the denigration of pornography as something inherently "dirty," for the "rough" men of the working classes, pervaded nineteenth- and twentieth-century judgments about porn (Cocks, 2004).[6] But capitalism has greatly facilitated the commodification and commercialization of sexualities across the spectrum, opening global markets in previously unimagined ways. Pornography has long been and remains a controversial issue. Researchers and activists have weighed in with arguments about how porn is linked to the degradation of women, violence against women, and the perpetuation of inequalities. The apparent flip side is represented by arguments about freedom of speech and the democratization of pornography. In this chapter, we will focus on men, women, and what pornography shows us about how our culture sees, sells, and uses sex.

PORN IN CONTEXT: RESEARCH AND THEORIZING

Social science researchers have tended to focus on the *effects* of pornography, conceptualized in these central questions:

Does pornography produce sexual arousal?
Does it affect consumers' attitudes, especially toward women and violence?
Does it affect criminal or violent behavior of users?
Does it affect consumers' sexual behavior?

Note that these questions have an uncritical heterosexual/heterocentric point of view. Researchers' gazes have not really been directed at gay or lesbian porn and consumers of these genres. The questions also ignore women consumers by failing to ask whether porn affects women's attitudes toward women, violence, sex, and men. We also need to ask *who* uses pornography. Some people never seek it, use it, see it, or purchase it. Some people see it incidentally, like when a friend has some or a partner suggests it. People may watch DVDs at home but never visit Web sites or buy magazines; consumption of one form does not imply consumption of all forms of pornography.

To answer the question of who uses porn, Timothy Buzzell (2005) analyzed data from the 1973, 1994, and 2002 General Social Survey (GSS), a biennial random, representative sampling of Americans.[7] Respondents were asked if they had seen a pornographic film in the previous year, or if they had visited a Web site in the preceding month (obviously asked only in 2002). In 1973, they were asked about having seen a film in a theater, while in 1994, people were asked whether they had been to a theater or used a VCR. He found that, regardless of available technology, the demographic characteristics of consumers were the same. About 22 percent of respondents in 1973, 1994, and 2002 reported having used films or Web sites. Not surprisingly, it was more men than women. The basic characteristics were: male, young, nonwhite, higher income, and completed high school, defying the stereotype of "the dirty old man." In 2002, 14 percent of the male respondents reported having visited a porn Web site in the previous 30 days. Only 4 percent of female respondents had done so.

Instead of a *systematic* review of the research addressing each of the four questions about effects, let's take a few shortcuts. Does pornography produce sexual arousal? Obviously pornography produces arousal. How can I be so sure? An industry that brings in billions of dollars annually, that only grows, that takes advantage of every technology thus created is clearly making products that work. Since pornography *is meant* to arouse and this is its main purpose, clearly pornography is doing its job very well. Does pornography arouse everyone? Obviously not. If we accept Buzzell's GSS analysis, then it is clear that not everyone uses porn. Maybe those who do not are people who would not find it arousing, among other reasons.

Does porn affect consumers' attitudes, especially toward women and violence? Twenty-plus years of research on this subject *does not* reveal any promising links between porn and men's attitudes (e.g., Duggan, Hunter, and Vance, 1985; Davis and Bauserman, 1993; Strossen, 1995).[8] In other words, there is no strong connection. This is not surprising, because by the time men would be recruited for quasi-experimental and experimental social psychology studies, they would already have had 18-plus years of socialization into U.S. culture. Being socialized into a culture with subtle and overt sex-based inequalities may affect men more. In other words, men who have already learned negative attitudes toward women may choose and perceive pornography differently than men with neutral or positive attitudes. One study found that men's choice of porn themes (e.g., "erotic," woman-as-insatiable, violent/aggressive) was related to intelligence and aggressive/antisocial tendencies (Bogaert, 2001).[9] Lower intelligence (measured as IQ score) and higher aggressive/antisocial tendencies were linked to choosing violent porn, but the majority of the men actually chose "woman-as-insatiable" porn.

Does porn affect criminal or violent behavior of users? The statement of convicted serial murderer Ted Bundy notwithstanding—that pornography had influenced him to do what he did (he was also diagnosed as sociopathic)—there *may* be some connection. But this connection seems to exist primarily for men with pre-existing (before consuming porn) hypermasculine gender roles and attitudes (e.g., Mosher and Anderson, 1986),[10] those who endorse rape myths, and those who believe that aggression is arousing for aggressor and victim (e.g., Malamuth, 1989).[11] Activist and author Andrea Dworkin has written that pornography, in its essence, is messages about violence against women. ". . . Pornography is violence against the women used in pornography and pornography encourages and promotes violence against women as a class" (1994: 153).[12] Sexual violence, sexual sadism, rape, sexual assault, and less extreme forms of *misogyny* (hatred of women) are far more complex than what researchers can uncover simply by exploring porn consumption.

Does porn affect consumers' sexual behavior? This question has not been addressed well or effectively. Often, researchers will design studies as experiments or quasi-experiments, where (male) subjects complete a survey about their sex lives, then watch a short porn film, and are assessed after the film. Too few studies have actually queried porn consumers about what they think about what they view, what they learn or glean from it, and how it might connect to their sexual lives. Technically, porn is "just" entertainment, similar to video games like "Grand Theft Auto," television shows like *South Park* and *Desperate Housewives,* and music like 50 Cent's and Bob Marley's. Researchers endlessly pursue the question of the effects of *all* forms of media. Does *Desperate Housewives* inspire women to have affairs, commit suicide, develop eating disorders? Does "Grand Theft Auto" inspire crime sprees, murder of police officers, and rape of women? Does Bob Marley's music inspire revolution, social consciousness, and marijuana smoking? But is porn different from these other forms of media? The short, glib answers are yes, porn probably is different, and yes, porn probably can affect people's behavior, but let's explore a little further.

Pornography as Education

What do people, especially men, think about pornography? What do they learn from it, if anything? Porn does seem to be a source of sex education for some people in the United States; men report that sources like *Playboy* have been influential sexually and intellectually (Beggan and Allison, 2003).[13] One study of 175 students showed that men seemed to learn more from pornographic sources than did women (Trostle, 1993; Trostle, 2003). More men reported that at least some of their knowledge on certain topics came from pornography: foreplay (54 percent vs. 25 percent of women), homosexuality (21 percent vs. 14 percent of women), masturbation (31 percent vs. 21 percent of women), mechanics of sex (47 percent vs. 16 percent of women), oral or anal sex (52 percent vs. 31 percent of women), and women's anatomy (51 percent vs. 11 percent of women). Nonetheless, respondents ranked pornography low in its general importance; peers were the "most important" source of sexual information (Trostle, 2003).[14]

A Swedish study revealed gender differences and consumption differences (Haggstrom-Nordin, 2005).[15] More men who watched porn daily or weekly were aroused by, fantasized about, or tried to perform acts from a film. In two related studies, Haggstrom-Nordin asked young adults, "Do you consider yourself becoming influenced in your sexual behavior by pornography?" Respondents who answered yes also explained how porn had influenced them. Men who answered "yes" seemed to have more positive regard, saying that porn provided inspiration, new ideas, and increased self-confidence. Women who answered "yes" also indicated that they had gained inspiration and new ideas, but described how porn had a negative influence, promoting uncertainty and a sense of incumbent sexual demands (e.g., being willing to perform certain behaviors, being sexually experienced in particular ways, and being generally available for sex). Women were much more likely to indicate that porn had given them a distorted picture of sex (39 percent vs. 13 percent of men). When asked, "Do you consider others becoming influenced in their sexual behavior by pornography?," respondents answered yes, but that they themselves had not been influenced. This is not surprising. Most of us like to think that we are wholly individual and only nominally socialized—that everything about us is the result of autonomous, informed choices.

It may be that it is difficult to know exactly how pornography influences us. If you play "Grand Theft Auto" and are asked whether the game has negatively affected you, you would know unequivocally whether you have begun committing the kinds of crimes depicted in the game. Therefore that would be an easier question to answer.

Most people do not commit serious felony crimes, but many people are sexually active at some point in their lives. Pornography depicts some activities that some of us actually engage in, so ultimately it may be difficult to know exactly how it influences us. If it is true that we are not really influenced by it at all—that it is only "other people" who are seduced by it—then we may be indirectly affected anyway.

Let's say that *you* do not use pornography in any form. You know what it is—you saw a few minutes of a film once at someone's party—but you have no interest in it. But what if you date someone who does use porn and who would say that they have been influenced, that they have learned something from porn? You may thus be sexually involved with a person whose fantasies, desires, and turn-ons owe something to pornography. If these fantasies and behaviors enter your shared activities, then it would seem that pornography is influencing you as well. For example, in a 1990s *Rikki Lake* talk show episode, "Help! My Man's Addicted to Porn!," one woman describes how her husband watches "his tapes" and then comes to bed with ideas and scenarios he wants to try out with her, including taping their activities.

It may be helpful to revisit the concept of socialization and theories about sex. Since the "Monty Python" film scene in chapter 4 does not represent how we *actually* learn about sex, we know that our preporn learning can be indirect, inferential, euphemistic, and vague. (It can of course be more direct, via consensual childhood sex explorations or nonconsensual incest/assaults.) Scripting theory argues that we develop our sexualities in interaction and via subcultural and cultural scripts. On the cultural level, we are all influenced by the fact that pornographic forms, images, and ideas have proliferated (Dines and Jensen, 2004).[16] What are the implications of knowing that pornography involves billions of dollars, millions of consumers, and thousands of films?

Interpersonally, we can and do learn about pornographic depictions of sexuality from partners and peers, as in the example above. Haggstrom-Nordin (2005) found that young men who used a lot of porn and whose first PVI was early in life had a broader range of behaviors in their scripts. Social learning theory would enable us to pose a chicken-and-egg question: which came first, early sexual activity and use of porn? Or early sexual activity and high interest in sex? In other words, we don't know if interest in sex predicts use of porn, and we don't know if use of porn precedes a broader range of conduct. In terms of scripting theory, on the intrapsychic dimension, we do not know precisely how pornography intersects with fantasies and arousal (beyond knowing that porn is arousing to those who use it).

Let's think a little more broadly. We are exposed to myriad representations of sex via *all* the sources listed at the start of the chapter—music, Hollywood movies, magazines, advertising, and so on. If we consume sexual representations from multiple sources, including porn, how can we know what is really influencing us? When we imagine "sex"—our fantasies, scenarios, and arousing ideas—how much of what we imagine is really from our cultural reference points—scenes from movies, advertisements, and so forth? This may be partly responsible for young lesbian women saying that they had difficulty labeling their feelings as "sexual" (e.g., Tolman, 2002; Diamond, 2003; Ussher, 2005).[17] Without cultural reference points depicting a range of scenarios, with no imaginings to write into their script, lesbian and bisexual women may be affected differently than heterosexual women. We will address gay men a little later in this chapter.

Pornography as Private and Public

Focus on Men

The study of pornography is a history of masculinity, men's sexualities, and men's fantasies. "Men consume pornography, using pornographic images for sexual arousal, usually without considering the relationship between what's in the pictures of stories and the sexual pleasure we seek. What matters with pornography is its utility, its capacity to arouse" (Kimmel, 1990).[18] Pornography is literally defined by its ostensible goal or outcome—remember that it is "sexually explicit" and "intended to cause sexual arousal"? Kimmel is arguing that when men use pornography, they do not really consider the medium itself, abstracted from how arousing it is. But *we* need to do two things: consider the medium and assess why and how it is arousing.

What is it about pornography that is arousing to many, though not all, men? What kinds of images arouse only a handful of consumers? What kinds of images arouse a lot of consumers? Are there differences in pornography for straight men and gay men? Why are there *so many* different kinds of images, characters, activities, settings, and stories?

What's between the Sheets: The Content of Porn

If you have ever looked at an "adult" magazine, you probably reacted similarly to my high school friend who found the porn stash in the woods, at least the first few times. "Wow! There are naked women in there!" Women who are willing to take their clothes off and smile while doing so, looking shyly but assertively into the camera, or dreamily into the distance, eyes fixed on a point somewhere outside the photograph. If you have ever done an aesthetic or artistic comparison of printed porn, you may have noticed that magazines that are sold on regular newsstands, like *Playboy* or *Penthouse*, seem to be better made than other adult magazines. Hard-core and specialty publications mostly sold at adult bookstores, such as *Hustler* and *Juggs*, are less glossy, less stylized. These magazines make no attempt to intersperse photos with news, features, and current events.

A content analysis of 430 *Playboy* centerfolds ("Playmates") found that the magazine maintained certain parameters of explicitness (Bogaert, Turkovich, and Hafer, 1993).[19] While breasts were almost always exposed in the centerfolds, there was a certain coyness—if a model's legs were spread, her genitalia would be covered, whether by a hand or by clothing. If pubic hair and breasts were shown, legs would be kept closed. But the Playmates have been critiqued as agents of harm for men, creating unrealistic expectations about women and enhancing men's alienation from their sexualities (e.g., Brooks, 1995).[20] Other studies have compared centerfold models' measurements to other women's, and naturally, the Playmates are thin for their height, with large breasts and tiny waists. The argument is that they present unrealistic body shapes and standards that negatively affect other women (e.g., Owen and Laurel-Seller, 2000).[21] *Playboy* and *Penthouse* do present a fairly narrow range of women and body types (mostly white and all fit/thin/curvy), but many other kinds of women are represented in more hard-core pornography. Women with body hair, large women, women of all races and ethnicities, older women, women with disabilities—there is no permutation unrepresented in porn, whether on a Web site or in a magazine. Magazines like *Bizarre* feature extreme portrayals of "mad" and "gross" sex, according to its spine.

A study of soft-core British magazines further delineates how bodies are presented (Attwood, 2005).[22] "Within soft-core narratives, the real remaining taboo is on male penetration; while women are routinely penetrated in every orifice, male bodies remain intact. Men in contemporary soft core also continue to be portrayed as machine-like; theirs are hard bodies which shoot 'massive jets of come' 'like machine-guns'" (p. 87). So men are represented in heterosexual porn in narrow ways as well, merely as objects or technicians of sex. Gay porn perpetuates this further, in publications that glorify the "prototype" of the hypermasculine, muscular, square-jawed beautiful man with a large penis (Mercer, 2003).[23] These portrayals can have an effect on consumers (Duggan and McCreary, 2004).[24] A survey of 101 men's consumption patterns revealed that exposure to pornography was positively correlated with body anxieties for gay men.

Film and Video

Imagine watching hundreds of hours of all kinds of sex for a research project, coding for instances of every kind of violence imaginable, every sex act, body language, facial expressions, and the kind of "dialogue" found in most pornographic films. The context of research on films has changed as technology has changed, enabling researchers to move from the adult movie theater of the past to a television, a VCR/DVD, and a remote. Several researchers have recently undertaken these analyses, most looking to answer the question of whether pornography depicts violence against women. Monk-Turner and Purcell (1999) wanted to study "the treatment of female characters in videocassette pornography."[25] Using 209 vignettes from 40 randomly sampled videos, the authors did find dehumanizing or degrading content, but they also found intimacy in movies with white actors (29 percent of the vignettes). The dehumanizing content in the vignettes included status inequalities (19 percent), vulgar references to women (15 percent), and subordination (39 percent)—but there was only one instance of "extreme violence."

Films follow a formula, a script, that clearly mimics the elements of some men's fantasies (Dines and Jensen, 2004). The formula includes three basic themes: (1) women always want sex from men; (2) women like everything men do or want; (3) women can easily be persuaded if they are at all reluctant.

Dines and Jensen describe what they suggest is a representative example of the exact scenarios:

"Delusional" is a release from the Vivid studio, whose videos are considered the upscale end of the hardcore market. The plot concerns Lindsay, who, after discovering her husband cheating on her, has been slow to get into another relationship, saying she is waiting for a sensitive man. A case of mistaken identity leads to her first step back into sex with a woman, which leads to another sexual encounter with the woman and a man. In the final sex scene, the lead male character Randy, professes his love for Lindsay: "I just want to look out for you." They embrace and after three minutes of kissing and removing their clothes, Lindsay begins oral sex on Randy while on her knees on the couch, and he then performs oral sex on her while she lies on the couch. They then have intercourse, with Lindsay saying, "fuck me, fuck me, please" and "I have two fingers in my ass—do you like that?" This leads to the usual progression of positions: She is on top of him while he sits on the couch, and then he enters her vaginally from behind before he asks, "Do you want me to fuck you in the ass?" She answers, "Stick it in my ass." After two minutes of anal intercourse, the scene ends with him masturbating and ejaculating on her breasts (pp. 374–375).

Scenes like the one Dines and Jensen describe are "the aspect of porn work that is the most routine, mundane, and scripted" (Abbott, 2004: 382).[26] Porn films depicting heterosexual activity tend to include vaginal and anal penetrations, oral sex, and the requisite ejaculation onto the woman, the "cum shot" or "money shot" (Nagel, 2002).[27] The money shot is so-named because without it, male actors do not get paid; the ejaculation is the proof of completion (Abbott, 2004). In fact, "stunt dicks" can be called in to provide the money shot if the main actor (or "talent") cannot do so. But no research has directly explored how men feel about seeing porn actors who are generally well endowed and who, as far the viewer knows, *always* ejaculate after just enough sex has transpired (namely, never "prematurely").

Another crucial element of porn films is the "creation of a porn persona" (Abbott, 2004: 387). "Porn personas must be desirable, convey the impression that the work is enjoyable, and portray sex as authentic and pleasurable. Perhaps most importantly, however, the created persons must feed the fantasies of the imagined viewer" (p. 387). Dines and Jensen describe scenes from their qualitative studies of porn films (Dines, Jensen, and Russo, 1998; Dines and Jensen, 2004).[28] They describe women whose personas seem punctured by their private selves, whose faces belie their feelings, women who seem "on the verge of crying" in scenes of anal sex (2004: 374). Indeed, Abbott reported that good working conditions included "working with 'nice guys,' having an 'easy scene' (no anal), and getting through a scene quickly" (2004: 383).

But without good actors—giving the appearance of authentic enjoyment, being seemingly insatiable, wanting anything and everything—porn would not necessarily capture the sexual imaginations of the average (heterosexual) viewer—male, younger, with at least a high school education (Buzzell, 2005). Filmmakers appear to rely on their own perceptions of what would be arousing to this "average viewer." For example, when black women are depicted in interracial porn, they are the objects of violence more often than are white women (Cowan, 1995; Monk-Turner and Purcell, 1999).[29] Black men are uncritically portrayed as animals, as little more than a penis, in scenes uniformly lacking intimacy (Dines, 1998; Monk-Turner and Purcell, 1999).[30] Women of other ethnicities are depicted in accordance with cultural stereotypes—the fiery Latina, the Asian "china doll," and the exotic animalistic black woman (Mayall and Russell, 1993).[31] The uncritical reinforcement of sexual and racial stereotypes is embedded in a medium that most consumers are unlikely to critique. The average watcher is unlikely to drop what he's doing, aghast at the stereotyping.

In terms of other stereotypes, gay porn treads a fine line between exaggerating and stereotyping gay men's sexuality and representing the main genre in which that sexuality can be expressed in a positive light (e.g., Burger, 1995; Thomas, 2000).[32] There are arguments suggesting that regardless of actual content, anything that shows men having sex with men is at least one step above the total repression of gay men's sexualities (e.g., Green, 2000).[33]

So what do we know about porn thus far? Films feature formulaic scenarios, sexual diversity, "insatiable" women. Magazines feature hegemonically attractive women, seductively posed. Porn reinforces and (re)presents stereotypes of women, race, and men. The one-dimensionality of male actors, who are paid far less than women in heteroporn, is worth noting. Male "talent" are rendered merely as (large) penises, sources of "money shots," and aggressors with one thing on their minds. An episode of the BBC program "Weird Weekends" featured host Louis Theroux learning about the American porn industry. The single most important elements of success for a male actor? "Get wood" and then keep it up until the money shot. Men are paid less than women, have shorter careers overall, and are not given many chances. If they lose their erections frequently they will have trouble being hired for other scenes in other films.

The Internet

Thousands of hard-core pornographic Web sites are a mere mouse click or unsolicited pop-up away, showing every fantasy imaginable, including bondage, bestiality, and group sex. Internet pornography is a $2.5 billion business in the United States, with more than 4 million Web sites, according to Family Safe Media, a company that sells parental control products for computers. The company, which compiled statistics from various outlets and studies, claims that the average age of first exposure to Internet porn is 11, and that children between ages 12 and 17 constitute the largest group of viewers of online porn (English, 2005).[34]

The Internet has been hailed as the great democratizing force of sexual representations. With an Internet connection, anyone, even 11-year-olds, can access these four million (and counting) Web sites. People in offices, homes, libraries, and cybercafes around the world can check out what's new in online sex. Did you know that 70 percent of the adult content Web site traffic occurs during the 9-to-5 work day (Delmonico, Griffin, and Carnes, 2002)?[35] So what do consumers see? When I was doing research for this book one day, a banner ad popped up, advertising "college girls pooping and farting." (I checked it out, of course.) There are Web sites catering to every possible niche of the sexual imagination—animals (bestiality), every aspect of BDSM, "messy" sex (food, oil, mud, and so on), people dressed like babies, women with every sex toy imaginable, women having sex with women, and transwomen with various stages of pre- and postoperative bodies. There are sites depicting men masturbating, having sex with other men, wearing leather, and using every sex toy imaginable. Barron and Kimmel (2000) point out that it is far cheaper for an entrepreneur to create basic Internet pornography than to publish a magazine (tens of millions of dollars needed) or even make a video ($3,000 for a shoestring budget).[36]

Not many scholars have undertaken systematic content analyses of the Web. Research is complicated by the sheer volume of sites and the fact that most porn sites charge access or membership fees. There is also the question of how to do random sampling from a population whose parameters are not fully known. Mehta and Plaza (1997) did manage to get a random sample of pornographic images, downloaded from Internet newsgroups.[37] The authors compared their content analysis to studies of magazine and video porn to determine whether computer porn differed. They found more images of fellatio, homosexuality, and group sex, compared to magazines and videos. The most prevalent themes included erect penises (35 percent), fetishes (33 percent), and masturbation (21 percent).

The "Triple A Engine" of accessibility, affordability, and anonymity has combined to make the Internet especially attractive to those interested in sex generally, and in niche markets and specialized interests (Cooper, 2004).[38] Remember the "slash" fiction that introduced chapter 7? The Internet has enabled slash fiction to proliferate and find broader audiences (Salmon and Symons, 2004).[39] "Slash" can be written in very explicit and very sexual ways, and in any case, involves sexual pairings of two male characters. The pairings unite characters who are otherwise depicted as heterosexual in their original television shows or movies, as in the Captain Kirk/Mr. Spock example. Since slash entails male-male sex but is almost exclusively written by women, it has been described as a type of romance, similar to Harlequin novels. The male characters have deep friendships that progress toward sexual intimacies; one is often "an anal virgin" (Salmon and Symons, 2004).

In contrast to the strict explicitness parameters of *Playboy* over the last 40-plus years (Bogaert et al., 1993), the Internet certainly includes a much broader range of sexual representations. Compared to "college girls pooping and farting," *Playboy's* coy discretion of not showing Playmates' genitalia seems almost quaint. One reason why there may be such differences is the way in which people access the pornography. The

Internet can be entirely accessed within the privacy of one's home. No one else needs to know what any individual downloads, views, or searches for. Accessibility and privacy combine to (re)create fears about porn that transcend the content—fears of Internet porn addiction, compulsive cybersexing, and "cyber-cheating." There are numerous articles focused solely on these negatives. "The sheer volume of these troublesome tales and the ease with which they circulate in popular culture clearly illustrate a moral bias that continues to color understandings of the intersection of sex and technology" (Waskul, 2004: 105).[40] There is a fear that Internet porn facilitates impersonal, dehumanized sexual relations. In some ways this is really a larger concern about U.S. culture. Social scientists have been particularly concerned about the ways in which social bonds have weakened over the last half-century (e.g., Putnam, 2000; Pappano, 2001).[41]

This concern evokes the children's morality tale wherein Chicken Little keeps claiming that the sky is falling because acorns are dropping on his head. In this case, we keep crying that our culture is falling, and Internet sexual representations are the bellwether, the acorns. This concern is a feature of the complex, contradictory and confusing messages we socially construct about sexualities. Other commentators say that the downfall of our society is exemplified by the endemic levels of STI and HIV/AIDS. Cybersex—even cyber affairs and "cheating"—are by definition "safer sex," if they remain entirely within the confines of the computer. It would be the safest form of partnered sex we could imagine—there is no opportunity for infection or body fluids to pass. So why not advocate cybersex as a form of safer sex? The Goldilocks theory may be operating here as well, though it is hard to tell what a "just right" amount of computer-mediated sexuality would be. Only one hour while at work, and only during lunch and coffee breaks? Only the amount that does not disrupt one's "real world" sex life?

One qualitative study of computer sex participants describes cybersex addiction in a way that implies that the computer may be incidental (Schneider, 2000).[42] In other words, the computer can be a tool for self-destruction, degradation, and addiction—just like any other modern object (e.g., shopping, eating, "real-time" sex, alcohol, and so on). The "Chicken Little/sky is falling" concerns with Internet porn as a symbol of the downfall of society are an extension of *other* cultural anxieties about sex—*moral panics*. Those who focus on young adults worry that today's adolescents are at risk from more than just STIs, HIV, and teen pregnancy (e.g., Zillman, 2000).[43]

The bigger fears relate to discourses of monogamy, sex as an extension of love, and normativity. The key question is, will people develop a deep callousness toward sex and a sense that it is merely a means to an end devoid of intimacy?

The Power of Taboos

So just what is arousing about women having sex with animals? Or women sitting on the toilet? Or men dressed in diapers, holding baby bottles and rattles? Or one woman surrounded by five or ten men, all ejaculating on her, calling her *slut* and *bitch*? Or 12 men in a daisy chain, sucking, touching, and fucking? The answers to these questions are beyond the scope of this chapter, but one common element is the power of the *taboo* (e.g., Sigel, 2000; Fisher and Barak, 2001).[44] Many elements of heterosexual interaction are taboo (forbidden by social or cultural mores), given that we have constructed a fairly narrow cultural script: one man, one woman, if not married at least "in love," committed, monogamous, engaging in "normal" sex. The "what" and "how" of the hegemonic script are straightforward, "vanilla"—missionary position, maybe woman-on-top, penile-vaginal intercourse to orgasm (his, at least), in a private place. Though it appears that many men have fantasies of multiple partners (e.g., Kimmel and Plante, 2002), culture has not caught up with the intrapsychic in this regard.[45] Those fantasies are not sanctioned, enabling them to retain some of their naughtiness, their taboo spark. But for the average inexperienced sexually interested young adult, simply seeing someone naked might be exciting, let alone actually having some kind of sex with them!

It is hard to tell exactly how and why sexual imaginations progress and adapt, facilitating the growth of so many pornographic representations of "sex." Regardless of anyone's subjective feelings—judging particular acts as "disgusting" or judging particular forms as "degrading"—the enormity and complexity of the human animal's sexual imagination has to be appreciated, at least in the abstract (Rubin, 1984; Califia, 1994; Morin, 1995).[46] We are not content to stop at basic PVI, man-on-top, darkened bedroom sex. Nor are we content to simply accept the real vicissitudes of desire, the reality that most people are *not* sexually hungry, active, and interested all the time. Pornography enables us to construct whatever we want from the realm of our imaginations. "Heteroporn presents a world of male defined, male dominated sexual abundance, an escapist sexual fantasy with starkly misogynist and objectified images of women and female desire. The world of the sexual act is separate and distinguished from the narrative and sexual scenes are not integrated into the narrative" (Fejes, 2002: 101–102).[47] But Fejes also notes that "gayporn" includes "separated utopias," where masculine, attractive men are sexually disconnected from each other, reduced to nothing more than a hand stroking one's own penis, masturbating in a room of men but not really interacting.

All of this highlights the ultimate context of pornography. Modern pornography exacerbates the public/private tensions we have built into our sexualities. The image of the "dirty old man" furtively sneaking off to the adult bookstore or X-rated theater, themselves depicted as sticky-floored, stark environments, is not far from our current concerns about porn. We have built onto the foundation of the image of the old man, replacing him with a somewhat younger man furtively downloading niche porn at work or after his family is in bed. Technology enables modern pornography to enter our homes—and our sexual imaginations—in ways that the underground pornographers of the nineteenth and twentieth centuries never imagined. And where our collective eyes see the computer screen or the plasma TV we also see a major element of porn that often defies our logic: masturbation.

The man jacking off alone is a staple of gay porn (e.g., Fejes, 2002). We can imagine the viewer at home, masturbating along with the actor, some intimacy potentially exchanged between consumer and the character in the film. But the fact is that when researchers ask about the effects of porn, they omit central questions that might uncover the relation of porn to solo sex. Leonore Tiefer suggests that a major reason for the blanket assumption that women's use of porn is "harmful" is the "discomfort with the idea of women masturbating" (Tiefer, 2004: 144).[48] Admittedly, we have a culturally ambivalent perception of men masturbating, but Tiefer is suggesting that we are much more uncomfortable with the idea of women's solo sex.

Responding to Pornography: Cultural Concerns

Research about reactions and perceptions typically focuses on women. This is probably due to the argument that pornography is harmful to women on every dimension (e.g., Dworkin, 1981; Small, 1990).[49] Though men are the primary producers and consumers of the medium, there is a paucity of information about their feelings and interpretations. Any attempt to discern how men feel about porn seems limited to the previously discussed questions of whether heterosexual men interpret porn as violence against women. Haggstrom-Nordin (2005) found that her young adult respondents generally felt that sex was separated from intimacy in pornography. This perception represents yet another conundrum of modern Western societies where hooking up and friends-with-benefits (FWB) can certainly entail sex without intimacy. Indeed, 50 percent of the men and 33 percent of the women in Haggstrom-Nordin's study had engaged in some sort of FWB sex. These mixed feelings, exemplified as sexual excitement, guilt, disgust—especially among the young women in her study—are indicative of the ways in which the erotic remains enormously complex. In Sweden, Norway, and Finland, for example, both men and women have experience with porn, with about

85 percent of Scandinavian men and about 63 percent of Scandinavian women reporting ever having seen any form of it (Træen, Spitznogle, and Beverfjord, 2004; Haggstrom-Nordin, 2005).[50] But both studies report that young and adult women have mixed reactions to porn—it is disgusting but also arousing sometimes.

Sexual disgust and curiosity are strange bedfellows, but for women, make a compelling story: "I am grossed out by [any activity] but strangely drawn to it because my partner is into it. . . ." In this narrative, the muted tones (that ambivalent/missing discourse) of young women's desires are the central element of the reaction to porn. So researchers may also focus on women's responses because of the socialized inequalities in men's and women's desires. Men are given more cultural permission to access theirs, to see themselves as sexual creatures from a young age, and to masturbate. It may also be that women's lived experiences do not really square with what is portrayed in porn films. When my students talk about porn and analyze it, the women tend to focus on whether anyone is actually enjoying themselves. Perhaps they extrapolate from their own experiences and fantasies. They ask why there is always a facial cum shot, anal penetration, why there is so much double penetration. Someone always asks, "Doesn't that hurt?" Reading Sharon Abbott's (2004) description of actors/talent as workers helps; the students understand that sex work is work like any other, that, for example, an "easy scene" does not include anal sex (let alone double penetration).

When my male students write about pornography, they almost uniformly express little disgust. Some may say they do not seek it out, or that they only see pornography in a social context, because "someone else had it," but they are not offended by it. Outnumbered in sexuality and gender classes, the men rarely admit in class that they enjoy porn, that they use it, masturbate to it. But a key difference between men's and women's reactions to porn lies in the socially constructed sexual imagination, I think. If women's desires have romance, beautiful beaches, boyfriends or girlfriends, and love as central elements, leaving us to "guess the rest," then we could argue that pornography represents "the rest." Whether gay, straight, fetishized, niche, or any other sort of porn, what we *see* when we really look at porn is men's desires. Dines and Jensen (2004) write:

> It hurts to know that no matter who you are as a woman, you are reducible to a thing to be penetrated and that men will buy movies about that. It hurts women, and men like it. Knowing that makes it difficult to avoid the hurt, even if one has found ways to cope with the injuries from male violence in other places. It is one thing to deal with acts, even extremely violent acts. It is another to know what thoughts, ideas, and fantasies lie behind those acts.

In pornography, we are forced to confront the sexual imagination of a significant number of men (p. 369).

Though their focus is on violent acts, there is an analysis beyond violence. The contrast between women's fantasies and film of, for example, a woman squatting in a bathtub urinating on someone while another person stands and urinates on her is the stuff of a cognitive meltdown. It is difficult for many heterosexual women to process the fact that men—men they become involved with, fall in love with, and desire intimacy with—could collectively create these images, respond to them, and masturbate to them.

Capitalism and "The Fairer Sex": Women Creating Representations

Porn has always depended on the contributions of women as "talent." The development of the video camera and the Internet have enabled women to participate in the creation and dissemination of porn. Women's entrepreneurial efforts run the gamut from developing "one-off" Web sites of themselves to creating porn film companies as Candida Royalle, a former porn star, has done. Women have created sexuality information Web sites and adult Web bulletin boards. In New York and Los Angeles, women have created "sex parties" for attractive, sexually experimental singles and couples (such as Cake and One Leg Up, both in New York City). The virtual communities inspired by the parties are nurtured on Web sites, of course. Women have also created printed porn, such as *Sweet Action: Porn for Girls*, which has fuzzy, artsy pictures of naked skinny rocker and artist "boys" with erections. The first issue sold out its print run, and the second issue featured a letter from "Doris":

> Ladies: Enclosed is a check for $10.00 to cover cost of an issue of your magazine plus mailing. I am over 18 years of age. Although I am 80 years old, I am not in my second childhood. If your magazine is as advertised, I've been waiting for such a one for many a year. My email address is . . . (*Sweet Action* #2, 2004: 1).

Other woman-made printed porn has been available since the mid-1980s, in the form of *On Our Backs*, a sex-positive magazine of "dyke sex." The magazine features articles about everything from fisting to cruising for lovers to power and BDSM games, along with pictorials of a variety of women. "It makes [lesbian] desires visible, and by doing that it normalizes them," wrote the editor of *OOB*, Diana Cage (2004).[51] Women have also created a number of sex-positive sex-related companies, which, though not pornographic, bear mentioning. Joani Blank started "Good Vibrations," as a "friendly, clean, well-lighted alternative to conventional 'adult bookstores'" (Hall, 2000).[52] The store sells sex toys, books, videos, lubricants, and other sexual accessories, offering "tester" vibrators and staff educated about sexualities; their catalog business and advertising extends their reach well beyond California. Other sexual entrepreneurs include performance artist and activist Annie Sprinkle, who has done shows in which the audience lines up to see her cervix via a speculum, and Betty Dodson, who pioneered a movement exhorting women to learn to masturbate (e.g., Dodson, 1996).[53] Dodson has run workshops for small groups of women who gather to learn exactly how to masturbate (using their own Hitachi Magic Wand vibrators). The emphasis of these efforts is clearly to make sex accessible to women, to destigmatize everything from sexual products to sex toys to women's bodies.

Jane Juffer (1998) refers to this as a "domestication" of porn—the marketing of pornographic images and discourses to women and to couples.[54] Sanitizing sexual representations by calling them "erotica," she argues, does not obscure the fact that porn for women (and other sexual products, like those described) exists within cultural contexts that have already defined sexual scripts. Karen Ciclitira (2004) interviewed British women about porn and discovered that awareness of this context has created some ambivalence and discomfort about porn.[55] A 35-year-old white respondent said that she had looked at porn with a boyfriend, and on her own, until discovering feminism, in her late teens:

> . . . I felt I was fulfilling *his* fantasy about women fancying other women. . . . It was a bit like reclaiming my own sexuality I suppose, it was like saying well in fact if it turns me on then you know that's okay, then that's, that's for me, but I'm not gonna be part of his fantasy about it, because I didn't feel that that was *equal* anymore. . . . I don't feel that I want to be or have to be available, or sexual all the time, or wear [garter belts], or masturbate with candles, or you know be any of that stuff (p. 292).

This woman is describing one way in which we can adapt our sexual scripts, interpersonally and intrapsychically. But more importantly, she describes the essential conundrum—the sticky wicket—of women's reactions to and interpretations of porn. In first coming to the medium as a young woman, learning about her own sexuality while also seeing sex represented pornographically, her responses were filtered through her first boyfriend's enjoyment of porn. In saying that she doesn't want to "have to be available, or sexual all the time" with her current boyfriend, she is referring to the overarching narratives of heteroporn's depiction of women. But rejecting those depictions does not mean that other depictions are readily available, despite the efforts of the porn and sexuality entrepreneurs described above.

Some Thoughts on the Future of
Porn and Sexual Representation

Apparently, things have not been good in Chicago at the *Penthouse Magazine* headquarters (Fine and Kerwin, 2005).[56] General Media, the parent company, filed for bankruptcy in 2002, and founder Bob Guccione's 45-room Manhattan condo went on the market for $40 million ("Sales Fall at Spicier Penthouse," 2002).[57] *Penthouse's* transformation from a "gentleman's magazine" (like *Playboy*) to a more hard-core, explicit publication did not work. Circulation dropped from 5 million copies in the 1970s to 382,019 by the end of 2003. *Penthouse* was bought in late 2004 by investors who will need to spend about $80 million save the magazine, but brand manager Robert Passikoff observed that "male consumers 'are not out there looking for a toned-down skin magazine'" (Fine and Kerwin, 2005). The explanation for the downfall of a magazine that clearly was once very successful—the Internet did it in. Without the brand reputation of *Playboy* and the iconic figure of Hugh Hefner, *Penthouse* lost readers though its content went from soft-core to hard-core and very explicit.

This is symbolic of the future of porn, I think. The movement from more public experiences of porn to more private experiences has already changed the way sexualities are represented. The glass-fronted booth of the adult bookstore peepshow has been replaced by computer cameras trained on women sitting in their rooms, in their apartments and houses, waiting for cybersex customers. Why buy a magazine that has flat, 2-D photos of penetration and the "insatiable woman" when a real, live, "nude girl" or guy can be purchased on the Internet? Sex can be as close as one's computer and its little camera, and a person can be naked and masturbating within the comfort of their own home. The question is, is it a bad thing that *Penthouse* might disappear from the newsstand, having been supplanted by hard-core, ultra-explicit Internet depictions of sex? Is it a bad thing that people might seek, purchase, and enjoy the sexual marketplace from their homes? One could even see this as an improvement in women sex workers' working conditions—no penetration, no body fluids, no risks of

STIs, pregnancy, assault, violence, and the ability to control work hours by simply turning off the computer and/or camera.

The irony of this is that sex has been made so public through capitalism—it is essential to advertisements, movies, television (especially cable), and music. In shifting from public sexual marketplaces to private homes and offices, we do run some risks as a society. First is what we might call the "Jacking Off Alone" problem (apologies to Putnam's 2000 book *Bowling Alone*). Though both public and private settings can afford at least the illusion of anonymity, the fact is that public sexual marketplaces offered consumers an odd sense of belonging. Those "dirty bookshops" and movie theaters were, at their best, places where men's desires could exist outside the boundaries of hegemonic scripting. Once his car was parked behind the privacy fence and he was inside the windowless building, a man could be free to experience his fantasies, see them represented in magazines and on VCR movie boxes. Could the Internet, through its solitary, anonymous appeal, actually "drive pornography underground [again], socially or psychically"? Will the Internet "come to represent the notion that sex is dirty" (Steinberg, 1990: 58)?[58]

While the Internet may negatively change the dynamics of porn consumption for individuals, it seems likely that the future will herald a different attitude towards the stars of heterosexual pornography. Gay porn stars are already held in positive regard (Fejes, 2002). The sex "soap opera" *Wet Palms,* available via download or DVD, features an intern's diary, where he describes what the guys are really like off-camera, along with outtakes, including one actor's penis with a "talking peehole." Through these adjuncts to the porn itself, the actors are humanized, rendered as celebrities, objects of fascination in the same way that *Entertainment Tonight* shows "the inside scoop" on Brad Pitt's latest motorcycle purchase. A young man named "Jason Curious" touts his Web site as "a way for people to live vicariously through someone who knows every porn star you've ever wanted to sleep with—female, male, straight, gay, everything in-between!" Jason interviews stars, hangs out with them, has sex with some of them, and describes it all in his diary and on the site.

Cowan and Polk (1996) explored 259 students' stereotypes of women in heterosexual porn compared to women celebrities, prostitutes, and women in general.[59] Porn actors were seen more negatively than celebrities and women in general, but more positively than prostitutes. But this may be changing as well. Porn stars have begun to infiltrate mainstream Hollywood; longtime actor Ron Jeremy was featured on VH1's *The Surreal Life,* living in a house with the very Christian Tammy Faye Bakker (Stanley, 2004).[60] Porn star Jenna Jameson has been seen on a 48-foot-high Times Square billboard and on E! Entertainment Television and the ubiquitous *Entertainment*

Tonight. Her autobiography, *How to Make Love Like a Porn Star,* was released in 2004 (yes, she slept with some rock stars, and no, porn is not everything it's cracked up to be). She has a contract with Vivid Video, which has made a reputation by branding itself as the company with the most attractive female stars ("there's no girl like a Vivid girl!") and the best production quality. This has led to the publication of a how-to book by "the Vivid Girls"—*How to Have a XXX Sex Life.*

The book exists because of the presumption that the average person might like to have a sex life like that of "the Vivid girls." In it they describe their likes, dislikes, sexual interests, and so on. The book is noteworthy for several reasons. That there is an audience for a sex book by porn stars, supplementing (or replacing?) the usual how-to book by a sex therapist or physician is symbolic of at least a subcultural shift. But who is that audience? Is it women who in other contexts might describe their feelings or reactions to porn as generally mixed, ambivalent, disgusted, and/or aroused? In a way, the book unintentionally captures *stars'* mixed interpretations of porn. For example, when Dasha describes g-spot orgasms that culminate in her ejac-ulations, she is clearly referring to her role as "talent": "I do it whenever I feel like it. Often a director asks me, 'Can you do it right now?' But it doesn't work that way. Sometimes my body's not in the mood, especially if I am dehydrated. Generally, though, if it's really passionate and the guy is really excited about the scene, then it works" (Vivid Girls, 2004: 174).[61] But when Kira says, "I like oral sex, but not for very long. Get me going, then I want something else" (2004: 85), is she talking about her off-screen or on-screen preferences?

"It's a way to prove your liberalness to not be freaked out by porn," said one media executive (Stanley, 2004). The clout of being "liberal," or at least open-mind-ed, cannot be underestimated when we consider the future of sexual representations. Yale University students started an unofficial group, "Porn 'n Chicken," in an effort to, well, eat fried chicken and rent X-rated movies ("Finger Lickin' Good," 2001).[62] Their "Ivy League porn" movie, *The StaXXX,* included a junior who volunteered to have sex with her girlfriend on camera. Amateur porn films, starring "real people," and celebrity sex tapes (think Paris Hilton and Pam Anderson and Tommy Lee) make news but do not seem to have any negative effects. The appeal of a few minutes of personal fame, along with the confessional impulse—the desire to reveal ourselves and see others revealed—is fundamental to these "amateur" forms of representation (Barcan, 2002).[63] The continuum of pornographic discourse includes "average guy" casting calls for men to star in gang-bang films, *The Howard Stern Show* interview-ing porn stars, and "college girls" baring themselves in *Girls Gone Wild!* videos. The blurred boundaries of this acceptability, of the porn star becoming a celebrity, may shift our perceptions of how, when, where, and why sex should be represented. The Yale student body was unseduced by the lure of *The StaXXX,* by the way; students were more worried about their futures, and how they would be impacted by having been nude in a college sex tape. The future of representation will almost certainly include more exhortations to watch and reveal ourselves, to show our sexualities in complex and contradictory manners.

CONCLUSIONS AND IMPLICATIONS

If we apply the Goldilocks theory to porn consumption, we see that it clearly operates for heterosexual men. They should cultivate the ability to appreciate it, to utilize it within particular boundaries. Appreciation of porn will help to prove that he is a hegemonic man—that he is heterosexual *and* sexual—but he should not overappreciate it or overidentify with it. What about heterosexual women consumers? Is there a just-right amount of porn that heterosexual women should seek? As subjects of heterosexual porn, women consumers are in a very different position than heterosexual men, who typically make and distribute sexual representations (Smith, 2002).[64] Women in porn are rendered as the women of heterosexual men's fantasies: active, assertive, dominant; lusty, "in touch" with themselves . . . and willing and interested in being splashed with ejaculate and called a slut, if not worse. The women of porn are rendered as slutty vixens. In this way porn and other sexual representations hinge on the existing discrepancies between all men's and women's desires, fantasies, and socialization. What are the implications of the different ways in which we are represented and choose to represent? Do we learn from porn in the same way that we learn from other agents of socialization? If so, what do we learn—about heterosexuality, homosexuality, race, capitalism, and gender?

Questions to Ponder

1. "It's a way to prove your liberalness to not be freaked out by porn," said one media executive." What do you think of this statement? Do you agree or disagree? Is there pressure for people to be into porn, or at the least, not freaked out by it?

2. There is no video series called *Guys Gone Wild!*—why? If there were such a series, who would host? What would the guys do? Who would the audience be?

Suggested Projects

1. Interview men and women about pornography. (Some age diversity might be useful so that you could compare and contrast.) Try to get a sense of respondents'

feelings and attitudes about pornography. What do they think about how men, women, and sexuality are portrayed in such media?

2. Create a visual collage or display of representations of sexuality, including those from a wide range of sources (i.e., pornographic and nonpornographic). How do men's and women's bodies appear? How is nudity used? In what ways is sex mixed with commercialism or capitalism?

9

Screwing with Sex

SOME POLITICS OF SEXUALITIES

It was a fairly small bar and it was packed. There were men everywhere I looked— older guys, younger guys who looked like they had to have fake IDs to get in, and guys in little more than leather jockstraps, with thick leather straps crisscrossing their chests. Most of the men were focused on the tiny stage in the corner, with its two spotlights bathing the area in yellow. On stage, an attractive man in a tiny g-string danced, working the crowd clustered at the stage's edge. He jumped off and moved through the men in the bar, gyrating against them, shaking his ass, and collecting money in his green, shiny g-string. By the end of the entirely forgettable song, he was totally nude, having stroked himself out of his thong, much to the crowd's satisfaction.

Ten minutes later, as I was standing at the bar collecting surveys on AIDS and condom use, he sidled up to me. Still wearing only the g-string, he was hairless, tanned, and oiled. "So," he said, "I haven't seen you here before. Can I buy you a drink?" After some back and forth about how I couldn't accept a drink because I was working, and no, I wasn't really a local, I told him I was a little confused.

"How did you end up in a strip show called 'Nine Inch Males'? How do you decide you're the right guy for the job?"

"Money. That's how I ended up here. Stripping for women really wasn't paying enough, but these guys—they don't care what I am, just that I'm not doing any false advertising, you know . . . ?" He gestured to his crotch. "When I finish college I'm sure I won't keep stripping but it really does pay my bills."

What does it mean to think about sexuality as political? Who cares about some random college guy who strips in gay bars? A quick glance around the world reveals a proliferation of the sexual marketplace we began exploring in chapter 8. On every continent we can see evidence of the collision of sex, capitalism, and representation. It makes sense to examine these issues further. In this chapter, we will focus on the medicalization of sex, particularly Viagra and the politics of orgasm and sexual "dysfunctions." With these examples we will be able to see how to connect the personal with the political, thus gaining an understanding of how sex operates in the world and in ourselves. The other goal of this chapter is to bring together some of the ideas scattered throughout the book, to provide some final conclusions and implications. And you will *definitely* learn why you should care about a guy in a shiny green g-string.

THE SEXUAL WORLD

Are there any sexual universals? Is there anything that happens around the world, over and over again? The basics of global sex are the same as the basics of sex in the United States: sperm and egg need to meet (somewhere, even in the lab) for conception to take place; every culture recognizes the existence of at least two sexes; when people engage in sexual acts, no matter where they are, the *mechanics* or hydraulics are the same though the meaning of the acts differ; and women are disproportionately victimized by all forms of sexual violence. It is difficult to discern precisely what else might constitute a sexual universal, but luckily that is not our purpose here.

We do know that most current societies, across time and space, define some elements of sex as problematic (Plummer, 2004).[1] Not every society defines every issue similarly; there is room for enormous variation. The "shapes" and meanings will differ. In the Western world, and especially in the United States, we have the luxury of defining "sexual dysfunction" as a social problem. We delineate that further to include the sexual body. So why address these issues in a chapter on the politics of sex? Since we regularly import Western sexual attitudes to other cultures, addressing them will shed some light on the future of global sexualities.

The Sexual Body: Bits, Pieces, and Ohhhhhh!

Where do we find sexuality? Is it in our heads, in our hearts, somehow, in our bodies, or in these and other locations? The body has traditionally been located as the site of sexuality. Sexual feelings are located in our physiology. As discussed in chapter 2, Masters and Johnson laid the foundation for the modern and continuing perception that physiology is the bedrock of human sexuality. "Human sexual response," as they called it, is generated by a pattern of quantifiable and general connections between stimulus and response. Touch this spot, get this result. Rub that spot, get that result. It is no exaggeration to suggest, as Tiefer has (2004), that Masters and Johnson are in large part responsible for our current situation: we are disconnected, bodies separated from our heads and minds.[2] Human sexuality textbooks always have several chapters on the sexual body—cross-sections of vaginas and testes abound—but a chapter on the mind and the brain is hard to find.

In the standard approach, the body is *the* site of sexuality. The "feelings" of sexuality happen there—the "real" effects of lust, desire, libido, carnality—they all take root and blossom in the body. Medicalization and moralizing about sexuality are focused on the body as well. *Medicalization* can be defined as "a gradual social transformation whereby medicine, with its distinctive modes of thought, its models, metaphors, and institutions, comes to exercise authority over areas of life not previously considered medical" (Conrad and Schneider, 1980, as cited in Tiefer, 2004).[3] We have seen increasing monolithic medical and moral control over the body and sexuality (e.g., Foucault, 1978).[4] This is visible in the explosion of erection-related pharmaceuticals—Viagra, Cialis, and Levitra. The attempt to medicalize women's sexualities, through things like the Eros, a suction cup device that creates a vacuum on the clitoris (thus engorging it with blood), also reveals the cultural focus on the sexual body—at the expense of better understanding mental, social, and other factors impacting our sexualities (Fishman and Mamo, 2001).[5]

The National Health and Social Life Survey (NHSLS)—the national, random, representative survey of about 2,500 Americans—asked respondents about particular sexual problems (Laumann, Paik, and Rosen, 1999).[6] About 43 percent of the female respondents—nearly half—had experienced at least one of several problems: lacked interest in sex, could not achieve orgasm, or experienced pain during sex. On average, about 30 percent of women between 18 and 59 had lacked interest in sex in the preceding 12 months; about 25 percent had experienced trouble having orgasms, and about 14 percent had experienced pain. For men between 18 and 59, about 14 percent had lacked interest in sex in the preceding 12 months; about 8 percent had experienced trouble having orgasms, and about 11 percent had experienced "erectile dysfunction."

But is experiencing a problem the same as being bothered by it? Some people may simply accept sexual difficulties, whether due to age, life circumstances, or something else. John Bancroft, head of the Kinsey Institute, interviewed heterosexually active women (by telephone) to ascertain whether those sexual problems were a source of "marked distress" (Bancroft, Loftus, and Long, 2003).[7] Only 24 percent of the subjects were upset by missing desire, arousal, or orgasms. It may be that not everyone with definable sexual problems perceives them as negative. But it may also be that Bancroft, Loftus, and Long did not correctly conceptualize "distress," having euphemistically and indirectly asked respondents, "During the past four weeks, how much distress or worry has your sexual relationship caused you?" and "During the past four weeks, how much distress or worry has your own sexuality caused you?" (p. 196).

On the other hand, in the NHSLS, only 29 percent of the women reported always having an orgasm with a partner in the preceding year, but 41 percent of women also reported that they were "extremely physically satisfied" by sex (Laumann et al., 1994).[8] Slightly fewer—39 percent—reported that they were extremely emotionally satisfied. Hmmm . . . this suggests that orgasm may not be the most important thing about sex! What about men? Not surprisingly, about 75 percent claimed that they "always" had an orgasm with a partner. Guess what? About 47 percent were extremely physically satisfied by sex, while 42 percent were extremely emotionally satisfied. Apparently a person can feel sexually satisfied even without always having an orgasm (yes, there is a touch of sarcasm here). This is striking to most observers precisely because it highlights how little we really know about the phenomenology of sex in Western countries. How *do* men and women experience sex? How do we feel about our sexual bodies?

Focus on the Penis and Penetration

Freud was among the first modern commentators on the significance of the penis. It is so figuratively huge that when little girls realize they "lack" one, he asserts, they develop a *penis envy* that is essentially unquenchable. The erection specifically is interpreted as the very essence of a man (Potts, 2000).[9] We certainly see this in pornography, which operates on the mantra of "the bigger the better." Even *Sweet Action*, the porn magazine created by young women, shows men with sizeable hard-ons. The penis is given the weight and responsibility of symbolizing the essence of "sex":

> Sex and sexuality are inscribed on the penis—it remains the "organ of copulation"—but never, in English language definitions [are sex and sexuality inscribed] on the vagina, and only sometimes on the clitoris[. O]nly half the definitions of the clitoris—the organ designed solely for sexual pleasure—mention or even imply sexuality. Indeed, both the vagina and the clitoris are overwhelmingly "organs" of *location*, i.e. their definition and meaning is primarily derived from their location in a female body. Moreover, the vagina and clitoris continue to be defined in relation to an implicit penile norm—they are either a homologue of the penis, small in comparison to the penis, or the receptacle for the penis (Braun and Kitzinger, 2001a: 223).[10]

The penis is defined by intercourse and penetration, and the clitoris and vagina are defined by the penis as well.

As the "organ of copulation," the penis becomes responsible for upholding what is taken to be the most important element of heterosex—penile-vaginal intercourse (Jackson, 1984).[11] The "coital imperative" is the socially constructed expectation that "sex" is defined by or as PVI (McPhillips, Braun, and Gavey, 2001).[12] In an interview study of 30 adult New Zealander men and women, the authors asked about the place of intercourse in heterosexual relationships. Not surprisingly, respondents generally stated that "Intercourse is the 'ultimate,' 'logical conclusion' of sex, the 'obvious' progression; simply, the normal thing to do at the end of it'" (p. 233).

Erections especially are taken as proof of masculine sexuality, of arousal, and are given hundreds of slang terms denoting the importance, power, and awe-inspiring properties of the average phallus (Braun and Kitzinger, 2001b).[13] In Braun and Kitzinger's study, British university students offered examples of slang, which though "British-ized" clearly reflect broader Western thinking about the erection: big guy, meat, harpoon, joystick, purple monster, veiny bang stick, manhood, and of course, wood (2001b: 149). "Manhood" and "big guy" seem particularly revealing, supporting Annie Potts's argument that "hard-on" has been equated to "man." She references a Robin Williams comedy routine that exemplifies the way many men learn to think about their penises—as the captain of the ship, in a sense:

> Men, you know you have a tiny creature living between your legs that has no memory and no conscience. You know that. You know you have no control.

There is no control over this tiny beast. You wake up in the morning, he's been up five minutes before you, like "How you doing?" No conscious control. He's there . . . You have no control! It should be a separate creature. You should be able to take it off. . . . We're driven! We're driven by this desire. By this strange creature. Wouldn't it be nice sometimes . . . if you could go into a bar, buy him a drink once in a while. There'd be a big bar up here, a little bar down here for him. Go into the bar. Here, pull him out. He's looking up at you with his one good eye, like "How you been, baby? Sorry about last night. I guess I got nervous. Fired off a couple of warning shots" . . . "I am not an animal, I am a sexual organ!" (*Robin Williams Live,* 1986).[14]

So the penis controls its "owner," and as a "strange creature," it is unfathomable and single-minded ("driven"). Williams distinguishes, however, between a mere animal and a penis, implying that animals are beneath us, and that though this penis is a "creature" and a "beast," it is *not* an animal. It may even be "six feet long and hard as steel" (Zilbergeld, 1992), but it is not a mere animal—the penis is at least equal to its "owner," if not superior.[15]

This is an interesting twist on the penis. The man has no control over the organ—it has the proverbial mind of its own—yet a primary tenet, or expectation, of masculinity is bodily control (e.g., Roberts et al., 1995).[16] Heterosexual men are especially subject to the discourse of control, given that sexual scripting and socialization still teach that *he* should direct sexual encounters.

Up the Creek without an Erection

"The penis has [a] . . . more supercharged symbolic value in our culture. Its 'thrusting,' 'forceful,' 'penetrative' nature has been seen as the very model of active male sexuality" (Weeks, 2003: 51).[17] So what is a man to do if he has trouble getting or maintaining an erection? Prior to the advent of Viagra in 1998, men had a few choices: surgeries, penile implants, drugs injected directly into the penis (e.g., Caverject), and vacuum erection tubes. The increasing medicalization of sexuality had a ready market in men insecure about their "manhood." So medicine—with metaphors and models—has rushed in to classify, diagnose, and prescribe on behalf of men's sexualities. Even the term *impotence* is metaphorical; the dictionary definition is "lack of strength or power." Indeed, it is not surprising that this term would be applied to the symbolically supercharged phallus. Without the ability to get an erection, how is masculinity possible?

Erections are generally seen as a purely physical response, a somewhat complex nervous-system occurrence that has "normal," and thus "abnormal," parameters. For problems with this physiology, men can partake of any of the current pharmaceutical solutions—Viagra, Cialis, or Levitra—and regain this physical response. Through the last decade, as scientists were moving closer to synthesizing Viagra, sexologists and urologists began *retreating* from their previous position that 80 percent of impotence problems were due to emotional inhibitions:

> Perhaps the most important development in the treatment of erectile dysfunction has been the nearly complete reversal of the long-held belief that in 80% of cases the problem was due to psychological factors. It is now recognized that about 70% to 80% of cases have a physical cause, and that emotional factors like anxiety about sexual performance, undue stress or guilt are common causes of impotence only among the relatively few young men with erectile dysfunction (Brody, 1995).[18]

So a socially constructed problem of the body—"impotence"—was first defined as a mental problem when it was culturally meaningful to do so. As sexuality has become increasingly medicalized, it has been redefined as a chemical, bodily problem with a pharmaceutical solution. Set on scientifically regimenting and conceptualizing sexuality, we depart from actual psychological contributions to erectile difficulties for men of all ages—such as having internalized negative messages about sexualities. Men who agree with Robin Williams's assessment, that the "strange creature" is "out of control," could experience erectile difficulties due to the disconnection and disembodiment at which his example hints.

Brody wrote that "emotional factors like anxiety about performance, undue stress, or guilt" are thought to affect the sexual bodies of the *few* young men with physiological problems. Ostensibly that would include 39-year-old Viagra pitchman, baseball player Rafael Palmeiro (subsequently found to have steroids in his system). These "emotional factors" are less problems of the body and more problems or issues of the brain. We worry ourselves into sexual difficulties—revealed in the loss of interest or desire, or lack of orgasm. But we tend to separate the mind from the body, especially men, who are assisted by the "new view" of *erectile dysfunction* (ED). This new view, a shift from previous thinking, stipulates that the "current medical consensus on erectile dysfunction is 10–30 percent psychogenic [mental, psychological], and 70–90 percent organic [physiological]" (Loe, 2004: 29; citing Pfizer Pharmaceutical training materials).[19]

In what Kleinplatz calls "the Viagra mindset" (2004), the new emphasis on the body as the site of function and "dysfunction" ignores the subjective experiences of men.[20] By ignoring the real conditions in which erection is difficult or impossible (e.g., not feeling aroused, feeling pressured, feeling tired or stressed, not feeling comfortable with a partner), this mindset reinforces the idea that men's sexuality is simplistic, simply a matter of making penile blood vessels stay engorged. Even after competition from Levitra and Cialis (introduced in 2003 and 2004, respectively), Viagra still had $919 million in U.S. sales, even at $88 for a bottle of ten (bought via drugstore.com). Twenty million men around the world have used the drug since 1998 (Herper and Lagorce, 2003).[21] Because women's sexualities have not been medicalized to this extent, women may be more able to see the sexual connections between mind and body:

> It is important, sex is. You see kitty cats and they are all fat and you know they are not having sex. Really. And it's the same with people. It is a really good calorie burner. My doctor told me to see my gynecologist about Viagra for women. I would, but my SO [significant other] says I don't need a thing. It's chemistry that turns me on, and maybe it takes me longer than when I was younger, but then again, it's all between our ears, isn't it?—Bette, a 69-year-old woman (Loe, 2004: 309–310).[22]

Although I doubt that "kitty cats" are "fat" solely because they get spayed or neutered, I agree with Bette that a lot of sex is "between our ears." But her perspective is unusual, and the Viagra mindset certainly does not enhance this mode of thinking for men.

One way to continue keeping our minds and bodies disconnected is to continually remind us that sexuality is only located in the body/genitalia, as Pfizer does in marketing Viagra. When we get ready for a date or a night out, we focus on our bodies, women especially. Women dress in a "sexy" way, we primp, we highlight, we fetishize the body; women's bodies become the "playing field" of sexuality (Roberts et al., 1995). When people *discuss* sexuality, we often describe the basic script—what happened last night, in what order, how many orgasms—thus keeping it physical. We might talk about losing control of our bodies, our responses, or of being betrayed by our bodies. We don't often talk about feelings or emotions, however.

When we learn about sexuality in formal settings, in high school and college, we usually figure out by chapter two or three of the textbook that physiology is supreme. Here we see male and female genitalia from the inside out and the outside in. The pathways of blood vessels, musculature, and nerves are visible in the images. But what is usually left out of this picture? The brain, except when it is convenient. When brains *are* depicted in sexuality textbooks, they are shown with the physiological contributions to sexuality, the parts of the brain believed to be responsible for specific sexual functions, hormones, and so on. What we do not see is a map of the brain with vast gray areas to reflect what is probably more accurate about the brain's contribution to our sexualities.

But how *does* the brain contribute, beyond its physiology? When do we ask the brain to enter the calculus? The most obvious moment of entry, I think, is when parents and others ask teenagers—or more accurately, teen women—to stop and "think" before they engage their sexualities. Teen women are told that the mentality of sexuality is more important than the physicality: the mind trumps the body. The mind needs to "be ready" for what the body has in store for it. The teen mind is not ready, even if the teen body is seen as fully ready. Clearly what the beseechers of teenagers are referring to is something more than physiology. This is important—because when sexuality is seen as something merely physical, it is denigrated. If sex is purely physical, and not emotional or intimate, then it is cheapened. We can see the paradox here: for men, the body is most important to sexuality, but for women, the brain, the mind, and the emotions should be most important.

An example of how the brain—how mentality—can be ahead of the body in processing sexuality is in Reinholtz and Muehlenhard's (1995) study of college students' perceptions of genitalia and various sexual activities.[23] Women expressed more negative perceptions of their and their partners' genitals than did men. Women were more negative about giving and receiving oral sex, saying that they felt more degraded by both activities. Heterosexual men expressed the opinion that female partners were degraded by giving and receiving oral sex. Negative perceptions of genitalia were correlated with decreased sexual experience and decreased sexual enjoyment. The authors' (asociological, clinical) suggestion is for therapists to help partners (in couples) develop positive feelings toward their own and their partners' genitalia—which *might* happen *if* the "genitally negative" couple was living in a cultural vacuum. In this vacuum, there would be no competing, negative messages. (Remember that women are sold "feminine deodorant spray" to perfume the genitalia, while men have no such "masculine deodorant spray.")

There are several ironies, of course. The genitalia may be the most socially constructed body parts we have (recall Kessler's example of babies born with intersex attributes, in chapter 3). Sexuality is not linked to the body on the whole but specifically to the genitals; heterosexuality is especially focused on the joining or merging of the genitals. Yet the mind is subject to the cues of a culture that suggests that genitalia (particularly women's) are not quite hygienic. A range of bodily functions distract when we think about genitals: urination, menstruation, ejaculation, lubrication. Is it because we want to avoid these material realities of the sexual body that we tend to separate the mind and the body? So how do we get out of this conundrum? How do we link the body and the mind?

THE BIG OHHHHHH!

When I was about seven or eight, I remember seeing a slim little book on one of my mother's bookcases, called *The Job of Sex* (McConnachie, 1974).[24] I snuck it off the shelf and into my room one day, sat down on my bed to flip through it, and quickly got confused. I didn't understand anything in the book. The pictures were weird—a man was wearing a suit in one of them, but his penis was hanging out and he was talking to a fully dressed woman. The book had headings like "dow-jones" and "skivvies." I thought it was a book about sex! Eventually I returned it to my mom's bookcase, but I made sure that it came with me when I moved out for good (sorry Mom, I stole your book). Luckily it is now clear to me that *The Job of Sex* was *National Lampoon*'s parody of *The Joy of Sex* (Comfort, 1972), a wildly popular book that almost all of your parents likely owned at one time.[25] Comfort took a cookbook approach, with various sexual activities divided into aspects of a "meal"—"starters" and "main courses," for example. For example, he wrote that "multiple orgasm comes easily to many if not all women if they are responsive enough and care to go on" (1972: 61). *The Job of Sex* handled the topic of orgasms a bit differently:

> . . . This book explodes, once and for all, the absurd mystique of "the two orgasms." Under clinical, sanitized laboratory conditions, beneath Klieg lights, with X-ray machines, electroencephalograph equipment, two-way mirrors, and the finest medical hardware federal grant money can buy, it has been established that there is only one kind of orgasm, and that even it is rare except among convicted exhibitionists . . . for centuries, males have felt inadequate, or cheated, by achieving only the so-called "penile" orgasm, while the Holy Grail of the so-called "scrotal" orgasm eluded them (1974: 15).

Obviously *The Job of Sex* is spoofing the idea that we believe there are several different kinds of orgasms women should aspire to have. The reference to "laboratory conditions" reminds us of the typical way in which scientists have studied orgasm—not as an individual, interpreted experience, but mainly as a physiological phenomenon.

Western culture has linked the sexual self to the performance of the body (Scully and Bart, [1978] 2003; Moore and Clarke, 2001).[26] Parody notwithstanding, we tend to take the "job" of sex very seriously. When our bodies do not do what we want them to, we can develop performance anxiety, aversion to partnered sexual activities, and frustration and stress. The contours of men's and women's sexualities are considered to be dependent on the body, not so much on the mind. The stress of performance and the need to control the body can lead to some people faking orgasms (Roberts et al.,1995; Wiederman, 1997).[27] Most faking, or pretending, is done by heterosexual women (though as in other areas of sexual science, we know very little about same-sex identified men and women). Wiederman surveyed 161 women aged 18 to 27 and found that more than half had faked orgasm during heterosexual intercourse. These women were more likely to view themselves as attractive, had intercourse at a younger age, had more sexual partners than those who had never faked, and had higher sexual self-esteem. Women believe that a stigma is attached to women who cannot (easily) have orgasms (Lavie and Willig, 2005).[28] ". . . Our society . . . perceives them as women who are frigid, cold, sexually frustrated women who do not like sex, who are tense and not open" (p. 120).

Given the existence of Viagra, and the importance of the erection, the penis, and the "money shot" in pornography, how can we explain the fact that the minimal research on the subject focuses on women faking orgasms? It seems as if (heterosexual) men would be more likely than women to report ever having faked. *Cosmopolitan* magazine, which features a variety of articles about women's sexualities (including both how to masturbate and have an orgasm and how to fake an orgasm!), addressed the subject of heterosexual men who fake:

> Nick, 28, can definitely relate. "As I take on more career responsibilities, I'm finding myself totally taxed," he says. "But no self-respecting dude will ever acknowledge that he sometimes would rather catch up on sleep than roll around with a naked chick. To get it over with when I'm just not in the right frame of mind, I have to speed sex along by faking."
>
> "After my girl and I start messing around, all I can think is, Am I doing it right? Is she turned on? Will she blab about me to her friends or make a demand I can't fulfill?" says Patrick, 26. "By the time she has her orgasm, I can be so mentally exhausted, I may fake my own grand finale" (Koli, 2004: 128).[29]

No "self-respecting dude" would ever talk the way these men do (it's safe to guess that magazine quotes are embellished!), but the issues they raise are still germane. Nick brings up several things—that one primary aspect of hegemonic masculinity is working hard, and another is appearing to always be ready and interested in "rolling around" with a "naked chick." Patrick clarifies the performance pressure many heterosexual men are subjected to, being expected to initiate, choreograph, and orchestrate both partners' orgasms.

The concept of "fake(d)" orgasms brings to mind the ultimate symbolism of the Viagra mindset. In this conceptualization of what Tiefer has called the "perfect penis," men and their penises, orgasms, and pleasure are subject to games of pretense. The *Cosmo* examples above illustrate the idea that hegemonic, masculine sexuality goes beyond men simply faking orgasms. The men are pretending that sex is more important than sleep, or that her pleasure and needs are more important than his self-consciousness or his pleasure. Indeed, men are expected to "trade" orgasms with their partners (Braun, Gavey, and McPhillips, 2003).[30] Even if the quotes themselves are "faked," they nonetheless encompass what Potts (2005) calls cyborg masculinity—the idea of man-as-machine, maybe with a Viagra-induced erection that stays firm for hours (unlike non-drug-enhanced erections that wax and wane).[31] Men who have used Viagra are conscious of hegemonic cultural discourses about men's sexualities, discourses that likely infuse decisions about whether to fake orgasm (Rubin, 2004).[32] Masculinity, power, virility, and instrumental sexuality are paramount here. For many men, sex can easily become the "job" referred to in *National Lampoon*'s spoof.

That said, are Viagra, Cialis, and Levitra "bad" drugs? Is there anything wrong with taking drugs to help the penis fill with blood (and retain that blood), thereby creating an erection?

> [These] drugs provide a relatively safe and effective option for increasing penile vasocongestion. . . . They are surely a valuable option for clinicians and their patients who want to ensure predictable, reliable erections. The problem is with the idea that the view centered on mechanics and hydraulics represents the only way of looking at big, hard penises. Pharmaceutical companies have rapidly come to dominate the discourse on male sexual problems and their solutions. It is disconcerting that the biophysical model—just that and no more—has assumed hegemony over our conceptions of sexuality in general and erectile dysfunction in particular (Kleinplatz, 217).

The bigger problem is the hegemony—the lack of cultural discourse about any other aspects of sexualities, combined with the assumption that drugs will solve all problems. The singularity of this approach is evident within therapeutic approaches to sexual difficulties (Winton, 2001).[33] In Winton's study of 187 articles from four major sexology journals, he found that sex therapy for women's sexual problems was becoming medicalized, with treatments focusing on "correct genital functioning" to the exclusion of therapy about relationships and contextual issues.

Women's Orgasms and Sexual "Dysfunction"

Evolutionary psychologist Donald Symons (1979) wrote that "female orgasm" "inspires interest, debate, polemics, ideology, technical manuals, and scientific and popular literature solely because it is so often absent," compared to "the male orgasm, which exists with monotonous regularity and for the most part is interesting only to people directly involved in one" (p. 85).[34] This comment reflects the longstanding belief that women's orgasms are more varied and complex than men's. In their 1960s study of "human sexual response," Masters and Johnson even identified several more orgasmic pathways for women than for men.[35] Obscuring the diversity of men's orgasms and pleasurable feelings, while emphasizing the variety of ways in which women can be orgasmic is consequential. The most obvious consequence is that we ignore the ways in which relationship, context, feelings, and emotions impede or enhance both men's and women's orgasmic capabilities (e.g., Mah and Binik, 2005).[36] Indeed, the assumption that men's orgasms and ejaculations are ubiquitous dovetails with the belief that orgasm can only occur with a rock-hard erection (in fact, erection is not necessary). We attach too much significance to gender and sex differences when discussing orgasms. Writer Jonathan Margolis (2004) drew from a variety of sources to create his history of orgasm.[37] He described a study of orgasm descriptions—"powerful," "intense," and "pleasurable" were the most popular terms chosen by men and women. Another study revealed that 70 gynecologists, psychologists, psychiatrists, and urologists could not correctly establish the sex of a person based solely on self-authored orgasm descriptions.

For women, the issue of orgasm is especially fraught with misinformation, misinterpretation, and performance pressure. Scientists study how women's brains operate during orgasm, the link between orgasm and conception, and various forms of pleasurable stimulation (e.g., G-spot, via penetration, via oral sex, and so on).

Evolutionary psychologists debate about whether women's orgasms really matter because, unlike ejaculation, it is not a "necessary" variable in conception (see Eschler, 2004, for a brief review).[38] Biologist Elisabeth Lloyd offers a challenge to this traditional thinking in her book addressing bias in evolutionary theorizing (2005).[39] There are consequences to this "debate," including the perpetuation of a belief that men's sexuality is superior because of the importance placed on ejaculation. This is to say nothing of the inherent assumptions of heterosexuality and reproductivity. Clearly, ejaculation and sperm are not so important for the millions of regularly occurring sex acts that do not involve reproduction (e.g., contracepted PVI, anal sex, oral sex).

A less obvious consequence is the kind of performance pressure to which many Western women (but certainly also men) are now subject. Pressures to perform, be responsive, and be orgasmic are not new. Though the diagnosis of "female hysteria" and the use of vibrators as a medical, physician-administered cure have disappeared, the underlying ideology has not (Maines, 1999).[40] Women have long been expected to be responsive to penetrative activities (Ericksen, 1999),[41] raising questions about sex-linked power imbalances, heterosexuality, and lesbians' orgasmic activities (Bolsø, 2005).[42] Fake orgasms can result from heterosexual women's desire to please their partners, or from the awareness that men are expected to work for women's orgasms, among other reasons, including exhaustion, stress, discomfort, and lack of interest (Roberts et al., 1995; Wiederman, 1997). But we have also constructed more extensive typologies of orgasms, especially for women, on whom we have turned our sexual attention like a bright, unforgiving spotlight: multiple orgasms, vaginal orgasms, clitoral orgasms, uterine orgasms, G-spot, Z-spot, female ejaculation, and orgasms during anal sex. Though women can learn about all these orgasms, we also learn that asserting ourselves sexually is unfeminine. It may be that women learn to be less orgasmic than they could be solely from a physiological standpoint, through socialized inhibitions, fears, and gender roles.

Earlier in the book, I introduced the *Diagnostic and Statistical Manual*, 4th ed. (DSM-IV), the text that is the standard for psychiatric and mental health-related diagnoses. Leonore Tiefer (2004) points out that "classification sets into motion processes that often include intimidating and stigmatizing certain groups, setting and enforcing norms, creating culturally dominant language and imagery, and not least, creating and shaping individual desires and needs. As revolutionaries have pointed out, *naming is power*" (p. 132). The DSM classifies everything from schizophrenia to narcissistic personality disorder to sexual "disorders," as discussed in chapter 2. Between 1952 and 1994, the coverage of sexual disorders has increased, going from zero pages in the first

DSM to nineteen pages in the current DSM, the fourth edition (Tiefer, 2004). An example of why coverage has increased can be found in an argument about diminishing the importance of individuals' subjective experiences of sexual "dysfunction" (Althof, 2001).[43] Coverage of sex disorders has increased in part because of the continuing value placed on "scientific rigor" in accurately "characterizing" sexual problems. This requires scientists and physicians to continue defining what disorder is, independently of individual distress or concerns (Althof, 2001).

In this view, definitions and classifications appear to have essential qualities, existing beyond individual context. But the problem with this ideological approach is that in order to define *dis*orders or *dys*functions, we would need to know what "normal" sexual functions are. Unfortunately, we have little such information, researchers' imaginations having been limited by narrow paradigms, biased points of view, and culturally inadequate language for studying the subjective aspects of sex.

A nationally representative study of the self-reported sexual "dysfunction" of 1,056 Swedish women, ages 18 to 65, calls into question the concept of "normal" sexual response (Oberg, Fugl-Meyer, and Fugl-Meyer, 2004).[44] The majority of women—from 60 to 90 percent—reported at least *some* dysfunction related to desire and interest, orgasmic capabilities, and/or vaginal lubrication. Over one-third reported pain with PVI (*dyspareunia*). Nearly 45 percent with low interest, desire, and/or orgasmic difficulties were distressed by these things. About 65 percent of those with lubrication problems and/or dyspareunia were distressed by these things. Age had little to no influence on sexual functioning, similarly to the findings of Laumann, Paik, and Rosen (1999) in the NHSLS. Another study, using an Internet convenience sample (simply, those respondents who replied, without regard to representativeness) of women, found that most respondents had, at some time, experienced low desire (77 percent), low arousal (62 percent), and difficulty achieving orgasm (56 percent) (Berman et al., 2003).[45]

What can we make of these findings? "Dysfunction" seems far more usual than unusual, at least for women. Distress seems prevalent as well, though perhaps not as common as we might guess or assume. Why would anyone be distressed by how their sexualities function? Our expectations about how our bodies should operate and appear are directly connected to cultural messages dictating and scripting expectations. An illustration of this involved a convenience sample study of 50 adult women, all of whom worked at a hospital (Schober, Meyer-Bahlburg, and Ransley, 2004).[46] Women aged 20 to 56 were asked to describe their clitorises, their vaginas, and their sexual sensitivity. In assessing the size of the vaginal opening (*introitus*), 78 percent chose "adequate for sexual penetration" and 16 percent (n = 8) chose "just large enough to insert finger or small object . . . " (but not large enough for other things, including a regular-sized tampon). While 48 percent indicated that their clitoris was "moderate-sized and raised," the rest of the sample chose other descriptions, such as large, long, or small. Schober, Meyer-Bahlburg, and Ransley remarked that "only two-fifths of the women indicated a clitoral size [i.e., "small"] that would typically be regarded as normal" (p. 593). Physicians are trained to see "moderate-sized" clitorises—the size indicated by 48 percent of this sample—as "too large."

Recall Suzanne Kessler's discussion about size determinations for intersexed babies with large clitorises (chapter 3). Physicians believed that they could discern the "normal" size range for a clitoris; this discernment appears to have been based solely on social conventions. But how do any of us know what is too large? Philosopher Nancy Tuana teaches a large lecture course on sexuality. She writes:

> I have discovered that the students in the class know far more about male genitals than they do about female genitals. Take, for example, the clitoris. The vast majority of my female students have no idea how big their clitoris is, or how big the average clitoris is, or what types of variations exist among women. Compare to this the fact that most of my male students can tell you the length and *diameter* of their penis both flaccid and erect, though their information about the average size of erect penises is sometimes shockingly inflated—a consequence, I suspect, of the size of male erections in porn movies. That is, both women and men alike typically know far more about the structures of the penis than they do about those of the clitoris (2004: 198).[47]

She does note that her students can, by and large, draw "relatively accurate rendition[s]" of vaginas, uteruses, fallopian tubes, and ovaries. This is probably due to having learned about sexual anatomy in biology classes.

What has been omitted from most of the discussion about orgasms, erections, and sexual dysfunctions is context. Most of the research is hampered by several assumptions. Researchers either assume that sexual orientation, race/ethnicity, and class are meaningless, or they specifically select heterosexuals. Most of the studies require respondents to be in sexual relationships, assuming that most dysfunction occurs with a partner. (But some people have different patterns of response and arousal depending on whether they are alone or with another person.)

Then there is the foundational assumption that orgasms, erections, arousal, and interest are relatively constant, free from the influence of mood, partner, setting, life circumstances, and so forth. The questions researchers pose reveal the assumption that there is a baseline norm and that most people recognize it and experience it, to the extent that they would then recognize any variation from that norm. So it is assumed that most men know the difference between the Goldilocks orgasm/ejaculation, happening at the just right time, and the occasional "too soon" or "too late" climax. In simply documenting "sexual dysfunction" without exploring the *causes* of the dysfunction, researchers reinforce the belief that sexuality is located mainly in the body. Why *do* some men have erection difficulties or ejaculate before they want to, or not at all? Why *do* some women have difficulties having orgasms, feeling aroused, or being lubricated? Why is dysfunction relatively consistent across adult age groups?

Because research on dysfunction has largely ignored the complexities and nuances of sexualities, we only know about self-reported prevalence of difficulties and self-reported "distress." It is likely that sexual difficulties have a variety of sources, only a few of which are physiological or uniquely psychological. But the research does not consider the possibility that sexual dysfunction exists because, well, sex itself is not very functional. Penile-vaginal intercourse is not an especially efficient or direct way to promote women's orgasms. We learn little about how to explore our sexualities to figure out what *would* feel better. Since we are not taught *how* to discuss our sexual interests, when we try, the available language can be awkward and incomplete. What else about sex is just not very functional? A short list: alcohol-soaked hook-ups; mixing sex with guilt, shame, embarrassment, and/or fear; the problems of contraception and disease prevention; one-night stands, casual sex, and friends-with-benefits, which may not create conditions that would easily enhance orgasms and sexual functioning; and pressure to keep each partner "satisfied" (e.g., Nicolson and Burr, 2003).[48] By now you could certainly add to this list.

A New View of Sexualities

At the start of this chapter, I suggested that we could explore some global concerns about sex—the collision of sex, capitalism, and representation—by focusing on Viagra, orgasm, and sexual dysfunctions. We now need to explore how we can connect the personal with the political, and I still need to let you know why you should care about that college guy in the shiny green g-string!

Sexuality is global, to be sure, but more explicitly, sexuality is fundamental to the economies, politics, and gender roles of most of the world's nations. Viagra is sold around the world, though pharmaceutical advertising is illegal in Europe (unlike in the United States), and is available from Saudi Arabia to Mexico to Japan and everywhere in between (Loe, 2004). Pfizer, the maker of Viagra, commissioned a global study of sexual dysfunction, seeking to manufacture new demand and create new markets. That study, which included NHSLS researcher Edward Laumann, included data from 29 countries (Nicolosi et al., 2004).[49] A standardized questionnaire was given to 27,500 men and women aged 40 to 80. Overall, about 80 percent of men and 65 percent of women had had intercourse in the preceding year. Men were most concerned with early ejaculation (14 percent) and erectile difficulties (10 percent), while women were most concerned with lack of interest (21 percent), inability to orgasm (16 percent), and lubrication problems (16 percent). About 39 percent of women and 28 percent of men were impacted by at least one sexual dysfunction. This is less than the overall proportions reported in smaller studies focused on Western nations, suggesting that there may be different sociocultural sexual scripts. Indeed, the prevalence of sexual problems differed from region to region, with East Asian and Southeast Asian respondents reporting the most difficulties (e.g., lack of interest in sex, early ejaculation, and so on) (Nicolosi et al., 2004).

In this attempt to document global sexual dysfunction, it is important to note that 191,310 people were contacted in the 29 countries, but only 145,380 were really eligible to participate, and only 27,500 completed the questionnaire. While most of the men (82 percent) and women (76 percent) agreed that "satisfactory sex is essential to maintain a relationship," fewer agreed that they were "in favor of the use of medical treatments to help older people enjoy sexual activity." Only 68 percent of men and 60 percent of women agreed with this, but in developing countries, there was even less agreement. This finding may represent the extent to which medicalization has taken hold in Western and developed countries, making us more likely to accept the diagnoses and interventions offered by medical stakeholders and those with the power to define sexualities. It is significant that the same stakeholders who now promote and benefit from pharmaceutical solutions to sexual dysfunctions maintained (until the 1990s) that most instances of erectile disorder were psychological, not physiological.

But without significant private funding sources to study sexualities anywhere in the world, we will continue to see private, for-profit stakeholders such as Pfizer bankrolling research (Allina, 2001).[50] The implications are grave. Is it reasonable to assume that researchers funded by (sexual dysfunction) drug manufacturers will be free from bias? Instead, a corporate, medicalized research agenda is promoted. Pfizer can glance at Nicolosi et al.'s findings—that 34 percent of female East Asian respondents had experienced some lack of interest in sex—and begin developing a marketing campaign for a pill to solve the problem. In fact, drug companies and other multi-national corporations using sexuality to sell or to make money depend on academics and researchers (Fishman, 2004).[51] Women's health activist Amy Allina (2001) points out that private funders enable researchers to circumvent the much bigger problem, at least in the United States: entrenched cultural conservatism, mixed messages, and confusion about sex. This combines with disrespect for individual choices, fear of youthful sexualities, and rhetoric about "family values" that prioritizes ineffective abstinence-only "sex" education (e.g., Levine, 2002).[52] All of this leads to minimally creative, banal sexual research agendas and knowledge production that support the status quo.

Globally, we see other likely contributions to unhappy sexual lives, sexual dysfunctions, and diminished intimacies (e.g., Ogden, 2001).[53] Women and men are subject to local and global inequalities on numerous dimensions—financial, legal, spiritual, emotional, educational, intellectual, and so on (e.g., Nagel, 2003).[54] Threats to women's and girls' abilities to develop healthy sexualities and relationships abound. Rape (acquaintance, marital, stranger, and as a war crime), sexual assault, domestic abuse, destructive genital mutilation, and childhood sexual assault disproportionately affect women and girls (e.g., Gavey, 2005).[55] Global capitalism and consumerism is revealed in sexual slavery, sexual trafficking, sex tourism, and sex work (e.g., Kempadoo and Doezema, 1998; Clift and Carter, 2000).[56] Heterosexually active men and women are thus differentially affected by the ways in which we have institutionalized sexualities and gender.

"The majority of people on a global scale still have to struggle with getting their daily bread, against the exigencies of extreme poverty, famine, drought, war, authoritarian governments, corruption and violence. Compared to these questions, concerns about sexuality and the body and a sense of self may seem fairly trivial when most people have to struggle just to survive; [these concerns appear to be] the worries of the . . . educated middle class rather than the preoccupations of the embattled majority" (Weeks, 1998: 40).[57] It is true that concerns about sexual selves and healthy relationships may seem trivial when epidemics of poverty, war, famine, violence, AIDS, and childhood diseases threaten billions of people. Indeed, it is quite a luxury to have the time, freedom, and resources to contemplate things like "the end of the heterosexual/homosexual binary divide" and "the queering of identities" (Weeks, 1998: 49). Even the concept of an *identity*, a self-concept connected to sexual practices, attractions, and interests, is outside the scope of consideration for most people in the world. In the United States we have the (odd) luxury of being able to treat issues of homosexualities, gender diversities, and teen sexualities as "moral" crises.

Because we believe we have our citizens' basic needs met, we feel we can afford to view sexualities as individual choices, made by people lacking proper morals, discipline, and so forth.

This view disables us from thinking more broadly about sexualities. If we assume that everything sexual results from individual, (im)moral choices, we will miss the bigger context. Sociocultural structures and institutions provide the blueprint for the sexualities individuals may develop. For example, the reality of sexual violence in all its forms is larger than any individual or their choices. There are other contextual variables as well, such as laws and customs discriminating against or honoring sexual and gender variation, and attitudes about marriage and nonmarital sexuality, and cultural levels of gender equality. If we accept this reasoning—that individual sexualities develop within broader cultures—then we may start to see how the personal is political in Western countries. Looking at global sexualities enables us to see the reverse—how the political becomes personal.

Sociological Imagination C. Wright Mills

CONCLUSION

Regardless of how we come to understand ourselves sexually and regardless of our preferences, practices, feelings, desires, interests, and attitudes—we each want to be free to develop these things within ourselves. We do not normally think of ourselves as subject to any external influences. But clearly our freedom to develop *is* subject to forces outside our direct control. We all bear the weight of accumulated cultural confusion, contradictions, and mixed messages. We are all subject to conceptions of sexualities and definitions of "normal" and "abnormal." Labeling, classifying, and naming affect each of us in ways both visible and invisible. Which brings me back to the dancer in the shiny green g-string. . . .

I think he represents many of the issues we have explored in this book. He was a heterosexually identified man dancing nude in a "gay bar." But what was his sexual orientation? Was he "really" straight? After all, he was letting other men stare at his endowment, touch him, and dance with him. He was getting an erection knowing that other men would be looking at him. In his performance of sexuality, he was selecting elements of a script that he knew would be arousing, showing off his large erection, a hairless chest, and his muscular physique. The main point of his dancing was to make money (for college) selling his particular portrayal of sex. In short, he epitomizes modern, Western sexualities: flexible, commercial, scripted, individual, conformist, structured, and unique—all of this (and more), all at once. We *do* have the luxury of being able to piece together aspects of culture and explore our sexualities. Sex is *not* a natural act, as Leonore Tiefer has written, but knowledge-seeking can become one. Using critical thinking and creativity, I hope your continuing academic *and* personal explorations will be rewarding, challenging, and fascinating.

Questions to Ponder

1. Can heterosexual women "have sex" like heterosexual men? What are the implications of gender differences in prevalence of sexual violence and commercialism (broadly defined)?

2. What are the pros and cons of the medicalization of sexualities? In what other realms do we see the rise of this paradigm (besides in drugs for erectile disorder and other sexual "dysfunctions")?

Suggested Projects

1. Search for op-ed newspaper articles that address any aspect of sexualities. Analyze carefully, using critical thinking as your guide. What are the author's assumptions? What information and evidence are offered? Does the author discuss any policy changes, social activism, or political ramifications of the issue?

2. Choose one global sexuality issue and research it further. How will you combine evidence and information in your paper? Can you find first-person narratives to supplement scholarly and other research? What are the bigger implications of the issue you have chosen?

Acknowledgments

I am fortunate to live and work in a productive, vibrant, engaged community—Ithaca, New York. Here is where I have landed the job a sexualities scholar dreams of—given the chance to teach about sex without fear, censorship, or guilt. Many thanks to my entertaining and challenging colleagues in the Sociology Department, who painstakingly laid the foundation for the Gender (and Sexuality) Concentration in which I now work. Special thanks to Vikki Hammond and Jonathan Laskowitz, who facilitated various kinds of support for this task, including course release time and research assistance. Many others deserve mention as well:

• My students. I first taught a sex course as an undergraduate, at Hampshire College, but the bulk of my pedagogy was developed with the indulgence of students at the University of New Hampshire, Wittenberg University, and Ithaca College. For this project, Scott Goldman and Steve Mardenfeld read chapters and gave feedback.

• Autumn Miller, who served in several capacities as a research assistant, a student of "sexology," and a reader. Her assistance, enthusiasm, and friendship were invaluable.

• My "mentors," who have been in my corner for many, many years. Michael S. Kimmel has been a teacher, advisor, collaborator, and friend. Peter Adler, Leonore Tiefer, Francis Dodoo, Jim Ennis, and Peggy Kleinplatz are mensches, one and all.

• My mentoring groups at Ithaca College, with shifting memberships but singular purpose—support and feedback in the incredibly profound endeavors of the academic. Special thanks to Susanne Morgan for working to make this, and more, happen.

• My friends, professional and personal, and my parents. Evan Cooper provided many excellent excuses to take my laptop and leave the house. He is a true mensch. Lis Maurer and Braeden L. Sullivan were thoughtful foils for many of my ideas; Lis read chapters and gave feedback as well. To my other friends—please forgive me for being such a bad correspondent while I was distracted by this book and other things.

My parents have always been eternally supportive of the daughter with the avant-garde interests. And Brody Burroughs made it *all* happen—1,000 things, 1,000 ways.

• The professionals at Westview Press. Being part of Westview's list is actually a professional dream come true. Jill Rothenberg (now with SEAL) pitched the idea to me and had faith in me and the project, and Steve Catalano ably stepped in to make it come together in the last year. All new authors should have such caring, dedicated, intelligent, and fun editors. Thanks also to the production, marketing, and design crews, along with Westview's publisher, Cathleen Tetro.

Please note that all errors or omissions in the book are entirely mine. I welcome your feedback about any aspect of it: rplante@ithaca.edu.

—Rebecca F. Plante

Ithaca, New York
September, 2005

Notes

Introduction

1. I am taking the liberty of changing the author's name, so as not to inundate her blog with hits, but I read blogs on blogspot.com and livejournal.com.

2. Gagnon, John, and William H. Simon. 1973. *Sexual Conduct: The Social Sources of Human Sexuality.* Chicago: Aldine.

3. Retrieved from "Position Statements." http://www.siecus.org/about/abou0001.html.

Chapter 1

1. Halperin, David M. 1990. "Sex before Sexuality: Pederasty, Politics, and Power in Classical Athens." Pp. 37–53 in *Hidden from History: Reclaiming the Gay and Lesbian Past*, ed. M. Duberman, M. Vicinus, and G. Chauncey. New York: Meridian.

2. Karras, Ruth Mazo. 2000. "Review Essay. Active/Passion, Acts/Passions: Greek and Roman Sexualities." *American Historical Review* 105(4): 1250–1266.

3. Keuls, Eva. 1993. *The Reign of the Phallus: Sexual Politics in Ancient Athens.* Berkeley: University of California Press.

4. Carroll, Joseph. 2005. "Society's Moral Boundaries Expand Somewhat This Year." News release, 5/16/05. Retrieved from www.gallup.com.

5. Turley, Jonathan. "Of Lust and the Law." *Washington Post*, 9/5/04, p. B1.

6. Pennington, Jon C. 2003. "It's Not a Revolution but It Sure Looks Like One: A Statistical Accounting of the Post-Sixties Sexual Revolution." *Radical Statistics* 83: 104–116.

7. Loftus, J. 2001. "America's Liberalization in Attitudes toward Homosexuality, 1973 to 1988." *American Sociological Review* 66: 762–782.

8. Barash, David P., and Judith Eve Lipton. 2001. *The Myth of Monogamy: Fidelity and Infidelity in Animals and People.* New York: W.H. Freeman.

9. Laumann, Edward O., John H. Gagnon, Robert T. Michael, and Stuart Michaels. 1994. *The Social Organization of Sexuality: Sexual Practices in the United States.* Chicago: University of Chicago.

10. Cornog, Martha. 1986. "Naming Sexual Body Parts: Preliminary Patterns and Implications." *Journal of Sex Research* 22: 393–398.

11. Richter, Alan. 1987. *The Language of Sexuality.* Jefferson, NC: McFarland and Company.

12. De Sousa, Ronald, and Kathryn Pauly Morgan. 1988. "Philosophy, Sex, and Feminism." *Atlantis, A Journal of Women's Studies* 13(2): 1–10. Retrieved from http://www.chass.utoronto.ca/~sousa/sexphil.html.

13. Ibid.

14. Baker, Robert. 2000. "The Language of Sex: Our Conception of Sexual Intercourse." Pp. 277–281 in *Gender Basics: Feminist Perspectives on Women and Men,* 2nd ed., ed. A. Minas. Belmont, CA: Wadsworth. [Abridged version of "'Pricks and Chicks': A Plea for 'Persons'," 1975, in *Philosophy and Sex,* eds. R. Baker and F. Elliston. Buffalo, NY: Prometheus Books.]

15. Kitzinger, Celia. 2005. "'Speaking as a Heterosexual': (How) Does Sexuality Matter for Talk-in-Interaction?" *Research on Language and Social Interaction* 38: 221–265.

16. Kinsey, Alfred C., Wardell B. Pomeroy, and Clyde E. Martin. 1948. *Sexual Behavior in the Human Male.* Philadelphia: W.B. Saunders; Kinsey, Alfred C., Wardell B. Pomeroy, Clyde E. Martin, and Paul H. Gebhard. 1953. *Sexual Behavior in the Human Female.* Philadelphia: W.B. Saunders.

17. D'Emilio, John, and Estelle B. Freedman. 1988. *Intimate Matters: A History of Sexuality in America.* New York: Harper and Row.

18. Godbeer, Richard. 2004. "Courtship and Sexual Freedom in Eighteenth-Century America." *OAH Magazine of History* 18(4): 9–12.

19. Bloch, Ruth H. 2003. "Changing Conceptions of Sexuality and Romance in Eighteenth-Century America." *William and Mary Quarterly* 60(1): 44. 10 March 2005, http://www.historycooperative.org/journals/wm/60.1/bloch.html.

20. Misra, Ranjita, and Steven Hohman. 2000. "Trends in Abortion Attitude among Young Adults: 1977–1993." *American Journal of Health Studies* 16: 85–99.

21. Harding, David, and Christopher Jencks. 2003. "Changing Attitudes toward Premarital Sex." *Public Opinion Quarterly* 67: 211–227.

22. Retrieved from http://webapp.icpsr.umich.edu/GSS/.

23. Herek, Gregory. 2002. "Gender Gaps in Public Opinion about Lesbians and Gay Men." *Public Opinion Quarterly* 66: 40–67.

24. Huberman, Barbara. 2005. "Rights, Respect, Responsibility: A Vision for Our Youth." Presented at the New View of Women's Sexuality Conference, "Women and the New Sexual Politics: Profits vs. Pleasures," July 10, Montreal, Canada.

25. Landry, David J., Lisa Kaeser, and Cory L. Richards. 1999. "Abstinence Promotion and the Provision of Information about Contraception in Public School District Sexuality Education Policies." *Family Planning Perspectives* 31(6):280–286.

26. "Low-Income Parents Support Sex Ed Too." 2002. *Contemporary Sexuality* 36(11): 8.

27. Saad, Lydia. 2004. "Abortion Divides Public; Not a Top Issue for Voters." Gallup News Service release. Retrieved from http://www.gallup.com/poll/content/?ci=11461&pg=1.

28. Robison, Jennifer. 2002. "Feminism—What's in a Name?" Gallup News Service Release. Retrieved from http://www.gallup.com/poll/content/?ci=6715&pg=1.

29. Saad, Lydia. 2001. "Women See Room for Improvement in Job Equity; But are Generally Satisfied with Their Lives." Gallup News Service Release. Retrieved from http://www.gallup.com/poll/content/?ci=4561&pg=1.

30. Kelly, Gary F. 2004. *Sexuality Today: The Human Perspective* (7e, updated). Boston, MA: McGraw-Hill.

31. Catalano, Shannan M. 2004. "Criminal Victimization." *National Crime Victimization Survey.* Working Paper No. 205455, Bureau of Justice Statistics, Washington, DC.

32. Seidman, Steven. 2004. *Beyond the Closet: The Transformation of Gay and Lesbian Life.* New York: Routledge; Savin-Williams, Ritch. 2005. *The New Gay Teenager.* Cambridge, MA: Harvard University Press.

33. Wloszczyna, Susan. 2003. "It's In to Be 'Out' These Days." *USA Today.* Retrieved from http://www.usatoday.com/life/2003–06–01-in-out_x.htm; see also www.sexetc.org for details.

34. "Opinion Polls on Marriage Equality Yield Widely Varying Results." 2005. GLAAD Eye on the Media Center. Retrieved from http://www.glaad.org/media/newspops_detail.php?id=3800&.

35. McLean, Renwick. 2005. "Spain Approved Same-Sex Marriage Bill." *New York Times,* June 30. Retrieved from www.nyt.com.

36. Kamen, Paula. 2002. *Her Way: Young Women Remake the Sexual Revolution.* New York: Broadway Books.

37. Grigoriadis, Vanessa. 2003. "The New Position on Casual Sex." *New York,* January 13. Retrieved from http://newyorkmetro.com/nymetro/nightlife/sex/features/n_8227/.

38. Robinson, B. A. 2005. "Wal-Mart's Refusal to Stock the 'Morning-After' Pill." Ontario Consultants on Religious Tolerance. Retrieved from http://www.religioustolerance.org/abo_walm.htm.

39. "Daily Reproductive Health Report." 2005. Henry J. Kaiser Family Foundation. Retrieved from http://www.kaisernetwork.org/daily_reports/rep_index.cfm?hint=2&DR_ID=31345.

40. Huberman, Barbara. 2005. "Rights, Respect, Responsibility: A Vision for Our Youth." Presented at the New View of Women's Sexuality Conference, "Women and the New Sexual Politics: Profits vs. Pleasures," July 10, Montreal, Canada.

41. Pinker, Steven. 2002. *The Blank Slate: The Denial of Human Nature and Modern Intellectual Life.* New York: Viking Press.

42. Buss, David. 1994. *The Evolution of Desire: Strategies of Human Mating.* New York: Basic Books.

43. Herdt, Gilbert. 1999. "Clinical Ethnography and Sexual Culture." *Annual Review of Sex Research* 10:100–120.

44. "Sexual Relations among Young People in Developing Countries: Evidence from WHO Case Studies." 2001. Geneva: World Health Organization. Retrieved from http://www.who.int/reproductive-health/publications/RHR_01_8/.

45. Darroch, Jacqueline E., Susheela Singh, and Jennifer J. Frost. 2001. "Differences in Teenage Pregnancy Rates among Five Developed Countries: The Roles of Sexual Activity and Contraceptive Use." *Family Planning Perspectives* 33: 244–256.

46. Mackay, Judith. 2001. "Global Sex: Sexuality and Sexual Practices around the World." *Sexual and Relationship Therapy* 16: 1468–1479.

47. "Into a New World: Young Women's Sexual and Reproductive Lives." 1998. New York: Alan Guttmacher Institute.

48. Bland, Lucy, and Laura Doan (eds). 1998. *Sexology in Culture: Labelling Bodies and Desires.* London: Polity.

49. Margolis, Jonathan. 2004. *O: The Intimate History of the Orgasm.* New York: Grove Press.

50. Scriven, Michael, and Richard Paul. Undated. "Defining Critical Thinking." Critical Thinking Foundation. Retrieved from http://www.criticalthinking.org/aboutCT/definingCT.shtml.

51. Paul, Richard, and Linda Elder. 2001. *The Miniature Guide to Critical Thinking: Concepts and Tools.* Dillon Beach, CA: The Foundation for Critical Thinking.

52. Tiefer, Leonore. 2004. *Sex Is Not a Natural Act and Other Essays.* 2nd ed. Boulder, CO: Westview Press.

CHAPTER 2

1. Ladas, A. K., B. Whipple, and J. D. Perry. 1982. *The G Spot and Other Recent Discoveries about Human Sexuality.* New York: Dell; Zaviacic, M., A. Zaviacicova, I. K. Holoman and J. Molcan. 1988. "Female Urethral Expulsions Evoked by Local Digital Stimulation of the G-Spot: Differences in the Response Patterns." *The Journal of Sex Research* 24: 311–318; Schubach, G. 2001. "Urethral Expulsions during Sensual Arousal and Bladder Catheterization in Seven Human Females." *Electronic Journal of Human Sexuality* 4. Retrieved from http://www.ejhs.org/volume4/Schubach/.

2. Carroll, Joseph. 2005. "Society's Moral Boundaries Expand Somewhat This Year." News release, 5/16/05. Retrieved from www.gallup.com.

3. Schutt, Russell. 2004. *Investigating the Social World.* Thousand Oaks, CA: Pine Forge.

4. Dworkin, Shari L., and Lucia O'Sullivan. 2005. "Actual versus Desired Initiation Patterns among a Sample of College Men: Tapping Disjunctures within Traditional Male Sexual Scripts." *Journal of Sex Research* 42: 150–59.

5. Laumann, Edward O., John H. Gagnon, Robert T. Michael, and Stuart Michaels. 1994. *The Social Organization of Sexuality: Sexual Practices in the United States.* Chicago: University of Chicago.

6. See http://www.socialpsychology.org/expts.htm.

7. Wiederman, Michael W. 2001. *Understanding Sexuality Research.* Belmont, CA: Wadsworth.

8. Downey, Lois, Rosemary Ryan, Roger Roffman, and Michal Kulich. 1995. "How Could I Forget? Inaccurate Memories of Sexually Intimate Moments." *Journal of Sex Research* 32: 177–193.

9. Jaccard, James, Robert McDonald, Choi K. Wan, Vincent Guilamo-Ramos, Patricia Dittus, and Shannon Quinlan. 2004. "Recalling Sexual Partners: The Accuracy of Self-Reports." *Journal of Health Psychology* 9: 699–712.

10. Anonymous. 2001. Wave III Codebook, Section 16: Sexual Experiences and STDs. Retrieved from http://www.cpc.unc.edu/projects/addhealth/codebooks.

11. Manning, Wendy D., Monica A. Longmore, and Peggy C. Giordano. 2005. "Adolescents' Involvement in Non-Romantic Sexual Activity." *Social Science Research* 34: 384–407.

12. Szasz, Thomas. 2000. "Remembering Krafft-Ebing." *The Freeman* 50(1). Retrieved from http://www.fee.org/vnews.php?nid=4523.

13. Tiefer, Leonore. 2004. *Sex Is Not a Natural Act and Other Essays.* 2nd ed. Boulder, CO: Westview Press.

14. LeVay, Simon. 1991. "A Difference in Hypothalamic Structure between Heterosexual and Homosexual Men." *Science* 253: 1034–1037.

15. Weis, David. 1998. "Conclusion: The State of Sexual Theory." *Journal of Sex Research* 35: 100–114.

16. Hogben, Matthew, Mark G. Hartlaub, and Lauren R. Wisely. 1999. "Searching for a Common Core: An Examination of Human Sexuality Textbook References." *Teaching of Psychology* 26: 131–134.

17. Storr, Merl. 1998. "Transformations: Subjects, Categories and Cures in Krafft-Ebing's Sexology." Pp. 11–26 in *Sexology in Culture: Labelling Bodies and Desires,* eds. L. Bland and L. Doan. Chicago: University of Chicago Press.

18. Oosterhuis, Henry. 2000. *Step Children of Nature: Krafft-Ebing, Psychiatry, and the Making of Sexual Identity.* Chicago: University of Chicago Press.

19. Katz, Jonathan Ned. 1995. *The Invention of Heterosexuality.* New York: Plume.

20. Katz, Jonathan Ned. 2004. "'Homosexual' and 'Heterosexual': Questioning the Terms." Pp. 44–46 in *Sexualities: Identities, Behaviors, and Society*, eds. M. S. Kimmel and R. F. Plante. New York: Oxford University Press.

21. Pfeiffer, Carl J. 1985. *The Art and Practice of Western Medicine in the Early Nineteenth Century*. Jefferson, NC: McFarland.

22. Dixon-Woods, Mary, Joanne Regan, Noelle Robertson, Bridget Young, Christine Cordle, and Martin Tobin. 2002. "Teaching and Learning about Human Sexuality in Undergraduate Medical Education." *Medical Education* 36: 432–441.

23. Masters, William, and Virginia Johnson. 1966. *Human Sexual Response*. Boston: Little, Brown.

24. Tiefer, Leonore. 1995. "Historical, Scientific, Clinical, and Feminist Criticisms of 'the Human Sexual Response Cycle' Model." Pp. 41–58 in *Sex Is Not a Natural Act and Other Essays*, 2nd. ed., by L. Tiefer. Boulder, CO: Westview.

25. "Frequently Asked Questions." Official Website of the American Psychiatric Association. Retrieved from http://www.psych.org/research/dor/dsm/dsm_faqs/faq81301.cfm.

26. Lovgren, Stefan. 2004. "Could Kinsey's Sex Research Be Done Today?" *National Geographic News*, November 16. Retrieved from http://news.nationalgeographic.com/news/2004/11/1116_041116_sex_research.html.

27. Hogben, Matthew, and Donn Byrne. 1998. "Using Social Learning Theory to Explain Individual Differences in Human Sexuality." *Journal of Sex Research* 35: 58–71.

28. Laumann, Edward O., Stephen Ellingson, Jenna Mahay, and Anthony Paik, eds. 2004. *The Sexual Organization of the City*. Chicago: University of Chicago.

29. Sprecher, Susan. 1998. "Social Exchange Theories and Sexuality." *Journal of Sex Research* 35: 32–43.

30. Gagnon, John, and William H. Simon. 1973. *Sexual Conduct: The Social Sources of Human Sexuality*. Chicago: Aldine.

31. Gagnon, John, and William H. Simon. [1973] 2004. "The Social Origins of Sexual Development." Pp. 29–38 in *Sexualities: Identities, Behaviors, and Society*, eds. M. S. Kimmel and R. F. Plante. New York: Oxford University Press.

32. Rich, Adrienne. 1980. "Compulsory Heterosexuality and Lesbian Existence." *Signs: Journal of Women in Culture and Society* 5: 631–660.

33. Rubin, Gayle. 1984. "Thinking Sex: Notes for a Radical Theory of the Politics of Sexuality." Pp. 267–319 in *Pleasure and Danger: Exploring Female Sexuality*, ed. C. S. Vance. Boston: Routledge.

34. Allen, Paula Gunn. 1986. *The Sacred Hoop: Recovering the Feminine in American Indian Traditions*. Boston: Beacon Press; Anzaldúa, Gloria, 1987. *Borderlands/La Frontera: The New Mestiza*. San Francisco: Aunt Lute Books; Collins, Patricia Hill. 1990. *Black Feminist Thought, Knowledge, Consciousness, and the Politics of Empowerment*. Boston: Unwin Hyman.

35. Moraga, Cherrie. 1983. *Loving in the War Years*. Boston: South End Press; Faderman, Lillian. 1992. *Odd Girls and Twilight Lovers: A History of Lesbian Life in Twentieth-Century America*. New York: Penguin; Newton, Esther. 1993. *Cherry Grove, Fire Island: Sixty Years In America's First Gay and Lesbian Town*. Boston: Beacon Press.

36. hooks, bell. 1982. *Ain't I a Woman: Black Women and Feminism*. Boston: South End Press; Butler, Judith. 1990. *Gender Trouble: Feminism and the Subversion of Identity*. New York: Routledge.

37. Marshall, James. 1990. "Foucault and Educational Research." Pp. 11–28 in *Foucault and Education: Discipline and Knowledge*, ed. S. Ball. London: Routledge.

38. Foucault, Michel. 1980. *Power/Knowledge: Selected Interviews and Other Writings 1972–1977*. New York: Pantheon.

39. Plummer, Ken. 1995. *Telling Sexual Stories.* London: Routledge.

40. Gamson, Joshua, and Dawne Moon. 2004. "The Sociology of Sexualities: Queer and Beyond." *Annual Review of Sociology* 30: 47–64.

41. Stein, Arlene, and Ken Plummer. 1996. "'I Can't Even Think Straight': 'Queer' Theory and the Missing Sexual Revolution in Sociology." Pp. 129–144 in *Queer Theory/Sociology,* ed. S. Seidman. Cambridge, England: Blackwell.

42. Jagose, Annemarie. 1996. "Queer Theory." *Australian Humanities Review,* December. Retrieved from http://www.lib.latrobe.edu.au/AHR/archive/Issue-Dec–1996/jagose.html.

CHAPTER 3

1. Rhode, Deborah L. 1997. *Speaking of Sex.* Cambridge, MA: Harvard University Press.

2. See http://www.sickkids.ca/childphysiology/cpwp/Genital/genitalintro.htm.

3. Bornstein, Kate. 1994. *Gender Outlaw: On Men, Women and the Rest of Us.* New York: Routledge.

4. Burr, Vivien. 1995. *An Introduction to Social Constructionism.* London: Routledge.

5. Perry, Della, and Ruth Keszia Whiteside. 2000. "Women, Gender and Disability—Historical and Contemporary Intersections of 'Otherness.'" Paper presented at the Abilympics International Conference, September 1995. Retrieved from http://www.wwda.org.au/whites.htm.

6. "What Is Intersex?" Retrieved from www.isna.org/faq/what_is_intersex.

7. Preves, Sharon. 2003. *Intersex and Identity: The Contested Self.* New Brunswick, NJ: Rutgers University Press.

8. Kessler, Suzanne. 1998. *Lessons from the Intersexed.* New Brunswick, NJ: Rutgers University Press.

9. Dreger, Alice Domurat. 1998. *Hermaphrodites and the Medical Invention of Sex.* Cambridge, MA: Harvard University Press.

10. Morris, Esther. 2000. "The Missing Vagina: An Additional Monologue." Retrieved from http://www.mrkh.org.

11. Beck, Max. 2001. "My Life as an Intersexual." Retrieved from http://www.pbs.org/wgbh/nova/gender/beck.html.

12. Costich, Jim. 2003. "An Intersex Primer: Our Lives." *The Empty Closet,* published by the Gay Alliance. Genesee Valley, NY.

13. Wilchins, Riki. 2004. *Queer Theory, Gender Theory.* Los Angeles: Alyson Publications.

14. Reid, Guynel Marie. 1994. "Maternal Sex-Stereotyping of Newborns." *Psychological Reports* 75: 1443–1451.

15. Kuebli, Janet, Susan Butler, and Robyn Fivush. 1995. "Mother-Child Talk about Past Emotions: Relations of Maternal Language and Child Gender over Time." *Cognition and Emotion* 9: 265–283; Burns, Ailsa, and Ross Homel. 1989. "Gender Division of Tasks by Parents and Their Children." *Psychology of Women Quarterly* 13: 113–125; Adams, Susan, Janet Kuebli, Patricia A. Boyle, and Robyn Fivush. 1995. "Gender Differences in Parent-Child Conversations about Past Emotions: A Longitudinal Investigation." *Sex Roles* 33: 309–323.

16. Hoffman, Lois W., and Deborah D. Kloska. 1995. "Parents' Gender-Based Attitudes toward Marital Roles and Child Rearing: Development and Validation of New Measures." *Sex Roles* 32: 273–296.

17. Leve, Leslie, and Beverly Fagot. 1997. "Gender-Role Socialization and Discipline Processes in One- and Two-Parent Families." *Sex Roles* 36: 1–21.

18. Raffaelli, Marcela, and Lenna L. Ontai. 2004. "Gender Socialization in Latino/a Families: Results from Two Retrospective Studies." *Sex Roles* 50: 287–300.

19. Terman, Louis, and Catherine Miles. 1936. *Sex and Personality: Studies in Masculinity and Femininity.* New York: McGraw Hill.

20. Kimmel, Michael S. 2004. *The Gendered Society*, 2nd ed. New York: Oxford University Press.

21. Rice, Thurman B. 1948. *In Training, for Boys of High School Age.* Chicago: American Medical Association.

22. Newport, Frank. 2001. "Americans See Women as Emotional and Affectionate, Men as More Aggressive." Gallup News Service release. Retrieved from http://www.gallup.com/poll/content/default.aspx?ci=1978.

23. Kimmel, Michael S. 2004. "A Black Woman Took My Job . . . " *The New Internationalist,* November. Retrieved from http://www.findarticles.com/p/articles/mi_m0JQP/is_373/ai_n7584532.

24. Bornstein, Kate. 1994. *My Gender Workbook.* New York: Routledge.

25. Retrieved from http://www.ftmaustralia.org/basics/tg/identities.html.

26. Osborne, Judy. 2005. "Growing Up Transgender." *Transgender Tapestry* 108: 22.

27. Lantz, Barbara. 2003. "Is the Journey Worth the Pain?" Pp. 7–11 in *Trans Forming Families: Real Stories about Transgendered Loved Ones,* ed. M. Boenke. Hardy, VA: Oak Knoll Press.

28. Sullivan, Braeden L. and Rebecca F. Plante. "I Love My New Clitdick: Trans People's Sexualities and Selves." Presented at the annual meeting of the Society for the Study of Symbolic Interaction, August 13, Philadelphia, PA.

29. Hale, C. Jacob. 2002. "Whose Body Is This Anyway?" Pp. 250–252 in *GenderQueer: Voices from beyond the Sexual Binary,* eds. J. Nestle, C. Howell, and R. Wilchins. Los Angeles: Alyson Books.

30. Roughgarden, Joan. 2004. *Evolution's Rainbow: Diversity, Gender, and Sexuality in Nature and People.* Berkeley: University of California Press.

31. Retrieved from http://trans-academics.org/forum/lofiversion/index.php/t59.html.

32. Ekins, Richard, and Dave King. 1999. "Towards a Sociology of Transgendered Bodies." *The Sociological Review* 47: 580–602. Retrieved from http://search.epnet.com/login.aspx?direct=true&db=sih&an=2178766.

33. Berg. 2004. Message forum post at www.butch-femme.com.

34. Thomas, Wesley, and Sue-Ellen Jacobs. 1999. "'. . . And We Are Still Here': From Berdache to Two-Spirit People." *American Indian Culture and Research Journal* 23(2): 91–107.

35. Epple, Carolyn. 1998. "Coming to Terms with Navajo Nadleehi: A Critique of Berdache, 'Gay,' 'Alternate Gender,' and . . . " *American Ethnologist* 25: 267–290.

36. Nanda, Serena. 1998. "The Hijras of India: Cultural and Individual Dimensions of an Institutionalized Third Gender Role." Pp. 226–239 in *Culture, Society and Sexuality: A Reader,* eds. Richard Parker and Peter Aggleton. London: UCL Press.

37. Nanda, Serena. 1999. *Neither Man nor Woman: The Hijras of India,* 2nd ed. Belmont, CA: Wadsworth.

38. Schmidt, Johanna. 2001. "Redefining Fa'afafine: Western Discourses and the Construction of Transgenderism in Samoa." *Intersections: Gender, History and Culture in the Asian Context* 6 (August). Retrieved from http://wwwsshe.murdoch.edu.au/intersections/issue6/schmidt.html.

39. Martin, Emily. 1991. "The Egg and the Sperm: How Science Has Constructed a Romance Based on Stereotypical Male-Female Roles." *Signs: Journal of Women in Culture and Society* 16: 485–501.

40. Fausto-Sterling, Anne. 2000. *Sexing the Body: Gender Politics and the Construction of Sexuality*. New York: Basic Books.

41. Freud, Sigmund. 1962. *Three Essays on the Theory of Sexuality*. James Strachey, trans. New York: Basic Books.

CHAPTER 4

1. Monty Python's *Meaning of Life*. 1983. Universal Studios.

2. Moore, Susan M., and Doreen Rosenthal. 1993. *Sexuality in Adolescence*. New York: Routledge.

3. Pascoe, C. J. 2005. "'Dude, You're a Fag': Adolescent Masculinity and the Fag Discourse." *Sexualities* 8: 329–346.

4. Haroian, Loretta. 2000. "Child Sexual Development." *Electronic Journal of Human Sexuality* 3. Retrieved from http://www.ejhs.org/volume3/Haroian/body.htm.

5. Lamb, Sharon. 2004. "Sexual Tensions in Girls' Friendships." *Feminism and Psychology* 14: 376–382.

6. Savin-Williams, Ritch. 2005. *The New Gay Teenager*. Cambridge, MA: Harvard University Press.

7. Stekel, Wilhelm. [1950]2004. *Auto-Eroticism: A Study of Onanism and Neurosis*. Reprinted, London: Kegan Paul.

8. Gagnon, John H. 1977. *Human Sexualities*. Glenview, IL: Scott, Foresman and Company.

9. Measor, Lynda. "Young People's Views of Sex Education: Gender, Information and Knowledge." *Sex Education* 4: 153–166.

10. Pluhar, Erika, and Peter Kuriloff. 2004. "What Really Matters in Family Communication about Sexuality? A Qualitative Analysis of Affect and Style among African American Mothers and Adolescent Daughters." *Sex Education* 4: 303–321.

11. Lehr, Sally T., Alice S. Demi, Colleen DiIorio, and Jeffrey Facteau. 2005. "Predictors of Father-Son Communication about Sexuality." *Journal of Sex Research* 42: 119–129.

12. Paikoff, R. L., A. McCormick, and L. M. Sagrestano. 2000. "Adolescent Sexuality" Pp. 416–439 in *Psychological Perspectives on Human Sexuality*, eds. L. T. Szuchman and F. Muscarella. NY: John Wiley and Sons.

13. Rucibwa, Napthal Kaberege, Naomi Modeste, Susan Montgomery, and Curtis A. Fox. 2003. "Exploring Family Factors and Sexual Behaviors in a Group of Black and Hispanic Adolescent Males." *American Journal of Health Behavior* 27: 63–74.

14. Pryor, Richard. [1971]2001. *Live & Smokin'*. Distributed by MPI Home Video.

15. Doswell, Willa M., Yookyung Kim, Betty Braxter, Jerome Taylor, Julius Kitutu, and Yu-Hun Alice Hsu. 2003. "A Theoretical Model of Early Teen Sexual Behavior: What Research Tells Us about Mother's Influence on the Sexual Behavior of Early Adolescent Girls." *Journal of Theory Construction and Testing* 7: 56–60.

16. Smith, Carolyn. 1997. "Factors Associated with Early Sexual Activity among Urban Adolescents." *Social Work* 42: 334–346; Browning, Christopher R., Tama Leventhal, and Jeanne Brooks-Gunn. 2004. "Neighborhood Context and Racial Differences in Early Adolescent Sexual Activity." *Demography* 41: 697–720.

17. Beaty, Lee A. 1999. "Identity Development of Homosexual Youth and Parental and Familial Influences on the Coming Out Process." *Adolescence* 34: 597–402.

18. D'Augelli, Anthony R., Arnold H. Grossman, and Michael Starks. 2005. "Parents' Awareness of Lesbian, Gay, and Bisexual Youths' Sexual Orientation." *Journal of Marriage and Family* 67: 474–482.

19. Durham, Meenakshi Gigi. 1998. "Dilemmas of Desire: Representations of Adolescent Sexuality in Two Teen Magazines." *Youth and Society* 29: 369–389. Retrieved from http://www.infotrac.com.

20. Guilamo-Ramos, Vincent, James Jaccard, Juan Pena, Vincent Goldberg. 2005. "Acculturation-Related Variables, Sexual Initiation, and Subsequent Sexual Behavior Among Puerto Rican, Mexican, and Cuban Youth." *Health Psychology* 24: 88–95.

21. Rostosky, Sharon, Mark D. Regnerus, and Margaret Laurie Comer Wright. 2003. "Coital Debut: The Role of Religiosity and Sex Attitudes in the Add Health Survey." *Journal of Sex Research* 40: 358–367.

22. McCree, Donna Hubbard, Gina M. Wingood, Ralph DiClemente, Susan Davies, and Katherine F. Harrington. 2003. "Religiosity and Risky Sexual Behavior in African-American Adolescent Females." *Journal of Adolescent Health* 33: 2–8.

23. Adam, Mary B., Jenifer K. McGuire, Michele Walsh, Joanne Basta, and Craig LeCroy. 2005. "Acculturation as a Predictor of the Onset of Sexual Intercourse among Hispanic and White Teens." *Archives of Pediatrics and Adolescent Medicine* 159(3): 261–265.

24. Regan, Pamela C., Ramani Durvasula, Lisa Howell, Oscar Ureno, and Martha Rea. 2004. "Gender, Ethnicity, and the Developmental Timing of First Sexual and Romantic Experiences." *Social Behavior and Personality: An International Journal* 32: 667–676.

25. Miller, B. C. and S. C. Leavitt. 2003. "Sexuality in Adolescence." Pp. 1471–1476 in *International Encyclopedia of Marriage and Family*, 2nd ed., ed. J. J. Ponzetti. NY: Macmillan Reference USA.

26. Upchurch, Dawn M., Lene Levy-Storms, Clea Sucoff, and Carol S. Aneshensel. 1998. "Gender and Ethnic Differences in the Timing of First *Sexual* Intercourse." *Family Planning Perspectives* 30(3): 121–128.

27. Swann, Stephanie K., and Christina A. Spivey. 2004. "The Relationship between Self-Esteem and Lesbian Identity during Adolescence." *Child and Adolescent Social Work Journal* 21: 629–646.

28. Amico, Michael. 2005. "Gay Youths as 'Whorified Virgins.'" *Gay and Lesbian Review Worldwide* 12(4): 34–36.

29. Mac an Ghaill, Mairtin. 1994. *The Making of Men: Masculinities, Sexualities and Schooling.* Buckingham, UK: Open University Press.

30. Connell, R. W. 2000. *The Men and the Boys.* Berkeley: University of California Press.

31. Walker, Barbara M., and Saville Kushner. 1999. "The Building Site: An Educational Approach to Masculine Identity." *Journal of Youth Studies* 2: 45–58.

32. Mac an Ghaill, Mairtin. 1999. "'New' Cultures of Training: Emerging Male (Hetero)Sexual Identities." *British Educational Research Journal* 25: 427–443. Retrieved from http://search.epnet.com/login.aspx?direct=true&db=aph&an=2403323.

33. Way, Niobe. 2004. "Intimacy, Desire, and Distrust in the Friendships of Adolescent Boys." Pp. 167–196 in *Adolescent Boys: Exploring Diverse Cultures of Boyhood*, eds. Niobe Way and Judy Y. Chu. New York: New York University Press.

34. Harper, Gary W., Christine Gannon, Susan E. Watson, Joseph A. Catania, and M. Margaret Dolcini. 2004. "The Role of Close Friends in African American Adolescents' Dating and Sexual Behavior." *Journal of Sex Research* 41: 351–362. Retrieved from http://search.epnet.com/login.aspx?direct=true&db=aph&an=15567779.

35. Didion, Joan. 2003. *Where I Was From.* New York: Knopf.

36. Messerschmidt, James. 2000. "Becoming 'Real Men': Adolescent Masculinity, Challenges and Sexual Violence." *Men and Masculinities* 2: 286–307.

37. Retrieved from www.atkol.com/forums/replies.asp?forum=2&topic=2973.

38. Mac an Ghaill, Mairtin. 1999. "'New' Cultures of Training: Emerging Male (Hetero)Sexual Identities." *British Educational Research Journal* 25: 427–443.

39. Kimmel, Michael S. 1994. "Masculinity as Homophobia: Fear, Shame, and Silence in the Construction of Gender Identity." Pp. 119–141 in *Theorizing Masculinities*, ed. H. Brod. Thousand Oaks, CA: Sage Publications.

40. Harris, Anita. 2004. *Future Girl: Young Women in the Twenty-First Century.* London: Routledge.

41. Brown, Jane D., Jeanne R. Steele, and Kim Walsh-Childers. 2002. "Introduction and Overview." Pp. 1–24 in *Sexual Teens, Sexual Media: Investigating Media's Influence on Adolescent Sexuality*, eds. J. D. Brown, J. R. Steele, and K. Walsh-Childers. Mahwah, NJ: Lawrence Erlbaum Associates.

42. David, Prabu, Glenda Morrison, Melissa A. Johnson, and Felecia Ross. 2002. "Body Image, Race and Fashion Models: Social Distance and Social Identification in Third-Person Effects." *Communication Research* 29: 270–294; Schooler, D., L. M. Ward, A. Merriwether, and A. Caruthers. 2004. "Who's That Girl: Television's Role in the Body Image Development of Young White and Black Women." *Psychology of Women Quarterly* 28: 38–47.

43. Goodman, Robyn J. 2002. "Flabless Is Fabulous: How Latina and Anglo Women Read and Incorporate the Excessively Thin Body Ideal into Everyday Experience." *Journalism and Mass Communication Quarterly* 79: 712–727; Pompper, Donnalyn, and Jesica Koenig. 2004. "Cross-Cultural-Generational Perceptions of Ideal Body Image: Hispanic Women and Magazine Standards." *Journalism and Mass Communication Quarterly* 81: 89–107; Vander Wal, Jillon S., and Nancy Thomas. 2004. "Predictors of Body Image Dissatisfaction and Disturbed Eating Attitudes and Behaviors in African American and Hispanic Girls." *Eating Behaviors* 5: 291–301.

44. Garner, Ana, Helen Sterk, and Shawn Adams. 1998. "Narrative Analysis of Sexual Etiquette in Teenage Magazines." *Journal of Communication* 48: 59–78.

45. Kim, Janna L., and L. Monique Ward. 2004. "Pleasure Reading: Associations between Young Women's Sexual Attitudes and Their Reading of Contemporary Women's Magazines." *Psychology of Women Quarterly* 28: 48–58.

46. Durham, Gigi. 1996. "The Taming of the Shrew: Women's Magazines and the Regulation of Desire." *Journal of Communication Inquiry* 20: 18–31.

47. Peril, Lynn. 2002. *Pink Think: Becoming a Woman in Many Uneasy Lessons.* New York: W. W. Norton.

48. Carpenter, Laura. 2001. "The Ambiguity of 'Having Sex': The Subjective Experience of Virginity Loss in the United States." *Journal of Sex Research* 38: 127–139. Retrieved from http://search.epnet.com/login.aspx?direct=true&db=sih&an=5290293.

49. Sander, Stephanie, and June Machover Reinisch. 1999. "Would You Say You 'Had Sex' If . . . ?" *Journal of the American Medical Association* 281: 275–277.

50. Gonzalez-Lopez, Gloria. 2004. "Fathering Latina Sexualities: Mexican Men and the Virginity of Their Daughters." *Journal of Marriage and Family* 66: 1118–1130.

51. Carpenter, Laura. 2001b. "The First Time/Das Erstes Mal: Approaches to Virginity Loss in U.S. and German Teen Magazines." *Youth and Society* 33: 31–61.

52. Fine, Michelle. 1988. "Sexuality, Schooling, and Adolescent Females: The Missing Discourse of Desire." *Harvard Education Review* 58: 29–53; Tolman, Deborah. 1994. "Doing Desire:

Adolescent Girls' Struggles for/with Sexuality." *Gender and Society* 8: 324–342; Thompson, Sharon. 1995. *Going All the Way: Teenage Girls' Tales of Sex, Romance, and Pregnancy.* New York: Hill and Wang.

53. Tolman, Deborah L. 2002. *Dilemmas of Desire: Teenage Girls Talk about Sexuality.* Cambridge, MA: Harvard University Press.

54. Holland, Janet, Caroline Ramazanoglu, and Sue Sharpe. 1994. "Power and Desire: The Embodiment of Female Sexuality." *Feminist Review* 46: 21–38.

55. Moore, Kristin A., Anne K. Driscoll, and Laura Duberstein Lindberg. 1998. *A Statistical Portrait of Adolescent Sex, Contraception and Childbearing.* Washington, DC.: The National Campaign to Prevent Teen Pregnancy.

56. Bay-Cheng, Laina Y. 2001. "SexEd.com: Values and Norms in Web-based Sexuality Education." *Journal of Sex Research* 38: 241–251.

57. Thomson, Rachel. 2004. "'An Adult Thing'? Young People's Perspectives on the Heterosexual Age of Consent." *Sexualities* 7: 133–149.

58. Faulkner, Sandra L. 2003. "Good Girl or Flirt Girl: Latinas' Definitions of Sex and Sexual Relationships." *Hispanic Journal of Behavioral Sciences* 25: 174–200.

59. Diamond, Lisa M. 2003. "What Does Sexual Orientation Orient? A Biobehavioral Model Distinguishing Romantic Love and Sexual Desire." *Psychological Review* 110: 173–192; Ussher, Jane M. 2005. "The Meaning of Sexual Desire: Experiences of Heterosexual and Lesbian Girls." *Feminism and Psychology* 15(1): 27–32.

60. Ussher, Jane M. 1997. *Fantasies of Femininity: Reframing the Boundaries of Sex.* London: Penguin.

61. Wilkins, Amy. 2004. "'So Full of Myself as a Chick': Goth Women, Sexual Independence, and Gender Egalitarianism." *Gender and Society* 18: 328–349.

CHAPTER 5

1. Haffner, Debra W., ed. 1995. *Facing Facts: Sexual Health for America's Adolescents.* New York: SIECUS.

2. *Teens Talk about Sex: Adolescent Sexuality in the 90's.* 1994. (Poll by Roper Starch Worldwide for SIECUS.) New York: SIECUS.

3. Bellafante, Ginia. 2005. "Facts of Life, for Their Eyes Only." *New York Times* June 5. Section 9 (Style), pg. 1. Accessed via LexisNexis.

4. Flaake, Karin. 2005. "Girls, Adolescence and the Impact of Bodily Changes." *European Journal of Women's Studies* 12: 201–213.

5. Shipman, G. 1971. "The Psychodynamics of Sex Education." Pp. 326–339 in *Adolescent Behavior and Society: A Book of Readings,* ed. R. E. Muuss. New York: Random House.

6. Frankel, Loren. 2002. "'I've Never Thought About It': Contradictions and Taboos Surrounding American Males' Experiences of First Ejaculation (Semenarche)." *Journal of Men's Studies* 11: 37–56.

7. Adegoke, Alfred A. 1993. "The Experience of Spermarche (the Age of Onset of Sperm Emission) among Selected Adolescent Boys in Nigeria." *Journal of Youth and Adolescence* 22: 201–209.

8. Diorio, Joseph A., and Jennifer A. Munro. 2000. "Doing Harm in the Name of Protection: Menstruation as a Topic for Sex Education." *Gender and Education* 12: 347–366.

9. Martin, Karin. 1996. *Puberty, Sexuality, and the Self: Girls and Boys at Adolescence.* New York: Routledge.

10. Moore, Susan M. 1995. "Girls' Understanding and Social Construction of Menarche." *Journal of Adolescence* 18: 87–104.

11. Lovering, K. M. 1995. "The Bleeding Body: Adolescents Talk about Menstruation." Pp. 10–31 in *Feminism and Discourse: Psychological Perspectives*, eds. S. Wilkinson and C. Kitzinger. Thousand Oaks, CA: Sage.

12. Koff, Elissa, and Jill Rierdan. 1995. "Preparing Girls for Menstruation: Recommendations from Adolescent Girls." *Adolescence* 30: 795–811.

13. Teitelman, Anne M. 2004. "Adolescent Girls' Perspectives of Family Interactions Related to Menarche and Sexual Health." *Qualitative Health Research* 14: 1292–1308.

14. Kinsey, Alfred C., Wardell B. Pomeroy, and Clyde E. Martin. 1948. *Sexual Behavior in the Human Male*. Philadelphia: W.B. Saunders.

15. Kinsey, Alfred C., Wardell B. Pomeroy, Clyde E. Martin, and Paul H. Gebhard. 1953. *Sexual Behavior in the Human Female*. Philadelphia: W.B. Saunders.

16. Ostovich, Jennifer M., and John Sabini. 2005. "Timing of Puberty and Sexuality in Men and Women." *Archives of Sexual Behavior* 34: 197–86.

17. Cornog, Martha. 2003. *The Big Book of Masturbation: From Angst to Zeal*. San Francisco: Down There Press.

18. DeLamater, John. 1987. "A Sociological Perspective." Pp. 237–256 in *Theories of Human Sexuality*, ed. J. H. Geer and W. T. O'Donohue. New York: Plenum.

19. Smith, Anthony M. A., Doreen A. Rosenthal, and Heidi Reichler. 1996. "High Schoolers' Masturbatory Practices." *Psychological Reports* 79: 499–509.

20. Laumann, Edward O., John H. Gagnon, Robert T. Michael, and Stuart Michaels. 1994. *The Social Organization of Sexuality*. Chicago: University of Chicago Press.

21. Hex, C. 1999. "Sex and the Thinking Girl: Betty and Celina Get Wired." Part II. Pp. 93–95 in *The BUST Guide to the New Girl Order*, eds. M. Karp and D. Stoller. New York: Penguin Books.

22. Reinholtz, Rhonda K., and Charlene L. Muehlenhard. 1995. *Journal of Sex Research* 32: 155–165.

23. Baumeister, Roy F., Kathleen R. Catanese, and Kathleen D. Vohs. 2001. "Is There a Gender Difference in Strength of Sex Drive?" *Personality and Social Psychology Review* 5: 242–273.

24. Regan, Pamela R., Elizabeth R. Kocan, and Teresa Whitlock. 1998. "Ain't Love Grand! A Prototype Analysis of Romantic Love." *Journal of Social and Personal Relationships* 15: 411–420.

25. Blumstein, Philip, and Pepper Schwartz. 1983. *American Couples: Money, Work, Sex*. New York: William Morrow.

26. Monto, Martin. 2001. "Prostitution and Fellatio." *Journal of Sex Research* 31: 140–145.

27. Leitenberg, Harold, and Kris Henning. 1995. "Sexual Fantasy." *Psychological Bulletin* 117: 469–496.

28. Kimmel, Michael S., and Rebecca F. Plante. 2002. "The Gender of Desire: The Sexual Fantasies of Women and Men." *Advances in Gender Research* 6: 55–77. Note: my discussion is adapted from this work.

29. Masters, William H., and Virginia E. Johnson. 1966. *Human Sexual Response*. Boston: Little, Brown; Masters, William H., and Virginia E. Johnson. 1970. *Human Sexual Inadequacy*. Boston: Little, Brown; Kaplan, Helen Singer. 1974. *The New Sex Therapy: Active Treatment of Sexual Dysfunctions*. New York: Brunner and Mazel.

30. Chick, David, and Steven R. Gold. 1987–1988. "A Review of Influences on Sexual Fantasy: Attitudes, Experience, Guilt, and Gender." *Imagination, Cognition and Personality* 7: 61–76.

31. Ellis, Bruce. J., and Donald Symons. 1990. "Sex Differences in Sexual Fantasy: An Evolutionary Psychological Approach." *Journal of Sex Research* 27: 527–555.

32. Freud, Sigmund. [1949]1975. *Three Essays on the Theory of Sex*. Translated by J. S. Strachey. New York: Basic Books.

33. Follingstad, D. R., and C. D. Kimbrell. 1986. "Sex Fantasies Revisited: An Expansion and Further Clarification of Variables Affecting Sex Fantasy Production." *Archives of Sexual Behavior* 15: 475–486.

34. Barclay, A. M. 1973. "Sexual Fantasies in Men and Women." *Medical Aspects of Human Sexuality* 7: 205–216; Iwawaki, S., and G. D. Wilson. 1983. "Sex Fantasies in Japan." *Personality and Individual Differences* 4: 543–545; Knafo, D., and Y. Jaffe. 1984. "Sexual Fantasizing in Males and Females." *Journal of Research in Personality* 18: 451–462.

35. Zurbriggen, Eileen L., and Megan R. Yost. 2004. "Power, Desire, and Pleasure in Sexual Fantasies." *Journal of Sex Research* 41. Retrieved from http://search.epnet.com/login.aspx?direct=true&db=sih&an=14514724.

36. Mednick, R. A. 1977. "Gender Specific Variances in Sexual Fantasy." *Journal of Personality Assessment* 41: 248–254.

37. Wilson, G. D., and R. J. Lang. 1981. "Sex Differences in Sexual Fantasy." *Personality and Individual Differences* 2: 4, 343–346.

38. Stock, W. E., and J. H. Geer. 1982. "A Study of Fantasy Based Sexual Arousal in Women." *Archives of Sexual Behavior* 11: 33–47; Follingstad, D. R., and C. D. Kimbrell. 1986. "Sex Fantasies Revisited: An Expansion and Further Clarification of Variables Affecting Sex Fantasy Production." *Archives of Sexual Behavior* 15: 475–486.

39. Dubois, Stephanie L. 1997. "Gender Differences in the Emotional Tone of Written Sexual Fantasies." *The Canadian Journal of Human Sexuality* 6. Retrieved from http://proquest.umi.com/pqdweb?did=391712011&sid=1&Fmt=3&clientId=12342&RQT=309&VName=PQD.

40. Friday, Nancy. [1973]1998. *My Secret Garden*. New York: Pocket Books; Friday, Nancy. [1980]1998. *Men in Love*. New York: Delta.

41. Rose, Tricia. 2003. *Longing to Tell: Black Women Talk about Sexuality and Intimacy*. New York: Picador.

42. Lehne, Gregory K. 1978. "Gay Male Fantasies and Realities." *Journal of Social Issues* 34: 28–37; Billingham, Robert E., and Stewart L. Hockenberry. 1987. "Gender Conformity, Masturbation Fantasy, Infatuation, and Sexual Orientation: A Discriminant Analysis Investigation." *Journal of Sex Research* 23: 368–373.

43. Dean, Karol E., and Neil M. Malamuth. 1997. "Characteristics of Men Who Aggress Sexually and of Men Who Imagine Aggressing: Risk and Moderating Variables." *Journal of Personality & Social Psychology* 72: 449–455.

CHAPTER 6

1. www.ym.com. Retrieved from http://boards.ym.com/thread.jspa?threadID=103917& messageID=751753.

2. Dunn, Lillian. 2004. "The Linguistic Side of Tonsil Hockey." *The Phoenix*, January 29. Retrieved from http://phoenix.swarthmore.edu/2004–01–29/living/13594.

3. Manning, Wendy D., Monica A. Longmore, and Peggy C. Giordano. 2000. "The Relationship Context of Contraceptive Use at First Intercourse." *Family Planning Perspectives* 32: 104–110.

4. Lavinthal, Andrea, and Jessica Rozler. 2005. *The Hookup Handbook: A Single Girl's Guide to Living It Up*. New York: Simon Spotlight Entertainment.

5. Kleinplatz, Peggy. 1992. "The Erotic Experience and the Intent to Arouse." *Canadian Journal of Sexuality* 1(3): 133–139.

6. Sherman, Alexa Joy, and Nicole Tocantins. 2004. *The Happy Hook-Up: A Single Girl's Guide to Casual Sex*. Berkeley, CA: Ten Speed Press.

7. Dubberley, Emily. 2005. *Brief Encounters: The Women's Guide to Casual Sex*. London: Fusion Press.

8. Bass, Jonathan. 2005. *How to Get Laid: The Gay Man's Essential Guide to Hot Sex*. Los Angeles: Alyson.

9. Brass, Perry. 1999. *How to Survive Your Own Gay Life: An Adult Guide to Love, Sex, and Relationships*. Bronx, NY: Belhue Press.

10. Caster, Wendy. 2003. *The Lesbian Sex Book*. Revised by Rachel Kramer Bussel. Los Angeles: Alyson.

11. Newman, Felice. 2004. *The Whole Lesbian Sex Book,* 2nd ed. San Francisco: Cleis Press.

12. Cage, Diana, ed. 2004. *On Our Backs Guide to Lesbian Sex*. Los Angeles: Alyson.

13. Risman, Barbara, and Pepper Schwartz. 2002. "After the Sexual Revolution: Gender Politics in Teen Dating." *Contexts* 1(1): 16–24.

14. Reisberg, Leo. 1999. "More Students Eschew Political Extremes, Preferring to Call Themselves 'Middle Of The Road.'" *Chronicle of Higher Education,* January 29, 45(21). Retrieved from http://search.epnet.com/login.aspx?direct=true&db=aph&an=1475414.

15. McGinn, Daniel. 2004. "Mating Behavior 101." *Newsweek,* October 4. Retrieved from http://www.msnbc.msn.com/id/6100311/site/newsweek/.

16. Maticka-Tyndale, Eleanor, Edward S. Herold, and Dawn Mewhinney. 1998. "Casual Sex on Spring Break: Intentions and Behaviors of Canadian Students." *Journal of Sex Research* 35: 254–264; Paul, Elizabeth L., Brian McManus, and Allison Hayes. 2000. "'Hookups': Characteristics and Correlates of College Students' Spontaneous and Anonymous Sexual Experiences." *Journal of Sex Research* 37: 76–88. Retrieved from http://search.epnet.com/login.aspx?direct=true&db=aph&an =298 4996; Hughes, Mikayla, Kelly Morrison, and Kelli Jean K. Asada. 2005. "What's Love Got to Do with It? Exploring the Impact of Maintenance Rules, Love Attitudes, and Network Support on Friends with Benefits Relationships." *Western Journal of Communication* 69: 49–66.

17. Munson, Marcia, and Judith P. Steboum. 1999. "Introduction: The Lesbian Polyamory Reader: Open Relationships, Non-Monogamy, and Casual Sex." *Journal of Lesbian Studies* 3(1/2): 1–7.

18. Anonymous. 2004. "Trends in Reportable Sexually Transmitted Diseases in the United States, 2003—National Data on Chlamydia, Gonorrhea and Syphilis." Retrieved from http://www.cdc.gov/std/stats/trends2003.htm.

19. Wiederman, Michael. 1997. "The Truth Must Be in Here Somewhere: Examining the Gender Discrepancy in Self-Reported Lifetime Number of Sex Partners." *Journal of Sex Research* 34: 375–386.

20. Maticka-Tyndale, Eleanor, Edward S. Herold, and Martin Oppermann. 2003. "Casual Sex among Australian Schoolies." *Journal of Sex Research* 40: 158–169. Retrieved from http://search.epnet.com/login.aspx?direct=true&db=aph&an=10226599.

21. Agostinelli, Gina, and David Wyatt Seal. 1998. "Social Comparisons of One's Own with Others' Attitudes toward Casual and Responsible Sex." *Journal of Applied Social Psychology* 28: 845–860.

22. Herold, Edward S., Eleanor Maticka-Tyndale, and Dawn Mewhinney. 1998. "Predicting Intentions to Engage in Casual Sex." *Journal of Social and Personal Relationships* 15: 502–516.

23. Egan, Cari E. 2001. "Sexual Behaviors, Condom Use and Factors Influencing Causal Sex among Backpackers and Other Young International Travellers." *Canadian Journal of Human Sexuality* 10: 41–57.

24. Conner, Mark, and Dina Flesch. 2001. "Having Casual Sex: Additive and Interactive Effects of Alcohol and Condom Availability on the Determinants of Intentions." *Journal of Applied Social Psychology* 31: 89–112.

25. Hingson, Ralph, Timothy Heeren, Michael Winter, and Henry Wechsler. 2005. "Magnitude of Alcohol-Related Mortality and Morbidity among U.S. College Students Ages 18–24: Changes From 1998 to 2001." *Annual Review of Public Health* 26: 259–279.

26. Cooper, M. Lynne. 2002. "Alcohol Use and Risky Sexual Behavior among College Students and Youth: Evaluating the Evidence." *Journal of Studies on Alcohol Supplement* 14: 101–107.

27. Buunk, Bram P., Pieternel Dijkstra, Detlef Fetchenhauer, and Douglas T. Kenrick. 2002. "Age and Gender Differences in Mate Selection Criteria for Various Involvement Levels." *Personal Relationships* 9: 271–278.

28. Buss, David. 1994. *The Evolution of Desire: Strategies of Human Mating.* New York: Basic Books.

29. Steele, Claude M., and Robert A. Josephs. 1990. "Alcohol Myopia: Its Prized and Dangerous Effects." *American Psychologist* 45: 921–933.

30. Jones, Barry T., Ben C. Jones, Andy P. Thomas, and Jessica Piper. 2003. "Alcohol Consumption Increases Attractiveness Ratings of Opposite-Sex Faces: A Possible Third Route to Risky Sex." *Addiction* 98: 1069–1075.

31. Fredrickson, Barbara L., and Roberts, Tomi-Ann. 1997. "Objectification Theory: Toward Understanding Women's Lived Experiences and Mental Health Risks." *Psychology of Women Quarterly* 21: 173–206.

32. Wiederman, Michael. 2000. "Women's Body Image Self-Consciousness during Physical Intimacy with a Partner." *Journal of Sex Research* 37: 60–68.

33. Dove, N., and M. W. Wiederman. 2000. "Cognitive Distraction and Women's Sexual Functioning." *Journal of Sex and Marital Therapy* 26: 67–78.

34. Faith, Myles S., and Mitchell L. Schare. 1993. "The Role of Body Image in Sexually Avoidant Behavior." *Archives of Sexual Behavior* 22: 345–356.

35. Holmes, Tabetha, Parri Chamberlin, and Michael Young. 1994. "Relations of Exercise to Body Image and Sexual Desirability among a Sample of University Students." *Psychological Reports* 74: 920–922.

36. Davison, Tanya E., and Marita P. McCabe. 2005. "Relationships between Men's and Women's Body Image and Their Psychological, Social, and Sexual Functioning." *Sex Roles: A Journal of Research* 52: 463–475. Retrieved from www.infotrac.com.

37. Allen, Louisa. 2002. "'As Far as Sex Goes, I Don't Really Think about My Body': Young Men's Corporeal Experiences of (Hetero)Sexual Pleasure." Pp. 129–138 in *The Life of Brian: Masculinities, Sexualities and Health in New Zealand,* eds. H. Worth, A. Paris, and L. Allen. Dunedin, New Zealand: University of Otago Press.

38. Conner, Mark, Charlotte Johnson, and Sarah Grogan. 2004. "Gender, Sexuality, Body Image and Eating Behaviours." *Journal of Health Psychology* 9: 505–515.

39. Glenn, Norval, and Elizabeth Marquardt. 2001. "Hooking Up, Hanging Out, and Hoping for Mr. Right—College Women on Dating and Mating Today." Research report posted at www.iwf.org. Retrieved from http://www.iwf.org/news/010727.shtm.

40. Paul, Elizabeth L., and Kristen A. Hayes. 2002. "The Casualties of 'Casual' Sex: A Qualitative Exploration of the Phenomenology of College Students' Hookups." *Journal of Social and Personal Relationships* 19: 635–661.

41. Chng, Chwee Lye, and Alan Moore. 1994. "AIDS: Its Effects on Sexual Practices among Homosexual and Heterosexual College Students." *Journal of Health Education* 25: 154–160.

42. Johnson, Pamela. 2002. "The Truth about Casual Sex." *Essence*, June 33(2): 126–128; 130; 168–170.

43. Træen, Bente, and Dagfinn Sørensen. 2000. "Breaking the Speed of the Sound of Loneliness: Sexual Partner Change and the Fear of Intimacy." *Culture, Health and Sexuality* 2: 287–301.

44. Stigum, Hein, Per Magnus, J. R. Harris, Sven O. Samuelsen, and Leiv S. Bakketeig. 1997. "Frequency of Sexual Partner Change in a Norwegian Population: Data Distribution and Covariates." *American Journal of Epidemiology* 145: 636–643.

45. Retrieved from a blog at www.blogspot.com.

46. Potts, Annie. 2002. "The Man with Two Brains: The Discursive Construction of the Unreasonable 'Penis-Self.'" Pp. 105–115 in *The Life of Brian: Masculinities, Sexualities and Health in New Zealand*, eds. H. Worth, A. Paris, and L. Allen. Dunedin. New Zealand: University of Otago Press.

47. Retrieved from www.livejournal.com.

48. Impett, Emily A., and Letitia Ann Peplau. 2003. "Sexual Compliance: Gender, Motivational, and Relationship Perspectives." *Journal of Sex Research* 40: 87–100.

49. Kimmel, Michael S., and Rebecca F. Plante. 2002. "The Gender of Desire: The Sexual Fantasies of Women and Men." *Advances in Gender Research* 6: 55–77.

50. Lewin, Tamar. 2005. "Are These Parties For Real? "*New York Times*, June 30: G1. Retrieved from http://proquest.umi.com/pqdlink?did=860711571&Fmt=7&clientId=12342&RQT=309&VName=PQD.

51. Jackson Susan M., and Fiona Cram. 2003. "Disrupting the Sexual Double Standard: Young Women's Talk about Heterosexuality." *British Journal of Social Psychology (insert)42*: 113–127.

52. Williams, Alex. 2005. "Casual Relationships, Yes. Casual Sex, Not Really." *New York Times*, April 3. Retrieved from http://proquest.umi.com/pqdlink?did=816298601&Fmt=7&clientId=12342&RQT=309&VName=PQD.

53. Laumann, Edward O., John H. Gagnon, Robert T. Michael, and Stuart Michaels. 1994. *The Social Organization of Sexuality*. Chicago: University of Chicago Press; Sprecher, Susan, and Pamela C. Regan. 1996. "College Virgins: How Men and Women Perceive Their Sexual Status." *Journal of Sex Research* 28: 397–408; Baumeister, Roy, and Dianne Tice. 1998. *The Social Dimension of Sex*. Boston: Allyn and Bacon.

54. Izugbara, C. Otutubikey. 2004. "Notions of Sex, Sexuality and Relationships among Adolescent Boys in Rural Southeastern Nigeria." *Sex Education* 4: 63–79.

55. Weis, David L. 1998. "Interpersonal Heterosexual Behavior." Pp. 91–144 in *Sexuality in America: Understanding Our Sexual Values and Behavior*, eds. P. B. Koch and D. L. Weis. New York: Continuum.

CHAPTER 7

1. Cavalcante, J. S. "The Word Withheld." Retrieved from http://www.kardasi.com/KSOF/Stories/word_withheld.htm.

2. Miller, Elaine. 2004. "A Short Explanation of BDSM." Retrieved from http://elainemiller.com/write/backcheck1.html.

3. Foucault, Michel. 1978. *The History of Sexuality: An Introduction.* New York: Pantheon Books.

4. Katz, Jonathan Ned. 1995. *The Invention of Heterosexuality.* New York: Plume.

5. Gagnon, John H. 1977. *Human Sexualities.* Glenview, IL: Scott, Foresman.

6. Kinsey, Alfred C., Wardell B. Pomeroy, and Clyde E. Martin. 1948. *Sexual Behavior in the Human Male.* Philadelphia: W.B. Saunders.

7. Laumann, Edward O., John H. Gagnon, Robert T. Michael, and Stuart Michaels. 1994. *The Social Organization of Sexuality.* Chicago: University of Chicago Press.

8. Kauth, Michael R., and Seth C. Kalichman. 1995. "Sexual Orientation and Development: An Interactive Approach." Pp. 81–103 in *The Psychology of Sexual Orientation, Behavior, and Identity,* eds. L. Diamant and D. McAnulty. Westport, CT: Greenwood Press.

9. Bem, Daryl J. 1997. "Explaining the Enigma of Sexual Orientation." Invited presentation at the annual meeting of the American Psychological Association, August 15–19, Chicago, IL.

10. Most of these studies were carried out within the last several years, and most were done by psychologists, evolutionary psychologists, and within the hard sciences.

11. Weeks, Jeffrey. 2003. *Sexuality,* 2nd ed. London: Routledge.

12. Plummer, Kenneth. 1975. *Sexual Stigma: An Interactionist Account.* London: Routledge.

13. Lemert, Edwin. 1951. *Social Pathology: A Systematic Approach to the Theory of Sociopathic Behavior.* New York: McGraw-Hill.

14. Goffman, Erving. 1963. *Stigma: Notes on the Management of Spoiled Identity.* Englewood Cliffs, NJ: Prentice Hall.

15. Whisman, Vera. 1996. *Queer by Choice: Lesbians, Gay Men, and the Politics of Identity.* New York: Routledge.

16. Plummer, Kenneth. 1995. *Telling Sexual Stories: Power, Change, and Social Worlds.* London: Routledge.

17. Connell, R. W. 2000. *The Men and the Boys.* Berkeley: University of California Press.

18. Gagnon, John, and William H. Simon. 1973. *Sexual Conduct: The Social Sources of Human Sexuality.* Chicago: Aldine.

19. Feinberg, Leslie. 1998. *Trans Liberation: Beyond Pink or Blue.* Boston: Beacon.

20. Rochlin, Martin. Undated [1972?]. Original source unclear, but it has been reprinted in numerous printed sources and on the Internet.

21. Bell, Alan P., Martin S. Weinberg, and Sue Kiefer Hammersmith. 1981. *Sexual Preference: Its Development in Men and Women.* Bloomington: Indiana University Press.

22. Diamond, Lisa M. 2005. "A New View of Lesbian Subtypes: Stable versus Fluid Identity Trajectories over an 8-Year Period." *Psychology of Women Quarterly* 29: 119–128.

23. Stein, Arlene. 1989. "Three Models of Sexuality: Drives, Identities and Practices." *Sociological Theory* 7: 1–13; Golden, Carla. 2003. "Improbable Possibilities." *Psychoanalytic Inquiry* 23: 624–641.

24. Ussher, Jane. 1997. *Fantasies of Femininity: Reforming the Boundaries of Sex.* London: Penguin.

25. Retrieved from http://www.advocate.com/currentstory1_w_ektid18848.asp.

26. Rich, Adrienne. 1980. "Compulsory Heterosexuality and Lesbian Existence." *Signs: Journal of Women in Culture and Society* 5: 631–660.

27. Jackson, Stevi. 1999. *Heterosexuality in Question.* London: Sage.

28. Hattori, Ayako. 1999. "Heterosexism and Women's Lives in Japan." *Off Our Backs,* November. Retrieved from http://www.findarticles.com/p/articles/mi_qa3693/is_199911/ai_n8858403.

29. Thompson, Beverly Yuen. 2000. "Being Bi in a Mono-Culture: Towards a More Inclusive Perspective on Race and Sexuality." *The Multiracial Activist*. Retrieved from http://www.multiracial.com/readers/thompson.html.

30. Bindel, Julie. 2004. "If We Wanted to Be Straight, We Would Be." *The Guardian*, December 14. Retrieved from http://www.guardian.co.uk/gayrights/story/0,12592,1373326,00.html.

31. Pharr, Suzanne. 1988. *Homophobia: A Weapon of Sexism*. Little Rock, AR: Chardon Press.

32. Eyre, Linda. "Compulsory Heterosexuality in a University Classroom." *Canadian Journal of Education* 18: 273–284.

33. Pascoe, C. J. 2005. "'Dude, You're a Fag': Adolescent Masculinity and the Fag Discourse." *Sexualities* 8: 329–346.

34. Herek, Gregory. 1986. "On Heterosexual Masculinity: Some Psychical Consequences of the Social Construction of Gender and Sexuality." *American Behavioral Scientist* 29: 563–577; Kimmel, Michael. 1994. "Masculinity as Homophobia: Fear, Shame, and Silence in the Construction of Gender Indentity." Pp. 119–141 in *Theorizing Masculinities*, ed. H. Brod. Thousand Oaks, CA: Sage.

35. Flood, Michael. 1997. "Homophobia and Masculinities among Young Men (Lessons in Becoming a Straight Man)." Presented at the O'Connell Education Centre, April 22, Canberra, Australia. Retrieved from http://www.xyonline.net/misc/homophobia.html.

36. Chodorow, Nancy. 1999. Address on homophobia. Presented to The Public Forum, American Psychoanalytic Foundation. Retrieved from http://www.cyberpsych.orghomophobia/noframes/chodorow.htm.

37. Rust, Paula. 1996. "Managing Multiple Identities: Diversity among Bisexual Women and Men." Pp. 53–84 in *Bisexuality: The Psychology and Politics of an Invisible Minority*, ed. B. A. Firestein. Thousand Oaks, CA: Sage.

38. Delany, Samuel R. 2004. "Some Queer Notions about Race." Pp. 199–223 in *Queer Cultures*, eds. D. Carlin and J. DiGrazia. Upper Saddle River, NJ: Pearson/Prentice Hall.

39. Chen, Anthony S. 1999. "Lives at the Center of the Periphery, Lives at the Periphery of the Center: Chinese American Masculinities and Bargaining with Hegemony." *Gender and Society* 13: 584–607.

40. Retrieved from an Internet source that remains anonymous.

41. Hutchins, Loraine, and Lani Ka'ahumanu, eds. 1991. *Bi Any Other Name: Bisexual People Speak Out*. Los Angeles: Alyson.

42. Meyer, Michaela D. E. 2005. "Drawing the Sexuality Card: Teaching, Researching, and Living Bisexuality." *Sexuality and Culture* 9: 3–13.

43. Diamond, Lisa M. 2003. "Was It a Phase? Young Women's Relinquishment of Lesbian/Bisexual Identities over a 5-Year Period." *Journal of Personality and Social Psychology* 84: 352–364; Diamond, Lisa M. 2005. "A New View of Lesbian Subtypes: Stable vs. Fluid Identity Trajectories over an 8-Year Period." *Psychology of Women Quarterly* 29: 119–128.

44. Klein, Fritz. *The Bisexual Option*, 2nd ed. Binghamton, NY: Haworth Press.

45. Retrieved from www.girlsgonewildcom.

46. Herek, Gregory M. 1988. "Heterosexuals' Attitudes toward Lesbians and Gay Men: Correlates and Gender Differences." *Journal of Sex Research* 25: 451–477; Horn, Stacey S., and Larry Nucci. 2003. "The Multidimensionality of Adolescents' Belief about and Attitudes toward Gay and Lesbian Peers in School." *Equity and Excellence in Education* 36(2): 136–147.

47. Kimmel, Michael, and Rebecca F. Plante. 2002. "The Gender of Desire: The Sexual Fantasies of Women and Men." *Advances in Gender Research* 6: 55–77.

48. Chauncey, George. 1994. *Gay New York: Gender, Urban Culture, and the Making of the Gay Male World.* New York: Harper; Valocchi, Steve. 1999. "Riding the Crest of a Protest Wave? Collective Action Frames in the Gay Liberation Movement, 1969–1973." *Mobilization* 4: 59–73.

49. Faderman, Lillian. 1981. *Surpassing the Love of Men: Romantic Friendship and Love between Women from the Renaissance to the Present.* New York: William Morrow.

50. Herdt, Gilbert. 1981. *Guardians of the Flutes: Idioms of Masculinity.* New York: McGraw-Hill.

51. Herdt, Gilbert. 1997. *Same Sex Different Cultures: Exploring Gay and Lesbian Lives.* Boulder, CO: Westview Press.

52. Rubin, Gayle. 1984. "Thinking Sex: Notes for a Radical Theory of the Politics of Sexuality." Pp. 267–319 in *Pleasure and Danger: Exploring Female Sexuality*, ed. C. Vance. Boston: Routledge and Kegan Paul.

53. Halpin, Sean, and Michael W. Allen. 2004. "Changes in Psychosocial Well-Being during Stages of Gay Identity Development." *Journal of Homosexuality* 47(2): 109–126; Cross, Malcolm, and Franz Epting. 2005. "Self-Obliteration, Self-Definition, Self-Integration: Claiming a Homosexual Identity." *Journal of Constructivist Psychology* 18: 53–63.

54. Valentine, David. 2003. "'I Went to Bed with My Own Kind Once': The Erasure of Desire in the Name of Identity." *Language and Communication* 23: 123–138.

55. Rodriguez Rust, Paula C. 2001. "Two Many and Not Enough: The Meanings of Bisexual Identities." *Journal of Bisexuality* 1(1): 31–68.

56. Baumeister, Roy F. 2000. "Gender Differences in Erotic Plasticity." *Psychological Bulletin* 126: 347–374.

57. Ault, Amber. 1994. "Hegemonic Discourse in an Oppositional Community: Lesbian Feminists and Bisexuality." *Critical Sociology* 20(3): 107–122; Stein, Arlene. 1997. *Sex and Sensibility: Stories of a Lesbian Generation.* Berkeley: University of California Press.

58. Carey, Benedict. 2005. "Straight, Gay or Lying? Bisexuality Revisited." *New York Times*, July 5, F1. Retrieved from http://proquest.umi.com/pqdweb?did=862665651&sid=1&Fmt=3& clientId=12342&RQT=309&VName=PQD.

59. Rieger, Gerulf, Meredith Chivers, and J. Michael Bailey. 2005. "Sexual Arousal Patterns of Bisexual Men." *Psychological Science* 16: 579–584.

60. Bailey, J. Michael, Kathleen T. Bechtold, and Sheri A. Berenbaum. 2002. "Who Are Tomboys and Why Should We Study Them?" *Archives of Sexual Behavior* 31: 333–341; Bailey, J. Michael. 2003. *The Man Who Would Be Queen: The Science of Gender-Bending and Transsexualism.* Washington, DC: Joseph Henry Press/The National Academies.

61. Chivers, Meredith L., Gerulf Rieger, Elizabeth Latty, and J. Michael Bailey. 2004. "A Sex Difference in the Specificity of Sexual Arousal." *Psychological Science* 15: 736–744.

62. Bailey, J. Michael. 2002. "Response to the *Washington Times* Article on My Research on Female Sexual Arousal." Retrieved from http://www.psych.northwestern.edu/psych/people/faculty/ bailey/ responsetimes.htm.

63. Weinrich, James D., and Fritz Klein. 2002. "Bi-Gay, Bi-Straight, and Bi-Bi: Three Bisexual Subgroups Identified Using Cluster Analysis of the Klein Sexual Orientation Grid." *Journal of Bisexuality* 2(4): 109–139.

64. Gaffney, Catherine. 2005. "Re: Gay, Straight or Lying . . . " *New York Times*, July 12, F2. Retrieved from http://proquest.umi.com/pqdweb?did=865774741&sid=1&Fmt=3&clientId= 12342&RQT=309&VName=PQD.

65. Lever, Janet. 1994. "Sexual Revelations: The 1994 *Advocate* Survey of Sexuality and Relationships: The Men." *The Advocate*, August 23: 18–24; Stokes, Joseph P., Will Damon, and David

J. McKirnan. 1997. "Predictors of Movement toward Homosexuality: A Longitudinal Study of Bisexual Men." *Journal of Sex Research* 34: 304–312.

66. Blumstein, Philip, and Pepper Schwartz. 1976. "Bisexuality in Men." *Urban Life* 5: 339–358.

67. Eigenberg, H. M. 1992. "Homosexuality in Male Prisons: Demonstrating the Need for a Social Constructionist Approach." *Criminal Justice Review* 17: 219–234; Hensley, Christopher, Richard Tewksbury, and Jeremy Wright. 2001. "Exploring the Dynamics of Masturbation and Consensual Same-Sex Activity within a Male Maximum Security Prison." *Journal of Men's Studies* 10: 59–71.

68. Weinberg, Martin S., Colin J. Williams, and Douglas W. Pryor. 2001. "Bisexuals at Midlife: Commitment, Salience, and Identity." *Journal of Contemporary Ethnography* 30: 180–208.

69. Haslam, Nick. 1997. "Evidence That Male Sexual Orientation Is a Matter of Degree." *Journal of Personality and Social Psychology* 73: 862–870.

70. "'Stella' Inspiration Breaks Silence." 2005. ABC-News, July 12. Retrieved from http://abcnews.go.com/GMA/story?id=930609&page=1.

71. Wellington, Elizabeth. 2005. "Taking Her Groove and Moving On." *Philadelphia Inquirer*, July 10. Retrieved from http://www.philly.com/mld/inquirer/entertainment/12084947.htm.

72. Laumann, Edward O., Stephen Ellingson, Jenna Mahay, Anthony Paik, and Yoosik Youm. 2004. *The Sexual Organization of the City.* Chicago: University of Chicago Press.

73. Collins, Patricia Hill. 2000. *Black Feminist Thought: Knowledge, Consciousness, and the Politics of Empowerment,* 2nd ed. New York: Routledge.

74. Battle, Juan, and Anthony J. Lemelle, Jr. 2002. "Gender Differences in African American Attitudes toward Gay Males." *Western Journal of Black Studies* 26(3): 134–139; Nagel, Joane. 2003. *Race, Ethnicity, and Sexuality: Intimate Intersections, Forbidden Frontiers.* New York: Oxford University Press.

75. Gonzales, Alicia M., and Gary Rolison. 2005. "Social Oppression and Attitudes toward Sexual Practices." *Journal of Black Studies* 35: 715–729.

76. Boykin, Keith. 2005. *Beyond the Down Low: Sex, Lies, and Denial in Black America.* New York: Carroll and Graf Publishers.

77. King, J. L. 2004. *On the Down Low: A Journey into the Lives of "Straight" Black Men Who Sleep with Men.* New York: Harlem Moon/Broadway Books.

78. Leddick, David. 2003. *The Secret Lives of Married Men.* Los Angeles: Alyson.

79. "New Jersey Governor Quits, Comes Out as Gay." 2004. CNN Inside Politics, August 12. Retrieved from http://www.cnn.com/2004/ALLPOLITICS/08/12/mcgreevey.resigns/.

80. Higgins, Daryl J. 2004. "Differences between Previously Married and Never Married 'Gay' Men: Family Background, Childhood Experiences and Current Attitudes." *Journal of Homosexuality* 48(1): 19–41.

81. Whitley, Bernard E. 2001. "Gender-Role Variables and Attitudes toward Homosexuality." *Sex Roles* 45: 691–722.

82. Garber, Marjorie. 1995. *Vice-Versa: Bisexuality and the Eroticism of Everyday Life.* New York: Simon and Schuster.

83. Crawford, Isiaah, Kevin W. Allison, Brian D. Zamboni, and Tomas Soto. 2002. "The Influence of Dual-Identity Development on the Psychosocial Functioning of African-American Gay and Bisexual Men." *Journal of Sex Research* 39: 179–189. Retrieved from http://search.epnet.com/login.aspx?direct=true&db=sih&an=7708432.

84. Baker, Debra Fran. 2004. "The Slash Edge: Why 'Queer as Folk' Isn't Slashy." Retrieved from http://www.nightroadsassoc.com/qaf1.htm. Also, personal communication, 2005.

85. Braeden and I are readying these data, collected in 2004, for several publications.

86. Savin-Williams, Ritch. 2005. *The New Gay Teenager.* Cambridge, MA: Harvard University Press.

87. Seidman, Steven. 2004. Beyond the Closet: *The Transformation of Gay and Lesbian Life.* New York: Routledge.

88. Spillane, Eileen. 2005. "Same-Sex but Not 'Gay.'" *The Advocate*, August 16: 34–36.

CHAPTER 8

1. Margolis, Jonathan. 2004. *O: the Intimate History of the Orgasm.* New York: Grove Press.

2. Retrieved from www.bikiniscience.com/chronology/1965–1970_SS.

3. Slade, Joseph W. 2001. *Pornography and Sexual Representation: A Reference Guide.* Westport, CT: Greenwood Press; Paul, Pamela. 2004. "The Porn Factor." *Time*, January 19: 99–100.

4. Cooper, A., Irene P. McLoughlin, and Kevin M. Campbell. 2000. "Sexuality in Cyberspace: Update for the 21st Century." *CyberPsychology and Behavior* 3: 521–536.

5. Stanley, T. L. 2004. "Porn Crosses Over to Media Mainstream." *Advertising Age* 75(4): 4–6. Retrieved from http://search.epnet.com/login.aspx?direct=true&db=ufh&an=12146617.

6. Cocks, H. G. 2004. "Saucy Stories: Pornography, Sexology and the Marketing of Sexual Knowledge in Britain, c. 1918–70." *Social History* 29: 465–484. (Yes, I did cite an author named Cocks in a book about sex.)

7. Buzzell, Timothy. 2005. "Demographic Characteristics of Persons Using Pornography in Three Technological Contexts." *Sexuality and Culture* 9: 28–48.

8. Duggan, Lisa, Nan Hunter, and Carole Vance. 1985. "False Promises: Feminist Antipornography Legislation." Pp. 130–151 in *Women against Censorship*, ed. V. Burstyn. Vancouver, Canada: Douglas and MacIntyre Ltd.; Davis, Clive M., and Robert Bauserman. 1993. "Exposure to Sexually Explicit Materials: An Attitude Change Perspective." *Annual Review of Sex Research* 4: 121–209; Strossen, Nadine. 1995. *Defending Pornography.* New York: Anchor Books.

9. Bogaert, Anthony F. 2001. "Personality, Individual Differences, and Preferences for the Sexual Media." *Archives of Sexual Behavior* 30. Retrieved from www.infotrac.com.

10. Mosher, Donald L., and Ronald D. Anderson. 1986. "Macho Personality, Sexual Aggression, and Reactions to Guided Imagery of Realistic Rape." *Journal of Research in Personality* 20: 77–94.

11. Malamuth, Neil M. 1989. "The Attraction to Sexual Aggression Scale: Part 1." *Journal of Sex Research* 26: 26–49.

12. Dworkin, Andrea. 1994. "Why Pornography Matters to Feminists." Pp. 152–153 in *Living with Contradictions: Controversies in Feminist Social Ethics*, ed. A. Jaggar. Boulder, CO: Westview Press.

13. Beggan, James K., and Scott T. Allison. 2003. "'What Sort of Man Reads *Playboy*?' The Self Reported Influence of *Playboy* on the Construction of Masculinity." *Journal of Men's Studies* 11: 189–206.

14. Trostle, Lawrence C. 1993. "Pornography as a Source of Sex Information for University Students: Some Consistent Findings." *Psychological Reports* 72: 407–412; Trostle, Lawrence C. 2003. "Overrating Pornography as a Source of Sex Information for University Students: Additional Consistent Findings." *Psychological Reports* 92: 143–150.

15. Haggstrom-Nordin, Elisabet. 2005. "Worlds Apart? Sexual Behaviour, Contraceptive Use, and Pornography Consumption among Young Women and Men." Acta Universitatis Upsaliensis.

Digital Comprehensive Summaries of Uppsala Dissertations from the Faculty of Medicine 6: Uppsala, Sweden.

16. Dines, Gail, and Robert Jensen. 2004. "Pornography and Media: Toward a More Critical Analysis." Pp. 369–380 in *Sexualities: Identities, Behaviors, and Society*, eds. M. S. Kimmel and R. F. Plante. New York: Oxford University Press.

17. Tolman, Deborah L. 2002. *Dilemmas of Desire: Teenage Girls Talk about Sexuality*. Cambridge, MA: Harvard University Press; Diamond, Lisa M. 2003. "What Does Sexual Orientation Orient? A Biobehavioral Model Distinguishing Romantic Love and Sexual Desire." *Psychological Review* 110: 173–192; Ussher, Jane M. 2005. "The Meaning of Sexual Desire: Experiences of Heterosexual and Lesbian Girls." *Feminism and Psychology* 15(1): 27–32.

18. Kimmel, Michael S. 1990. "Introduction: Guilty Pleasures—Pornography in Men's Lives." Pp. 1–22 in *Men Confront Pornography*, ed. M. S. Kimmel. New York: Crown Publishers.

19. Bogaert, Anthony F., Deborah A. Turkovich, and Carolyn L. Hafer. 1993. "A Content Analysis of *Playboy* Centrefolds From 1953 through 1990: Changes in Explicitness, Objectification, and Models' Age." *Journal of Sex Research* 30: 135–139.

20. Brooks, Gary R. 1995. *The Centerfold Syndrome: How Men Can Overcome Objectification and Achieve Intimacy*. San Francisco: Jossey-Bass.

21. Owen, Patricia R., and Erika Laurel-Seller. 2000. "Weight and Shape Ideals: Thin Is Dangerously In." *Journal of Applied Social Psychology* 30: 979–990.

22. Attwood, Feona. 2005. "'Tits and Ass and Porn and Fighting': Male Heterosexuality in Magazines for Men." *International Journal of Cultural Studies* 8: 83–100.

23. Mercer, John. "Homosexual Prototypes: Repetition and the Construction of the Generic in the Iconography of Gay Pornography." *Paragraph* 26: 280–290.

24. Duggan, Scott J., and Donald R. McCreary. 2004. "Body Image, Eating Disorders, and the Drive for Muscularity in Gay and Heterosexual Men: The Influence of Media Images." *Journal of Homosexuality* 47(3/4): 45–58.

25. Monk-Turner, Elizabeth, and Christine H. Purcell. 1999. "Sexual Violence in Pornography: How Prevalent Is It?" *Gender Issues* 17(2): 58–67. Retrieved from http://search.epnet.com/ login.aspx?direct=true&db=aph&an=2339995.

26. Abbott, Sharon A. 2004. "Creating a Scene: The Work of Performing Sex." Pp. 380–389 in *Sexualities: Identities, Behaviors, and Society*, eds. M. S. Kimmel and R. F. Plante. New York: Oxford University Press.

27. Nagel, Chris. 2002. "Pornographic Experience." *Journal of Mundane Behavior* 3. Retrieved from http://mundanebehavior.org/index2.htm.

28. Dines, Gail, Robert Jensen, and Ann Russo. 1998. *Pornography: The Production and Consumption of Inequality*. New York: Routledge.

29. Cowan, Gloria. 1995. "Black and White (and Blue): Ethnicity and Pornography." Pp. 397–412 in *Bringing Cultural Diversity to Feminist Psychology: Theory, Research, and Practice*, ed. H. Landrine. Washington, DC: American Psychological Association.

30. Dines, Gail. 1998. "King Kong and the White Woman: *Hustler* Magazine and the Demonization of Black Masculinity." *Violence against Women* 4: 291–307.

31. Mayall, Alice, and Diana E. H. Russell. 1993. "Racism in Pornography." Pp. 167–178 in *Making Violence Sexy: Feminist Views on Pornography*, ed. D. E. H. Russell. New York: Teachers College Press.

32. Burger, John R. 1995. *One-Handed Histories: The Eroto-Politics of Gay Male Video Pornography*. New York: Harrington Park Press; Thomas, Joe A. 2000. "Gay Male Video Pornography: Past, Present, and Future." Pp. 49–66 in *Sex for Sale: Prostitution, Pornography, and the Sex Industry*, ed.

R. Weitzer. New York: Routledge.

33. Green, Leslie. 2000. "Pornographies." *Journal of Political Philosophy* 8: 27–52.

34. English, Bella. 2005. "The Secret Life of Boys: Pornography Is a Mouse Click Away, and Kids Are Being Exposed to It in Ever-Increasing Numbers." *Boston Globe*, May 12, D1. Retrieved from http://proquest.umi.com/pqdweb?did=837118401&sid=2&Fmt=3&clientId=12342&RQT=309&VName=PQD.

35. Delmonico, David L., Elizabeth Griffin, and Patrick J. Carnes. 2002. "Treating Online Compulsive Sexual Behavior: When Cybersex Is the Drug of Choice." Pp. 147–168 in *Sex and the Internet: A Guidebook for Clinicians*, ed. A. Cooper. New York: Brunner-Routledge.

36. Barron, Martin, and Michael S. Kimmel. 2000. "Sexual Violence in Three Pornographic Media: Toward a Sociological Explanation." *Journal of Sex Research* 37: 161–168.

37. Mehta, Michael D., and Dwaine Plaza. 1997. "Content Analysis of Pornographic Images Available on the Internet." *Information Society* 13(2): 153–161.

38. Cooper, Al. 2004. "Online Sexual Activity in the New Millennium." *Contemporary Sexuality* 38(3): 1–7.

39. Salmon, Catherine, and Don Symons. 2004. "Slash Fiction and Human Mating Psychology." *Journal of Sex Research* 41: 94–100.

40. Waskul, Dennis, ed. 2004. *Net.SeXXX: Readings on Sex, Pornography, and the Internet*. New York: Peter Lang.

41. Putnam, Robert D. 2000. *Bowling Alone: The Collapse and Revival of the American Community*. New York: Simon and Schuster; Pappano, Laura. 2001. *The Connection Gap: Why Americans Feel So Alone*. New Brunswick, NJ: Rutgers University Press.

42. Schneider, Jennifer P. 2000. "A Qualitative Study of Cybersex Participants: Gender Differences, Recovery Issues, and Implications for Therapists." *Sexual Addiction and Compulsivity* 7: 249–278.

43. Zillman, Dolf. 2000. "Influence of Unrestrained Access to Erotica on Adolescents and Young Adults' Dispositions toward Sexuality." *Journal of Adolescent Health* 27: 41–44.

44. Sigel, Lisa Z. 2000. "Name Your Pleasure: The Transformation of Sexual Language in Nineteenth-Century British Pornography." *Journal of the History of Sexuality* 9: 395–419; Fisher, William A., and Azy F. Barak. 2001. "Online Sex Shops: Phenomenological, Psychological, and Ideological Perspectives on Internet Sexuality." *Cyberpsychology and Behavior* 3: 575–590.

45. Kimmel, Michael, and Rebecca F. Plante. 2002. "The Gender of Desire: The Sexual Fantasies of Women and Men." *Advances in Gender Research* 6: 55–77.

46. Rubin, Gayle. 1984. "Thinking Sex: Notes for a Radical Theory of the Politics of Sexuality." Pp. 267–319 in *Pleasure and Danger: Exploring Female Sexuality*, ed. C. Vance. Boston: Routledge and Kegan Paul; Califia, Pat. 1994. *Public Sex: The Culture of Radical Sex*. San Francisco: Cleis Press; Morin, Jack. 1995. *The Erotic Mind: Unlocking the Inner Sources of Sexual Passion and Fulfillment*. New York: Harper Perennial.

47. Fejes, Fred. 2002. "Bent Passions: Heterosexual Masculinity, Pornography, and Gay Male Identity." *Sexuality and Culture* 6: 95–104.

48. Tiefer, Leonore. 2004. "Some Harms to Women of Restrictions on Sexually Related Expression." Pp. 139–146 in *Sex Is Not a Natural Act and Other Essays*, 2nd ed., by L. Tiefer. Boulder, CO: Westview Press.

49. Dworkin, Andrea. 1981. *Pornography: Men Possessing Women*. New York: Penguin; Small, Fred. 1990. "Pornography and Censorship." Pp. 72–80 in *Men Confront Pornography*, ed. M. S. Kimmel. New York: Crown Books.

50. Træen, Bente, Kristin Spitznogle, and Alexandra Beverfjord. 2004. "Attitudes and Use of Pornography in the Norwegian Population 2002." *Journal of Sex Research* 41: 193–200.

51. Cage, Diana. 2004. *On Our Backs Guide to Lesbian Sex*. Los Angeles: Alyson.

52. Hall, Dennis. 2000. "Good Vibrations: Eros and Instrumental Knowledge." *Journal of Popular Culture* 34(1): 1–7.

53. Dodson, Betty. 1996. *Sex for One: The Joy of Selfloving*. New York: Crown Trade Paperback.

54. Juffer, Jane. 1998. *At Home with Pornography: Women, Sex and Everyday Life*. New York: New York University Press.

55. Ciclitira, Karen. 2004. "Pornography, Women and Feminism: Between Pleasure and Politics." *Sexualities* 7: 281–301.

56. Fine, Jon, and Ann Marie Kerwin. 2005. "VC Unit Tries to Rescue 'Penthouse' from Hard Times with Soft Approach." *Advertising Age*, March 14, 76(11): 29.

57. "Sales Fall at Spicier Penthouse." 2002. *Contemporary Sexuality* 36(5): 9.

58. Steinberg, David. 1990. "The Roots of Pornography." Pp. 54–59 in *Men Confront Pornography*, ed. M. S. Kimmel. New York: Crown Publishers.

59. Polk, Roselyn K., and Gloria Cowan. 1996. "Perceptions of Female Pornography Stars." *Canadian Journal of Human Sexuality* 5(3): 221–228.

60. Stanley, T. L. 2004. "Porn Crosses Over to Media Mainstream." *Advertising Age*, January 26, 75(4): 4–6.

61. Vivid Girls. 2004. *How to Have a XXX Sex Life: The Ultimate Vivid Guide*. New York: HarperCollins.

62. "Finger Lickin' Good." 2001. *Contemporary Sexuality* 35(3): 7.

63. Barcan, Ruth. 2002. "In the Raw: 'Home-Made Porn' and Reality Genres." *Journal of Mundane Behavior* 3. Retrieved from http://mundanebehavior.org/index2.htm.

64. Smith, Clarissa. 2002. "'They're Ordinary People, Not Aliens from The Planet Sex!': The Mundane Excitements of Pornography for Women." *Journal of Mundane Behavior* 3. Retrieved from http://mundanebehavior.org/index2.htm.

CHAPTER 9

1. Plummer, Ken. 2004. "The Sexual Spectacle: Making a Public Culture of Sexual Problems." Pp. 521–541 in *Handbook of Social Problems: A Comparative, International Perspective*, ed. G. Ritzer. Thousand Oaks, CA: Sage.

2. Tiefer, Leonore. 2004. "Historical, Scientific, Clinical, and Feminist Criticisms of 'The Human Sexual Response Cycle Model.'" Pp. 41–66 in *Sex Is Not a Natural Act and Other Essays,* 2nd ed., by L. Tiefer. Boulder, CO: Westview Press.

3. Tiefer, Leonore. 2004. "The Medicalization of Impotence: Normalizing Phallocentrism." Pp. 195–208 in *Sex Is Not a Natural Act and Other Essays,* 2nd ed., by L. Tiefer. Boulder, CO: Westview Press.

4. Foucault, Michel. 1978. *The History of Sexuality: An Introduction*. New York: Pantheon Books.

5. Fishman, Jennifer R., and Laura Mamo. 2001. "What's in a Disorder: A Cultural Analysis of Medical and Pharmaceutical Constructions of Male and Female Sexual Dysfunction." Pp. 179–193 in *A New View of Women's Sexual Problems*, eds. E. Kaschak and L. Tiefer. Binghamton, NY: Haworth Press.

6. Laumann, Edward, Anthony Paik, and Raymond C. Rosen. 1999. "Sexual Dysfunction in the United States." *Journal of the American Medical Association* 281: 537–544.

7. Bancroft, John, Jeni Loftus, and J. Scott Long. 2003. "Distress about Sex: A National Survey of Women in Heterosexual Relationships." *Archives of Sex Behavior* 32: 193–209.

8. Laumann, Edward O., John H. Gagnon, Robert T. Michael, and Stuart Michaels. 1994. *The Social Organization of Sexuality: Sexual Practices in the United States.* Chicago: University of Chicago Press.

9. Potts, Annie. 2000. "'The Essence of the Hard On': Hegemonic Masculinity and the Cultural Construction of 'Erectile Dysfunction.'" *Men and Masculinities* 3: 85–103.

10. Braun, Virginia, and Celia Kitzinger. 2001a. "Telling It Straight? Dictionary Definitions of Women's Genitals." *Journal of Sociolinguistics* 5: 214–232.

11. Jackson, Margaret. 1984. "Sex Research and the Construction of Sexuality: A Tool of Male Supremacy?" *Women's Studies International Forum* 7: 43–51.

12. McPhillips, Kathryn, Virginia Braun, and Nicola Gavey. 2001. "Defining (Hetero)Sex: How Imperative Is the 'Coital Imperative'?" *Women's Studies International Forum* 24: 229–240.

13. Braun, Virginia, and Celia Kitzinger. 2001b. "'Snatch,' 'Hole,' or 'Honey-pot'? Semantic Categories and the Problem of Nonspecificity in Female Genital Slang." *Journal of Sex Research* 38: 146–158.

14. Williams, Robin. 1986. *Robin Williams Live.* Produced by V. Kaplan. Mr. Happy Productions.

15. Zilbergeld, Bernie. 1992. *The New Male Sexuality.* New York: Bantam.

16. Roberts, Celia, Susan Kippax, Catherine Waldby, and June Crawford. 1995. "Faking It: The Story of 'Ohh!'" *Women's Studies International Forum* 18: 523–532.

17. Weeks, Jeffrey. 2003. *Sexuality,* 2nd ed. London: Routledge.

18. Brody, Jane. 1995. "Personal Health: With More Help Available for Impotency, Few Men Seek It." *New York Times,* Aug. 2: C9.

19. Loe, Meika. 2004. *The Rise of Viagra: How the Little Blue Pill Changed Sex in America.* New York: New York University Press.

20. Kleinplatz, Peggy. 2004. "Beyond Sexual Mechanics and Hydraulics: Humanizing the Discourse Surrounding Erectile Dysfunction." *Journal of Humanistic Psychology* 44: 215–242.

21. Herper, M., and A. Lagorce. 2003. "Viagra vs. Levitra." www.forbes.com. Retrieved from http://www.usrf.org/ForbesArticle.html.

22. Loe, Meika. "Sex and the Senior Woman: Pleasure and Danger in the Viagra Era." *Sexualities* 7: 303–326.

23. Reinholtz, Rhonda K., and Charlene L. Muehlenhard. "Genital Perceptions and Sexual Activity in a College Population." *Journal of Sex Research* 32: 155–165.

24. McConnachie, Brian. 1974. *National Lampoon: The Job of Sex: A Workingman's Guide to Productive Lovemaking.* New York: Warner Books.

25. Comfort, Alex. 1972. *The Joy of Sex.* New York: Fireside Books.

26. Scully, Diana, and Pauline Bart. [1978]2003. "A Funny Thing Happened on the Way to the Orifice: Women in Gynecology Textbooks." Reprinted in *Feminism and Psychology* 13(1): 11–16; Moore, Lisa Jean, and Adele Clarke. 2001. "The Traffic in Cyberanatomies: Sex/Gender/Sexuality in Local and Global Formations." *Body and Society* 7: 57–96.

27. Wiederman, Michael. 1997. "Pretending Orgasm during Sexual Intercourse: Correlates in a Sample of Young Adult Women." *Journal of Sex and Marital Therapy* 23: 131–138.

28. Lavie, Maya, and Carla Willig. 2005. "'I Don't Feel Like Melting Butter': An Interpretive Phenomenological Analysis of the Experience of 'Inorgasmia.'" *Psychology and Health* 20: 115–128.

29. Koli, Anuradha. 2004. "Is Your Guy Faking It in Bed?" *Cosmopolitan* 237(2): 128.

30. Braun, Virginia, Nicola Gavey, and Kathryn McPhillips. 2003. "The 'Fair Deal'? Unpacking Accounts of Reciprocity in Heterosex." *Sexualities* 6: 237–261.

31. Potts, Annie. 2005. "Cyborg Masculinity in the Viagra Era." *Sexualities, Evolution and Gender* 7: 3–16.

32. Rubin, Rona. 2004. "Men Talking about Viagra." *Men and Masculinities* 7: 22–30.

33. Winton, Mark Alan. 2001. "Paradigm Change and Female Sexual Dysfunctions: An Analysis of Sexology Journals." *The Canadian Journal of Human Sexuality* 10: 19–24.

34. Symons, Donald. 1979. *The Evolution of Human Sexuality.* New York: Oxford University Press.

35. Masters, William, and Virginia Johnson. 1966. *Human Sexual Response.* Boston: Little, Brown.

36. Mah, Kenneth, and Yitzchak M. Binik. "Are Orgasms in the Mind or the Body? Psychosocial Versus Physiological Correlates of Orgasmic Pleasure and Satisfaction." *Journal of Sex and Marital Therapy* 31: 187–200.

37. Margolis, Jonathan. 2004. *O: The Intimate History of the Orgasm.* New York: Grove Press.

38. Eschler, Lara. "The Physiology of the Female Orgasm as a Proximate Mechanism." *Sexualities, Evolution and Gender* 6: 171–194.

39. Lloyd, Elisabeth A. 2005. *The Case of the Female Orgasm: Bias in the Science of Evolution.* Cambridge, MA: Harvard University Press.

40. Maines, Rachel P. 1999. *The Technology of Orgasm: "Hysteria," the Vibrator, and Women's Sexual Satisfaction.* Baltimore, MD: Johns Hopkins University Press.

41. Ericksen, Julia. 1999. "Compulsory Heterosexuality and 'Orgasm Inadequacy': A Brief History of the Problematic Nature of Female (Hetero)Sexual Desire." Presented at the annual meeting of the American Sociological Association, August 6–10, Chicago, IL.

42. Bolsø, Agnes. 2005. "Orgasm and Lesbian Sociality." *Sex Education* 5: 29–48.

43. Althof, Stanley. 2001. "My Personal Distress over the Inclusion of Personal Distress." *Journal of Sex and Marital Therapy* 27: 123–125.

44. Oberg, K., A. R. Fugl-Meyer, and K. S. Fugl-Meyer. 2004. "On Categorization and Quantification of Women's Sexual Dysfunctions: An Epidemiological Approach." *International Journal of Impotence Research* 16: 261–269.

45. Berman, L., J. Berman, S. Felder, D. Pollets, S. Chhabra, M. Miles, and J. A. Powell. 2003. "Seeking Help for Sexual Function Complaints: What Gynecologists Need to Know about the *Female* Patient's Experience." *Fertility and Sterility* 79: 572–576.

46. Schober, Justine M., Heino F. L. Meyer-Bahlburg, and Philip G. Ransley. 2004. "Self-Assessment of Genital Anatomy, Sexual Sensitivity and Function in Women: Implications for Genitoplasty." *BJU International* 94: 589–594.

47. Tuana, Nancy. 2004. "Coming to Understand: Orgasm and the Epistemology of Ignorance." *Hypatia* 19: 194–232.

48. Nicolson, Paula, and Jennifer Burr. 2003. "What Is Normal about Women's (Hetero)Sexual Desire and Orgasm?: A Report of an In-Depth Interview Study." *Social Science and Medicine* 57: 1735–1745.

49. Nicolosi, A., E. O. Laumann, D. B. Glasser, E. D. Moreira, A. Paik, and C. Gingell. 2004. "Sexual Behavior and Sexual Dysfunctions after Age 40: The Global Study of Sexual Attitudes and Behaviors." *Urology* 64: 991–997.

50. Allina, Amy. 2001. "Orgasms for Sale: The Role of Profit and Politics in Addressing Women's Sexual Satisfaction." *Women and Therapy* 24(1–2): 211–218.

51. Fishman, Jennifer R. "Manufacturing Desire: The Commodification of Female Sexual Dysfunction." *Social Studies of Science* 34: 187–218.

52. Levine, Janice. 2002. *Harmful to Minors: The Perils of Protecting Children from Sex.* Minneapolis: University of Minnesota Press.

53. Ogden, Gina. 2001. "The Taming of the Screw: Reflections on 'A New View of Women's Sexual Problems.'" *Women and Therapy* 24(1–2): 17–21.

54. Nagel, Joane. 2003. *Race, Ethnicity, and Sexuality: Intimate Intersections, Forbidden Frontiers.* New York: Oxford University Press.

55. Gavey, Nicola. 2005. *Just Sex? The Cultural Scaffolding of Rape.* London: Routledge.

56. Kempadoo, Kamala, and Jo Doezema, eds. 1998. *Global Sex Workers: Rights, Resistance, and Redefinition.* London: Routledge; Clift, Stephen and Simon Carter, eds. 2000. *Tourism and Sex: Culture, Commerce and Coercion.* London: Pinter.

57. Weeks, Jeffrey. 1998. "The Sexual Citizen." *Theory, Culture and Society* 15(3–4): 35–52.

Index

Abbott, Sharon, 252, 258
AIDS, *see* HIV/AIDS
Anal sex, xii, 43, 45, 114, 127, 198, 247, 252, 258, 280
Arousal, sexual, 55, 57, 130, 140, 143, 146, 149, 185, 200, 224–229, 237, 245, 249
Assumptions *(also* "Taken for granted"), xvi, 4, 34, 52, 58, 60–61,63, 85, 89, 114, 115, 170, 187, 197, 201, 208, 257, 279–280, 282–283
   critical thinking, 27–28, 29, 226–228
   sexual orientation, 40, 42, 51, 94, 197–198, 200, 215, 226–228, 233, 234–236

Bailey, J. Michael. *See also* Gerulf Rieger; Meredith Chivers, 224–229
Baker, Robert, 12, 13, 160, 237
Bancroft, John, 270
Baumeister, Roy *(also* plasticity), 223
Bay-Cheng, Laina Y., 129
BDSM
   (bondage/domination/sadomasochism), 196, 197, 206, 230, 237, 254, 259–260
Beck, Max, 76, 85
Bem, Daryl, 201
Birth control. *See* Contraception; Pill, contraceptive
Bisexual or bisexuality, 40, 111, 127, 197, 199, 215–236, 249
   concept of arousal, 226–229, 237
   defined, 216–217, 219, 224–225
   identity, 63, 116, 208, 211, 217–218, 222–229
   invisibility of, 217, 238
   race, 230–236
   "Straight, Gay, or Lying?," 224, 229, 234–235
"Bisexual Until Graduation" *(also b.u.g)*, 203
Blumstein, Philip, 229
Body or bodies, xi, xv, 5, 44–45, 50, 60–61, 104, 107, 112, 161, 269, 274–275, 277
   binary, 68, 74, 77, 85, 87, 134–135
   intersex, 71–72, 75, 76
   men, 89, 117, 119, 176–177, 191, 213–214, 250, 252, 273, 278
   transgender, 83, 88–90
   women, 70–71, 89, 92, 112, 126, 128, 138–139, 143–144, 176, 178, 180, 250, 252, 281–282
Bondage. *See* BDSM
Bornstein, Kate, 68, 82
Bourdieu, Pierre *(cultural capital)*, 232
Boykin, Keith, 232, 234, 235
Braun, Virginia, 271, 278
Buss, David, 23, 175

Carey, Ben, 224, 226, 227
Carpenter, Laura, 127–128
Casual sex. *See* Hooking up

Chauncey, George, 220
Chivers, Meredith, 224–229
Chodorow, Nancy, 214
Clitoris, 10, 69, 72, 74, 75, 89, 100, 110,
    124–125, 143, 210, 269, 271,
    281–282
Coital imperative, 271
Coitus. *See* Penile-vaginal intercourse
Collins, Patricia Hill, 231
Coming out. *See* Sexual orientation
Compulsory heterosexuality. *See also*
    Adrienne Rich, 59, 130, 209–210, 212,
    215, 223
Connell, R.W., 117, 205–206, 207
Contraception, 16, 21–22, 190
Contraceptive pill. *See* Pill
Cornog, Martha, 11, 142, 143
Cosmopolitan (also Cosmo), 21, 27, 126, 143,
    144, 221, 277–278
Cost-benefit analysis.
    See Social exchange theory
Critical thinking *(also* elements of thought),
    xvi, xix, 4, 6, 26–29, 33–47, 50–51,
    70–71, 148–152, 170,
    225–229
Cross-cultural sexualities
    Asia, 284
    Australia and New Zealand, 138, 173,
        176, 271
    Canada, 20, 174
    globally, 20, 23–24, 209–210, 244,
        268, 283–285
    India, 90
    Japan, 24, 56, 210–211, 284
    Native American, 13, 90
    Nigeria, 137
    Norway (Norwegian), 184, 190, 257
    Sambians of New Guinea, 220
    Sa'moa, 91
    Scandinavia, 257–258
    sub-Saharan Africa, 24
    Sweden, 247, 257, 281

United Kingdom *(also* Britain, British),
    24, 117, 118, 123, 129, 176, 250,
    271
Cybersex, 243, 259–261, 264

D'Augelli, Anthony, 111
Davis, Clive M., 245
De Sousa, Ronald, 11, 12
Desire. *See* Sexual desire
DeLamater, John, 142
D'Emilio, John, 13
Desperate Housewives, ix, 16, 246
Diagnostic and Statistical Manual-IV (also
    DSM-IV)*,* 49–50, 84, 197, 280–281, 290
Diamond, Lisa, 209, 217
Dines, Gail , 248, 251–252, 258
Domination. *See* BDSM
"Down low." *See also* Race; Sexual
    orientation*,* 230, 233, 235, 236
Dreger, Alice Domurat, 74
Drinking. *See* Alcohol
DSM-IV. *See Diagnostic and Statistical
    Manual-*IV
Durham, Meenakshi Gigi, 112, 126
Dworkin, Andrea, 246, 257
Dworkin, Shari, 35, 36

Ekins, Richard, 88, 89
Ellis, Havelock, 198, 236
Erectile dysfunction. *See also* Viagra,
    273–274, 278, 283, 284
Essentialism, essential, 44–46, 59, 95,147,
    201–202, 204–205, 281
    biological determinism, 77, 82, 202
    concept of "the Truth,*"* 205, 230
    sexual orientation, 202–208, 236
Evolutionary psychology, xiv, 23–24, 44, 87,
    95, 147, 152, 175, 225, 254, 279, 280
Fag. See Sexual orientation
Fausto-Sterling, Anne, 91
Feinberg, Leslie, 206–207, 208
Fine, Jon, 261

Fine, Michelle, 128
Fishman, Jennifer R., 269, 285
Foucault, Michel. *See also* Power, 59–62, 198
Freedman, Estelle, 13
Freud, Sigmund, 50–51, 53, 59, 94–95,
    106, 146–147, 198, 202–203, 270
    polymorphous perversity, 50–51, 94,
    202

Gagnon, John, xv, 9, 51–52, 54–55, 56–57,
    106, 198, 206, 208, 216
Gamson, Joshua, 62
Gavey, Nicola, 271, 278, 285
Gay, x-xi, xiv, 6, 8, 9, 12, 14–15, 19, 45,
    103–104, 111, 116, 119, 123, 127, 167,
    171, 177, 190, 203–206, 211, 221, 229,
    231, 236–237, 250, 262
Gay bashing. *See* Violence against men
Gender
    binary thinking, 10, 58, 63, 73, 74,
        77–80, 88, 91, 101–102, 201, 186
    desire, 23, 35, 128, 142–145, 148,
        159–161, 179, 189, 191, 209, 224,
        237, 258
    double standard, xii, 44, 189–190
    inequality, 246, 258, 285,
    menìs bodies, 119, 176–177, 191,
        213–214, 250, 252, 278
    menìs power, 160, 209–210, 251, 272
    objects, women as, 131, 152, 180, 210,
        222, 256,
    women's bodies, 70–71, 92, 126, 138,
        143, 144, 176, 178, 250, 252,
        281–282
Genitalia, xi, xv, 10–11, 50–51, 57, 68, 69,
    73–74, 75, 77, 82–83, 86, 89, 106,108,
    134, 142, 144, 153, 250, 274, 281–282
    perceptions of, 275, 281
Giordano, Peggy, 40, 165
Girls Gone Wild, 218, 224, 263
GLAAD (Gay And Lesbian Alliance Against
    Discrimination), 19

Global sexuality, 20, 23–24, 209–210, 244,
    268, 283–285
Goffman, Erving, 203
Golden, Carla, 209
Goldilocks theory of sex, 64, 128, 129, 181,
    189, 190, 191, 255, 264, 283
Gonzalez-Lopez, Gloria, 127
Grossman, Arnold, 111

Haffner, Debra, 134
Haggstrom-Nordin, Elisabet, 248, 257
Halperin, David, 6, 7
Hegemonic. *See also* Hegemony, 19, 85, 87,
    102, 112, 116–118, 123, 130, 144, 170,
    190, 203, 221, 231, 277
    masculinity, 118, 212–214, 221, 231,
        264, 278,
    scripts, 207, 212, 213–214, 214–215,
        234, 256, 278
Hegemony. *See also* Hegemonic, 130, 207,
    234, 256, 262, 279
Herold, Edward, 170, 173, 174
Heterosexism, defined, 213–214
Heterosexual, heterosexuality
    defined as "normal," 44, 74, 94,
        197–198, 200, 211, 221, 256
    evolution of the concept, 198–199,
        285,
    expectations of, 272
    identity, 102, 197, 201, 210–211, 236,
        275
    privilege, defined, 237
    "Questionnaire," 207–208, 210
Herdt, Gilbert *(also* Sambians of New
    Guinea), 220
Herek, Gregory, 14–15, 213, 219
HIV/AIDS, 230, 234, 255
    evaluation of educational efforts, 233
    research focus on, 171, 198
Holland, Janet, 128
Homophobia, 19–20, 211, 229, 233–236
    defined, 111, 123

Homophobia *(continued)*
  heterosexism, 212–215
  internalized, 111, 215, 233
  weapon of sexism, as a, 212
Hooking up
  alcohol, 168–169, 172–173, 174–178,
    180–181, 184
  "beer goggles," 175–176, 178, 181
  desire, 174, 176–177, 179–180, 182,
    183, 185, 190–191
  difficulties in defining, 163–166
  emotions, xiii, 166, 182, 184, 185, 187
  friends with benefits (FWB), xii–xiii,
    169, 170, 172, 174, 178, 182–186,
    187, 190, 192, 257
  fuckbuddies, 167, 169, 182
  gays and lesbians, 167, 171
  gender, 20–21, 166–167, 172,
    177–181, 184–185, 189–190
  how-to books on, 20, 166–167,
    178–179, 180, 183, 184, 187, 188
  peer influences, 173–174
  research, 168–173
  social exchange theory, 166, 182–185,
    187, 190
  thinking critically about, 168–170, 177
Huberman, Barbara, 16, 23
Human sexual response cycle (HSRC). *See
  also* Masters and Johnson, 31–32, 47, 49,
  64, 65, 269, 279, 281

Identity. *See* Sexual orientation
Impotence. *See also* Erectile dysfunction,
  272–273
Inequality , 59, 62, 93, 95, 122, 130, 161,
  200, 209–210, 211–212, 223, 231–233,
  236, 246, 251, 258,
Intercourse. *See* Penile-vaginal intercourse
Internet or Web, 20–21, 122, 129, 167,
  243–244, 245, 250, 253- 255, 259, 261,
  262
    bulletin or message boards, 43, 168

  sex sites, 253–255, 259
  blogs, xii–xiii, 61, 188, 215
Intersexuality, 63, 71, 73–74, 76, 77, 80, 83,
  89
Jackson, Stevi, 210
Jagose, Annemarie, 63
Jensen, Robert, 248, 251–252, 258
Johnson, Pamela, 182
Johnson, Virginia. *See* Masters and Johnson

Katz, Jonathan Ned, 48, 198, 213, 220
Kerwin, Ann Marie, 261
Kessler, Suzanne, 74, 75, 89, 275, 282
Kimmel, Michael, 80, 124, 146, 150, 152,
  180, 187, 189, 213, 219, 249, 254
King, Dave, 88, 89
Kinsey, Alfred, 13, 35, 39, 47, 64, 136, 140,
  147, 200
Kinsey scale, 47, 64–65, 199–200, 218, 226,
  227
Kitzinger, Celia, 13, 271, 278
Klein, Fritz, 218
Kleinplatz, Peggy, 166, 274, 278
Krafft-Ebing, Richard von, 39, 42, 47–49,
  64, 95, 198, 225
Kushner, Saville, 117–118

Labels, 203, 220, 229, 238
    classification and, 50, 93, 95, 197,
      280, 285
    process of labeling, 49, 197, 203–205,
      231, 234–235, 283
Lamb, Sharon, 105, 202
Laumann, Edward, 9,15, 52, 143, 191, 200,
  225, 229, 231, 269, 270, 281, 284
Lesbian, xviii, 12, 14, 19, 39, 45, 59, 63,
  64, 111, 116, 125, 127, 129–130
"Lesbian Until Graduation "*(l.u.g)*, 217,
  222, 223
LeVay, Simon, 45, 46
Loe, Meika, 273, 274, 284
Loftus, Jeni, 9, 270

Longmore, Monica, 40, 165
Love, 24, 25, 54, 107, 108, 115, 128–129,
  145, 151–152, 155, 172, 184–185, 219,
  234, 255–256, 258–259

Mac an Ghaill, Mairtin, 117, 123, 203
Mackay, Judith, 24, 188
Mamo, Laura, 269
Manning, Wendy, 40, 165
Martin, Emily, 91–92, 93, 94, 95
Master status, 221, 237
Masters (William) and Johnson (Virginia),
  31–32, 39, 47, 49–50, 64, 65, 269, 279
Masturbation, 49, 104, 144, 147, 261
  antimasturbation, 106
  gender, 106, 135–136, 140–146, 191,
    223, 256–258, 259, 260
  slang for, 141
Maticka-Tyndale, Eleanor, 170, 173, 174
McMillan, Terry, 230–231, 235
Medicalization of sexualities, 51, 268, 284
  defined, 269
  men, 272–273, 278
  stakeholders, 284
  women, 269, 274, 279, 280,
    282
Menarche, 134–144, 161
Monty Python, 99–101, 170, 248
Moon, Dawne, 62
Morgan, Kathryn Pauly, 11, 12
Morning-after pill. *See* Pill
MRKH Syndrome (Mayer-Rokitansky-
  Kuster-Hauser), 75

Nagel, Joane, 231
Nanda, Serena, 90
National Health and Social Life Survey
  (NHSLS). *See* Laumann, Edward
Nature/nurture. *See* Essentialism; Social
  constructionism
Nature perspective. *See also* Essentialism, 201
Nocturnal emission. *See* Semenarche

Objectification. *See* Gender, women as
  objects
Ochs, Robyn, 217
On Our Backs, 167, 259
Oppression. *See also* Inequality, xvi, xviii,
  59–60, 200, 209–210, 231–233
Oral sex, 45, 127, 158, 161, 165, 169, 181,
  201, 242, 251, 252, 263, 275, 279
Orgasm
  faking, fake, 277–278, 280
  gender, xii, 104, 106, 120, 140,
    142–143, 144, 179, 189, 199, 279
  G-spot (Grafenberg), xii, 241, 263,
    279, 280
  hooking up, 179, 189
  Masters and Johnson research, 31–32,
    39, 47–49, 64, 65, 279
  (as) "outlets," 149, 199
  sexual dysfunction, xii, 50, 64, 176,
    268–273, 279–281, 283–284
  sexual fantasies in, 149, 156, 158
O'sullivan, Lucia, 35, 36
Out of the closet. *See* Sexual orientation

Pascoe, C.J., 103, 213, 214, 219
Paul, Elizabeth, 168, 170–172, 178–180,
  186, 188
Penile-vaginal intercourse, xvii, 7, 11, 13,
  37, 40, 41, 58, 68, 91, 107, 111, 127,
  134, 160, 256, 271, 283
  PVI, 12, 89–90, 109, 113–116, 127,
    128, 161, 171–173, 175, 181, 184,
    185, 188, 190, 197, 201, 248, 256,
    271, 281, 283
Penis, xi, 40, 61, 72–74, 88, 89,106, 116,
  134, 242, 252, 270–272, 282
  phalloplasty, 89
  slang for, 10–11, 271
  (as) "strange creature," 271–272
  symbolism, 191, 220, 253, 271–274,
    277–279
Penthouse, 133, 250, 261

Pharr, Suzanne, 212

Pill, contraceptive, ix, 17, 21–22, 144, 187
    "morning-after," 20, 21–22

Playboy, x, 110, 133, 243, 247, 250, 254, 255, 261

Playmate (or "Bunnies"). *See also Playboy*, x, 134, 243, 250, 254

Pleasure, 7, 51, 94, 120, 126, 128, 142–144, 148, 150, 159, 160, 176, 179–180, 182–184, 191, 249, 271, 278

Plummer, Ken, 61, 63, 202, 205, 206, 268

Poll, public opinion, 7, 8, 9, 14, 17, 18, 19, 20, 24, 25, 43, 127

Pornography or porn, 110, 133, 278–279
    actors ("talent"), 251, 257, 262–263
    anal sex in, 252, 258
    arousal, 202, 225, 237, 245–249
    characteristics of users, 144, 245, 249
    cybersex, 243, 255, 261
    defined, 242
    depiction of bodies in, 250
    disgust, 256, 257, 258, 263
    fantasies, 243, 248–249, 251, 252, 256–259, 264
    film or video, 142, 144, 191, 228, 245, 251–253, 257, 258, 263
    gay porn, 249, 250, 252, 253, 256, 257, 262–263
    in history, 242–243
    industry, 243–244, 253–254, 259, 261
    Internet, 243, 245, 250, 253, 256, 257, 262
    masturbation, 142, 144, 257
    men, 110, 133, 191, 225, 245–247, 249–250, 258, 264
    Penthouse, 250, 261
    public/private dimensions, 249, 256, 258, 261–262
    race, 191, 225, 227, 228, 231, 237, 252–253
    research on effects of, 242–249
    sexual behavior, 246, 247–249
    sexual imagination, 252, 254, 255, 256, 258, 259
    taboo, 228, 249–250, 256, 261
    violence against women, 244, 245–246, 249–251, 252, 257, 258–259
    women consumers, 144, 245, 256, 259–260, 264

Potts, Annie, 187, 270, 271, 278

Power, xvi, 7, 13, 46–49, 59–63, 70, 95, 103, 138, 160, 177, 209–212
    culture, 59, 95, 102, 207, 232
    defined, 6
    Foucault on, 59–62
    in classifying and labeling, 47, 59, 64–65, 83–84, 92, 95, 103, 203, 221, 280, 284
    "personal is political," 286

Pregnancy. *See* Reproduction

Preves, Sharon, 73

Prostitution, 39, 53, 90, 231, 243

PVI. *See* Penile-vaginal intercourse

Queer
    bisexuality, 230–236
    defined, 196
    "genderqueer," 83, 84, 87
    homophobia, 214, 233, 234
    hooking up, 178
    inequalities, 59, 130, 209–210, 212, 214, 223
    Queer as Folk, xi, 237
    sexual fantasies, 150
    sexual orientation, 211, 214–215, 221, 227, 230–236
    social construction, 203, 231
    theory, 62–63

Race
    bisexuality, 230–236
    "down low," 235

gender, 35–36, 113, 117, 124–125, 127, 130, 141, 144, 151, 214, 222, 231–232, 251
homophobia, 214, 233, 234, 235–236,
inequalities, 59, 62, 93, 95, 122, 130, 200, 209–210, 212, 223, 231–233, 236, 251
language, xviii, 11
pornography, 191, 225, 227, 228, 231, 237, 252–253
sexual orientation, 211, 214–215, 221, 227, 230–236
social construction of, xvi, xviii, 5, 11, 207, 231–232, 253, 264
socialization, 16, 78, 110, 113–115, 119–120, 125, 129, 141, 143, 207
Ramazanoglu, Caroline, 128
Rape and sexual violence. *See also* Sexual assault; Violence, 18, 120, 130, 151, 210, 213, 214, 231, 232, 246, 248, 285, 286, 287
Rape, Abuse, and Incest National Network (RAINN), 18
Regan, Pamela, 115, 145, 191
Reproduction *(also* conception), 5, 13, 15, 45, 91–93,102, 135, 138, 139–140, 144, 198, 201, 220, 280
Research
college students, 35–36, 37, 40, 127, 150, 152, 167–181, 275
heterocentrism, 40, 42, 46–47, 151, 171, 178, 198, 201, 245, 277, 282
historical, 26, 48, 106, 205
hooking up, 168–173
on pornography, 244–249
(public) opinion polls, 8–9, 14, 17, 19–20, 34–35, 43, 95, 168
question bias, 39–40,
researcher bias, 42, 149, 171, 280, 284
respondent bias, 37–41, 150, 170–172, 206, 284
sexual fantasies, 149–151,152–153

sexual orientation, 197–198, 205, 224–230
thinking critically about, 34–46, 114, 152, 168–170, 231, 224–229, 270
use of penile strain gauges, 225, 226, 228, 237
Rich, Adrienne, 209
Rikki Lake Show, 144, 248
Rieger, Gerulf. *See also* Meredith Chivers; J. Michael Bailey, 224–229
Risman, Barbara, 167, 186
Rubin, Gayle, 59, 221, 256
Rust, Paula Rodriguez, 214, 223, 228

Saad, Lydia, 17
Sadism. *See* BDSM
Sambia. *See* Gilbert Herdt
Sa'moa, 111
Savin-Williams, Ritch, 18–19, 105, 111, 116
Schema, 81–85, 89, 197
Schwartz, Pepper, 167, 186, 229
Seidman, Steve, 18–19
Semenarche *(also* spermarche), 134, 136, 137, 140, 144, 161
Sex and the City, ix, xii, xiii, 20, 43, 141
Sex toys and vibrators, x,xii, 244, 260, 280
Sex work. *See also* Prostitution, 210, 258, 261, 285
Sexual assault. *See also* Rape; Violence, 17–18, 190
Sexual desire, 145, 161, 179, 191, 209, 224, 237, 256, 258, 262, 264, 269
gender, 35, 64, 126, 128–131, 138, 141–145, 148, 152, 159–161, 177, 179–180, 183, 185, 187, 191, 208–209, 224, 258, 260, 262, 264,
partners, 90, 143, 237, 248,
sexual dysfunction, 50, 270, 273, 281
sexual orientation, 4, 63, 94, 117, 129–130, 151, 196, 200, 208–209, 219, 223, 224, 249, 256, 260

Sexual dysfunction, xi, xiv, 268
  arousal difficulties, 50, 270, 281
  disembodiment, 273–274
  men, 274, 278
  mind/body, 274
  narrow conception of, 283
  orgasmic difficulties, 47, 50, 269–270,
    273
  physicians and power, 281
  social construction of, 273, 284
  women, 176, 269, 281
Sexual fantasies. *See also* Arousal;
  Pornography
  data collection, 149–151
  defined, 145
  fantasy partners, 155–156
  gender differences, 145–148, 152–161,
    179–180, 189, 191–192, 219, 243,
    259
  intrapsychic scripts, 145–146,
    148
  language, 154, 158, 160
  love, 145, 151, 152, 155, 258
  masturbation, 141, 134, 144–147
  research on , 146–153
  sexual orientation, 64–65, 160, 151,
    200, 202, 209, 216, 218–219, 223,
    225
Sexually explicit material (SEM). *See*
  Pornography
Sexual orientation. *See also* Hegemonic
  scripts), 25, 45–47, 56, 102, 108, 111,
  116, 129
  asexual, 197, 238
  assumptions, 40, 42, 94, 197–198,
    200, 215, 226–228, 233, 234–236
  binary categories, 63, 196, 200, 201,
    209, 216, 220–221, 229
  coming out (of the closet), 18–19, 235,
    238
  defined, 201–202, 204, 208, 216–217,
    218, 219, 224–225

  desire *(See also* Sexual desire), 211, 221,
    237, 249
  essentialism *(See also* Essentialism),
    45–46, 202–208, 236
  "fag," 103, 197, 203–205, 209,
    213–214
  heterosexual privilege, 237
  homophobia *(See also* Homophobia),
    214, 223, 229, 233, 234
  identity, 4, 51, 52, 63–64, 87, 111,
    116, 196, 221, 206–207, 218,
    236
  language, xvi, xviii, 4, 103, 196–199,
    207
  learning (theory), 203, 213, 274
  pansexual, 196
  peer context *(See also* Socialization),
    116, 121, 223
  race *(See also* Race), 211, 214–215,
  research, 197–198, 200, 205, 219,
    224–230
  slash fiction, 195–196, 216, 254
  social construction (concept of choice),
    116, 130, 204–208, 215, 209,
    211–212, 229, 247
Sexual scripts. *See also* Gender; Race;
  Sexual orientation, xviii, 175, 179,
  185–186, 216, 218, 229, 274, 286
  arousal, 55, 57, 228
  cultural, 56–58, 102, 106, 115, 130,
    166, 174, 186, 223, 230, 248, 249,
    256, 260, 279, 281, 284
  gender, 36, 57, 191, 210, 223–224,
    248, 249, 272
  interpersonal, 56, 58, 120, 129, 167,
    168, 237, 260
  intrapsychic, 56, 58, 134, 145–146,
    148, 151, 160, 161, 167, 168, 200,
    248, 256, 260
  subcultural, 56, 112, 115, 168, 236,
    248
  theory, defined, 54–58, 248

Sexual self, 56, 101, 134, 216, 220–221, 230, 237, 252, 277–278

Sexual violence.

See Rape and sexual violence

Sexuality, 197, 210

attitudes about, ix, xv, xvii, 6, 8–9, 13–15, 17, 19, 34, 39, 43, 52, 95, 102, 111, 113, 142, 161, 174, 183, 189, 214, 219, 236, 245, 246, 262, 286

the brain and, xv, 45–46, 202, 204, 228, 238, 269, 273, 275–276, 279

body. *See* Body

children (*See also* Socialization), 16, 18, 71–77, 104–106, 107, 135, 206, 253

classifying of , 48, 50, 59, 61, 63–64, 65, 83, 95, 211, 280

concept of the "Other," 93, 124, 197–198, 203, 211, 221, 231–232, 281

contradictory, confusing, ambivalent, ix, 9, 15, 17, 20, 23–25, 42, 102, 108, 115–116, 128, 145, 165, 169, 255, 283, 285

cultural capital, 232, 233

defined, xvii

globally, 20, 23–24, 209–210, 244, 268, 283–285

language, xvi–xix, 4–5, 10–13, 48, 61, 83–84, 92, 143, 150, 153, 158, 160, 165, 169, 203, 271

morality, 6, 9, 13, 95, 234, 256, 285–286

narratives, 95, 155, 203–207

phenomenology, 238, 283

politics of, 268

polyamorous, 171

social construction, xvi, 8, 202–206, 211, 275

social control, 5, 23, 59, 60–61, 94, 102–103, 106, 123, 192, 215, 223, 229, 232, 269, 286

Sexually explicit material (SEM). *See* Pornography

Sexually transmitted infections (STIs), 171, 190, 255

SIECUS, xvii, 16

Simon, William, xv, 54–55, 56–57, 206

Slang, 4, 11, 16, 21, 30, 40, 138, 141, 150, 153, 154, 159, 165, 169, 189, 216, 235, 271

research, 40–41, 150, 169–170

"suck my dick," xi, 11, 238

"Slut" (*also* slutty), 64, 103, 128, 130, 181, 183, 189–190, 213, 221, 256, 264

Social class, 5, 78, 105, 110–111, 119, 122, 143, 214, 221, 227, 244,

Social constructionism. *See also* Essentialism, xv, xviii, 7–9, 24, 29, 44–46, 48, 59, 62, 70–71, 77, 91, 95, 134, 199, 201, 203, 211, 230–231

socially constructed, xiv, xvii, 7–8, 29, 39, 56–57, 60, 65, 67, 70, 80, 84, 89, 92, 95, 102, 198–199, 208, 255, 258, 271, 273, 275

Social exchange theory, 53–54, 166, 182–185, 222

Social order, 87, 102, 200

Socialization, 74, 101, 112, 117, 160–161, 186–187, 212, 215

childhood, 5, 76, 78, 81, 85–86, 94, 102–109, 111, 112

defined, 5, 102–103

gender(ed), 44, 78, 80, 85–87, 94–95, 102, 112, 117–131, 134, 145, 156, 210, 229, 264, 272

parents (families) and, 16, 78

sexual , 94, 111, 116, 117, 145, 206, 229, 248

subcultural, 5–6, 24, 78, 104, 110–111, 114–117, 187, 189, 210, 227, 231, 236

Socioeconomic status (SES). *See* Social class

Sprecher, Susan, 53, 54, 191

Starks, Michael, 111

Stein, Arlene, 209, 223

Stereotypes or stereotyping, 21, 71, 78, 82, 84, 85, 87, 88, 93, 167, 197, 199, 231, 233, 245, 252, 253, 262

Stigma or stigmatization, 75, 127, 130, 203–204, 220, 229, 234, 237, 260, 277, 280

STIs. *See* Sexually transmitted infections

Szasz, Thomas, 42

Tewksbury, Richard, 230

Thompson, Sharon, 128, 130

Tiefer, Leonore, 29, 44, 49, 257, 269, 278, 280, 281, 287

Tolman, Deborah, 128, 129, 130, 189, 249

Transgender *(also* Trans), xviii, 63, 83–89, 178, 206, 221, 224
    alphabet soup, in the, 84, 196, 206, 221, 237
    defined, xviii, 83–84, 196, 198
    identity and, 85, 221, 237
    transmen, -women, -people, 84–89, 90, 237, 254

Ussher, Jane, 129–130, 209, 249

Viagra. *See also* Erectile dysfunction, xii, 242, 268, 272, 273, 277, 278
    Cialis and Levitra (as competition), 269, 273, 274, 278
    global market for, xiv, 274, 283–284
    "Viagra mindset," 274, 278

Violence (see also Sexual assault), 18, 210, 212, 213, 244, 245, 246, 251, 258–259, 268, 286

Violence against men (also "gay bashing"), 213–214, 233

Violence against women, 122, 214, 251–252, 257, 285

Walker, Barbara, 117–118

Ward, Monique, 126

Waskul, Dennis, 255

Weeks, Jeffrey, 202

Whisman, Vera, 204, 207, 208

Wiederman, Michael, 37, 176, 277

Wilde, Oscar, 3, 95, 196, 205

Will & Grace, ix, xi, xiv, 212

Zurbriggen (Eileen) and Yost (Megan), 147–148, 149, 150, 159, 161